Civil War Iowa *and the* Copperhead Movement

Civil War Iowa

AND THE

Copperhead Movement

Hubert H. Wubben

E
507.9
W8

THE IOWA STATE UNIVERSITY PRESS, AMES

562804

To Shirley

Hubert H. Wubben is Professor of History, Oregon State University, Corvallis, Oregon. He was graduated from Cornell College, Mt. Vernon, Iowa, and received the Master's and Ph.D. degrees from the University of Iowa.

Composed and printed by The Iowa State University Press, Ames, Iowa 50010

First edition, 1980

Library of Congress Cataloging in Publication Data

Wubben, Hubert H   1928–
    Civil War Iowa and the Copperhead movement.

    Bibliography: p.
    Includes index.
    1. Iowa—history—Civil War, 1861–1865.   2. Copperhead (Nickname)   I.   Title.
E507.9.W8   977.7′02   79–23407
ISBN 0-8138-1120-1

FRONTISPIECE. The Governor's Greys and Jackson Guards leaving Dubuque, from *Harpers' Weekly*, May 25, 1861. *(State Historical Society of Iowa)*

···❧▶◀[*Contents*]▶◀❧···

v

Acknowledgments

WHEN I first became intrigued by the Copperheads years ago, Allan Bogue raised the provocative and important question, "What can you say about Copperheads that Frank Klement hasn't already said?" While I know neither scholar personally, Klement and Richard Curry through their works have influenced nearly everything I've written or thought about Copperheads, although they are hardly to be blamed for my conclusions. The same should be said for the late Wood Gray.

William Appleman Williams wrote a detailed and helpful critique on a predecessor manuscript to this study. Two hours of conversation with Robert Dykstra during the summer of 1975 were a great stimulant. David C. Childs efficiently translated portions of certain German newspapers. Joyce Giaquinta, manuscript librarian at the Iowa Historical Society, saved me from making a bad mistake in my evaluation of the purposes of a group of Civil War Iowa home guardsmen. All students who have ever worked in Iowa history owe much to the late Mildred Throne of the Society, both for what she did to help those of us who were graduate students and for what she wrote as a scholar.

Oregon State University colleague Darold Wax, who erroneously claims to know little about the Civil War era and Copperheadism, has always known enough to keep me honest. So has Shirley Wubben who constantly raised pointed questions and objections which had to be raised.

Thanks also to *Civil War History* and Kent State University Press for permission to quote passages from my article, "Copperhead Charles Mason: A Question of Loyalty," 24 (March 1978): 46–65.

Finally I wish to acknowledge my indebtedness to Suzanne C. Lowitt, an editor of great skill and tact; to Julia Bruce who is an excellent typist of manuscripts; and to Oregon State University's General Research Fund which provided assistance in the form of several small grants.

H. H. W.

Corvallis, Oregon

Introduction

Few epithets in American history served their purpose more effectively than the word Copperhead during the Civil War. Employed loosely against nearly all opponents of the Lincoln administration, it lingered as a stigma for more than two decades after the war. Iowans who wrote the triumphant history of their state's participation on the winning side made much of the Copperhead theme. Most of them were Republicans, and they often portrayed the wartime Iowa Democratic party as a party dominated by Confederate sympathizers. Anyone taking a cursory look at the Iowa political record might well conclude that the state's voters got the message. They favored Republican candidates at the polls with almost monotonous regularity well into the twentieth century.

Use of the term Copperhead by scholars is paradoxical. Copperhead was a smear. Republicans used it as a code word for Southern sympathizer at the least, for traitor at the worst. Frank Klement calls Copperheads "Democratic critics of change and the Lincoln administration." Richard Curry calls them "conservative opponents of the Lincoln administration" who were also called Butternuts and Peace Democrats. Curry also draws a line between ordinary Copperheads and Peace Democrat Copperheads, holding that Peace Democrats were "those Copperheads unrealistic enough to believe that the Union could be restored if only North and South could be persuaded to come together at the conference table." Elsewhere he has called them Conservative Union Democrats. William Carleton has separated wartime Democrats into three categories. "War Democrats," he writes, "supported the war measures as vigorously as the Republicans and many of them . . . passed over to the Republican party." Majority Democrats stood solidy against disunion and favored war if necessary to end secession. Peace Democrats, a term he uses interchangeably with Copperheads, "with or without a cease-fire or an armistice" favored Northern initiatives leading to negotiations and a national convention to work out a nation-saving compromise. Less friendly to Copperheads is Wood Gray. Gray never specifically defines the word Copperhead, but he emphasizes the Copperheads' defeatism, their constant calls for peace, and their opposition to war. At one point he speaks of them as men "who gave aid and comfort to the Confederacy either through political maneuvering or revolutionary plotting,'' who made the Democratic party their instrument when they could. Irving Katz is closer to Gray than to Klement, Curry, or Carleton. He draws a distinction between some Civil War peace men and other peace men. The Copperheads, he says, were those peace men who were ''pro-Confederate.'' However, those historians who view the Copperheads more sympathetically have adopted the term simply as a matter of convenience to identify the Democratic critics of the Lincoln administration.[1]

But, so far as Iowa is concerned, one must make a distinction between some Democratic critics of the Lincoln administration and other critics. Iowa's Democrats were factionalized well before the war began over issues, patronage, and personalities. When war came, one faction, gingerly at first, but with increasing fervor, promoted the idea that negotiations with the Confederacy would restore the Union whereas continued war would not. Not all members of this faction, of course, opposed the war absolutely. In the early years particularly, they cheered the rare Union victories. But they also demanded that the administration explore peaceful means to end the rebellion. And they demanded that the South be restored with its privileges and institutions intact. By early 1863, they became known as Copperheads. The other faction, probably a majority in the party, was equally opposed to abolition but much less solicitous toward Southern feelings as the war dragged on. Most important, it resisted emphasis upon peace through negotiations without a corresponding effort to exert strong military pressure upon the South. Men of this faction objected so vociferously to the Copperhead label when Republicans applied it to them that they sometimes forced their opponents to acknowledge that there was a difference between themselves and Copperheads. They are properly called War Democrats. Frank Palmer, editor of the Des Moines *Iowa State Register,* probably the first to make it a practice to consistently stick Democrats with the Copperhead label, grudgingly admitted under pressure that while all Copperheads were Democrats, some Democrats were not Copperheads. Copperheads, he grumped, were those who favored ''peace through compromise and Restoration through Conciliation.''[2]

The story of Iowa's Copperheads is obviously part of a larger story of the Civil War era in Iowa. Thus, while this volume concentrates upon the tribulations of the Copperheads and their intraparty opponents, the War Democrats, in competition with the upstart Republicans, it also deals with the economic, cultural, and social life of the Iowa populace in wartime. Although the war was pervasive in its effects upon all Iowans, those effects were filtered through their everyday concerns, many of which were the same as they had been in peacetime. They still worked to live, talked about the weather, raised children, went to church, took an interest in their schools, worried about law and order, complained about taxes, got exasperated about dogs in the countryside and hogs in the streets, supported charities, formed clubs, sought entertainment, and looked closely at one another's manners and morals. The newspapers they read, particularly those in the eastern one-third of the state where the bulk of the population lived, are a primary source throughout. One should add also that their newspapers were often a mine of misinformation. Editors and reporters told as much of the who, what, when, where, why, and how as they wanted, which was often severely limited by their editorial viewpoints in a day when papers were much more party or individual mouthpieces than they are today. And many editors obviously knew nothing or cared nothing about the concept of a follow-up story. Still, their newspapers, carefully used, are invaluable sources; scholars who neglect them do so at their peril. The men who edited the Dubuque *Herald* and Dubuque *Times,* for instance, had important things to say about the nefarious influences of circuses and bawdy houses upon impressionable youth as well as about the activities of Iowa's political elite—and they said it loudly and clearly. Editorial comment on the penchant of Davenporters for moneymaking to the exclusion of other concerns, or about the fact that Oskaloosa was hardly the place to go for fun and games, can only enhance one's understanding of a state which contained large numbers of men and women who were intriguing mixtures of the earthy and the puritanical.

Much of the story has already been told. But not all of it by any means. Nor will this book complete the record. Iowa's history during the Civil War years will long remain fertile ground for those who want to better understand the development of this country's heartland and its influence upon the character of American life today.

Civil War Iowa *and the* Copperhead Movement

1

1850s: A Decade of Transition

THE Copperhead movement generated much sound and fury in Iowa. Yet it was never so potent a force politically as it was in the more populous western states, Ohio, Indiana, and Illinois. This weakness reflected the condition of the state's Democratic party which suffered from a series of developments and events largely beyond its control in the decade before the war. Copperheadism was not, of course, a "purely political" movement. But Copperheadism manifested itself most clearly in the political process. This was because the men who were Copperheads saw the political process as the best way to win the power needed to take Iowa into the peace camp.

In the 1850s a massive influx of settlers attracted by the well-publicized fertility of Iowa's soil entered the state. Prior to 1850, the southern Ohio River Valley region and the border states had supplied most of the migrants, heavily Democratic in politics. But in the 1850s the tide shifted substantially. Settlers coming primarily from the upper Ohio Valley, the Middle Atlantic states, and New England flooded the state. Mainly Whigs or Free-Soilers at first, by the mid- and late fifties they were Republicans. In 1856, the Iowa Republican party came into existence composed of a coalition of men from the two older parties plus nativists, abolitionists, temperance advocates, and antislavery Democrats, some of whom managed to combine nearly all of these elements in one person. Since the Iowa population exploded from 192,214 in 1850 to 674,913 in 1860, this changed population pattern could only have significant long-range effects upon the course of party politics as well as upon the state's social and cultural environment.[1] As early as September of 1854, one older Iowan of Northern background proudly asserted in John Greenleaf Whittier's *National Era*, "We are now no longer ashamed to be known as Iowaians. . . . The change is radical; it will last. . . . The incoming population is of the right sort."[2] The reason for this jubilation was the victory of James Grimes, a Whig running with Free-Soiler endorsement, in the gubernatorial election which brought an end to Democratic control of the state government. Arrival of several thousand foreign-born settlers, mostly Irish and German, countered the Whig–Free-Soil–Republican political trend somewhat, and the depression of 1857 with its aftermath slowed the migration into Iowa. But for the Democrats the damage was done. The numbers were to be increasingly against them.

Regardless of their origins or political leanings, what these settlers wanted— as had the earlier migrants—were homestead laws, internal improvements, and railroad land grants. They agitated unceasingly for them. The Democrats, the majority party until the mid-fifities, tried to oblige. In Congress, led by Senator George W. Jones, they struggled for years against the reluctance of the national party leadership to approve such measures. Unfortunately for them, Republicans controlled the governor's office and the state legislature when Congress in 1856 finally approved a railroad land grant for the state. The Republicans happily accepted the grant, emphasizing their own efforts in its behalf and skillfully underplaying the Democrats' years of labor toward the same end.[3]

Republicans consolidated their position as a result of the way they dealt with the shock of the depression. Real estate values and grain prices fell. Over two years there was a total of $5 million in business bankruptcies. Those who invested in railroad stocks or speculated in land lost heavily. Construction of railroads practically ceased. Gold and silver disappeared from circulation, leaving Iowans with depreciated bank bills from other western states. Heavy rains and an early frost brought widespread crop failures in 1858. During the crisis the Republican-dominated legislature passed a stay law. The law extended to nine months the period required of mortgagees between the date they filed default complaints and the date they could foreclose on debtors. It also extended the time during which a mortgagor could act to reclaim his lost property.[4]

Republicans handled the prickly railroad issue reasonably well during this period. Iowans yearned for railroads since the state's rivers were inadequate for carrying their growing agricultural production to the Mississippi. They voted big bond issues, incurring $18 million in local government debts in the process by 1857. These bonds they exchanged for railroad stocks. Promoters then sold the bonds to eastern investors to get construction and operating capital. With the coming of hard times this resource dried up. The citizens now tended to see the railroads in a less benevolent light. Consequently, the carriers began to look toward state aid as a way out of their difficulty. Republicans in the legislature, however, read voter sentiment accurately and resisted any suggestion that railroads get special help.[5]

Republicans also won favor by working successfully for the repeal of the 1846 constitution and its injunction against banks. When a constitutional convention met in 1857 to draw up a new state charter, the delegates inserted a provision which permitted banks. Many old line Democrats still feared wildcat banking and adamantly opposed the move, but a majority of voters wanted a change. From this came a state bank as well as measures which permitted a tightly circumscribed free banking system.[6] Republicans also profited from a rise in prohibition sentiment, engendered in part by nativism. In 1855 their Whig–Free-Soiler predecessors had pushed a limited prohibitory bill through the legislature which the voters approved by referendum, 25,555 to 22,645. Democrats generally opposed the measure, particularly in southern and western Iowa and in those areas along the Mississippi where Irish and German immigrants were concentrated. An 1857 revision of the law permitted the manufacture of certain types of alcoholic beverages and their sale for medicinal and sacramental purposes through designated outlets. As any reader of Iowa newspapers of the Civil War era can attest, Iowans construed the medicinal and sacramental restrictions liberally.[7]

Iowa Democrats, nevertheless, could not capitalize on the nativist issue during the 1850s as much as Democrats could elsewhere. James Grimes, one of the founding fathers of the Iowa Republican party, had a lot to do with this. Grimes, a Whig, became governor in 1854, the first non-Democrat to win a statewide election. During the 1854 campaign, although hitting hardest at the Kansas-Nebraska Act and its repeal of the Missouri Compromise, he also spoke against the Clayton amendment to the act. This amendment, which failed of passage, sought to bar alien voting and officeholding in the territory. Then, as he began to form a new party out of the victorious coalition of 1854, he made it clear that the new organization should try to capture the allegiance of the foreign born.[8] In 1856, Grimes won reelection, this time as a Republican. During the period 1854–1856, the nativist American party (more commonly called Know-Nothing) enjoyed a rapid growth, snaring some Democrats as well as Whigs. When the party underwent an equally rapid decline, the Republicans deftly co-opted much of its membership. They accomplished this by concentrating on the slavery extension issue rather than by catering to nativist doctrines. Later, when occasions arose in which Republicans could take a stand favorable to the foreign born, or could give them some tangible recognition within the party, they did so. When Massachusetts's Republican-controlled legislature passed an amendment to the state constitution which prohibited naturalized citizens from voting until two years after they had received their papers, the Iowa Republican central committee forthrightly condemned the act. That same year, 1859, Republican state convention delegates finessed their startled opponents by nominating German-born Nicholas Rusch to be their candidate for lieutenant governor, although not all Republicans were happy about it. Unlike James Grimes, Senator James Harlan did hedge slightly in response to angry German-Iowans' questions about his position on discrimination against the foreign born, naturalization laws, and the Massachusetts law in particular.[9]

Democrats of course were not totally inept in dealing with the nativist movement. Senator Jones also firmly opposed the Clayton amendment in the Senate. Democratic editors and politicians in Iowa constantly reminded the immigrants that the bulk of the Know-Nothings had, after all, become Republicans. And most Democrats opposed the Whig-Republican temperance forces who maintained that German and Irish drinking habits contributed to public disorder and desecrated Sabbaths.[10]

Nevertheless, a degree of nativism also infected some Democrats. Several normally Democratic southern tier counties, where foreign-born persons were rare, had pockets of Know-Nothing strength. Wartime Democrats who had been Know-Nothing members or sympathizers were Hugh Sample, a member of the Democratic state central committee in 1861, and John Wallace, the party's candidate for secretary of state in 1864.[11] And, following the close gubernatorial election of 1859 in which Republican Samuel Kirkwood defeated former Senator Augustus Dodge, the Davenport *Democrat* blamed Iowa's German Republicans for the loss. Nearly three months later, editor Thomas Maguire was still unhappy. Germans couldn't read English, he said; hence their intelligent but erring compatriots who edited the German language Davenport *Der Demokrat* (a Republican-leaning paper despite its name) led them around far too easily. Nor could Maguire get over the Republican selection of Rusch as Kirkwood's running mate. Personally he liked Germans, Maguire claimed, "But why they should take precedence both in the quality and number of official positions in this state over native-born citizens we cannot exactly appreciate . . . that they should take the lead and fill the most important offices we have never consented to and never will. . . ."[12] The animus of the *Democrat* toward foreign-born persons was nothing new by that time, however. When *Der Demokrat* eulogized John Brown, the Republican Davenport *Gazette* applauded the German paper. But the *Democrat* pronounced the tribute "disgusting." The editor in words that could only have caused Davenport's many foreign-born residents to wonder who their friends really were, wrote:

> These outward signs of inward hostility are unmistakable proof that there exists in this country a class of men who are anxiously awaiting a state of things which will warrant revolution and subversion to the government. . . . Many of them brought from Europe the wildest theories and the most dangerous political as well as religious principles. . . . We have fought the Know Nothings from the beginning, but if anything under the sun could make us one, it would be the impudent assumption of such as *Der Demokrat* and those it represents, that to them, *as Germans,* is committed the task of reforming our institutions.[13]

Even more scornful was the Democratic *Register* of LeClaire, a few miles up the river from Davenport. It sneered, "Would it not be proper for them [the *Demokrat*'s editors and the Davenport Germans] to wait at least until the filth and dirt of the ship and their smell of garlic should have worn off before they undertake to dictate to Americans how to make and administer laws."[14] Such selective examples of prewar antagonism toward the foreign born taken from two Iowa Democratic papers will not suffice, of course, to prove that rank and file Iowa Democrats were more antagonistic than rank and file Iowa Republicans. Most likely they were not. They simply show that the foreign born, constituting 15.7 per cent of Iowa's population, could not be expected to feel thoroughly at home with either party. Outnumbered as they were, the Democrats could ill afford such disaffection.[15]

The issue which did the most, however, to weaken the party arose out of the

Kansas-Nebraska Act; namely, slavery's possible extension into the West. Slavery extension had not struck such fire earlier. During the late 1840s most Iowans opposed the Wilmot Proviso. Their general assembly was the only free state legislature to take a stand against it. Most also favored the Compromise of 1850 and hoped that it would lay to rest the question of slavery extension. Senators George Jones and Augustus Dodge were two of only four Democratic senators who voted for all five parts of the compromise. Some Iowa Whigs did object to the fugitive slave law, but during the election campaign of 1852 both Whigs and Democrats stressed their support of the 1850 accord and their disavowal of "higher law" doctrines. There was, nevertheless, some resentment among elements of the electorate who believed that Jones and Dodge had gone too far in assuring the South that Iowans were thoroughly procompromise, anti–Free-Soil, antiblack, antiabolition, and, by extension, pro-Southern.[16]

To be sure, they were nearly as antagonistic to blacks as other westerners. This attitude changed only slowly, even under the impact of eastern and upper midwest migration. An Iowa Territorial Supreme Court decision of 1839 held that the Missouri Compromise forbade slavery in Iowa. This was the famous *Ralph* case in which Chief Justice Charles Mason, later to become a leading Copperhead, declared that a Missouri slave owner who allowed his slave to become a resident in free territory could not thereafter exercise ownership rights.[17] But this decision was no harbinger of any movement toward civil rights for blacks. In 1851, the legislature passed a law excluding black migrants, although no attempt to enforce it took place until 1863 when a federal district judge ruled the measure unconstitutional.[18] Furthermore, during the early 1850s, Iowa's small band of Free-Soilers thought it important to deny that they harbored abolitionist leanings. Thus, when Augustus Dodge spoke in support of the Kansas-Nebraska bill before the Senate in 1854, he could still complain about "the sickly sentimentality over slavery" and believe he expressed the dominant mood in the state. However, by that time abolitionists were more numerous in Iowa. Southern Iowa Quakers in particular were a thorn in the side of northern Missouri slave owners.[19] Moreover, antislavery and antislavery extension sentiments had grown to the point where it was unwise for Iowa's most important politicians to defend Southern doctrines and Southern objectives openly.

Iowans wanted the territory to their west organized, assuming that it would promote the state's growth and their own prosperity. But repeal of the Missouri Compromise was another matter. They believed that it unnecessarily revived the troublesome quarrel over slavery extension. To the consternation of Senators Jones and Dodge, petitions protesting the Kansas-Nebraska bill and its repeal provision flooded their offices. Throughout the rest of the year James Grimes and the Whigs capitalized successfully on the issue, charging that the act was a Southern plot to extend slavery. Their victory that fall resulted in Whig–Free-Soiler control of the legislature, control of Iowa's two seats in the United States House of Representatives, and Free-Soiler James Harlan replacing Dodge in the Senate.[20] Meanwhile, Iowa's population boom continued. From 326,500 in 1854, it climbed to 512,000 in 1856.[21] When the Kansas question refused to die, some citizens joined or otherwise aided the free-state forces moving into the disputed territory.

Through it all, Charles Mason, by then head of the United States Patent Office, became increasingly discouraged. The whole issue of squatter sovereignty was a "farce" in the first place, he wrote. "That the subject of slavery may be left to the people of the territories, I am willing to concede, not because they are to do just as they choose on all subjects, but because it is a method of getting past a very difficult subject."[22] Mason's judgment that the Kansas-Nebraska Act was simply an acceptable way out of a difficult subject bore no relation to what Iowans were thinking. Republicans had little difficulty keeping the slavery extension issue alive. In the 1856 election, Grimes' second term victory carried enough Republicans with him to take control of the state government. Thus strengthened, he permitted muskets in the Iowa arsenal to fall into the hands of those who materially backed the free-state forces in Kansas. The Iowa legislature also passed a law allowing blacks to testify in court.[23.]

Abolitionists were strong enough by then to establish a working Underground Railroad, aided by the disinclination of increasing numbers of Iowans to uphold the fugitive slave act.[24] Citizen concern for blacks had limits, nevertheless. During the constitutional convention of 1857, controversy raged over a proposal to grant them the suffrage. The convention sidestepped the issue by submitting it to a popular vote separate from the constitution. Democratic spokesmen and editors leaped to the attack. Among the relatively moderate voices was that belonging to the editor of the McGregor *North Iowa Times* who wrote, "Our sympathies for the black man are not less than those entertained by his loudest pitty-ers but we would not be so hypocritical as to tantalize him with political rights and then practice towards him the severest social exclusion."[25] In Muscatine, Congregational church parishioners demonstrated their reluctance to abide the presence of blacks in their midst. When a black woman applied for membership, aided by a letter in her behalf from the community's African church, the congregation turned her down. The church records state, "In the opinion of the majority of the Church, the reasons of the applicant for being received into this church rather than to labor for Christ in the church and among the people of her color are inconsistent."[26] It was hardly surprising, then, that the provision to legalize black suffrage should fail decisively, 49,387 to 8,489, while the proposed constitution scraped by 40,311 to 38,681.[27] Republicans did not push the suffrage measure. The observant McGregor editor summed up the general Iowa response to the possibility of black participation in the life of the state when he reported, "There is no man of our acquaintance, be his politics Republican or Democratic, who desires to have negroes come among us."[28] Even so, the Iowa legislature in 1858 did pass a law permitting black children to attend school with white youngsters if the affected white parents in the individual school districts unanimously agreed to allow it. This partially reversed an 1847 law which provided for free common schools for white children only. But the state supreme court disallowed the 1858 measure, holding that under the 1857 constitution only the state's board of education could regulate schools. Until 1874 when the high court ruled in a Keokuk case that black children had the right to attend school with whites, the situation was fluid, some communities having integrated schools, and others not.[29]

The *Dred Scott* decision aroused some antagonism in the state among both Republicans and Democrats. The state Democratic platforms of 1857 and 1858 failed to endorse it, while the 1859 platform defensively announced that the party bore no responsibility for high court judgments. Such a course reflected the discomfort many Iowans felt over anything which overtly protected slavery and, in the latter year, the internal Democratic upheaval coming in the wake of the split between President James Buchanan and Stephen Douglas over the Lecompton constitution issue.[30] The Lecompton controversy was the major point within the whole slavery extension issue which tore the Iowa Democrats apart more than any other, a situation which Republicans shrewdly exploited. Senator George Jones, due to be replaced in 1858 by James Grimes, aligned himself with the president and voted for Kansas's admission as a slave state contrary to "instructions" sent him in January, 1858, by the Republican-controlled general assembly. Though defending Jones against Republican demands that he resign, most assembly Democrats and the majority of the party throughout the state resented the proslavery Lecompton document and the manner in which its proponents rammed it through to ratification. Accordingly, they lined up with Douglas against Buchanan and Jones. Only one Democratic paper, the Dubuque *Northwest,* supported the administration.[31] Although Jones had no chance to retain his Senate seat when his term expired, he sought the empty honor of being the Democratic candidate when the legislators met to choose his successor. Judge Thomas S. Wilson, an old Jones foe in Dubuque, where both men lived, won the upper house caucus in a battle which everyone recognized as a test of strength between Douglas men and Buchanan men. The combined senate and house Democrats, however, rejected both Jones and Wilson, choosing lawyer Ben Samuels, also from Dubuque, to be the party's pro forma candidate.

In thorough disarray, the party was ill prepared to resist further Republican gains. Henry Clay Dean, orator, land speculator, and former Methodist minister from southeastern Iowa, who frequently took the stump for the Democrats, wrote in dismay:

> The negro question with which we have legitimately nothing under the Heavens to do, has cost us two Governors, two United States Senators, four Congressmen, and the whole of the Supreme Bench, and both Houses of the Legislature, for three successive sessions. We have imposed upon us a constitution in which nothing but the negro question was fairly discussed before the people.[32]

The party, now controlled by the antiadministration faction, suffered through the rest of 1858. Administration supporters, angered at the state convention's refusal to back Buchanan's Lecompton stand, held their own convention where they praised both Jones and the president.[33] From Spain, where he served as ambassador, former Senator Dodge wrote to an unhappy Jones that he hoped the party would submerge its differences long enough to support the nominees for state office even if they were Douglas men. "I trust," he wrote, "that you will act upon the principle that the meanest Democrat is better than the best Black Republican."[34] Regardless, the Democrats absorbed another licking, this time in races for minor state posts.

The year 1859 provided the Democrats with the last real opportunity to reestablish themselves in power. Prominent Republicans, smelling victory, hankered for party nominations. Some were miffed when Nicholas Rusch won the spot as Kirkwood's running mate. The Democrats nominated Dodge for governor. His absence overseas had kept him out of the Democratic bloodletting, making him acceptable to both factions. Dodge ran a strong race, but Kirkwood won, 56,532 to 53,332, while Rusch, despite some Republican fears, held his own against Democrat Lysander Babbitt, 55,789 to 52,722.[35]

Thereafter, having done their best behind Dodge, only to lose, Democratic unity dissolved once more. The year 1860 witnessed renewed fighting between the growing Douglas wing and the declining proadministration faction which made the party unable to mount a strong challenge in either the presidential election or the battle for minor state offices in 1860. Two events in early 1860 seemed to confirm their worst fears, that radicalism ruled in Iowa and that they could do little about it. The first came in Kirkwood's inaugural speech in which he declared that while Northerners condemned John Brown's raid on Harper's Ferry, they, nevertheless, admired and sympathized with Brown's "disinterestedness of purpose . . . and . . . the unflinching courage and calm cheerfulness with which he met the consequences of his failure." Democrats throughout the state reacted angrily. In the state legislature they tried unsuccessfully to defeat a resolution to print 7,500 copies of the address. The second was the Barclay Coppoc affair. Coppoc was one of two Iowa brothers who went east with Brown in the summer of 1859. Virginia troops captured Edwin Coppoc at Harper's Ferry. Barclay Coppoc, who guarded the raiders' supplies in Pennsylvania, learned of the debacle and fled to Iowa. When Virginia sought to extradite him, Kirkwood delayed, arguing that the extradition papers did not fulfill all legal requirements. Several Republican legislators got wind of the move and spirited Coppoc out of danger before Virginia authorities could meet Kirkwood's objections. When Democrats in the legislature charged that the Governor connived in the escape, Republicans submitted evidence to the contrary, then refused to allow their opponents to back out gracefully.[36] Both incidents, practically and symbolically, demonstrated the Iowa Democrats' weakness in the final year before the Civil War. For them, the future looked bleak.

That future was somewhat cloudy for all Iowans in one respect because they were still feeling the effects of the depression that began in 1857. Their location and their increasing dependence upon a market economy which extended well beyond state boundaries caused them to wonder how increasing sectional discord, perhaps culminating in war, might affect their livelihood.

Census figures for 1860 clearly revealed the primacy of agriculture. There were 88,628 farmers and 27,196 farm laborers in the state, constituting 62 per cent of the working populace. In contrast, only 6,307 people earned their living in the state's 1,939 manufacturing concerns. Iowa ranked seventh in the nation in corn production and eighth in wheat.[37] Most of the corn found its way to market as hogs or packed pork. By 1860, Iowans had begun to recognize the singular importance of corn-hog production as the basis of the state's prosperity. As early as 1858, John Wallace, executive secretary of the state's agricultural society, declared that in that bad year pork exports saved the citizens from bankruptcy.[38] Those counties not bordering the Mississippi regarded it as a milestone when farmers produced a surplus and ceased to rely on the home market for survival. Indeed, the Iowa farmer by the late 1850s was knowledgeable enough about the market system to know that his well-being depended not only upon national but also upon European consumption of his surplus.[39] As Dubuque businessman Solon Langworthy noted in the spring of 1859, ''Farmers in consequence of the War which has recently broke out between France and Italy are in High Hopes of good prices for produce and are enlarging their fields and planting more acres than any previous year.''[40] The year 1859 was not, however, a particularly good year. At best it was one of ''average prosperity'' according to Wallace. Farmers managed to lower their indebtedness, but not so much from sales as from ''the vastly improved habits of economy learned and practiced at home.''[41] And it took nine columns of the Iowa City *Reporter* in February, 1860, to contain the 109 separate notices from tax title buyer LeGrand Byington to different parties that he intended to foreclose the mortgages he held on their land and buildings.[42] Secretary Wallace at the end of 1860 felt slightly more optimistic. But he was not one to let farmers forget what he thought was a valuable, if also harsh, experience. ''When our farmers shall have learned not to ask it,'' he sermonized, ''and our business men not to grant credit to the enormous extent which has of late years characterized these transactions, then we may expect a *real* rather than an *apparent* prosperity and advancement in all that makes a State prosperous and wealthy.''[43]

Wallace's advice to farmers to be conservative in outlook and in practice was similar to the counsel some important Iowa newspapers freely offered their businessmen-readers. Reject the notes of shaky banks, they urged, to rid the state of worthless paper. Davenport *Democrat* editor David Richardson, who had replaced Thomas Maguire in early 1860, welcomed the failures of such banks. ''The wild-cat panic is coming,'' he exulted, ''and *let it come*. We welcome it. Let every weak backed institution be crowded to the wall and pinned there beyond hopes of resurrection.''[44] Meanwhile the Iowa State Bank and its branches were reported safe, not particularly astonishing news, however, in view of the tight reins applied by law to the branches, and the limited capital and field of action within which they could operate.[45] The economic climate may have improved somewhat for individual Iowans by the end of 1860. One would hope that the

Dubuque area farmer who got only $3.50 the previous September for a wagon-load of potatoes from a 40-mile round trip to market was doing better. The Dubuque *Times,* at any rate, was determinedly cheerful when it claimed that an upward tendency in produce prices was one indication that the postelection panic experienced by some was about "played out." But while it played, it hurt. As tenant farmer wife, Sara Kenyon of Delaware county told eastern relatives, the election "made awful work here. brought produce flat and what you did sell and get money for perhaps the money would be worthless when you were home."[46]

Railroad mileage in Iowa totaled 679.67 miles at the time of the 1860 census. Many of the roads, all located in the eastern one-third of the state, were in difficult financial straits. Most disappointing of all was the performance of the Mississippi and Missouri, recipient of the first Iowa railroad land grant. Starting from Davenport it had yet to reach Des Moines, much less the proposed western terminus at Council Bluffs. At this time the Rock Island bridged the Mississippi at Davenport; the Illinois Central reached Dunleith opposite Dubuque; and the Chicago, Burlington, and Quincy touched opposite Burlington. Cattle and hog raisers who lived close to these towns or close to their Iowa extensions and feeder lines counted themselves fortunate. Shipping costs by rail were low enough to leave them more profit than they could realize from the traditional method of selling to drovers. Complaints about freight rates were common all the same. "It is of very little consequence to us whether Eastern railroads pay large or small dividends, or whether they pay any at all or not. Cheap freights are what we want," wrote the editor of the Burlington *Hawk-eye* in a burst of candor in March of 1860.[47]

In the year and a half that preceded the war, the state's three major shipping points, Dubuque, Davenport and Burlington, partially recovered from the economic collapse of 1857. Dubuquers acknowledged that 1860 was a year of steady improvement. Shipments of wheat, flour, corn, eggs, potatoes, apples, hides, live and dressed hogs, wool, cattle, barley, and oats in and out of the city increased by 75 percent over those of 1859. *Herald* editor Dennis Mahony claimed that secession would bring no harm to Dubuque. The South would not interfere with the river trade; in fact, the Northwest would enjoy free trade through Mobile and New Orleans. Easterners, he crowed, dreaded the prospect.[48]

Dubuque's business people were optimistic for another reason. Racine and Milwaukee actively courted the city's trade on the eve of the war. Both cities sought to divert it from Chicago. Racine businessmen sponsored a train load of Dubuque business leaders, lawyers, editors, and political figures on an all-day excursion to let them see for themselves Racine's advantages as a trading partner. This culminated in a banquet at which both groups avowed their mutual interest in harmonious and widened trade. These dreams never materialized as Chicago continued to maintain its preeminence as Dubuque's primary trading outlet. The Racine episode was less noteworthy for results than it was as a revelation of the significance of North-South compared with East-West trade immediately prior to the war in the upper Mississippi Valley. This disclosure came in a speech by Judge

Thomas S. Wilson. Wilson reviewed the commercial history of Dubuque in detail, pointing out that until the middle 1850s when the railroad came to Dunleith, St. Louis was the only major outlet for its trade. St. Louis continued to delude itself, Wilson declared, in believing that Dubuque needed St. Louis. Following the depression of 1857, St. Louis business interests claimed Dubuque merchants failed to pay their debts and made it clear that St. Louis didn't need the upper Mississippi Valley trade anyway. They would get what they wanted from the Missouri River Valley. Now, Wilson gloated, St. Louis sang a different tune because the Hannibal to St. Joseph railroad had siphoned off most of the freight and passengers formerly destined for itself. St. Louis now suffered. "Its papers now say that trade with the Upper Mississippi Valley must be cultivated, and that Iowa is not such a bad state after all. This shows the folly of expecting a city to monopolize trade which has not railroads to meet the needs of the age, and of expecting water communication to take the place of them." Nevertheless, Dubuque had some stake in Southern trade. Responding in mid-December, months before Wilson's remarks at Racine, to what he believed to be a lack of concern with New Orleans markets, one Dubuque businessman sought to set *Herald* readers straight. Some Dubuque mills, he wrote, shipped all their flour to New Orleans because they had better markets there than in the East. The same was true for most corn and oats. "Flour goes South and wheat goes East as a general rule," he asserted.[49]

The Davenport *Democrat* claimed that the city was doing well in the fall of 1859. Farmers were better off, and the paper urged that easterners consider moving to Iowa.[50] But editor David Richardson was less sanguine after Lincoln's election the next year. A great crash lay ahead, he predicted, one which would leave "nothing but wrecks behind," in both North and South. He listed several ominous signs including bank suspensions; conversion of bonds, securities, and paper into specie; and specie-hoarding. Richardson printed figures purporting to show that Lincoln's election cost Scott county farmers $12,000 in less than two weeks' time. He estimated that the loss to all Iowa wheat growers, who probably sold two million bushels of wheat during that period, was $200,000.[51] In midwinter 1861, Davenport still looked South, hoping for secessionist outlets, partly because of currently high rail rates to Chicago. Corn dealers kept their stocks off the market, waiting for the Mississippi ice to melt. So did one wheat operator who held onto 57,000 bushels. A little over a month before the outbreak of war, one overstocked shipper sent loads of potatoes every day to deep South buyers via rail to Peoria and thence by river. He was not alone. In Burlington the *Hawk-eye* noted the heavy movement of produce to points south of St. Louis. As late as mid-March Davenport received a big order from Texas for 18,000 bushels of sacked corn.[52]

At Burlington by 1857, the Burlington and Missouri River Railroad tapped the produce to the west. Ferried across the river, it went mostly eastward via the Chicago and Burlington, later known as the CB&Q (the Chicago, Burlington, and Quincy). The city's meat packers by 1859–1860 were sending dressed pork to Cincinnati. Cattle came east on the Burlington and Missouri from as far as Ottumwa,

76 miles away. They also came by foot, and in that season Burlington claimed more drovers passed through on their way east than through any other river point north of St. Louis. Sometimes poor management cut into the drovers' profits. When a Texas group tried to get their herd of plains cattle to swim the river at Muscatine, the cattle panicked. Wisdom prevailed eventually, and the Muscatine ferry operator prospered accordingly. Near Vinton, hard driving killed 15 to 20 hogs in another drove.[53] During the winter of 1860, so long as the ice covered the river, Burlington did good business with Illinois farmers. They drove thousands of hogs across the ice to be slaughtered. In addition, they brought corn, wheat, hay, wood, butter, and poultry. Burlington traders used the ice also. After it began to melt, the ferry carried cattle to a point where the ice was still strong. There they debarked and headed across the frozen Illinois side.[54] In early November, 1860, the Burlington *Hawk-eye* professed to be less worried about the possibility of disunion and business failure and disruption of trade than did the *Democrat*. But by midwinter of 1861, the editor was less certain. The people could stand secession so long as it consisted only of resolutions, he wrote. But any Southern move to obstruct passage on the Mississippi was another matter.[55]

How important was North-South trade on the Mississippi River? Wood Gray has argued that by 1860 the South was of minimal importance to the Northwest, either as a consumer or as an exporter of its production. River trade with New Orleans, in short, counted for little compared with that between the Northwest and the great urban markets and export centers of the Northeast. But old assumptions died hard, he added. The average midwesterner still believed that his welfare depended upon access to Southern markets. Frank Klement, on the other hand, believes that Southern markets were yet vital to the region. Paul Gates also emphasizes the economic ties between West and South, particularly the dependence of the South upon the upper Mississippi Valley for foodstuffs by 1860. The South, he declares, having opted for cotton production on a grand scale, was emerging as a "food deficit area" in the two decades preceding the war. Gates also contends that New Orleans was a major exporter of western foodstuffs as late as 1859. So far as western exports flowing out of New Orleans to Atlantic coast and foreign ports is concerned, there is no doubt that the flow declined significantly in the twenty years prior to the war. Whereas in 1845 one-half of the Mississippi Valley's surplus went to New Orleans, in 1860 this share was down to 23 percent. One problem here is that of geographical definition. Everyone who deals with the West in discussing trade patterns in the prewar period uses "Northwest," "Upper Mississippi Valley," or "Midwest" to mean West. Generally one can take it to mean that region north of St. Louis, north and east of the Missouri River, north of the Ohio River, and west of Pennyslvania. "Upper Mississippi Valley" certainly means Iowa. But Gates also speaks of Indiana and Cincinnati as being in the "upper part of the Mississippi Valley."[56] The problem is simply that western products arriving at New Orleans came from a vast region. Parts of that region were to be more adversely affected than others by the wartime blockade of the Mississippi. Hence, to say that the West was hurt or not hurt, or that all of the prewar West profited by the South's becoming a food deficit area is to fuzz over the question: Which part or parts of the West were so or most affected?

However the word West may be defined, railroads, canals, and the Great Lakes by 1860 carried the bulk of its burgeoning production eastward. Moreover, the western states acquired many supplies like coffee from the East, which previously had come upriver.[57] Total imports into the West jumped from 360,000 tons to 900,000 tons between 1849 and 1860. But imports into the West from New Orleans included in these figures increased only from 125,000 tons to 200,000.[58] Bulk grain certainly moved East far more than South by 1860, to the near exclusion of New Orleans. Chicago that year received 50 million bushels, Milwaukee 10 million and New Orleans only 5,198,927. Furthermore, New Orleans in the 1860–1861 season exported a minuscule 2,189 bushels of wheat, 80,500 barrels of flour, and 224,382 bushels of corn, rye, oats, and small grains compared with New York's 23,859,147 bushels of wheat, 2,728,012 barrels of flour, and 9,268,729 bushels of corn.[59] Additional evidence of the decline of New Orleans as an important outlet for western surpluses is seen in the work of economist Albert Fishlow. Fishlow's studies show that in 1860, western foodstuffs reexported from New Orleans totaled only 3 percent of all surplus western foodstuffs. This included 3 percent of its flour, 2 percent of its corn, and 1 percent each of its meat products and whiskey. This was a striking drop from 1857, when 13 percent of all western foodstuffs shipped out of the West were reexported through the Crescent City.[60]

If New Orleans was relatively unimportant to the West by 1860 as an exporter of its surplus, and if the products sent upriver were less and less important in the total volume of western imports, was the New Orleans-served South, nevertheless, an important market for Iowa producers? Dubuque, or McGregor farther north, by 1860–1861 may have earned very little from Southern trade overall. Northern Iowa grain, for example, by 1860, usually went downriver only as far as LaCrosse, Wisconsin; Dunleith opposite Dubuque on the river; or Fulton, Illinois; thence by rail to the Lake ports.[61] The *Herald* unhappily admitted the unimportance of Southern trade to Dubuque. St. Louis, complained the editor, was responsible for this development, although he assigned a different reason than did Judge Wilson several months later at Racine. When the railroads reached the Mississippi River, St. Louis shippers gave up the contest. They could have been more than a match for eastern competitors. Now the Mississippi Valley had to depend upon seaboard cities, the writer complained, "paying them tribute without a reciprocal return of benefits," a common as well as an inaccurate assessment of the relationship.[62]

Further down the river, more Iowa products went south, but this traffic also declined in the 1850s. Burlington by 1855–1856 recognized that railroads had supplanted the river as the major carrier of products in and out of the city. In the fall of 1860 in those places where East-South competition was yet a factor, shippers kept a close eye on rates and acted intelligently, as they did a month before Lincoln's election, sending everything east because river rates were too high. A rise in the water level three weeks later caused some Burlington shippers to send some goods to St. Louis. But the *Hawk-eye,* even as it complained about high rail rates hurting the farmers, acknowledged that the St. Louis revival was only temporary, the market there being in a "declining state."[63] Fishlow believes such trade overall never was of major significance to the West or the South, adding, "The South was neither a major market for western producers nor in dire need of imported foodstuffs." By 1839, for example, at the high point of demand for western foodstuffs, the South purchased less than one-fifth of the total exports of the West.[64] Instead, he stresses the South's growing self-sufficiency and expanding intra-Southern trade which supplied increasing percentages of foodstuffs sent to New Orleans. The border states became major suppliers. Louisville, for example, exported one-fifth of the pork and bacon arriving at New Orleans by 1853 and one-third by 1860. And the South, 1840–1860, produced more corn, swine, cattle, peas, and beans per capita than the national average. In these foodstuffs there is striking evidence that western sales were small indeed by 1859–1860, compared with Southern production of the same. In 1860, Southern consumption of western corn was 1,590,131 sacks (two sacks to the bushel), compared with 340 million bushels produced in the South itself in 1859. That means that the South produced 99 percent of the corn it consumed. Southern-produced wheat consumed in the South (consumed as flour at five bushels to the barrel), amounted to 38 million bushels in 1859. Western wheat (1860) consumed in the South amounted to 4,250,000 bushels, or 11 percent of the total. Fishlow calculates that in 1860, western pork, bacon, and beef only accounted for 5 percent of the South's consumption of these items, the rest coming from the South itself. In short, if the South was a food deficit region, the deficit was small and easy to overcome by producing more foodstuffs and less cotton. However, western products consumed in the South were more significant to the West in terms of total western production—keeping in mind the unanswered question: significant to which part or parts of the West? In 1860, the South consumed 19 percent of the West's flour; 23 percent of its meat products; 17 percent of its corn; 39 percent of its whiskey; and overall, 14 percent of its foodstuffs. Nearly all of this came in at New Orleans. Nevertheless, Fishlow concludes: "The South was virtually self-sufficient in foodstuffs on the eve of the Civil War and the re-export trade had dwindled to insignificant proportions. Political overtures to the West were without economic content."[65]

Still, for some parts of the West, Southern consumption of its production was probably yet important, even if the great majority of that production went east. As a result of the 1857 crash and ensuing depression lasting into the early war years, most westerners lived in an economic climate in which there was no sure thing, no absolutely dependable hedge against economic disaster. They sold where they could, to the home market and to the East primarily, to the South secondarily. In any case, any sales were vital because the depression left them with no safety margin. Southern sales, limited though they were, probably provided the difference between an adequate living and an inadequate one—or worse— for some westerners, although how many or in what areas of the West are uncertain. Politicians of both parties could and did capitalize upon this concern, before and during the war. This is not to deny that people in some locations seemed less concerned about Southern sales. Dubuque looked more to the East and saw its prosperity coming mainly from eastern sales. Davenport and Burlington looked East also, but being farther downriver they watched the Southern market more closely. All river town newspapers regularly carried market reports from New York and Chicago. In addition, the great bulk of newspaper copy devoted to commerce did deal with grain, cattle, hogs, beef, and packed pork headed east by rail. St. Louis and New Orleans market reports appeared far less regularly. Nevertheless, significant loadings destined for St. Louis or New Orleans always received newspaper attention.

So did one other matter as the Confederacy assumed substance: tariffs. David Richardson compared the existing federal tariff with the low-rate revenue tariff levied by the Confederate congress and gloomily concluded that Great Britain and France would have "a very plausible excuse for recognizing the independence of the seceding states." The Burlington *Hawk-eye* editor speculated that if secession became a fact the Confederate tariff would attract imports at Savannah and New Orleans to the ruin of loyal cities like Baltimore and New York.[66]

Ultimately such concerns led to speculation about peaceful separation of North and South or of West and East in such a way as to avoid economic catastrophe. The *Hawk-eye* reported some talk about the formation of a Northern confederacy. But any such confederacy would require an open Mississippi. Iowa and the rest of the Northwest would stand for nothing less, the paper said. Dennis Mahony began to think of a different alignment. If significantly lower tariff rates prevailed in the South, would it be sensible for the Mississippi Valley states to "remain tributary to the interests of New York, New England and Pennsylvania? . . ." he asked. For a brief time, however, he professed to believe that President Lincoln was preparing the nation for a North-South separation, though moving slowly so as to not anger the North. Negotiate trade treaties with the seceders, he urged. Get uniform imposts and limited trade restrictions. Then grant the South de jure recognition. Too long a delay would prevent the North from getting the "commercial advantages and privileges which would not be easily secured." When that possibility seemed to fade, he returned to the idea that Iowa, with other "congenial elements," might split from the East, without specifying which elements he had in mind. Burlington banker W. W. White in private was both specific and emphatic. All states favoring "Constitutional government" should separate themselves "peaceably if possible, forcibly if necessary" from "Yankeedom," he wrote. And that might well mean Iowa's joining the South to enjoy the benefits of free trade.[67]

Speculations about Iowa's future and how Iowans would best serve their economic interests made sense only in light of the political developments in the fifteen months preceding the war. For the leading men of the Democratic minority, those developments had been a series of unmitigated disasters. For them, Murphy's law was apropos: "If anything can go wrong, it will."

2

Looming Crisis: 1860 to Fort Sumter, April, 1861

LAUREL SUMMERS, United States Marshal for Iowa, had a problem in early 1860. Appointed to office by Franklin Pierce in 1853, Summers served through the years of the Democratic debacle in Iowa. A willing laborer in the party's inner circle and a correspondent of many of its leaders, the Marshal remained a Buchanan loyalist without raising the hackles of the Douglas wing. Now, thanks to his position and the upcoming census, he had some balm to dispense to unhappy party workers—patronage jobs as census takers and their assistants.

That was the problem. Many eager Democrats demanded posts as their due, especially Buchanan men who frequently denounced competitors as Douglas apostates in terms usually reserved for Republicans. Reticent they were not. One issued a threat. Sometime newspaper editor, John Parrish of Harrison county, wrote that he would once again start up a Democratic organ if he won a post. Otherwise not. "I want to know whether you intend to help or pull down politically in this county. That's the question," he concluded belligerently.[1] Summers, a conscientious man, soon despaired of making sound choices on his own, so he solicited advice from other party leaders. Bernhart Henn from Fairfield and Augustus Dodge were helpful. They always recommended men who had remained loyal to Buchanan.[2] There was little else for Iowa Democrats to scramble for, certainly not at the top where the Iowa Legislature easily reelected James Harlan to the Senate over Dodge.

Iowa's Republican congressmen contributed to Democratic discomfiture by sending copies of Democratic congressional speeches to Republican papers. They were "so full of Slavery, Disunion and Treason," commented the Keokuk *Des Moines Valley Whig*, "that nothing else is considered likely to be as effective in bringing the people to a feeling sense of the true character of the Democratic party, and of the perils with which it has surrounded the country."[3] David Richardson recognized the damage such speeches could cause. Hence, he welcomed President Buchanan's recommendation that the United States at some future date acquire Cuba and occupy portions of Mexico's northern province to put an end to bandit raids from that quarter. Such bold steps would have the virtue of "crushing out and repressing dissension at home," he felt.[4]

Iowa sent a Douglas slate of delegates to the Charleston convention where Dubuque lawyer Ben Samuels was a leader in the successful fight to replace the Southern plank on slavery in the territories with one embodying Douglas's particular popular sovereignty concept. The Iowa delegation stuck with Douglas at the Baltimore convention, also, and in July the state convention endorsed him for president. Finally die-hard administration Democrats balked. Despite pleas from men in their own ranks like Richardson, who argued that Douglas was strong in Iowa whether he (Richardson) or they liked it or not, they held a Breckinridge convention. They also chose a set of Breckinridge electors. Beyond that, administration Democrats took little part in the campaign.[5] In late August, two weeks after the Breckinridge convention, forty to fifty Bell and Everett supporters met in Iowa City, announced that they were against sectional strife, and went home.[6] Meanwhile, moderate Republicans counseled the party to unite behind "men of conservative tendencies" and against extremists. They had to be, however, "inflexibly fixed in their opposition to the extension of slavery. . . ." Most Republicans were partial to William Seward; but there was early mention of Lincoln, and the Lincoln-Hamlin ticket was a popular choice.[7] Likewise with the Davenport Germans, complained Richardson. "[They] appeared to be generally pleased with the nomination," he wrote, "as the abolition proclivities of Mr. Lincoln are just the same as they openly profess."[8] Two other factors, however, were probably at least as important as their alleged abolition bias in motivating those Iowa Germans who lined up with the Republicans. First, the Republicans did not nominate Missouri's Edward Bates or Pennsylvania's Simon Cameron whom the Germans thought were nativist sympathizers. Second, the Republican platform contained a resolution opposing any changes in federal or state laws that might limit immigrant opportunity to become citizens.[9]

Douglas campaigned briefly in the state in October, making a major address at Iowa City. He denounced Republican opposition to popular sovereignty and charged that Northern and Southern sectionalists promoted disunion sentiments. Breckinridge Southerners, Douglas claimed, favored Lincoln's election so they would have an excuse for secession.[10] Republicans campaigned hard but with confidence. They attacked Buchanan's veto of the homestead bill, called for a Pacific railroad act, and reiterated their opposition to the further spread of slavery while denying that they intended to disturb the institution in those states where it existed.

Republicans, however, had no desire to appear overly sympathetic to blacks in slavery or in freedom. A campaign letter urged Southerners to listen to Republicans. "They will find," wrote Henry Scholte, a Dutch-born Pella editor,

that we too in the North are white men and have no desire to draw their black, brown, yellow or other colored servant, into our community or embrace. . . . We will keep in the North the unconstitutional Abolitionists down, let them keep in the South the unconstitutional Disunionists down, and we can yet be and remain a happy, contented and prosperous nation. . . .

Scholte also denied that Republicans ever promoted black interests. Eastern state Democrats, he said, were responsible for those citizenship and voting rights which blacks did possess.[11] The Council Bluffs *Nonpareil* made no such appeal to the South. But it agreed that Democrats, not Republicans, favored black equality and black suffrage. Moreover, Republicans bore no responsibility for the "production of Mulattoes, and for all the disgusting concubinage which prevails in the South." Had not Andrew Jackson, a Democrat, called Southern blacks "brethern" when he appealed for their help at the battle of New Orleans? Had not Democratic Vice-President Richard Johnson lived all his life with a black concubine? One can add that had the *Nonpareil* been the least bit soft on the black issue, it could have expected no quarter from its intracity rival, the *Bugle.* But there was another side to the *Bugle's* position on race, a side not dissimilar to that exhibited by other Democratic papers in the state. Editor Lysander Babbitt exploited racial issues— but he didn't want outsiders messing with Council Bluffs' free blacks. When kidnappers abducted John Williamson, Williamson's sister and brother-in-law, and took them to Missouri, Babbitt was outraged. Efforts of some Council Bluffs citizens (all Democrats, the editor claimed) brought about Williamson's return. Babbitt also demanded that the kidnappers be caught and punished. What makes Babbitt's position even more interesting is that Williamson had worked successfully for the Underground Railroad in western Iowa.[12]

Ambiguity on race questions was not exclusive with Democratic editors. During the campaign nearly everybody, Democrat or Republican, who said or wrote anything for public consumption about the place of blacks in American life agreed that that place was a position inferior to whites. Republicans and Democrats equivocated on slavery. Republicans attacked slavery but denied they were abolitionists. Democrats defended slavery on constitutional grounds while denying that they approved the institution personally. One who did not equivocate got blistered. That was Henry Clay Dean. Dean told a Fairfield audience that "Since the crucifixion of Christ there has not been so benevolent an institution known among men as African slavery." Nor had so many barbarians become civilized and Christianized as under Southern slavery specifically. The *Hawk-eye* promptly labeled Dean a "depraved wretch" and reminded readers that he was a Douglas elector. The story elicited an angry rebuttal from Stilson Hutchins, editor of the Des Moines *Journal.* Hutchins, later to become a bitter Copperhead given to antiblack diatribes, refused to believe that any minister could possibly utter such words.[13]

Slave stealing and even slaveholding among Iowans were occasional news items in Iowa that election year. Tabor citizens spirited four black fugitives North to freedom. A black man near Osceola was less fortunate. Though he claimed to be a free laborer and had $150 in his pocket, abductors dragged him across the Missouri line and jailed him at Princeton. The sheriff announced that he would hold the captive for three months. If not claimed, the black would go on the auction block. Argument raged in Iowa City early in the year over whether two black girls were really slaves of a local man and wife rather than bound apprentices as the couple claimed.[14]

As the election approached, Dubuque's *Der National-Demokrat* became more and more disturbed by the possibility of a Republican triumph. The editor tried hard to ensure that his readers would do nothing to help bring it about. One inflammatory article listed a series of scurrilous statements, purportedly voiced by prominent Republicans and their newspapers, under the headline "Rep Reichflaschen fur die Deutschen!" (Republican Smelling Bottle [Salts] for the Germans.) According to the paper, Ohio Republican Tom Corwin once declared, "It'll be the happiest day of my life when I wander knee-deep through the blood of the immigrants with both my hands digging out their bowels." Andrew Curtin, gubernatorial candidate in Pennsylvania, supposedly threatened to shoot someone he labeled a "God-damned German dog." A newspaper described only as the *Herald* apparently judged that "A nigger is far more intelligent than a Catholic." And "Judge Schurz" (probably Carl Schurz) reportedly sneered on one occasion, "The Germans and Irish Democrats are as dumb as this krauthead." (The unfortunate "krauthead" remained mercifully anonymous.) *Der National-Demokrat* also complained that Massachusetts pampered black voters while it denied many Germans the ballot. Meanwhile, German Republicans in Cincinnati, Chicago, and other western cities refused to be upset by such discrimination. *Der National-Demokrat* also tried to convince its readers that, contrary to the claims of German-Republican organs, slave labor was no threat to Northern white labor. Rather, northern and eastern workers benefited from Southern trade. Were this trade to cease, the Northern economy would suffer severely. The fact was, concluded the paper, that Northern white labor could exist very well alongside Southern slave labor.[15]

The Des Moines *Wochentliche Iowa Post,* as strong for Lincoln as *Der National-Demokrat* was for Douglas, was as sensitive about anti-German slights as the Dubuque paper. The difference was that it culled such slights from Democratic sources—Iowa ones at that. When the Bloomfield *Democratic Clarion* declared that Nicholas Rusch should have relinquished his lieutenant governor post in favor of a more qualified Republican, and that Rusch should quit frequenting beer parlors and singing German songs which native Americans couldn't understand, the *Post* reacted angrily. Nor did the editor take lightly a slur in the Keokuk *Journal* that Germans were a bunch of "beer drinking Dutchmen." The combative *Post* also scorned *Der National-Demokrat,* especially when the Dubuque paper proclaimed that most Iowa Germans were Democrats, not Republicans.[16] As usual, Dubuque Germans voted heavily Democratic, but in Burlington the *Hawk-eye* complimented the city's Germans for voting in what it claimed was "a solid phalanx" for Lincoln. A Keokuk correspondent told Kirkwood that but for the failure of a judge to hold court as promised to naturalize some German Republicans, Lincoln would have carried Lee county instead of losing it by seventeen votes.[17]

Democrats had whistled in the dark as November approached, professing to see a surge toward Douglas among the electorate. But in the end no one was surprised at the magnitude of Lincoln's victory. The Illinoisan collected 70,316 votes, Douglas 55,091, John Bell, 1,763, and Breckinridge 1,035.[18] Nor perhaps did all

Democrats care. Clearly the prominent but numerically impotent Buchanan regulars had no love for Douglas or his supporters. In August ex-Senator Jones denounced Ben Samuels, the party's candidate for Congress from the Second District, as "the unscrupulous and bitter reviler of Mr. Buchanan and his Adm." Douglas was even worse: "the most corrupt of all politicians."[19] Charles Mason was less a Douglas hater than Jones. Nevertheless, he viewed Douglas's defeat as "fitting retribution for the part he took in repealing the Missouri Compromise which opened the floodgates of strife and overwhelmed the Democratic party."[20] Douglas backer, J. B. Dorr of the Dubuque *Herald,* an acerbic critic of Buchanan and Southern fire-eaters, had few friends among old guard party men. When Dorr sold the *Herald* in May, 1860, they greeted his departure with pleasure.[21] Dorr, however, had the last word. In an arrangement as unusual as it must have been galling to new editor Dennis Mahony, Dorr announced that he would retain control of the "political department" until after the election. Dorr wanted to be certain that the *Herald* would be an unequivocal Douglas paper during the campaign. When Mahony espoused a view of popular sovereignty which, in Dorr's opinion, deviated too much from the Douglas position, he reminded readers that Mahony's views were not necessarily those of the *Herald.* For a time thereafter, Dorr signed all editorials with his initials.[22]

Democratic press reaction to defeat reflected all the diversity that existed within the party. The most optimistic—and most superficial—came from the Bloomfield *Democratic Clarion* which opined that Republican concern over slavery and its spread would cease now that the party was victorious. More gloomy and more accurate was the Lyons *City Advocate,* the only journal to back the Breckinridge-Lane ticket. The editor saw "disunionist sentiment . . . assuming shape and form that it never before had" as a prelude to civil war.[23] Dennis Mahony, at last in full command of the *Herald'*s political department, had strong words of advice for the South. The South should not, he declared, "suffer the compact which brought them into the Union to be violated with impunity and without means of redress; submit to incursions into their territory and trespass upon their property by Northern Abolitionists [nor look] . . . submissively upon every aggression upon their domestic institutions. . . ."[24]

Just as angry as Mahony at the outcome of the election was the editor of the Muscatine *Daily Review,* a Douglas paper. He blamed New York, Philadelphia, and Chicago papers for the nation's troubles. New York newspapers in particular lied when they portrayed Southerners as barbarians, he charged. Southerners expelled no Northern men from the South for expressing their political opinions. They hung no preachers for preaching on topics not related to the Gospel. Philadelphia and Chicago papers were equally inaccurate. He elaborated at length:

> The great men of the country are greater slaves than the negroes of the South; they are slaves to every newspaper, telegraph operator or correspondent in the country. If they have a mind of their own, they dare not speak it. The newspaper press rules everything from a quack doctor to the President of the

United States. The whole character of American journalism is intrinsically similar—if there is any favorable difference it depends on the local tastes or humors of the vicinity; they are merely politic adaptations. Some meretorious [sic] tendencies may be found in the rural districts, either from ignorance or simplicity of heart, but this does not qualify the hypothesis that everything is swayed to an[d] fro by the press.

The Southern press was just as bad. But if editors could create sectional feeling, they could also destroy it by suppressing "all and every line calculated to inflame the minds of our people."[25] *Der National-Demokrat* similarly complained about "tricky speakers" misleading the workers in preelection campaigning. Too many believed that the Republican victory would bring better times. Now, said the editor, citing the New York *Journal of Commerce*, 25,000 workers had lost their jobs since the election, and "rumors and reports recur about more worker lay-offs and closing factories."[26] One frustrated Democrat predicted to Laurel Summers that the incoming administration would appoint a new corps of abolitionist federal marshals "who will not regard an oath where a *nigger* is concerned. . . ." He recommended not very hopefully to Summers that Summers invoke divine guidance. "I wish you would *pray* three times for peace—it may help some. I have tried several times but they all act worse for it."[27]

Still, while all Iowa Democrats viewed Lincoln's election as a calamity, many of them rejected Southern secession out of hand. Wrote Davenport attorney James J. Lindley to Summers, "I am not with the South on this matter. . . . I do not believe in peaceable secession. The thing was not contemplated by the framers of the Constitution. The States came into the Union without conditions for all time."[28] J. B. Dorr lashed out at those Southerners "who by magnifying Southern wrongs have been deluding and misleading the citizens of the Southern states. . . . They aim at nothing but the destruction of the Government and the establishment of a Southern Confederacy. . . ."[29] Self-styled "Old Line Democrat" Enos Lowe told Charles Mason that no matter how bad a Republican victory was, Southern secession was worse. "No state," he wrote, "has a right to take back the power and authority delegated to the General Government without the consent of all the states." Secession angered Burlington's David Rorer, also. The mass of the Southern people, he hoped, would drive the traitors out and re-join the Union.[30] Judge J. M. Love also opposed secession, but he placed less hope in the efforts of Southern unionists. Better, he argued, to win the allegiance of the border states by pursuing a no-war policy. With the border states remaining loyal, unionists North and South would have the strength to reconstruct the nation.[31] Equally interesting were the reactions of two Democrats who were to wind up as Republican regulars before the end of the war. "We *National* Democrats," George C. Tichenor exhorted, "must buckle on the armor and once more gather the true patriots of the North beneath the glorious banner of 'Equal Rights to all' and gallantly throw ourselves into the breach and scatter, dismay, crush and exterminate the Hell hounds of fanaticism, give no quarter either to Abolitionist or weak kneed Democrats, but drive them to a common grave." William W.

Belknap, future Secretary of War in the Grant administration, who in the fall of 1861 would join the army, declared passionately that the flag was "disgraced when used by Abolitionists to aid in their hypocritical efforts in favor of what they call Union. A Union under the control and influence of a sectional party is but a Union in name—soon to be a mockery."[32]

Meanwhile, Iowa Republicans were jubilant over the election results and seemed not to grasp the extent of Southern bitterness. Addressing himself to both Southern and Northern Democrats, one of them wrote, "We out-voted you. We did not admit that you had the divine right to rule, and we promise you in advance a better administration than you have given us in the past four years. If not, your remedy is at the polls in 1864."[33] As secession loomed and Northern Democrats clamored for compromise, some Republicans grew more stubborn. Clark Dunham, *Hawk-eye* editor, was one. The party, he wrote, should not retreat "from the great central idea in the Chicago platform;—that slavery is a moral, social, political evil . . . and must not be extended over free territory."[34] Two days later the *Iowa State Register* seconded this position. The people of the free states "will not lay a finger upon the institutions of the Southern States," said the paper, "but they cannot be made to surrender the fruits of the recent victory. They will stand by their platform . . . and thus fulfill the glorious destiny of the Union, whether the cotton states are in it or out of it."[35] The Davenport *Gazette* fumed at secession preparations and charged that the South simply wanted to avoid paying debts owed Northern creditors. The editor also unburdened himself on another matter. Too long had Northern travelers been treated badly in the South. Too long had Northerners kept silent in order to keep the peace. Unlike the Muscatine *Daily Review* editor, the Davenport newspaperman believed the eastern press. "Northern men," he wrote,

> cannot travel in the South upon their ordinary business without they are prepared . . . to clothe themselves with cursing as with a garment, upon the mere utterance of the name of Abraham Lincoln . . . the faintest shadow of having exercised a freeman's right in the North in favor of free soil, free speech and human liberty, brings the lash, tar and feathers, and perhaps the hangman's rope or banishment. . . .[36]

Henry Scholte, now much more antagonistic to the South, voiced the same attitude. "It seems," he wrote, "as if we in the North have no freedom to express our opinion in reference to the institution of Slavery but that the Southern men have perfect liberty to curse and villify every Northern man. . . ."[37]

Many Iowa Republicans increasingly became hardened against the secessionists as the latter began to act on their threats. Shortly after the election James B. Howell, editor of the Keokuk *Gate City*, wrote that no one would disturb South Carolina if she departed the Union. But by early January Howell was applauding the movement to organize volunteer militia companies in Keokuk.[38] Dubuque businessman Solon Langworthy believed that eastern interference with the Southern people's local institutions was insufficient "to justify them in acts which would endanger the perpetuity of the only representative and free government on the earth."[39] If Charles Mason can be believed, Senator Grimes at first opposed efforts to force Southerners to stay in the Union. Since early December, however, he seemed to be "much more undecided on that subject," wrote the dejected Mason.[40] Still, Mason and other Democrats continued to hope that Republicans would come to their senses, that they might yet compromise on the slavery-in-the-territories issue so that the South might reverse course and decide to remain in the Union after all. The Sioux City *Register* viewed the territorial question as an "abstraction" only and believed that the South mainly needed assurance that the North was not at root hostile—that it would not agitate further against slavery. The Davenport *Democrat* also argued that a Republican retreat toward compromise on the territorial question would harm nobody since so little remaining territory was fit for slavery anyway. Charles Mason agreed. Even Arizona and New Mexico which had the proper climate would find Mexican labor cheaper. "We can therefore be just without any detriment to ourselves," he wrote. For a time after the election, Mason and Dennis Mahony clung to the idea that Southerners should have the right to take slaves into any territory. Later both accepted the Crittenden proposals. They demanded even more of the Republicans. The Dubuque editor put it succinctly; "Republicanism must be abandoned as a principle or the Union cannot be preserved."[41]

Iowa's Republican leaders would have none of it. Senator Grimes wrote that any concession would lead to other Southern demands, including annexation of Mexico. Equally important to Grimes was that the South renounce secession as a right.[42] Governor Kirkwood simply called secession treason. The *Iowa State Register* called it revolution and said flatly that there was no right to secede from the Union.[43] Sounding like Democrats Lindley, Dorr, and Lowe, the Burlington *Hawk-eye* argued that the Founding Fathers created no "temporary league." Rather, they formed "a perpetual Union . . . with ample power to protect itself."[44]

The Democratic Independence *Civilian* at the other extreme argued that a state could come into or walk out of the Union by choice.[45] Not Lysander Babbitt. He rejected secession by that route since, in his view, secession without congressional consent was illegal. Yet he saw a way to effect it. Let the Southerners draw up a constitution and submit it for voter ratification. If ratified, submit it to Congress where both governments could resolve differences and negotiate for peaceful separation. On the other hand, if the South Carolinians insisted on unilateral withdrawal, if they kept the peace, and if they kept their hands off federal property, Babbitt would let them go. Their leaving federal property alone was important to the *Bugle* editor. If they did not, he favored forceful action to teach them a lesson.[46] The Davenport *Democrat* was less permissive. If there was no power to hold states in the Union, David Richardson pointed out, then it was obvious that all federal laws could be nullified at any time and that any state could secede whenever it took a notion to do so. This was unacceptable. Congress might have to pass a force bill to prevent it.[47]

At this point the difference between Iowa Democrats who later became known as Copperheads and those who became War Democrats, at least in the judgment of those who tried honestly to draw such a distinction, began to appear. It put David Richardson in the war camp in opposition to fellow editors Mahony and Babbitt. After the November election, Mahony, Babbitt, Charles Mason, and others like them never entirely excused rebel behavior. They often said that the South should have remained within the Union awhile longer and worked with the Northern Democrats to try to win concessions from the incoming administration. But in the main they assumed that if the South acted too hastily, the South was correct in assuming that the administration would make no meaningful compromise.[48]

Nevertheless, those disgruntled Democrats who appeared to condone secession too readily and too outspokenly found themselves belabored by other embarrassed Democrats. This happened in Dubuque, "Gibraltar of the Iowa Democracy," in late November. The city's self-proclaimed National Democratic Club asserted that the "Confederate states" had no reason to believe the Lincoln administration would reject radicalism. Nor could they depend upon the "American mind" to support the Constitution and its binding obligations. Consequently, the Confederates were entirely justified in taking steps to maintain their rights, inside or outside the Union. Furthermore, if they could achieve greater internal unity they could count on the support of the Dubuque National Democrat body.

Even in Dubuque that was going too far. The National Democratic Club found itself in hot water. Spokesmen quickly denied that it favored secession and explained that the members only wished the Southerners to achieve success in their efforts to "vindicate their rights as freemen under the common Constitution. . . ." The explanation did not satisfy one disenchanted club member. The National Democratic Club was actually the Breckinridge and Lane Club, wrote Col. H. H. Heath to the *Herald,* and he for one opposed its stand. Mahony also reacted quickly. He felt that the club had invited the South to secede, a step too far too soon. There was, he cautioned, no justification yet for secession because there was one constitutional remedy yet untried—resort to the Supreme Court. Mahony agreed that a majority of citizens probably disputed Southern claims to slaveholding rights in the territories. But the Court should interpret that right. Then if either North or South rejected the decision, one could say that the Union was "virtually dissolved." In such case there was no need for an overt act by either side to annul the compact. Mahony condemned the Dubuque group's stand not once, but twice. On the other hand, he was not about to suggest that the South do nothing. "It is not the constitutionally recognized right of the majority to express its will with a view to enforcing it in some matters," he wrote. "The will of the majority may violate the fundamental rights of a minority, and it would be the right of the minority in that case to resist aggression."[49]

During this period Charles Mason, like Mahony, made a serious effort to think through the problems posed by secession. He believed that those states who wished to quit the Union had the right to leave if they took the "proper steps through [their] legally constituted authorities.'' "Voluntary allegiance,'' he added, "the result of mutual advantages derived from the Union, is all that we must rely upon to keep us one people.'' It was a principle which furnished "an efficient check upon the disposition of an overwhelming majority to tyrannize over the minority.''[50] But if Mason believed in the states' "sovereign capacity" to depart the Union, he also believed that separation would eventually cause great dissatisfaction in both North and South. Reunion would occur when moderate counsels regained authority. Judge Thomas S. Wilson was less sure. Besides, he welcomed the possibility of a new Union which would exclude New England whose "Yankeeism" and "twin brother abolitionism" weakened one's love of a united country in the first place.[51] W. W. White was so incensed by the election that he told Mason there was no further hope for civil, religious, or constitutional liberty "except in the superior moral and physical courage of Southern men.'' He doubted that "man—universal man" was fit for self government, Southern men possibly excepted.[52]

A contributor to the *Hawk-eye* who habitually signed himself as "Old Line Whig" presented the case for separation in a manner similar to Mason's. He believed that "If . . . an integral part withdraws its consent by the voice of an effective majority, coercion can never form a hearty union.'' Two republics were more feasible.[53] Lysander Babbitt speculated on the possibility of four republics. The four, respectively, might include: (1) New England, New York, New Jersey, Pennsylvania, and Delaware; (2) Maryland, Virginia, North Carolina, South Carolina, Georgia, Alabama, Mississippi, and Florida; (3) Ohio, Indiana, Kentucky, Illinois, Michigan, Wisconsin, Iowa, Minnesota, Tennessee, Arkansas, Missouri, Louisiana, Texas, Kansas, and the remaining territories east of the Rockies; (4) California, Oregon, and the remaining territories west of the Rockies. The third of these, he judged, would be powerful enough to control the destiny of the continent.[54] In Iowa City the *State Democratic Press* simply argued that the North ought to settle for a two-way split and recognize an "accomplished revolution.''[55]

Soon after South Carolina's secession, Iowans began to worry about the federal forts in Charleston harbor. Clark Dunham probably spoke for most Republicans when he wrote that action against the forts would lead to war.[56] Democrat David Richardson wavered for a time over whether to protect them or not. What he disliked most, however, was what he perceived to be the new administration's inability to act. Just before the batteries opened on Sumter, Richardson wrote that "the shedding of blood would have the effect to prove [at least that] we have a government. . . .''[57] Dennis Mahony's attitude toward the Sumter situation reflected Mahony's temperament. Whenever Southerners fired on the flag or took over federal property, he became angry. The government should meet such affronts "with stern yet paternal discipline,'' he declared. Mahony especially scorned traitorous federal officials in the South who turned United States government property over to the Confederates before they resigned their commissions. He counseled South Carolina to avoid violence against Fort

Sumter because it would provide the excuse Northern fanatics had long sought to start a war. And when the Irish editor began to hope for a peaceful separation of North and South in mid-March, he advocated federal evacuation of Sumter and other government territory in the South—but not before Washington had signed favorable commercial treaties with the Confederacy.[58] Charles Mason also watched developments around the forts carefully. Following a conversation with President Buchanan and Attorney General Stanton on November 18, he felt reassured. Buchanan planned to use military force if South Carolina attempted to seize the forts or if the United States Marshal there couldn't execute federal court judgments. On the other hand, he believed the federal government should abandon the forts as soon as the state was "fairly" [legally] out of the Union. Later he was to conclude that continued occupation of the forts had served no purpose except to irritate the South.[59]

Four days before the war started, Dennis Mahony offered his version of what the war would be about if it came. It would be more than a war between North and South, he wrote. On the one side were:

> those who are determined to subjugate the whole country to the domination of the Massachusetts school of politics, including the total abolition of slavery, the imposition of a high protective tariff, the substitution of specie money by paper currency, the legal and social distinction of classes in community and society by which captial shall become the ruler and poverty the serf. [On the other hand would be the patriots.] Those who favor the preservation of the Union, not by force, but by making it to the interests of every section and every state to become and remain a part of it; those who favor not only the equality of the States respectively in the Union but who favor the equality of individuals in the sovereignty of the State; those who are opposed to the imposition of indirect taxation upon the necessaries and conveniences of life, levied under the pretense of affording protection to certain branches of industry, but which, in reality, are imposed to make rich men richer, and consequently, poor men poorer.[60]

Clark Dunham's version written a week later was different. The war, contrary to Mahony's view, was simply a North-South war. It did not come because of the election of Lincoln or because of the "dominance of antislavery ideas." It came as a result of a struggle over political power. Northern population growth had changed the balance of power. When the South could no longer run the country, it wanted out. Dunham believed that rebel leaders had conspired to split the Democratic party in order to insure Lincoln's election. His victory became the pretense for "precipitating this revolution and overthrowing the Government."[61]

Dunham's denial that antislavery ideas were responsible for the war was doubtless a considered judgment. But antislavery ideas were important enough to provoke public debate in the winter and early spring of 1861. And such debate inevitably revealed that both slavery's attackers and its defenders saw it as no small factor in the growing rupture between North and South and between Northerners themselves. Southerners should remember, said the weekly *Iowa State Register,* that Northern state personal liberty laws only reflected the ideas of men in the free states that it was not their business to catch Southern runaways. "Regarding slavery as a great moral wrong," the editor wrote, "we cannot seek to eradicate that abhorrence of it which is a part of the religious education of a free people. . . ."[62] In Dubuque, the *Times* emphasized the moral question. "The whole Christian world," wrote the editor, "has been steadily advancing toward the deep-rooted sentiment and conviction that [slavery] is a gigantic crime against God and humanity, and a stain and disgrace to our civilization and our christianity."[63] The *Register* warned the South that even if it secured its independence for a time, its slave system would meet with "neither sympathy nor encouragement from the civilized world . . . [nor] be permitted to outrage the moral sense of Christendom. . . ." The *Hawk-eye* sounded a similar note, declaring that the South could not solve its problems by secession, for with slavery it would find itself friendless.[64]

Republican assertions that slavery was doomed because it was un-Christian had no effect upon Mahony, who asked Dubuque's abolitionist Presbyterian minister, John Holbrook, "Is the saving of the Nigger of more importance than the saving of souls?" Better, he jibed, to preach about "Christ and Him Crucified."[65] A *Herald* correspondent named "Lex" argued that "The abolition of slavery [should depend] upon more than the wish of the slave. The best interest of society, of both races, enter[s] into the right to be free. *Their superior condition in slavery to freedom* in the North must enter into it."[66]

How much influence such men as Dunham, Mahony, Mason, Dean, the editors of the *Times* and the *Register,* the Reverend Mr. Holbrook, and the self-assured "Lex" had on the thinking of the great mass of Iowans on this or any other subject is, of course, hard to determine. But as two scholars of political behavior have noted, "[I]nterest in history from the bottom up should not divert attention away from the locus of decision making or the interaction between political elites and the electorate."[67] In any event, Iowa's political elite—not excluding Holbrook and men like him whom angry Democrats always credited with a baleful influence over their congregations—always acted as if they might have some public impact at this critical point in American life.

3

Which Path to Tread? The Democratic Dilemma, 1861

Iᴇ I was not tied down here I would join you there at no remote day—and perhaps I will anyway in case of a dissolution of the Union—for then I confess there would be few attractions in the Abolition North of which Iowa has become part and parcel." So wrote Bernhart Henn, Fairfield banker and former congressman in early 1861 to Marcellus Crocker, rising young attorney who was half a month short of his twenty-fourth birthday. Crocker planned to move to the Pacific coast to regain his health and to establish a law practice. In his behalf Henn sent letters of recommendation to parties in California and one in Oregon to Senator Joseph Lane of the Breckinridge-Lane presidential ticket. Crocker, Henn declared, was a "warm and radical Democrat." Three months later warm and radical Democrat Crocker was one of the first to join the Second Iowa Infantry Regiment. Before the war ended, he was General Crocker, one of Iowa's legitimate war heroes, a confidant of leading Iowa Republicans, and a man who appeared destined for a luminous political and business career in the Hawk-eye state. Henn, on the other hand, was one of those who opposed the war and "black Republicanism" with all his heart until his death that fall. "He died a true democrat—and would not let an *abolitionist* visit him," wrote a friend approvingly.[1]

The Henn-Crocker episode and its aftermath is somewhat more than ironic. It exemplifies the drastic reshaping of personal and political fortunes and loyalties among many leading Iowans under the impact of war. Yet so astute an observer of men as Governor Samuel Kirkwood did not foresee such a result. Or, more likely, he could not conceive in the days immediately after the firing on Fort Sumter that there were men who had serious doubts that the war was necessary or just. "Ten days ago," he optimistically assured Simon Cameron, Secretary of War, "we had two parties in this state; today we have but one, and that is for the Constitution and Union unconditionally."[2]

Certainly the anger expressed in most newspapers, Republican and Democratic, the cries for retaliation, and the rush to the colors by hundreds of Iowans of military age promoted the illusion of unanimity. "Old Line Whig," the

Burlington *Hawk-eye* contributor given to labored disquisitions on the virtues of political moderation in tumultuous times, now demanded that the government "let loose the dogs of war" against traitors.[3] And W. W. White, who consistently defended the South and its course through the secession crisis, told Charles Mason, "Our interests are dependant [sic] upon maintaining the federal government under the Constitution; if we cannot do that now, what is to become of our country?"[4]

Yet all this was deceptive. Had Governor Kirkwood looked closely at the opposition press in the captial city he would have seen that the *Iowa State Journal's* angry young editor, Stilson Hutchins, stood against the war from the beginning. Hutchins, however, had too little support among Des Moines Democrats to stay in business. In a bitter valedictory note that fall he wrote that rather than modify his opinions he would be silent. This condition, unnatural for Hutchins, lasted only a short time. He soon joined Dennis Mahony in Dubuque where there were more kindred spirits.[5] County and township meetings of concerned Democrats in the spring and summer of 1861 also revealed less than citizen unanimity on the war. Poweshiek county Democrats had to call upon the sheriff to maintain order when war and peace proponents tangled in caucus. Some groups came out flatly for war. Others opposed invading the South, although they recommended stern action against any Southern incursion onto Northern territory. Others agreed to support the administration only if it strove for peace. Jefferson county Democrats required 2 ⅓ columns of small print to get across a series of twenty-four resolutions which: (1) condemned secessionists, Massachusetts politicians, Republicans, and Governor Kirkwood; (2) affirmed the impossibility of conquering the South; (3) praised Democrats and those others who had enlisted to protect Washington from Southern attack and "to sustain and preserve—not violate the Constitution and the laws"; (4) suggested that Republican politicians and editors do likewise, and, in particular, seek out front-line posts of greatest danger. Jefferson county Republican editor W. W. Junkin not unexpectedly found such resolutions "unpatriotic and truckling." Bellicose Lee county Democrat Thomas W. Clagett scorned Van Buren county Democrats as disunionists for relying "on praying to settle the present Civil War" rather than action.[6]

Democratic papers which had hoped for peace but now came out for war included *Der National-Demokrat* (Dubuque), *Des Moines News* (Keosauqua), Lyons *City Advocate,* Washington *Democrat, North Iowa Times* (McGregor), *South-Western Iowan* (Sidney), and *South-Tier Democrat* (Corydon). The Corydon editor, H. D'B. Cutler, damned both radicals and rebels at first. But he soon concluded that there was no recourse left except the sword. Practicing what he preached, Cutler announced in late June that he was joining the army and would sell half-interest in his organ to "any good Union man."[7] Others like the Iowa City *State Democratic Press* had to await a change in editors before they joined the war chorus. The Iowa City situation was touchy because businessman-land speculator LeGrand Byington and a small faction around him fought ceaselessly against any Democrat who did not share Byington's absolute revulsion toward all things Republican and abolitionist and toward the war.[8] In Davenport David Richardson was dubious at first about the prospects of achieving reunion through war and through Lincoln's assumption of extraordinary powers after the attack on Fort Sumter. But Richardson was above all a spread-eagle patriot who abominated secession as an offense against nature, and he was soon demanding that the administration make full use of the army to end it.[9] In western Iowa Lysander Babbitt initially blasted both Republicans and rebels. Slavery in the territories was the issue, and it wasn't worth either side fighting over, Babbitt cried. Yet, if someone had to give in, let it be the North where the issue should be unimportant. By early June, Babbitt decided that the war was illegal since Lincoln started it without congressional consent. A month later he foreclosed on Congress also. Now neither the president nor Congress had the constitutional right to make war in order to coerce a state.[10]

In Dubuque Dennis Mahony wanted it clearly understood "that among the journals of the country, the Dubuque *Herald* was opposed to giving practical effect in a fratricidal war to the dogma of the Republican party . . . that the American Union could not . . . exist part slave and part Free, territorially." Then he came to the point; it was conditional:

> The conflict . . . is but the practical development of this theory . . . and it is in that light that we shall regard it, and as such an issue, the subjugation of the South to the sentiment of partisan Republicanism or Dismemberment of the Union, we shall endeavor to meet the contest and to participate in the conflict which has been precipitated upon our beloved country and from a participation in which no Patriot can escape.

Mahony's prose was poorly coordinated in this passage. Yet the meaning was clear enough. He, like all patriots, must participate in the struggle. His conception of the origins of the struggle and his conception of the Republican administration's objectives would determine the way he participated. The next day he pressed for de facto recognition of the Confederacy. Mahony did believe that mutually beneficial economic relations might someday lead to reunion. For the immediate future, however, there was no hope, certainly not so long as a majority of the people approved the "despotic" president's course. But there was always another side to the Irish editor. Democratic generals won his praise early in the war, particularly Ben Butler. And he reported pridefully on April 26 that 200 of Dubuque's 15,000 residents had already left for military service while 100 others awaited orders. Democrats, he maintained, being truly earnest about preserving the Union, supplied most of the recruits.[11]

Dubuque's response to the crisis pleased one figure who frequently quarreled with Mahony. The Reverend C. Billings Smith announced from his Baptist pulpit that Dubuque's Catholics were indeed patriotic. Catholics, he now saw, were not in league with the nation's enemies, and he was glad to confess his error.[12] But one Iowan, Charles Mason, who rarely confessed error for anything, filled his diary with angry passages defending secession as a proper way to negate arbitrary federal power. Mason's belief, when he expressed it publicly three months later, was to cause him plenty of trouble. Already in trouble was David Sheward who within a year would be editing a peace paper in Fairfield, the *Constitution and Union.* Sheward's frankness wrung for him a backhanded compliment from W. W. Junkin. Sheward, he said, was at least an "open" traitor; there were others in Fairfield, but they tried to conceal the fact.[13]

Nevertheless, Kirkwood's early assumption that both parties were united behind federal efforts to halt secession was not disproved by the performance of most Democrats during the extra session of the state legislature. This he convened in order to meet looming federal obligations and to ratify his early extralegal steps to strengthen Iowa's militia. With a minimum of discord the legislature revamped the militia organization, authorized the selling of up to $800,000 in state bonds to finance the military buildup, and authorized counties to provide aid to soldiers' families. It also passed laws which prohibited civil suits against soldiers (primarily involving debt collection), and granted them continuances in pending suits until their being discharged from the service. The legislators did not, however, act on Kirkwood's request that it use its constitutional powers to punish those Iowans, if any, "who may feel disposed to furnish aid" to rebels.[14]

Republicans outnumbered Democrats 23 to 21 in the senate and 50 to 36 in the house. House Republicans initially bent over backward to achieve accord with the minority. They voted unanimously to eliminate party designations when that branch organized for business. Thomas Clagett chaired the committee on federal relations and Nathaniel B. Baker, Democrat from Clinton and former governor of New Hampshire, the one on military affairs. Three of the five seats on Clagett's committee went to Democrats.[15] Senate Republicans demonstrated a spirit of accommodation too. When both houses unanimously pledged to support federal efforts to "suppress treason and rebellion," they accepted Democratic Senator Gideon Bailey's move to limit the legislature's approval to "constitutional efforts."[16]

A majority of Democrats in the legislature approved all proposals designed to finance and equip Iowa's expanding volunteer regiments, to reorganize the militia, and to sell the state bonds. In the senate they never cast more than 5 nay votes on passage of such bills. House Democrats supported them even more strongly.[17] But Democrats, along with economy-minded Republicans, fought to contain the military budgets and the bond issue at what they considered reasonable levels.[18] Senate Democrats, more consistently than their house counterparts, urged tighter restrictions on use of Iowa regiments outside the state.[19] Democrats supplied the votes needed to turn back a soldier vote bill sponsored by a house Republican. But Republicans displayed no enthusiasm for soldier voting in 1861 either.[20] House Democrats tried to put the legislature on record favoring a federal amendment barring congressional action on state domestic institutions including slavery. With some Republican support they pushed such a resolution through the lower body. Only by a straight party vote in which Republicans needed their slender majority did the senate turn it down.[21] The same occurred to a peace resolution offered by Fort Dodge's Senator John Duncombe. Duncombe's resolution called for a national peace convention with a concurrent armistice. The resolution, a small political platform, warned against waging war to subjugate the South and to free the slaves, against the possible growth of military despotism, war-inflated public indebtedness, and loss of civil liberties. Senate Democrats, except for two absentees, lined up solidly behind it. Surprised Republicans buried this unwelcome development in the federal relations committee.[22]

Duncombe's near success did not escape the *Iowa State Register*'s attention. Henceforth, the paper warned, Republicans should retain the Republican label and forego concessions which Democrats would not reciprocate.[23] Even so, the *Register* and most Republicans praised Clagett and Baker. Baker in particular won quick recognition as the leader of those Democrats who strongly supported the war. When the legislature adjourned, Governor Kirkwood appointed him state adjutant general, a position he held until his death in the next decade.[24]

From the start of the war into the winter of 1861–1862, Iowa's economic picture was mixed. The state government suffered from its inability to collect delinquent taxes.[25] And efforts to sell Iowa state bonds in the East went for naught. The New York *Herald* claimed the bonds were a bad bargain. The paper cited the experiences suffered by many investors when several Iowa cities and counties defaulted on their railroad bonds following the 1857 depression. In Iowa some Democratic county conventions challenged the constitutionality of the bond law. The state Democratic convention of July 24 followed suit despite the fact that one of the bond commissioners, Charles Mason, was certain to be the party's gubernatorial candidate. From Dubuque the *Herald* challenged "patriot shouters" to buy the bonds. Iowans eventually did purchase some of them, while some suppliers of military equipment for Iowa troops accepted others in lieu of cash.[26] The commissioners only authorized $300,000 worth of bonds for sale. These eventually went for 94 cents on the dollar. Federal funding eliminated the need for further sales by the summer of 1862. For Governor Kirkwood and his agents, however, the first six months of the war were discouraging. Kirkwood borrowed money on his own credit to buy arms, and his agents sometimes had to sign personal endorsements for their suppliers.[27]

The state's citizens, like the Iowa government, were still recovering from the depression of 1857. Yet it is problematical whether the majority of them actually suffered a further setback with the coming of war. Some forecasters like David Richardson tended to expect the worst. They advised retrenchment. But the men who wrote county reports for the annual *Iowa Agricultural Report* at year's end seemed most disturbed at a population explosion among sheep-killing dogs. They generally expressed satisfaction with agricultural output and evinced great interest in attaining self-sufficiency in sorghum production. The agricultural society's executive secretary, John Wallace, dealt with more substantive topics—and complained more. He agreed that crops were abundant but contended that they brought only half the price they had a year or two earlier. He blamed the railroads for gouging the farmers through 30 percent to 40 percent rate increases. With the Mississippi blockaded they could do as they pleased, he wrote.[28]

Farmers and businessmen, of course, had worried about closure of the Mississippi in the event of war. But even before the blockade took effect, Dubuque shippers were sending flour and wheat eastward in far greater volume than they had a year earlier. April, 1860, flour shipments east were only 1,664 barrels compared with 10,834 in April, 1861. Wheat shipments east in April, 1860, were 13,902 bushels compared with 60,812 bushels a year later.[29] Grain shipments east continued heavy into May and a *Herald* writer exclaimed, ''Who says the country is going to wreck? North of Mason's and Dixon's line we are all right, and if we mistake not, our farmers will realize a higher price for grain next fall than for two years past—war or peace.''[30] When the blockade became official, river city editors grumbled and feared that a rise in Southern self-sufficiency would adversely affect their communities. Yet most seemed not to view the prospect as catastrophic. The blockade posed more of a problem for Keokuk in the extreme southeast corner of the state because it had no direct rail connection east, unlike the other major Iowa river cities. Most of its trade had been with St. Louis and New Orleans. Only in 1863 did it finally secure a good rail connection to the east when the Wabash and Mississippi reached the Illinois shore. But the city weathered this period satisfactorily, partly because it quickly became a rendezvous for military units on their way South. The city's business community moved with alacrity to acquire a telegraph connection when it feared that the War Department might move the rendezvous to some other location. Keokuk also captured some of the wholesale business which southeastern Iowa merchants formerly did with St. Louis.[31] In the Davenport area it was June 24 before the *Democrat* reported any specific negative effect by the blockade on any one locality, in this instance LeClaire, a small river town a few miles upstream.[32] Shipping companies which depended upon freight and passenger traffic up and down the Mississippi suffered, although the carrying of troops and supplies took up some of the slack. Downriver shippers soon found markets to the east, although they often discovered that rail, canal, and lake transport facilities could not always handle the abundant western production efficiently.[33]

However much Iowans feared a blockade, some saw war as a boon to the economy and they waxed optimistic, unlike Richardson. They advised farmers to plant heavily in order to reap a bonanza from sales to the army, to the East, and to Europe. The Council Bluffs *Nonpareil* even anticipated grain and meat sales to the ''erring brothers of the South'' who would starve without them.[34] Most insistent was an anonymous correspondent of the Dubuque *Herald* who urged farmers to plant every square foot of ground. Forget about current low prices, he said. Don't worry about depreciated currency. It would soon approach the value of specie. The only worry farmers really should have, he maintained, was a shortage of agricultural labor.[35] In West Union, peace advocate John Gharkey argued one week that the country had everything to lose by war. Yet seven days later he told farmers they had a responsibility to raise all they could. Prices for old wheat and corn-fed hogs would surely rise. Anyway, the war wouldn't be fought in Iowa.[36] Another writer believed that by maximum planting, farmers would not only serve the country but also pay off their debts. The Dubuque *Times* gave the same advice, but stressed service more and self less, "—not for selfish profit . . . but to aid and feed those who do the fighting."[37]

Richardson did not urge Davenport area farmers to plant heavily. He predicted unprofitable price levels in wheat, corn, barley, and oats. He also predicted that Iowa farmers might lose $4 to $5 million over the year. Consequently, he advocated "economy in living and frugality in general expenditures, not only among farmers but all classes." Farmhands' wages, however, began to climb. Farmers around LeClaire agreed in early July to try to hold the rate at $1.00 a day, as did farmers near Davenport and Muscatine. But Davenport area farmhands demanded $1.50. The *Democrat's* "locals" writer believed working a long, hot day was worth $1.50, but that both sides could afford to compromise at $1.25. Davenport had no lack of hands, he said. They were on every street corner. But the hands won, and he wryly noted that one could see farmers hauling them off by the wagonload to do a day's work for $1.50 and "rations." The paper also seemed mystified by an anomaly. The hard times and the prospect of low grain prices should result in decreased sales of farm machinery including reapers, threshers, power corn shellers, and separators. But sales were up over 1860 in Scott county and in portions of nearby Muscatine and Cedar counties. Reaper sales alone increased by 13 percent. Four Davenport firms manufactured most of the threshers. More understandable to the economically conservative Davenport reporter was the fact that these firms did a much greater business in repairing old machines.[38]

In south central Iowa near Ottumwa, farmers seemed to be hurting as badly as the *Democrat* anticipated. There were few buyers of butter and eggs, even at five cents a pound and three cents a dozen. In Harrison county on the western border where no railroad existed, farmers had to haul wheat 35 miles to get 35 cents a bushel. This was well below the 50 cents a bushel which more favorably situated Scott county farmers claimed was the cost of production. Harrison's corn growers either sold their production at 10 cents a bushel or burned it for fuel.[39] In the northern part of the state, Webster City had something of a building boom even though Hamilton county was still suffering hard times. Waterloo, too, was the scene of much building, and the *Courier* claimed that during the spring of 1861 merchants' sales tripled over those of any previous spring.[40]

For Iowans the start of the war made the already bad circulating currency problem worse. Some communities dealt with it better than others. In Fairfield local bankers prepared a list of thirty-eight Illinois banks whose notes were acceptable at par. The people cooperated, and poorly secured paper ceased to circulate. Keokuk bankers accepted notes from only twenty-seven Illinois banks, and like Fairfield bankers, rejected all Wisconsin bank notes. Davenport residents, prodded by Richardson, also moved toward note exclusion. Nevertheless, in the same issue of the *Democrat* one merchant could announce that he would refuse all Illinois and Wisconsin notes while another's advertisement proclaimed: "DISCREDITED Illinois money taken. . . . Bring on your rags." Finally, Davenport's bankers began to reject many Illinois notes they previously had accepted. On May 24, the city's merchants likewise agreed to reject all depreciated Missouri, Illinois, and Wisconsin paper. Davenport's branch of the Iowa State Bank remained strong, declaring a 10 percent dividend in June and adding 2 percent to its contingency fund.[41] In Dubuque, the *Herald* castigated the city's bankers for not following Keokuk's lead. At this time, mid-May, notes from thirty-five Illinois and twenty-four Wisconsin banks still circulated freely. Dubuque's lead miners association came out against accepting any paper money whatever, a stand which the *Herald* recommended to farmers. But the miners, along with many farmers, had to settle for the notes of eastern banks through much of the month. These also were depreciated badly. Soon, farmers began to sell wheat for 63 cents a bushel in gold, preferring it over 73 cents offered in paper currency. Later that year farmers were still skittish, despite the shortage of specie, and demanded payment in gold or in state bank notes.[42]

In the last quarter of the year eastern Iowa's economic outlook improved, although a December hog glut, brought on by two years of low corn prices, hit Burlington and Davenport.[43] In Davenport, thanks to an influx of United States treasury notes, money was "flush." Credit remained tight, however, and Richardson, though chary about borrowing, urged repeal of Iowa's stay and appraisement laws. There was a shortage of investment capital, he noted, and farmers, who actually had good security in land, couldn't get the loans they needed.[44] Land, however, was no great asset to Dubuque businessman Solon Langworthy who was under pressure from a creditor. Langworthy had hoped that creditor Daniel Limmer could get his money by selling some of Langworthy's land for him. Limmer, who was trying to collect from several borrowers, wrote that because of the war, land was nearly worthless in his area of Dubuque county. He was trying to get rid of one thousand good soil acres himself, but had no buyers.[45] Less genteel and more desperate were two hundred Irish railroad workers at McGregor. After receiving no wages for several weeks during the summer, they rioted in despair and tried unsuccessfully to hang the contractor.[46] Some Democrats did look hopefully to discontent among farmers and laborers to pave the way for electoral success that fall. Both groups would pay the major cost of the war if fighting continued, Lysander Babbitt asserted.[47] Richardson also worried about war costs and about who paid them. But he took a long view. The United States could acquire great wealth and power as an exporter of foodstuffs and cotton to Europe which needed both. Therefore, the struggle to achieve reunion was imperative. "We are not," he wrote, "fighting for a sentiment but for great pecuniary benefits. . . ."[48]

Although Richardson was not explicit, it is almost certain that the sentiment he referred to was abolition. But abolition attracted only sporadic attention in

1861 in Iowa compared with what was to come after the Emancipation Proclamation. Very early in the year the Dubuque *Times* declared that Democrats, not Republicans, were hung up on the "nigger question" since no sympathy existed between Republicans and abolitionists. Some hoped that black emigration would solve the problem. A *Times* reader suggested that the federal government appraise the value of all female blacks when they reached the age of twelve, buy them from their owners, and ship them to Liberia or some other suitable location. Immediately after the war started, the Burlington *Hawk-eye* recommended voluntary emigration to Haiti. Late in the year, the *Herald,* though calling emigration impractical, wished that it were not. Were it practical, the country should first deport the pure bloods; those with some white blood should go later, the paper said. What the river cities did not want was an influx of blacks from the border states or the South. In late April when a steamer from St. Louis carrying several hundred free blacks briefly touched at Dubuque, the *Herald* "locals" writer said, "We are glad that only a very few stopped in Dubuque."[49]

Republicans had to tread lightly on the subject of war aims to make certain that they did not include abolition. When the *Times* slipped, called for abolition, then reversed course three weeks later and declared "the war . . . is to be carried on purely and wholly for the sake of Union," the *Herald* quickly noted the inconsistency. A Clayton county Republican warned Governor Kirkwood that the *McGregor Press,* which claimed to be Republican and to have Republican patronage, was not controllable. The editor and his wife were too radical, he complained. From their writings readers got the impression that Republicans advocated abolition—and free love. Late in the year, the *Hawk-eye* reiterated the idea that "our armies are not sent . . . upon a mission of philanthropy to the Negro, but to compel submission to the laws by those in rebellion."[50]

Yet if Republicans couldn't be "sentimental" on the black issue, Democrats couldn't be too "hard." The *Herald* spoke for most of the party when it said it never advocated slavery; rather, it simply recognized slavery's legality. However, an entirely unexpected editorial in the Republican Davenport *Gazette* once gave David Richardson an opening he couldn't resist. He took it and got away with it. "Slavery was the greatest curse any nation could have," wrote the discouraged *Gazette* editor, but "Better were it . . . introduced into all our Territory than that this present awful state of affairs should have been inaugurated." Democrats across the state were astonished and pleased with such a stand from what Richardson called "heretofore, one of the most radical Republican papers in the state." Such accolades were unwelcome, and the *Gazette* quickly tried to recover lost face. Richardson, it cried, was a traitor who wanted to see slavery planted from Maine to Georgia. The *Democrat* editor knew when he'd won a round. "We are perfectly willing that . . . [the *Gazette* editor] should tell that yarn every day of the year . . . ," he cheerfully responded.[51]

Nevertheless, many Iowans probably assumed that the war, if it continued for any length of time, would doom slavery. As the *Times* put it, "the consequences of . . . war are not favorable to slave property." If the institution died as an incident or accident of war, so be it. Sara Kenyon, tenant wife in Delaware county, put it succinctly in October, 1861, when she wrote a relative, "There is no Secession about me or rank abolitionism. still now is the time to rid the country of the curse of Slavery I do hope and pray."[52]

Few Iowans in that year gauged loyalty by how one stood on the issue of slavery or freedom for blacks. Other issues sufficed, most of which could be categorized under the heading "war or conciliation." Not that any particular accuracy resulted from efforts by inflamed partisans to define loyal as opposed to disloyal or traitorous behavior. But it was easier to try. The editor of the *State Democratic Press* noted this in the late spring of 1861 when he wrote, "for God's sake, let not every vagabond in this community be permitted to make a definition of treason to suit himself, and then constitute himself accuser, jury, judge and hangman, and proceed to wreak his vengeance and indulge his spite upon any personal enemy whom he may choose to call a traitor."[53] For Democrats the problem was particularly painful. Bloomfield's state senator, Cyrus Bussey, soon to be appointed a military aide to Kirkwood and later to a field command, described a public meeting soon after the war started at which he vowed to support the Lincoln administration. "When the meeting closed," he recalled, "I was surrounded by excited Democrats who informed me that I had made a d____d fool of myself. They said, 'Don't you know this war was brought on by the republican party. Now let them fight it out.' I replied that if it was necessary for a man to be a traitor to his country to be a Democrat I should cease to be one."[54] Some individuals resorted to the press to deny that they were traitors, usually making matters worse and probably changing few minds in the process. Beleaguered B. B. Littleton in Jefferson county swore that he did not cheer when the rebels captured Fort Sumter. He only opposed an invasion of the South as he would oppose a rebel invasion of the North.[55] In Burlington, W. C. Wilson's earnest attempt to refute charges by J. H. Marshall that Wilson was a secessionist sparked a rejoinder from Marshall that Wilson obviously had a guilty conscience, but that he, Marshall, was glad to learn of Wilson's change of heart.[56] Charles Negus of Fairfield, the oldest member of the bar in Jefferson county, suffered ostracism when he refused to take the oath of allegiance to which the rest of the bar subscribed voluntarily in the heat of passion after Sumter. Members of the bar immediately reacted to his refusal by requesting that he absent himself from a bar social function. A letter from the sponsors said in part, "You are publicly invited not to attend our supper this evening . . . we loath and despise traitors who refuse to renew their allegiance to the United States. Negus explained at length and in vain that he had taken the oath officially three times in his public career. Demands that he take it unofficially constituted an aspersion on his character.[57]

When Republican members of Jefferson county's board of supervisors voted for a $1,000 appropriation to support families of volunteers and Democrats did not, the Fairfield *Ledger* editor was disgusted. While there was plenty of evidence that some Democrats sympathized with the South, he wrote, he was surprised to see them "place themselves upon the record so glaringly."[58] Dubuque's Dennis Mahony was not about to let the opposition define loyalty and patriotism for him. Loyal and patriotic men, he said, were those who tried to persuade their countrymen not to fight a disastrous war, even as the war waged. They should continue to "exercise their reason, judgment and [offer] understanding counsel" to the government, counsel "which seems to them best for the preservation of the Government itself." When this had little effect upon his opponents, he exploded, "To talk peace is treason; to petition Congress for restoration of peace is treason. In a word it is treason to be a patriot, and patriotic to be a traitor."[59] The Washington *Democrat* reacted similarly to two columns of abuse in the Washington *Press* by reminding the *Press* that it was not treasonous to say that the nation was distracted, not united; that commerce was paralyzed and trade "annihilated"; and that men in both North and South trampled on the Constitution.[60]

In Davenport the local home guard unit thought to establish a vigilance committee, a move sidetracked by United States District Attorney W. H. F. Gurley. Gurley said that the established authorities could maintain order on their own. Nevertheless, some persons in Davenport, at least briefly, constituted themselves as a secret group with the intent of ferreting out traitors, a move which angered both the *Democrat* and *Der Demokrat*.[61] In late August, the *Hawk-eye*, without defining loyalty, announced that there were some few in Burlington who were doubtful cases. The community's patience was near an end, wrote an editor, and while he wanted no violence, it was now clear "that no man's personal safety can be assured for one moment after the conclusion shall have been . . . arrived at that he is a traitor." A letter to the *Hawk-eye* from "Vox Populi" was more explicit about how many the few were. There were, he said, twenty-one "known secessionists" and fifteen "suspected secessionists" in Burlington.[62] Charles Mason tried to refute charges that he had expressed disloyal sentiments to his relatives in the East shortly after the war started. "Neither my wife nor my daughter ever stated that I strongly sympathized with the South," he said in a letter to the *Hawk-eye*. All he had said was that much of the country's misfortune could be laid at the door of the New York *Tribune* and the abolition party.[63] On the other side, W. W. Junkin of the Fairfield *Ledger* objected to name-calling by Democrats. Stop all this "party cant" about abolitionists, he demanded. Some were volunteers, some sent their sons to the army, some freely gave money to help soldiers' families. "To class such men with the 'fire-eaters' of the South who are in rebellion against the government, is a gross insult. . . . Let denunciation be meted out to traitors, not to loyal citizens."[64]

Not only labels but also material symbols could damage men who opposed the war. Mahony sensed this well. Some "friends of Peace" in Dubuque had adopted the white flag to show their feelings. Don't give the war party such an advantage, he warned. Use only the Stars and Stripes. Let "Rebels and Abolitionists and Revolutionaries" choose another.[65] There was no room in the teaching profession for white flags either, so to speak, a University of Iowa professor told the Iowa State Teachers Association convention, although Prof. Oliver M. Spencer's perspective differed from Mahony's. Teachers, said the professor, should love the country second only to God and should instill the same in their students, especially in times of civil dissension.[66] State Adj. Gen. Nathaniel Baker attempted to determine just how much war sentiment existed among a number of leading Iowa citizens including Mahony and Dubuque's Catholic Bishop Clement Smyth. The Bishop's response was entirely satisfactory. He replied that he was for Union and for peace, but that he "would not consent to purchase peace at the sacrifice of principle." Baker's letter to the Irish editor was not a model of tact. It alluded to charges that he was disloyal and that he had discouraged enlistments. Baker asked if Mahony would "devote [his] energies to put down the rebellion—to sustain the Union and put forth [his] best efforts to aid me in raising a regiment from this State. . . ." Mahony's answer must have been a surprise. "My services," he replied, "are at your command as the representative of the government to aid in raising a regiment from this state or in any other way that they may be best employed to put down rebellion, to sustain the Union, to make the American flag respected whether abroad or at home."[67] This response was not consistent with Mahony's usual antiwar stance. Bedeviled as he was by Republicans and by war proponents within his own party, he may have thought that his answer would rid him of the need to defend himself against what he believed was unfair criticism. Not clear in either Baker's or Mahony's letters is whether helping to raise a regiment might also mean taking command of one. One anxious Dubuque Republican so construed it. He hastily warned Baker against such a possibility. Future election opponent and, eventually, long-time United States Senator William B. Allison believed Mahony would hurt the cause of Union. At the very least, he contended, before giving Mahony a command, Baker should require that he retract his "treason" and insist that he put loyal men in charge of the *Herald*.[68] There is some evidence that a meeting took place in September, 1861, in Dubuque attended by Baker, Mahony, Bishop Smyth, and other Dubuque citizens. According to C. C. Flint, a Dubuque recruiter, Mahony at that time was promised a commission to raise and command an Irish regiment. Flint appealed to Kirkwood to do now (in August, 1862), what had been considered a year earlier. Mahony would accept a commission, Flint said, because he was poor and ambitious. Challenged by such a task, he would channel his energies into a better cause. Flint summed up his appeal eloquently, saying, "I have fought him for years politically. He is an opponent not to be despised—and an ally worth having."[69] But that was by then out of the question. For a year already Kirkwood had taken care to appoint no one to any position, major or minor, whose loyalty was suspect.[70]

Certainly in the spring and summer of 1861, Mahony had reason to feel besieged. At a patriotic rally in Dubuque on April 15, the Reverend C. Billings Smith announced that secessionists were few in Dubuque. "Their leader, thank God," Smith added, "is not a native . . . and if he had his just desserts he would be hanging from the nearest lamp post." When Mahony protested that this story, along with two others in the rival *Times* on the same day, were open incitements to riot against the *Herald,* the *Times* denied it. However, *Times* editor, Jesse Clement, declared that Dubuque was in no mood to listen to those who abused the war effort while the nation was in peril. A *Times* contributor signed "Iowa" echoed that sentiment. "Forebearance may cease to be a virtue in his [Mahony's] case," he wrote.[71] Such verbal warfare came to a head on July 12. On that day the *Times* printed a letter calling for a public meeting "to counsel as to those means, which might rightly be used to rid us of the reproach and injury [the *Herald*'s] existence brings upon us." Before the day was out a group of *Herald* enemies attempted to rush the paper's office. But city and county lawmen aided by a company of soldiers stopped them short of their goal. Two months later came news that the *Herald*'s enemies had persuaded St. Louis military authorities to interdict its circulation in that region.[72] Mahony also worried that increasing enmity between him and the paper's advertisers might cause him serious financial problems. Accordingly, he appealed to regional conservatives for support. In September, self-styled "Union Democrats" established the *Evening Union* in an effort to win away the *Herald*'s patrons. But the *Evening Union* died in December as Mahony's frequent appeals for support began to bear fruit.[73]

Similar although less intensive intracity warfare between rival papers occurred in Council Bluffs and in Davenport. In Fort Dodge, when John Duncombe started the *Democrat,* opponents threatened to destroy his press. Should that happen, he told Charles Mason, his friends would retaliate in kind.[74] One Republican editor, Charles Aldrich of the *Hamilton Freeman* in Webster City, suggested that the leading Democratic organs in Iowa were indeed a sorry lot. They exhibited, he maintained, "a venemous hatred of the National Administration which seemingly makes them crave for its downfall. . . ." In contrast, Aldrich declared, were "Democratic officers and Democratic privates . . . in the ranks of the Iowa volunteers, ready to hazard life, if necessary, in defense of the Government. . . ."[75]

Soldier recruitment was no great problem at the start of the war. Outfitting and arming those soldiers was, however. But under Kirkwood's and especially Baker's management, the state fielded sixteen infantry and four cavalry regiments, and three batteries of light artillery, a total of 19,105 men by the end of 1861.[76] With some notable exceptions, Democratic Dubuque, like the rest of Iowa, caught war fever. Some citizens were so eager to militarize the city that they pushed for the enrollment of all men able to bear arms into a seven-company home guard unit headed by a "field marshal" who would run local affairs, aided by a secret guards committee and a major. Although meant to be taken seriously, some residents thought it was a joke. The proposal died quickly as the community became involved in the real business of preparing units destined for duty against the South.[77]

Whether Republicans volunteered in greater numbers proportionately than

Democrats was and still is a matter of dispute. Two evenhanded county histories, those of Hamilton and Audubon, both in the western part of the state, reported that Democratic volunteering lagged throughout the war. In Hamilton county, J. W. Lee attributed this to a feeling of ill will against the party in power, not to disloyalty. The Audubon writer offered no explanation for the alleged Democratic deficiency. He believed it did account for Audubon becoming one of the few counties to switch to the Democrats during the war. Yet his account demonstrated a distaste for Republican zealots.[78] Stilson Hutchins believed sources who told him in the summer of 1861 that most of the men going into the army were Republicans. Their departure would help close the gap between the two parties "to a small number," Hutchins felt, although not enough for the Democrats to win the fall elections.[79] On the other hand, a LeClaire contributor to the Davenport *Democrat* claimed that of 30 recent local enlistees, 26 were Democrats, 3 were Republicans, and 1 an 1860 Constitutional Unionist.[80] The LeClaire writer may have been correct as to the political composition of LeClaire's recruits. He was far more specific than most. But one must discount nearly all newspaper reports which generalized about one or the other party's adherents having a better or a worse volunteer record. Too often one reads something like the report of "A True Republican" from Sigourney (Keokuk county), which charged that leading Democrats there tried to organize a military home guard unit that would decrease the number of volunteers available for war against the rebels. In this case "A True Democrat" responded that a large number of the volunteer company which recently departed Sigourney were Democrats, and that a Democrat raised the money to equip them.[81] Enthusiasm for military service declined later in the summer, partly as a result of the state's refusal to accept enlistments for any less than a three-year term after enlistment of the First Iowa Infantry, a ninety-day unit.[82] Occasionally young women tried to spur enlistments into guard units or into the infantry regiments by announcing their resolve to marry none but volunteers.[83]

There was some fear, even in 1861, of a draft. But Dennis Mahony favored a draft on the grounds that it would sweep up the rich and the "leading men of the community" who encouraged others to go to war. "Let the drafting process be put into motion at once," he wrote. "We want to see the sincerity, fidelity and patriotism of some of our war-favoring revilers put to the test." When Baker queried him about his loyalty, Mahony reiterated his belief in the draft, this time excluding the sarcasm. "[I]t is the right of the Government," he maintained, "to demand the service of every citizen, to be used in such a manner as it thinks may be most conducive to the public weal, more especially so in times of danger and of peril. . . ." What is strange about this antiwar man's support of the draft was his belief that "If rich men were drafted and did not choose to comply with the requisition, they could [at least] pay for a substitute. . . ." Later on, Mahony's views on the need for equality of risk between rich and poor eliminated this loophole in his thinking.[84] Mahony declared he would claim no exemption to which he might be entitled were he called. This spirit was in sharp contrast to that of Laurel Summers. Summers left his LeClaire home in September to avoid a draft which he thought was imminent. Two fascinating letters in his correspondence reveal what Summers was thinking and what his correspondents thought of him.[85]

Sept. 23, 1861

Dear Lal:

Of course you will not, for the present return. I think that you need have no fear. *They* have sent down a list of names, whether yours or my names are included I know not, but I think it is the *evident* intention to take none except *able bodied men* of good statue [sic], large, solid men—they will take the *runts* when they can do no better.

For all this I would be at some point *accessible* to Canada; you are not constitutionally capable of bearing arms any more than I am and I *know* my capacity.

Among the names gone down I learn are Jacob King, Bob Close and one or two others whom I have forgotten.

Jake leaves *instanter* for parts unknown. . . .

HENRY

Sept. 24, 1861

Dear Lal

I don't believe a word of any drafting in this state at this time. Though it may be we don't intend to worry ourselves but if the issue is made [we will] meet it when it comes and try to do our duty. . . .

I will not say where your address is.

EDWARDS
[of Parker and Edwards
law firm, Davenport]

Charles Mason, who made some effort to get a commission in the army, although he thoroughly disapproved the war and hoped the rebels would defeat the invading North, had nothing good to say privately about anybody who entered the Northern military service. Officers were monarchists at heart. Enlisted men joined only to gain a means of livelihood; having once tasted and enjoyed the excitement of army life, they would be unwilling to return to peaceful pursuits. Mason professed to believe they could be mustered out only if authorities bribed them with gifts of slaves and plantations stolen from a prostrate South.[86]

While most Iowans saw the major enemy as the distant rebel South, those who lived near Missouri sometimes felt as if they were in the front lines. Fremont county in the extreme southwest experienced problems through December, 1860, and January, 1861, when troubles in Atchison county, Missouri, spilled over the border. Unionist Jayhawkers from Missouri rode into Fremont several times to harass suspected rebel sympathizers, many of whom had left the state in the first place to avoid such treatment.[87] After the war started many border-county Iowans anticipated assaults from northern Missouri ''secesh.'' They wrote Kirkwood requesting arms and ammunition. Three Amity (Page county) citizens couldn't understand why they were targets. "[N]ot one negro has ever been stolen or even harbored by any citizen of Amity," they wrote, "but for some reason a bitter hatred of our place is felt by the proslavery part of Northern Mo."[88] Other Iowans wanted arms for use against alleged local rebel sympathizers who, they claimed, had organized themselves into secret societies.[89] When unrest in northwestern Missouri became more open, Kirkwood offered Iowa militia troops to Gen. John Pope, Union commander in that area. He might need them, Pope answered.[90] Units from Iowa did venture near or into northwest Missouri three times that summer in response to reports of rebel concentrations. No contact resulted.[91] Southeast Iowa militiamen from Keokuk, however, tasted combat in the one formal military action which occurred on the Iowa border during the war. That was at the "Battle of Athens" (Missouri) on August 5, 1861, when they helped a Missouri militia force withstand a rebel attack on Athens, a Union recruiting and training center. The battle ended when the rebels fled, but not before they had lobbed a few cannon balls across the Des Moines river at the small town of Croton, Iowa, the Keokuk troops' fire base.[92] Two months later Adjutant General Baker issued General Order No. 41 which provided for the systematic organization of guard units to protect the southern border.

While the Iowa government in 1861 prepared for war with what appeared to be the backing of the great majority of its citizens, Iowa's Democratic party leaders embarked upon a war with each other that was to outlast the Civil War itself and insure long-term Republican domination of the state. While so engaged they sometimes seemed to be practicing politics in a vacuum, concerned only with forcing the principles of one or another set of true believers down each others' throats. To be sure they addressed themselves to the economy, civil liberties, corruption in government, taxation, tariffs, the currency, conscription, the growth of federal power, and the future of blacks in American life. On these they tended to agree. What they did not agree on was how the Union should be restored—by war or by conciliation and compromise. That occupied the bulk of their time and energy. Iowa's Republicans couldn't have hoped for anything more helpful.

Two men put the big issue in stark and contrasting terms. Former Sen. George Jones wrote Laurel Summers that he favored Union, but not one maintained by force and run by abolitionists. He would, he declared, fight for the South under those circumstances. On the opposite end of the spectrum was H. D'B. Cutler, editor of the Corydon *South-Tier Democrat*. Secessionist treason, not abolition nor Southern rights, was the problem, he wrote. War was the only way to smash it.[93] Attempts to hammer out a consensus devolved, then, upon strong spirits who presumed to speak for party opinion, or else claimed to know what party opinion should be. Strongest of these was Mahony, former minority leader in the legislature and state party chairman from the summer of 1859 through the summer of 1860. One month after the presidential election Mahony had called upon Iowa's Democrats to meet in convention to consider the national crisis. There was little response. On January 12, 1861, he tried again, with the same result.[94] The "coercionist-compromiser" split narrowed when South Carolina batteries bombarded Fort Sumter, but not much. If the coercionists saw the bombardment as deplorable and inexcusable, the compromisers saw it as deplorable but understandable.

In the meantime, the state central committee seemed paralyzed. Once more the worried Mahony took matters into his own hands. On June 8, he called for an official Democratic convention to meet July 10 in Des Moines to nominate candidates for governor and the other state offices. Two features of this call were significant. First, Mahony issued it "by order of the State Democratic Committee," signing himself as chairman pro tem. Second, he declared emphatically what Democratic policy should be, namely: opposition to secession; opposition to the war policy of the federal executive; and opposition to executive "subversion" of the Constitution and the government.[95] Mahony wanted action, and he got it. Scores of heretofore dispirited Democrats angrily attacked the Irish editor for "illegally" attempting to assume control of party machinery and for presuming to define party policy. Mahony defended himself by claiming that state party chairman, Henry Altman of Davenport, had granted him the authority to call the convention during Altman's absence from the state. He denied that he intended to dictate party policy, although he admitted that the call contained his personal view on the issues.[96] The quarrel over Mahony's right to call a convention took a comic twist in early July when another member of the committee, Keokuk's Hugh W. Sample, soon to be an Iowa unit commander at the Battle of Athens, unilaterally assumed the acting committee chairman's post and rescinded Mahony's action. Sample charged Mahony with expressing "sentiment entertained by *none* but enemies to our party and the country." Sample in turn came under heavy fire from Mahony's friends for his "illegal" rescinding order and "improper assumption" of the acting chairmanship. Meanwhile, Altman had departed Iowa for good and was settled in Colorado. Hearing of the controversy, he wrote a letter to Iowa Democrats giving his version of events which led to Mahony's assumption of authority. Mahony printed the letter, then appended a restrained critique of Altman's explanation. What comes through most clearly in this labored exchange is that Altman, who probably had his mind on the move West, was not much concerned with the timing of the convention, nor had he any intention of enunciating party policy vis-a-vis the war. Mahony, in contrast, was both deeply concerned and eager to enunciate.[97] Finally the rest of the state central committee summoned up enough energy to function. It shifted the convention date from July 10 to July 24 without committing itself on the Mahony policy proposals. Even so, many counties sat out the convention. These included Scott (Davenport), Linn, Allamakee, and Clayton, all of which frequently voted Democratic or had strong Democratic minorities.[98]

On July 24, what was to be commonly known as the "Mahony Convention" assembled in Des Moines.[99] With relatively little difficulty the largely antiwar delegates selected candidates and wrote a platform. Charles Mason, Mahony's choice, headed the slate as the gubernatorial nominee. The platform made no concessions to the Republicans nor to the Lincoln administration. War resulted from the doctrine of irrepressible conflict which "arrayed Northern sentiment in antagonism to the Constitutional rights of the people of the slave states," the delegates declared. While they denounced secession as "a political heresy unwarranted by the Constitution," they warned that no Union formed in peace could survive through war without the advent of military despotism. Individual states, they agreed, were not creatures of the federal government, hence were not indebted to it for their position in the Union. And they urged that a national convention of states meet to promote legislation which would "secure equal and full rights to all sections of the Union."[100]

Republicans immediately proclaimed that in the Iowa Democratic ranks were significant numbers of disunionists, Southern sympathizers, and traitors. Though they angrily rejected these labels, many Democrats were embarrassed by the "Mahony platform." "Mahony-Mason Platform" is more accurate. Mahony wrote Mason that he had tried to draw up a document consistent with Mason's principles. There was nothing strange about this. Mason had been Mahony's choice all along for gubernatorial candidate. And, during this era, almost all Iowa Democratic leaders genuflected before Mason, longtime leader in bar, business, and political circles. He was at the time a patent lawyer in Washington, but he maintained his official residence in Burlington. All these leaders seemed to believe that Mason had unusual political insight and intelligence. His diary and his writings during the war reveal the falsity of the first assumption. As to the second, Mason was obviously very intelligent. But Mahony's own editorials in the *Herald* demonstrated that he was at least Mason's intellectual equal. What Mason had in spades, earned over the years, was "standing."[101]

Despite the aura of the Mason connection, a majority of the central committee were discomfited enough by Mahony's moves and by the convention he fathered to call for another convention, this one to be the "official" Democratic state convention.[102] In fact, there was enough discontent among some Iowans of both parties who desired the formation of a true nonpartisan ticket that moves toward that end were already underway. On July 25, thirty delegates representing seven counties assembled in a "Union Convention" at Des Moines. They nominated no candidates, but did, with some difficulty, draw up a platform pledging support to the federal government's efforts to maintain the Constitution and suppress the rebellion.[103] This group by early August professed to be dissatisfied with the results of the Republican convention of July 31 which renominated Kirkwood for governor. Accordingly, the "Union Convention" members convened again, a day ahead of the official Democratic convention. Now calling themselves the "People's Convention," they nominated Nathaniel B. Baker for governor. Keeping their pledge to field a nonpartisan ticket they nominated an 1860 Constitutional Union man and a Republican for the other two offices at stake, lieutenant governor and state judge. The People's Convention adopted a platform similar to the one of July 25 and took "Union Party" as its official name.[104] Baker and Reuben Noble, the candidate for judge, protested their nominations—but they didn't reject them.

On August 26, the official Democratic convention of 1861 met in Des Moines. To the chagrin of those favoring a tough stance against the South, the Mahony wing again controlled events. Though the "Mahonyites" allowed a war proponent, Lincoln Clark of Dubuque, to chair the convention, they denied him the right to select members of the resolutions committee. This task the convention at large assigned to itself. Predictably it rejected a minority report from the committee which condemned secession and demanded that Democrats support the war. Instead the delegates accepted the majority report which differed little from the platform produced at the Mahony convention. They now blamed both Northern and Southern sectionalism for the war rather than Northern sectionalism exclusively. "Real grievances" of the South became "real or supposed grievances." Whereas the Mahony convention adamantly opposed suspension of the writ of habeas corpus by any authority, the delegates now said that Congress could do so in case of rebellion or invasion "depending upon the needs of public safety." The majority conceded one other point to the minority which only slightly mollified that unhappy faction. The Mahony convention's nominee for lieutenant governor had been Clayton county farmer Maturin L. Fisher. When Fisher fortuitously withdrew from contention, the official convention replaced him with Lt. Col. William Merritt, a veteran of the battle of Wilson's Creek. By this time, however, Clark and a number of other delegates had walked out, angered by the adoption of what they described as a "secessionist platform."[105]

On September 1, then, Iowans found three tickets in the field vying for their support: that headed by incumbent Governor Kirkwood, advanced by the Republicans who bore down on the theme that Republicans alone represented Union sentiment and the Democratic party represented treason; the ticket headed by Mason, running on a platform rejected by many Democrats who believed it reflected unfairly upon the loyalty of the mass of the party; and that nominally headed by Baker who wouldn't say yes or no to a dissatisfied group of nonpartisans whose strength and position was not clear, even to themselves. The two major groups disavowed the third as neither fish nor fowl. Even so, leading Republicans and Democrats alike privately favored the Union party's existence, believing it would weaken their opponents.[106]

Dennis Mahony had good reason for satisfaction by September. The Iowa Democrats were on record against an all-out war to subdue the Confederacy. And his personal choice, Charles Mason, headed the party ticket. Mahony was not unhappy with the slightly revised platform of the official convention of August 29. Though he modestly disclaimed parentage, his *Herald* printed the judgment of the McGregor *North Iowa Times* that the official convention came through with a "Mahony ticket and Mahony resolutions."[107] But those Democrats who favored stern measures against rebels refused to accept defeat. Mahony expected to ride out the storm. Mason was more timid. After the Mahony convention, rumblings of discontent from several areas caused him to embark on a hurried trip through

Fairfield, Ottumwa, Keokuk, and the southern part of the state to take political soundings. The results reassured him, and he wrote a letter accepting the nomination on August 8.[108]

Republicans jumped to the attack. Mason's letter, they charged, plainly revealed him to be a disunionist. In particular they challenged his views on citizen obedience to the federal government and on the government's authority to deal with rebellion. Mason had written that citizens must obey the federal government if that government acted within Constitutional limitations. Mason's "if" was a big one. Coercion of mobs, rioters, and insurrectionists was constitutional, he argued. But coercion of one-third of the "Sovereign States" whose only aim was "to secure the happiness and security of their citizens by changing their form of government in a manner established by the Declaration of Independence" was not.[109]

One month later there were several new casts of characters performing on the Iowa electoral stage. Mason was not among them. Object of intense pressure, both to step down and to stand fast from warring factions in the party, he announced unhappily on September 20, "Circumstances have induced me to withdraw my name as a candidate for Governor."[110] A significant circumstance was Merritt's rising star among War Democrats coupled with Baker's belated rejection of the Union party nomination. Baker's move came on September 4. Five days later Merritt rejected his nomination for lieutenant governor on the Democratic ticket and threw his support to Baker whose rejection was not yet common knowledge.[111] This reactivated the nonpartisan Union party whose central committee on September 18 chose Merritt for the spot vacated by Baker. Following Mason's announcement, Union party and Democratic committeemen agreed to field a joint slate headed by Merritt with Laurin Dewey, Union party man, in second spot (Dewey had supported Bell for president in 1860), and James Ellwood, original Mahony convention nominee, for state judge.[112]

Two maverick slates squeezed onstage before the month ended. Union party men who refused to back Merritt chose a ticket headed by Lincoln Clark. A rump Democratic group composed of Democrats attending the state fair in Iowa City on September 26 picked a slate headed by Ben Samuels, himself a strong Mason supporter. Promoter of this last-gasp entry was Iowa City's LeGrand Byington, soon to win distinction as Iowa's number one irreconcilable in the peace ranks.[113] Mason's friends regarded his withdrawal under pressure as a bad mistake, and they told him so. Mason regretted it also within twenty-four hours, but too late to retrieve the nomination.[114]

Republicans were delighted. In the campaign they rarely attacked Merritt, but they belabored the platform as a "Mahony" or "disunionist" document. They expected to win handily—with good reason. In the election, Kirkwood rolled over Merritt easily, 59,853 to 43,245. Ben Samuels received 4,492, Henry Clay Dean, 463, Mason, 119, and Lincoln Clark, 50. In the First congressional district, Fairfield Republican James F. Wilson defeated state senator Jairus E. Neal of Knoxville, 28,133 to 20,328, in a special election to fill the vacancy caused by the resignation of Samuel R. Curtis who had joined the army. Neal did not have full Democratic support because of what some believed to be his pro-Southern course during the extra session of the 1861 legislature.[115]

After his defeat Merritt sought to return to Kirkwood's good graces. This was not easy to do. During the course of the campaign, the *Cedar Valley Times* (Cedar Rapids) accused Kirkwood of profiteering from war contracts. Kirkwood reacted hotly. Creditors were then dunning him for debts amounting to $6,000, debts incurred when he mortgaged his property to help meet the payroll of various Iowa regiments. He accused Merritt of fostering the *Times'* attack. Merritt admitted writing occasional articles for the paper on which his firm held a mortgage. But he denied responsibility for the assault on Kirkwood. Another situation of Merritt's own making irritated the Governor. Merritt had resigned his colonelcy and left the military service after he completed three months of active duty. After the election he decided to reenter the army, preferably as a brigadier general. He prodded Kirkwood to support his application for such a commission. Kirkwood sharply reminded Merritt that when he had declined the Democratic nomination for lieutenant governor, he gave as one reason the fact that he might want to return to the army. Then when Kirkwood offered him command of the First Iowa, his original unit, Merritt refused that in order to enter the campaign for governor. Now, Kirkwood concluded, "[You] almost challange [sic] my support of your present application as a right." One other Merritt statement is interesting. He told the Governor that he ran for governor on the Union ticket only, a revelation which would have been startling news to over 40,000 Iowa Democrats at that late date.[116]

4

The Problem of Loyalty: 1862

IOWA Democratic fears in the fall of 1861 that solidly entrenched Republicans would use their power to suppress dissent or take action against those suspected of pro-Southern sympathy were not entirely unfounded. The United States State Department, acquiring extralegal powers from President Lincoln to make political arrests, often used federal officials in the various states to effect that purpose. One of these officials was United States Marshal for Iowa, Herbert M. Hoxie. Hoxie, a resident of the state since 1840, was nearing thirty-two. Behind him lay experience as district court clerk for Polk county, tavern keeper, Underground Railroad activist, gold seeker, and holder of successive Republican party positions culminating in chairmanship of the state central committee in 1860. By this time Hoxie had also become an associate of Council Bluffs' Grenville M. Dodge. Together they were to rise after the war as successful railroad builders in the West and South. On his death in 1886 the Old Settlers Association of Boone county recalled that Hoxie had been hospitable at his tavern, helpful to people in the snow and mud, patriotic, generous, public spirited, and gentle.[1] These were qualities which political opponents during the war denied that Hoxie ever possessed.

In the summer of 1864, General Marcellus Crocker spent a furlough in Des Moines where he visited Hoxie. Crocker's genial description of the Marshal and his attitude toward his work is worth quoting. Crocker wrote General Dodge:

> Hub sends his regards. he lets on to be very busy and I supose that he is, he says that he has a kind of general supervision of affairs civil and military in the state and has diverstimes threatened me with arrest. And since I find his office a very convenient place to sponge stationary and envelopes & c. I have not seen proper to dispute his authority.[2]

Kirkwood's recommendation of Hoxie in early 1861 for Marshal did nothing to alleviate Democratic suspicions that Republicans were unprincipled opportunists. Even Republican Secretary of State Elijah Sells despised the nominee. Sells described him as ''suspicious, treacherous, and as corrupt as the devil wants him to be'' in a forthright protest letter to Kirkwood.³ Two Hoxie letters to Dodge likewise contribute little to Hoxie's image as a public servant. Shortly after his appointment, he wrote Dodge saying, ''There must be money in this war some place and we ought to have our share. How shall we go to work on it? That is the question.'' And from Washington, on February 24, 1865, after he had resigned his post and joined Charles Durant and the Union Pacific, he wrote, ''I am impelled to do this first because we had a fight in the delegation and 2nd because I can make more money [here]. The office [of Marshal] is not worth having and I have been a fool to keep it. True it is power—but what is power after all.''⁴

In October, 1861, Secretary of State William Seward encouraged Hoxie to be vigilant and thorough in his police role. The State Department had information, wrote Seward,

> that persons in the State of Iowa are disloyal and co-operating with those in arms against the authority of the Government of the United States, and that others are engaged in transporting gunpowder across the state for the insurrectionists . . . please confer with the United States district attorney and arrest and commit to military custody any such persons and report to this Department.⁵

By that time Hoxie had already gone to work, making what may have been the first political arrest of the war in Iowa. The victim was George Frane of Rochester in Cedar county who had for some time fought local abolitionists over their attempt to enroll a black child in the district school. Frane aroused suspicion in the Rochester post office when he scrutinized a map to find an address for a letter he was mailing to a northwest Missouri sheriff. This occurred in midsummer of 1861 near the time when a troop train in that region of Missouri plunged through a guerilla-sabotaged bridge into the Platte River. Frane's adversaries tried to forge a treasonous link out of these circumstances. Arrested by Hoxie and brought to Dubuque on October 21, Frane went before the grand jury. That body brought in no bill against him, and he was freed two days later. The whole Frane incident is more than a little muddy. The *Herald*'s coverage is partly at fault. Thoroughly friendly to Frane, it implied that Frane intended his letter to alert the Missouri sheriff to a slave-stealing expedition out of Iowa, one member of which was Barclay Coppoc. The *Herald* itself pointed out that the post office incident occurred about the time of the sabotage on the Platte bridge. Coppoc was in Missouri then, but not on a slave-stealing venture. He was a lieutenant in the Fourth Kansas Volunteers and died in the wreck of the troop train over the Platte.⁶ Hoxie also made his presence felt later that year in two instances, one minor and one major. The minor one merely involved his presence in Council Bluffs. Nathan Dodge, with obvious delight, wrote his brother, ''Hoxie is here—Sesseshers look pale and want to know who he is after. I tell them he is not going back without company.''⁷ The major incident was the Hill case in which a purloined letter led to a serious and prolonged civil liberties disaster.

William Hill of Magnolia was the Harrison county clerk. When war came, Mrs. Hill was visiting her family in Virginia. Hill, believing that she would be unable to leave the South without his assistance, went east to help. The Iowan later claimed that he feared Virginia authorities might not permit his wife to cross the picket lines unless he could win their sympathy. The method he used was calamitous. Hill wrote a letter to the *Union Democrat* of Union, Virginia, which castigated abolitionists, claimed Northern conservatives wished the South well in its efforts to resist invasion, claimed western Iowa would supply no troops for the federal army, and praised Virginia volunteers. Thanks to the war's disruption of the mail, the letter, dated May 14, 1861, got no further than Washington. While Hill was still in the East trying to get his wife out of Virginia, postal officials returned the letter to Magnolia where Hill's deputy opened it and passed it to local Republicans. Published in several Iowa papers, the contents created an enormous stir and demands that Hill be tried for treason. A federal grand jury in Des Moines soon indicted Hill, and trial was set for January 7.

In mid-December, however, Kirkwood, Hoxie, Sells, and other leading Republicans began to fear that the panel of prospective jurors contained too many "rebel sympathizers." A trial jury chosen from its ranks might free Hill. Accordingly, they wired Seward to recommend that United States Attorney for Iowa, W. H. F. Gurley, enter a nolle prosequi in the case, releasing Hill from the civil courts under the Department of Justice, thus clearing the way for action by the State Department. Gurley, then in Washington, consulted with the Attorney General about dropping the case and won his approval on December 27. The State Department took jurisdiction on December 28. Hill, knowing nothing of this, arrived in Des Moines on January 7 to stand trial, only to learn that Gurley had entered a nolle prosequi. His relief was short-lived. Late on the seventh or very early in the morning of the eighth, Hoxie arrested Hill and hustled him off to Fort Lafayette, New York, ignoring a writ of habeas corpus issued in his behalf in Davenport. Republicans wanted to make an example of the Harrison county man, arguing that his release would dismay loyal citizens and embolden those who opposed the war. Hill tried desperately to secure his freedom, but found himself blocked at nearly every turn. His admission that the sentiments in his letter were imprudent but that he wrote them only to ease his wife's passage out of Virginia had no effect upon authorities. Nor did his declarations of loyalty, offers to get character witnesses by the "thousands," nor his willingness to take a loyalty oath and stand trial for treason in Iowa. Secretary of War Stanton, who took over the responsibility for political arrest cases in February, believed Hill was a spy. By this time, C. C. Cole, Hill's lawyer, acting in what he thought was Hill's best interests, had filed a suit for damages against Hoxie; Hoxie thus had less reason than ever to want Hill released.

Eventually Senators Grimes and Harlan, beginning in February, interceded in Hill's behalf. Because of their efforts he won his freedom on April 29. Hill had to take a loyalty oath and to agree to take no legal action against Hoxie. Stanton was a real roadblock for Hill, delaying the release for as long as he could and once suggesting to Henry Halleck, military commander of the West, that Hoxie be instructed to arrest Cole also, arguing that it would have a "salutary effect." Halleck, like Grimes and Harlan, was skeptical about the government's case and did nothing. He mistakenly believed that the Hill affair stemmed from what he called a newspaper quarrel, and he thought Hoxie was too thin-skinned. "I permit the newspapers to abuse me to their heart's content and I advise you to do the same," he wrote the Marshal.[8] Hoxie, who is generally condemned by Iowa historians for his high-handed violation of civil liberties during wartime, came in for such strong criticism during the course of the Hill case that he tried to explain his actions in a widely circulated public letter. The letter suggested that Seward was the one who wanted Hill arrested and sent East.[9] The explanation is spurious. Hoxie, Kirkwood, Sells, and many others wanted Hill's hide, and the first two wrote Seward directly suggesting just how he could help them get it. The consequences to Hill were severe according to Joe H. Smith, Harrison county writer. Hill felt disgraced, and signs of mental breakdown occurred shortly after his release. He tried to commit suicide in 1879 and died insane in 1881. Smith blamed Republicans for Hill's problems, adding, ". . . authors of this misfortune stalk abroad in this county, as of this writing, not seeming to think that they were the authors of so great a misfortune . . . outrage and wrong . . . the saddest incident in all the history of the county."[10]

The Hill case coincided with another which was even more of a shock to Democrats and even more of a political windfall for their opponents. On December 20, 1861, federal agents under Seward's order arrested former Senator George Jones in New York and imprisoned him in Fort Lafayette for making "treasonable communication" with the enemy. The arrest occurred two weeks after Jones returned from South America. After Jones lost his Senate seat in 1859, President Buchanan appointed him minister to Colombia, a post he held until the fall of 1861 when a Republican replaced him. That year, while still in Colombia, Jones wrote two letters to Jefferson Davis, dated May 17 and May 23, plus a note written May 27, which he enclosed in the May 23 letter. The letter of May 23 also contained a copy of the May 17 letter because Jones feared that the first mailing might not reach Davis. Another Jones letter, written August 1 to Isaac E. Morse, a Louisiana friend and former United States congressman, also figured in Jones's difficulty, as did letters to Jones from his wife and from one of his sons. How the government got hold of the letters is not clear. One source says they were discovered on his person when he returned, which is surely inaccurate. The Chicago *Times* reported that Jones apparently enclosed them by mistake in a package he personally delivered to the State Department upon his return. However, the Department's report on the affair speaks of two separate mailings from Colombia. Letters from the family to Jones from Dubuque written in April, June, July, August, and September may have been intercepted before being sent on to Jones, if they were sent on at all.[11]

Only the Jones letters to Davis and Morse figured in the newspaper coverage. A letter to Laurel Summers, also written on May 17, the date of the first letter to

Davis, does not surface in the controversy. What Jones actually wrote was the subject of speculation until July when the government released some of the letters to the press. Prior to this, Jones's family in Dubuque had tried without success to get copies.[12] Enough of their contents leaked out, however, to inflame Dennis Mahony. "If he wrote such letters as the reports say of him he is an _____ traitor and should be dealt with accordingly," Mahony told Charles Mason. Republican comment was equally astringent and more voluminous. Some persons gave Jones the benefit of the doubt including former presidents Buchanan and Pierce.[13] So long as the government withheld the actual letters, in fact, Jones was better off. Their release brought him even greater abuse from all sides. The portions of Jones's letter of May 17 (the only Davis letter released at that time), which attracted the most critical comment revealed what Jones intended to do if war came.

> But let what may come to pass [he wrote] you may rely upon it as you say that neither I nor mine will be found in the ranks of our (your) enemies. May God Almighty avert civil war, but if unhappily it shall come you may—I think without doubt—count upon me and mine and hosts of other friends standing shoulder to shoulder in the ranks with you and our other Southern friends and relatives whose rights like my own have been disregarded by the abolitionists. I love Wisconsin and Iowa for the honors conferred by them on me and because I served them always faithfully; but I will not make war with them against the South whose rights they shamefully neglected. . . . The dissolution of the Union will probably be the cause of my own ruin as well as that of my country, and may cause me and mine to go South.

Jones made even clearer what he would do in his letter to Morse which he wrote after he knew the war had started. Strangely, it caused less of a stir. He said he was anxious to return to his family, "'my sons having left them to come down South to fight for the maintenance of the Constitution, the laws and the rights of the people of the South as I intend to do if required to fight at all. . . .'" At that it was probably fortunate for Jones that his letter to Summers reached Summers only.

> No Laurel, [he wrote] I will not do battle against them [the Southern people] and rather than do so I will leave my own beloved Iowa and go south. . . . Great God has it come to this that I am to be impressed into a northern army at the bidding of Kirkwood, FitzHenry Warren or other abolition cowards to go down south with a rifle on my shoulders to do battle against the only brothers whom I have . . . or turn my back upon the state which has honored me so highly? . . .[14]

Jones got a thrashing from some Democratic newspapers. The *Herald* alone put forth a limited defense. He was freed without trial in late February. After Thomas Clagett of the Keokuk *Constitution* read the Jones letters he wondered why the government ever let the ex-solon out of Fort Lafayette. David Richardson brushed aside Jones's explanation that he really opposed secession and that he meant that he would take up arms only against abolitionists. "There was treason in them [the letters] else we can't read the English language understandingly," Richardson concluded. Patrick Robb of the Sioux City *Register* said Jones was disloyal, while the *Cass County Gazette* called him a traitor. The Burlington *Argus* announced that Jones was no longer a Democrat. In Chicago, the *Times* said Jones' letters "lose [sic] in style as they are atrocious in sentiment" marked him as "worse than a southern rebel."[15] In Dubuque on his return, February 27, Jones had enough friends to give him a warm reception. But he did not lie low as many Democrats probably hoped he would. By mid-May he had appeared in Keokuk, Burlington, Davenport, and elsewhere, organizing resistance to federal tax collectors, guessed the scornful *Hawk-eye*. Thus, friend Summers, chairman of the party's central committee, felt impelled to hint that Jones should stay away from the party convention that year.[16]

With the Hill and Jones arrests obviously on his mind, Governor Kirkwood had strong words in his January, 1862, message to the legislature for those

> few . . . who, blinded by prejudice engendered by former political strife, cannot forget that the government is guided in this struggle for its life by the hands of political opponents, and who would rather see it perish than have it saved by their hands, who cry peace when there is no peace, and who will endeavor to turn us from the prosecution of this war by continually dwelling upon and exaggerating the misfortunes it has brought and will bring upon us.

Fortunately, judged the Governor, they had little influence.[17] Three days before Kirkwood's speech, the *Herald* reported with a hint of irony that several leading citizens, including a former Iowa governor (Stephen Hempstead), had voluntarily appeared before Col. J. F. Bates, a Democrat and a former commander of the First Iowa Infantry, to take an oath to support the Constitution. In Keokuk the *Gate City* complained that local "sympathizers" were giving special attention, food, luxuries, and fine clothes to wounded rebel prisoners in the local hospital. Rebels deserved humane treatment, but such extras, the paper declared, were offensive; the hospital director should set some limits.[18]

One small southern Iowa paper believed that resolutions approved at the Keokuk county Democratic convention were "less loyal" than those approved in 1861.[19] The Waterloo *Courier* was equally certain that while almost all Iowa Democrats were loyal, the state party leaders were not and would willingly accept humiliating peace terms. Only C. C. Cole, said the *Iowa State Register,* made a loyal speech at the party's state convention, and he got a cool reception. In Davenport *Der Demokrat,* less independent now but not yet completely committed to Republicanism, concluded that Iowa's Democrats were traitors and opposed to a free republic. Quick to notice deviation by any Germans from the course of clear loyalty, *Der Demokrat* excoriated one Hans Paulson for disgracing his fellow

Germans by making a drunken "Hurrah" speech for Jefferson Davis and Pierre Beauregard at a Davenport tavern.[20]

But Dubuque, so far as the rest of Iowa was concerned, remained the primary source of disloyal poison in the state. One of two 1861 legislators who left Iowa to join the Confederate army did come from Dubuque. That was James Williams. (The other was Cyrus Franklin from Wapello county.) Another Dubuque legislator created a stir when he admitted that he took no delight in either Northern or Southern victories. Elaborating further, however, John D. Jennings made it clear that he did not quite favor a draw. "I do not wish to see the people of the South crushed to the earth," he said. "They are Americans and I wish to see them acquit themselves in a manner worthy of American citizens and soldiers. I wish to see them conduct themselves with such vigor as to compel the North to yield such compromises in the end as will secure to them their constitutional rights. . . ." Jennings's admission was no surprise to the *Times* which was certain by then that the city's reputation as a "secessionist hole" had caused Washington to decree that the Pacific railroad would make no tributary connection with Dubuque.[21] Whether Washington was that concerned about Dubuque's political coloration is debatable. But Kirkwood was, and he eventually did something about it. Early in the war, the state established Camp Franklin on the outskirts of the city as a rendezvous for Iowa volunteers. According to writers who lived in the county at the time, "The citizens . . . did not properly care for the volunteers," who suffered much from sickness and inadequate quarters. Finally, in early 1863, the Governor publicly announced that no more Iowa troops would assemble at Camp Franklin because the county was "too secessionist."[22]

Considering the inflammatory rhetoric which pervaded the press, and Governor Kirkwood's direct challenge to opponents of the war in his legislative address, the 1862 regular session of the Iowa legislature did its work with less wrangling than might have been expected. Part of this resulted from the fact that the 1861 elections produced a decline in Democratic representation. Table 4.1 shows how great that decline was.

In the 1860–1861 legislature the 21 Democratic senators came from 49 of Iowa's 99 counties, and the 36 representatives from 39 counties. Considerably weaker in the 1862–1863 legislature, the 14 senate Democrats represented 37 counties and the 30 representatives, 18 counties.[23]

TABLE 4.1
PARTY REPRESENTATION, IOWA LEGISLATURE, 1860–61, 1862–63

Party	Branch	1860–61	1862–63
Republican	Senate	23	31
	House	50	65
Democrat	Senate	21	14
	House	36	30

Laws passed during the regular session established procedures for collecting the direct federal tax, tightened existing liquor control statutes, strengthened the militia law, provided aid for sick and wounded soldiers, exempted soldier property from taxes and forced sale while the owners were in service, and divided the state into six congressional districts, up from two, a result of the state's population growth.[24]

Once, in the 1862 regular session, Republicans backed Democrats into a politically awkward corner. House Republicans sponsored a resolution which was nothing less than a ringing endorsement of the Lincoln administration and which pledged "unwavering support" for the President's efforts to suppress rebellion and restore the Union. In the house, only 5 Democrats opposed it. Twenty-one, including some otherwise vitriolic critics of Lincoln, voted for the resolution. Most senate Democrats refused to bow before what may have been a deliberate effort by the majority to embarrass them. Only 2 voted with the Republicans.[25]

Democratic opposition to measures designed in one way or another to facilitate Iowa's contribution to the war was never clear cut. In the house, Democratic negative votes on final passage of such bills generally ranged from 5 to 17 in number. In the senate the range was normally between 7 and 12. As in the previous year, they opposed bills and resolutions and isolated provisions in them more in preliminary than in final balloting. This opposition, moreover, they directed primarily toward the technical content rather than the spirit of proposed legislation. They did not actively oppose the mobilization or equipping of Iowa regiments for use against the South. But they displayed much concern, along with some Republicans, about tables of organization, costs of materiel, and salaries for regimental officers.[26] At the conclusion of the session even so severe a critic as Frank Palmer of the *Iowa State Register* complimented the body for its "nonpartisan" spirit.[27]

Within five months Governor Kirkwood summoned the legislature to a special session, as he had in 1861. Faced with the prospect of additional federal calls for Iowa troops and a rise in state expenditures, Kirkwood requested legislative action on these and related matters. The lawmakers complied, whipping out thirty-nine bills in eight days. The most important provided for soldier voting in the field, increased appropriations for the executive department, additions to the militia law, and county authority to levy taxes to fund enlistment bounties and to pay support to soldiers' families.[28]

Democrats in both branches largely went along with the Governor's requests. Only one dared vote against the soldier vote bill, a measure many professed to favor enthusiastically. Before final passage, however, they fought to tighten voting procedures. Republicans accepted a Democratic modification of the oath prescribed for election officials. The change required them to swear not "to . . . influence or control the vote of any soldier." But they rejected Democratic demands that civilian voting commissioners be chosen on a nonpartisan basis. Senate Democrats split among themselves, 7 to 6, on a Democrat-introduced amendment to grant the vote to foreign-born Iowa soldiers who had applied for

United States citizenship but had not yet received their final papers. All Republicans rejected this proposal.[29] House Republicans rebuffed a Democratic resolution that proposed the establishment of military courts in Iowa to expedite the cases of persons arrested for alleged disloyalty. But House Republicans did show some concern for civil liberties. They quashed moves to require voter loyalty oaths and to bar persons "exhibiting favor for the principles, causes, or actors of the rebellion" from state office.[30]

The newspaper battle over loyalty, begun in 1860, waxed more furious in 1862, continuing to the end of the war. Almost any new Democratic publishing venture provoked immediate scrutiny by the opposition, and, more often than not, a swift judgment that the result was another Southern sympathizer rag. John Duncombe's Fort Dodge *Democrat*, for instance, inspired A. F. B. Hildreth of the St. Charles City *Intelligencer* to reject the customary exchange of copies between papers with the remark that "we fail to find a loyal sentiment in it. . . ."[31] These conflicts were especially abrasive in cities with competing party organs. In Dubuque, Jesse Clement and G. T. Stewart of the *Times* were ranged against a succession of *Herald* editors—Dennis Mahony, Stilson Hutchins, Patrick Robb (to a lesser degree), and M. M. Ham. In Keokuk, James Howell confronted Thomas Clagett. Frank Palmer of the *Iowa State Register* eventually got serious competition from William Merritt of the *Iowa Statesman*. Clark Dunham's adversary in Burlington was G. M. Todd of the *Argus*. Edward Thayer of the *Courier* battled with Republican John Mahin of the *Journal* in Muscatine. David Richardson fought with the Davenport *Gazette*'s Addison and Alfred Sanders and their successor Edward Russell, English-born abolitionist. In Council Bluffs W. S. Burke and W. W. Maynard of the *Nonpareil* took on Lysander Babbitt of the *Bugle*. And bitter warfare raged in Fairfield between the *Ledger*'s W. W. Junkin and David Sheward of the *Constitution and Union*. Other towns enjoying or enduring similar competition were Iowa City (*Republican* and *State Democratic Press*), West Union (*Public Record* and *Fayette County Pioneer*), Oskaloosa (*Herald* and *Times*), and Ottumwa (*Courier* and *Democratic Mercury*). Between Dubuque's *Der National-Demokrat* and Davenport's *Der Demokrat* existed a quarrel as to which was really loyal and which accurately represesented the thinking of Iowa's Germans.

Editors occasionally fought it out in the streets or in the courts. John Hodnett, a junior partner on the *Herald*, assaulted Clement. This won him a twenty-five day jail sentence which the Iowa Supreme Court upheld upon appeal.[32] Thayer and Mahin sued each other for defamation of character, but neither case reached the trial stage.[33] Clagett sued Howell for libel, prompting David Richardson to advise him to "withdraw the suit, and if you feel very bad, insist on Howell's running his nose against your fist a few times." Thayer employed Richardson's formula to chastise a reader who doubted his loyalty.[34] In Dubuque Mahony unsuccessfully sought a grand jury indictment against Stewart for calling him a traitor.[35] Republican editors could disagree on the question of opponents' loyalty. Clark Dunham declared unequivocally that there were no loyal Democratic papers in Iowa. But Frank Palmer, no softhearted judge of the opposition, corrected him. There were two, he said, the *Cass County Gazette* (Atlantic), and the Sioux City *Register*. Nor, Palmer, added, was the *Democrat* under Richardson so bad.[36]

One loyalty test was the army enlistment rate. Republicans often charged that Democrats failed to enlist in proportion to their numbers, while Democrats suggested that Republicans preferred profit making to going to a war for which they were responsible in the first place. In Dubuque there was a running battle between the *Herald* and *Times* over whether Dubuquers joined up in satisfactory numbers. The *Times* charged that the city and county failed to contribute their share. Many men enlisted in Dubuque only because it was a recruiting center; 90 percent of them came from adjacent counties and communities, the Republican organ claimed.[37] But quarreling over numbers could be beside the point. If the war became an abolition war, cried the Ottumwa *Democratic Mercury*, let the abolitionists and Southern traitors fight it. Democrats should fight only to preserve the Constitution and restore the Union.[38]

When Lincoln issued his call for 300,000 men in July, the questions who should enlist, who actually did, and who discouraged enlistments became daily topics of concern in many Iowa papers. In addition, whether lukewarm about the war or not, nobody wanted the onus of a draft hanging over the state. Hence, efforts to meet the Iowa quota of 10,000 men acquired an air of real and bitter urgency. The *Herald* asked, "How Many Republicans Will Answer the Call?" The great majority of the soldiers were Democrats, but those who brought on the conflict chose to serve "by becoming contractors, thieves and plunderers," the paper declared. It invited Dubuque Republicans, the "Allisons and Adamses, the Cooleys and Crams, the Lyons and Mills and Pollocks and the hosts of other talking warriors," to enlist. Two weeks later the Langworthys and the Stouts appeared on the list. The list grew longer, eventually containing Dubuque's Wide-Awake Republican club, the *Times* editorial writer, Dubuque delegates to the state Republican convention, the entire state Republican convention, and the editor of the Davenport *Gazette* ("He is a coward, with a coward's soul and a coward's brutality"—then the clincher—"He is an abolitionist").[39] David Richardson, with less rancor, likewise suggested that certain unnamed Davenporters enlist including "half a dozen lawyers, two or three doctors, a hotel clerk, and a large number of 'gentlemen.' "[40] Some Democratic papers which positively encouraged enlistments were the *North Iowa Times* (McGregor), Sioux City *Register*, Keokuk *Constitution*, and Muscatine *Courier*. Edward Thayer spoke at an enlistment rally in Wilton Junction. Thayer and Thomas Clagett, like Mahony, encouraged "patriot shouters" to enlist.[41]

One who clearly did not encourage enlistments was Fairfield's David

Sheward. As the enlistment campaign swung into high gear and as some counties began to offer enlistment bounties Sheward wrote,

> "Go tell your King he has not gold enough to buy me," said one of the patriots of '76; and that should be the reply of every Democrat and true lover of the country, to king Abraham, when an office or other bribe, military or civil, is tendered for the purpose of winning him to the side of the usurper. . . . Tell him he has not gold enough, nor honors enough to bestow to make you a traitor.

"We would have it distinctly understood," Sheward wrote in another editorial in the same issue, "that we are as much opposed to the war and the policy of the administration as ever, and that we will not forego an opportunity to strike a blow at it." Do something about Sheward, demanded the Dubuque *Times* editor after reading this polemic.[42] Something soon was.

Bounties did help where county supervisors provided them. Dubuque county recruits signing up between August 19 and September 1 got $50, provoking charges that few of them were really patriotic. Democratic supervisors in Des Moines county refused to pay bounties, angering the *Hawk-eye*. But Republican-dominated boards in Jackson and Delaware counties also refused.[43] Recruiters could be devious. George Noland, Republican farmer near Colesburg in Delaware county, wrote a furious letter to the *Herald* explaining how one of them tricked his son into enlisting. The Noland boy refused to volunteer that summer, but he did sign his name to some paper as an inducement to others to join, assuming that his own signature did not constitute an enlistment. On December 16, one Thomas Robinson hired him, ostensibly to help drive hogs to Davenport. When they reached Davenport, Robinson turned the youth over to the Sixth Iowa Infantry. "Instead of being hired to drive hogs my son is himself driven to the slaughter," cried young Noland's father.[44]

Another not-so-happy recruit was Solon M. Langworthy of the Dubuque Langworthys, one of the targets of Mahony's enlistment barbs about those who encouraged their "poorer Democratic neighbors" to go to war. In Langworthy's case, the Irish editor may have struck home. Langworthy enlisted at age forty-eight in September as quartermaster of the Twenty-Seventh Iowa. Captured in December and paroled in January, he returned to service with his regiment in June of 1863. He was still unhappy years later when he wrote, "I . . . sacrificed on the alter of my country years of uninterrupted business prosperity during which many of my business friends and acquaintances had made themselves rich."[45]

The Noland family's problem was distantly related to that of some Dubuque Irish soldiers who enlisted with the understanding that they would be formed into an all-Irish regiment. When intense recruiting failed to bring in enough men for the proposed regiment, 17 privates secured writs of habeas corpus from Judge Stephen Hempstead in an effort to get out. In the meantime, however, their units, the Forty-Second Iowa, and the Forty-Third Iowa were assimilated into the

Seventh Iowa Cavalry. The Seventh then went into the federal service. Accordingly, the men were remanded back to the army to serve three years or the duration of the war. Dennis Mahony's arrest in mid-August probably contributed to Irish reluctance to enlist. After Henry O'Connor of Muscatine, Kirkwood's choice to command the regiment, failed to win enough recruits, the Governor authorized John O'Neil and George M. O'Brien to assume the recruitment chores. They failed also.[46]

Iowa aliens generally faced growing pressure in 1862. On August 16, Kirkwood issued orders appointing draft commissioners in the various counties. They were to compile enrollment lists from which aliens could exempt themselves. The results were predictable. When many aliens chose exemption, there was intense reaction in some quarters, Democratic as well as Republican. By far the angriest in print was David Richardson. When many of Davenport's foreign-born residents secured exemptions, Richardson began to list them and their places of birth. On September 4, he called his roll the "Coward List," printing names of 29 exemptees from England, Ireland, Scotland, and Canada; 33 appeared under the heading "Germany, Prussia, Denmark, France, etc." The Democratic-dominated city council promptly and unanimously passed a resolution, introduced by an Irish member and seconded by a German, to deny public employment to any man on the list. Richardson urged citizens to study the list to see if it contained any voters; those recognized as voters should be reported for perjury. By September 6, there were 53 names on the British origins list and 73 on the German and continental list, under a new head, "Sneak List." The *Democrat* now reported formation of a committee which proposed to find out where the exemption claimants worked and which ones ran businesses. Loyal employers would fire the workers. Customers of those in business would be advised to take their trade elsewhere. Some exemptees began to withdraw their claims. As they did, the paper removed their names. On September 8, seven new names appeared on the British list and three on the German and continental. On September 9, the paper reported that the draft was off for the present, and it printed the "Sneak List" for the last time. By then, counting additions and drops, it stood at 53 for British origins claimants and 56 for Germans and other continentals.[47]

Richardson's methods earned him praise from the Burlington *Hawk-eye,* Sioux City *Register,* and the *Iowa State Register.* The Des Moines paper announced that those Polk county voters claiming exemptions would now be stopped at the polls. On October 11, the Dubuque *Times,* following Richardson's lead, printed the full list of Dubuque county exemption claimants. Dubuque city's six wards totaled 140 names and the eighteen rural townships 393 for a grand total of 523. As in Davenport, the paper urged citizens to use the list to challenge alien voters. It also urged them to inform the draft commissioner if any aliens who showed up to vote had taken out naturalization papers after the date of the draft enrollment. As in Davenport, Germans and Irish dominated the list. In Cedar Rapids, editor C. M. Hollis described Linn county's "Bohemians and Irish" who claimed exemptions as "despicable."[48]

James Howell was no less bilious than Richardson about aliens who wanted the best of two worlds as he saw it. Howell wrote:

On account of the large number of our laboring classes, who have left the city and county for the army, our farmers and others needing help begin seriously to feel the want of hands at living prices. Many a "Patrick" who is cursing the administration and the war, but who is sure to save his hide intact unless that abominable "dehraft" comes along is demanding and receiving better wages for his work than ever before. That's the way it is "ruining" him.[49]

Richardson not only opposed alien exemption claimants, he also opposed Quakers who lobbied for a bill to exempt members of the sect from the draft. When the bill failed to pass, he was delighted, as were many Iowans, judging from newspaper coverage of the Quakers' efforts. The *Democrat*'s legislative reporter called the unpopular Quakers "broad-brims" and "shad bellies."[50]

During August, when fear of a draft first reached a peak, many draft-age males left home temporarily. There was a noticeable exodus from Dubuque's heavily Irish first ward. Other places experienced the same phenomenon. Sioux City authorities picked up five Hamilton county men suspected of draft evasion. They claimed to be elk hunting, an explanation which brought a snort from the *Hamilton Freeman* editor who wrote, ". . . there are men enough camped out in northwest Iowa to form a regiment—all claiming to be in pursuit of that noble game." At Council Bluffs and Dubuque, provost marshals tried to stop the departure of draft-age men by instituting a pass system whereby those who wanted to cross the rivers had to prove that they didn't intend to evade the draft.[51]

State officials meanwhile were under great pressure to meet Iowa's share of the federal calls of July 2 for 300,000 men for three-years' duty and of August 4 for 300,000 for nine months of militia service. Kirkwood opposed the nine-months enlistment on the grounds that troops would be discharged just at the point when they could be effective in the field. So Iowa accepted only three-year enlistments. Halfway through September the 21,140 men required for the combined calls had signed up. These all went to newly constituted regiments. Harder to get were the approximately 8,000 recruits needed to fill the ranks of the old regiments. Thus, the threat of a draft to fill them hung over the state through the rest of 1862, 1863, and into the fall of 1864 when the first and only Iowa draft occurred.[52]

Building up the army in 1862 caused different kinds of worries for a few people. Charles Mason believed that the country could never safely disband a large army once it had one. He also saw such a force as a tool for Republican revolutionaries. One worried chaplain expressed another point of view after several months service in the Third Iowa. Many officers, he wrote, were patriotic and God-fearing and looked after their men's morals. But some were such bad influences that those troops unlucky enough to serve under them would return home as "walking personifications of obscenity and profaneness. . . ." The

Reverend E. C. Byam of Mount Vernon hoped to preserve some soldiers from such a fate. He proposed recruitment of a temperance regiment commanded by a Christian, a unit "free from the vices much too prevalent in the regiments generally. . . ."[53]

The year 1862 was a year in which dissident Democrats began to feel the force of state and federal power to silence them. The Jones and Hill cases served as portents. Some Republicans looked for legal grounds to shut up alleged rebel sympathizers. Those writing to Governor Kirkwood received a standard response from Nathan Brainerd, his secretary. Brainerd told them that mere expression of sympathy for rebels or, somewhat less accurately as events were to prove, holding meetings "for whatever purpose" were legal. Authorities could only act when there was evidence of treason. By mid-August, Brainerd added to the list of punishable offenses the acts of discouraging enlistments and interfering with an officer in line of duty.[54] Buttressing this was Edwin Stanton's August 8 order to federal officials to arrest and try before a military commission those persons "seeking to discourage volunteering, giving aid and comfort or through writing, speech or act engaging in any disloyal practice." Kirkwood, who worked closely with Hoxie and a host of deputy marshals and provost marshals, believed this insufficient to meet the disloyalist threat in Iowa. He wrote Lincoln asking that Hoxie be given more power. Lincoln's proclamation of September 24 in effect repeated Stanton's instruction and, in addition, authorized suspension of the habeas corpus privilege for those arrested.[55] Representative James F. Wilson's late July letter to Stanton may have helped spur that official's order. Wilson reported that four men at Rome in Henry county had threatened to hang a disabled recruiting officer if he didn't leave town. The congressman suggested that since no one knew for certain whether state authorities could detain those accused of discouraging enlistments, Stanton should grant such power to federal officers. Wilson, like Brainerd, drew a distinction between denunciation of the government and discouraging enlistments. Authorities could act against the latter, he said.[56] Other reports of violence or threats of violence related to recruiting activities or a possible draft reached Kirkwood from LeClaire and DeWitt. In LeClaire, according to J. W. White, "secesh" sympathizers tore down a flag at a recruiting office and vowed to resist a draft to the death. Near DeWitt, one Reuben Perry allegedly said that "He wished all those who volunteered to fight the South would get killed and if he enlisted he would go south and enlist under Jeff Davis by God. . . ." Informant William McKim told the governor that those who strove to get enlistments found such expressions "very unpleasant to say the least."[57]

Linked with discouraging enlistments as a stimulus to action was the belief that secret societies of Southern sympathizers had gained a foothold in Iowa. Foremost among these was presumed to be the Knights of the Golden Circle (KGC). Worried Iowans believed the Knights were well organized, disciplined, and prepared to aid the rebels. Even before the outbreak of war, Governor

Kirkwood sought to learn whether there were any such active secret groups in the state, particularly KGC lodges. The response was largely negative. Appanoose county Democrat Nathan Udell reported that few if any functioned there, although some had existed a few years earlier. But alarmist James Matthews of Knoxville claimed that Marion county indeed had many such organizations. Two Fairfield citizens argued in print over whether secret societies existed there without attracting more than passing attention.[58]

Throughout the rest of 1861, however, there was relatively little talk about secret societies in Kirkwood's or Adj. Gen. N. B. Baker's correspondence or in the state's newspapers. Then in April, 1862, the subject arose again. Jesse Clement charged that Dubuque harbored a KGC lodge, without supplying any evidence, despite demands that he do so. In May the Chicago *Tribune* and the New York *Tribune* repeated the charges, the Greeley organ adding that federal officials had the society's ringleaders under surveillance and that the society planned to resist federal tax collectors. Again the *Herald* denied the charges and demanded an investigation. None occurred, which didn't prevent Republican editors from splashing the story all over Iowa. Reports cropped up purporting to confirm the existence of societies in other parts of the state. The *Times* claimed active lodges existed in Jones and Linn counties. Marion county papers asserted that Pella and Red Rock townships harbored lodges. Josiah Grinnell, campaigning for the Fifth District congressional seat in southern and southwestern Iowa, excitedly informed Kirkwood that border county secret societies were numerous, armed, and prepared to resist the draft and tax collectors. Even the Davenport *Democrat* believed secret societies to be active in the state. "We are sorry to say," wrote the editor, "that they exist among those who profess to be Democrats."[59]

But when Marshal Hoxie, his deputies, provost marshals, home guard units, sheriffs, and city marshals began to move, they concentrated first on those accused of discouraging enlistments, of threatening recruiting officers, and of general disloyalty. Keokuk's home guard unit's General Orders No. 2 exhibited the spirit behind the arrests. Claiming to act on War Department instructions, the guard commander, Major Torrence, ordered every company commander to appoint a committee of three to five "prudent and discreet persons" to investigate any complaints about anyone "entertaining disloyal sentiments towards the government." If they judged the complaints to be valid, they were to report them to headquarters along with the names of suspects. Thus, the appointment soon after of J. M. Hiatt of Keokuk as Provost Marshal for Iowa, caused Thomas Clagett to feel better. Iowa didn't really need a provost marshal, Clagett believed, but if the state had to have one, Hiatt was a good choice. Similarly, the appointment of John E. Henry of Davenport as Deputy United States Marshal evoked praise from Richard Sylvester of the *State Democratic Press* who liked Henry and said jovially that he knew of no man by whom he'd rather be arrested. More perceptively, David Richardson responded that Sylvester just might get his wish, considering the current state of public opinion. Clagett hoped that Hiatt's appointment would relieve Keokuk citizens "from the rule of certain illegal bodies of men who have undertaken for some days past to control our city . . . it is better that we have military law than mob law.''[60]

Nevertheless, arrest victims soon had good reason to doubt that any kind of law operated to protect their rights. Inefficient officials arrested some by mistake. Some experienced difficulty learning the charges against them. Others were denied legal assistance until they had spent days or weeks behind bars. Some arrest cases confused arrestees, arresters, and jailers alike. The *Constitution* reported a situation which had all the elements of low comedy except that there was nothing funny about it so far as the victims were concerned. Four Davis county farmers in search of a stolen horse came upon both the horse and the thief at Eddyville. In response to the thief's cry that he was a Union man, that his opponents were Missouri jayhawkers, and that the horse was a "secession horse," the confused Eddyville home guard bundled the four farmers off to Keokuk to let Marshal Hiatt make what sense he could out of the affair.[61]

Former Muscatine Alderman William Kennedy, attempting to recruit men for a company, ran afoul of a jealous fellow recruiter who feared Kennedy might win a post which he coveted in the company. Kennedy found himself jailed in Davenport, charged with discouraging enlistments, until he could prove that he was a victim of spite. One Des Moines man, jailed for discouraging enlistments, won release after investigators learned that he was a newly commissioned first lieutenant trying to fill the ranks of his company by enticing recruits away from another unit.[62] When Patrick Cody accused H. W. Sample of refusing to pay his bounty subscription in anything but corn and potatoes, the angry Sample called Cody a liar and scuffled with him. Even angrier after being fined $3 and costs for committing a breach of the peace, Sample appealed the verdict, then issued a formal complaint against Cody accusing him of discouraging enlistments. Marshal Hiatt heard the complaint and quickly ruled against Sample. Nevertheless, Cody, who claimed to be encouraging enlistments, felt it necessary to establish the fact that he was unimpeachably loyal by voluntarily taking the oath of allegiance.[63] Compared with some federal and state officials Hiatt was a judicious man; yet it was not wise to arouse his ire. One person who spouted "disloyal language" quickly found himself in the Marshal's custody. He won his release only when a recruiter for the Fifteenth Iowa assured Hiatt that the man was a volunteer who committed the indiscretion while in his cups.[64] Volunteering, or promising to do so at the first opportunity, got several persons off the hook who were accused of draft evasion or being disloyal. Kirkwood suggested this for four Jasper county men who were so charged. E. M. Dean, Louisa county recruiter, claiming to have sufficient evidence to warrant Levi Gibson's arrest, gave Gibson a choice of joining the army or winding up in Hiatt's care. Two men supposedly trying to avoid the draft by striking out for Canada decided to enlist instead when picked up by Deputy Marshal Henry in Davenport.[65]

It is impossible to tell how many persons charged with disloyalty, or in some way impeding or discouraging enlistments, or being "Missouri secessionists" suffered arrest during August. About three dozen is probably a reasonable estimate.

Most prominent were Dr. Gideon S. Bailey of Van Buren county, a former state legislator, Dennis Mahony, and David Sheward. Bailey was more fortunate than most. Arrested on August 22 for discouraging enlistments and sent to St. Louis where friends, including Lt. Col. W. W. Belknap interceded, Bailey won his release without trial. After three weeks' confinement, he was home again.[66] Nine other arrest victims accompanied him on the trip to St. Louis that August. When they won release is not clear. It does not appear, however, that they remained in captivity into November as did Mahony and Sheward in Washington, and others held at Camp McClellan in Davenport. Mahony and Sheward, personally arrested by Marshal Hoxie and hustled off to Old Capitol Prison, tried in vain to learn the charges against them. Intercession by Charles Mason did them no good until after the fall election and until both took the oath of allegiance and signed a pledge not to sue Hoxie.[67] Despite the government's failure to bring formal charges against the two editors, the ostensible cause was discouraging enlistments. In Mahony's case, any attempt to use his *Herald* editorials and the paper's news coverage of recruiting activities against him might well have resulted in a triumphant Mahony day in court, one good reason for seeing that he never got it. Mahony approved the draft if it were to be run fairly. He counseled Dubuque citizens not to flee but to stay and ''meet it like men,'' and he gave a special boost to one recruiting officer who was a combat veteran.[68]

All this activity, none of which snared any Republicans unless by mistake, began to make even war supporters like Clagett, Richardson, and Thayer have second thoughts about just how far they were prepared to go to see dissent against the war—or the appearance of it—punished. Some means, Clagett declared, were not acceptable even in pursuit of a good end.[69] Now they were less inclined to be quite so open-minded as to admit at first glance that arrest victims might be getting what they deserved. Mahony and Sheward, of course, posed special problems. Both were controversial and acerbic. Everybody correctly viewed them as hostile to the war, a position not shared by the many Democrats who had no desire to see their party tarred with the charge that it was soft on rebels. Still, to observe the United States Marshal for Iowa, who was also the state Republican chairman, acting so enthusiastically against them was disquieting.

At the same time, late August, the *Iowa State Register* began again to fan the smoldering concern over the KGC. Arrests from then on sometimes included men believed to be Circle members despite the fact that nothing turned up to verify the assumptions of alarmists that there were thousands of members in scores of lodges all over Iowa working secretly to subvert the war. What little evidence there was that appeared to be authentic pointed to one county, Madison, and one town, Winterset, as centers of KGC activity. That was where Hoxie and Kirkwood expected trouble. Why they expected it there is clear. Hoxie had an informer, George Rose (an ''experienced detective,'' the Marshal called him) in the middle of a group of antiwar Democrats whose meetings and whose talk, as Rose reported them, sounded subversive. On the strength of a Rose deposition, Hoxie arrested seven Madison men: Joseph K. Evans, William Evans, V. M. Gideon, Joseph

Gideon, Jack Porter, David McCarthy, and James Keith, plus Polk county's Christopher Mann, a vociferous and constant annoyance during the war to local and state authorities. This mid-September haul was only the beginning of many, Hoxie believed. He wrote Kirkwood that he would smash the state KGC network by arresting their leaders at their headquarters in a few days. Such a sweep depended, however, on his getting more assistance from the War Department and from the state. Without such help, he told the Governor, he would have to let the culprits go.[70] This grand stroke never materialized because no such effective network existed. Even so, talk about the KGC and other alleged secret societies continued to excite the public from time to time during the next two years.

George Rose's deposition which gave Hoxie the excuse to move was colorful and detailed. Rose said the Madison county lodges intended not only to strengthen the Democratic party but also to resist the draft and federal tax collectors, and to support rebel recruiting efforts. Rose listed forty-eight names and reported the boast of one man that there were eight hundred lodge members in the county, organized in part by the ubiquitous Mann.[71] Hoxie's "detective" had some reason to be talkative. He was a Madison resident who had been arrested in Missouri for smuggling arms. Turned over to Hoxie, he won his release by telling the Marshal about KGC activities and by agreeing to act as an informant. One account, given in 1928, claims that Rose and a companion were captured late one night by two Missourians who were returning home after a meeting of loyal "Minute Men" in Pleasanton, Iowa. Taken back to Pleasanton and interrogated at the Masonic hall, Rose at first refused to talk. The "Minute Men" then allegedly hung him until he lost consciousness. After being revived, Rose cooperated freely, eventually winding up in Hoxie's service.[72]

Christopher Mann popped up in two more depositions that fall. One was a detailed account by an angry recruiter for the Twenty-Third Iowa who described Mann's efforts to obstruct his work. The other testified that Mann said one KGC objective was to put down abolitionists.[73] By that time Mann and the seven alleged Madison Knights were unhappy residents of the guardhouse at Camp McClellan. Some other arrest victims also wound up there. Others went to Keokuk. Few were as fortunate as John Strohl, a Centralia (Dubuque county) farmer. Dubbed a "loud-mouthed brawling secessionist" by the Times, Strohl never spent any time in a cell. Accused of discouraging enlistments and organizing men to oppose the draft, Strohl was allowed to stay with a friend for one night, take an oath of allegiance, post a good behavior bond, and go home the next day. There is reason to believe that officials took special pains to deal carefully with Dubuque dissenters, as with Strohl, or speedily as in Mahony's case. Hoxie, several assistant marshals, and a squad of soldiers rousted the editor out of bed at four in the morning and hustled him onto the steamboat Bill Henderson before Mahony's many allies could come to his aid.[74]

Although these arrests met the approval of many citizens, there was enough of a reaction against them to give Republican leaders some pause. James Howell defended Governor Kirkwood, saying that federal officials, not the Governor, were responsible. Kirkwood, however, had requested more powers for Hoxie when he became worried about the KGC and opponents of the draft. And the War Department, which first praised Hoxie's activities, especially his moves against the KGC, had second thoughts when the Marshal couldn't muster satisfactory reasons for his many arrests.[75] Friends often treated arrest victims like heroes on their return. Thousands greeted Mahony on the levee the evening of November 15. Bonfires blazed and stores remained lit. A big parade, music by the Germania band, and speeches in his honor highlighted the giant celebration. A month later Anamosa Democrats honored him also. Sheward got the same treatment in Burlington and Fairfield that Dubuque gave Mahony. Two hundred Winterset Democrats gave Madison county's seven returnees a joyous welcome, as did Des Moines Democrats for Christopher Mann.[76]

Imprisonment did nothing to moderate either Mahony's or Sheward's editorial positions. Mahony also wrote scornful letters to both Lincoln and Kirkwood, and eventually published an angry prison memoir called *Prisoner of State*. Mahony had good reason for anger. In a homecoming speech at Burlington, Sheward told his supporters that while he had received a brief hearing and examination at the hands of the Judge Advocate in Washington, Mahony had not. The Madison county returnees' descriptions of their arrest and imprisonment were equally bitter. Like Mahony and Sheward they got no satisfaction from their honorable discharges without trial. While held at Camp McClellan, they had complained about getting no change of clothing for seven weeks. Hearing of their complaints, Kirkwood told Hoxie to remedy the situation. Hoxie replied that he would do so at once. But the ex-prisoners credited the Davenport guard captain's wife with seeing that they received a change of clothing.[77] At the end of the year, Edward Thayer was moved to write, "We plead for the old order of things—for freedom of speech—freedom of the press—the preservation of individual rights—the re-establishment of the civil power—and the overthrow of military tryants."[78]

Free speech during the war did not usually include "hurrahing for Jeff Davis," especially if the scene of the hurrahing was a strongly "Union" town or tavern. But in Dubuque, one could be sure to find a spot where one could hurrah for whomever one pleased, much to the disgust of wartime visitors. Editors could treat such incidents with a degree of humor. "It was a big fight, caused by traitorous proclivities, backed up by bad whiskey, and resulted in bruised heads," said the Fairfield *Ledger* of one big brawl at Abingdon. At Red Rock, in Marion county, however, an Iowa volunteer shot and killed a local "sympathizer" who hurrahed too often, refused to take an oath of allegiance, then resorted to a knife against his opponents.[79] Forced oath-taking, a patriotic exercise invoked by zealous unionists on opponents of the war, became an increasingly common occurrence as the conflict dragged on. Henry Clay Dean suffered such an indignity, in early 1862, at the hands of a group of soldiers when Dean addressed a Ladies Aid Society fund-raising meeting in Mount Pleasant. Later that evening, after another altercation with the soldiers at his home, Dean filed assault and battery charges against his tormentors. The local justice of the peace wisely took advantage of Dean's temporary absence from Mount Pleasant and the imminent departure of the soldiers' regiment to avoid taking action that he believed could lead to a further and possibly more serious confrontation between the antagonists. The same unit, the Fourth Iowa Cavalry, was a party to a similar incident a week later in Mount Pleasant. Jones county volunteers celebrated their departure for the South in August by rounding up alleged peace partisans in the Clark's Grove area and forcing them to swear loyalty oaths. Kossuth county volunteers gave the same treatment to George Blottenberger who foolishly asserted in their presence that he hoped those going to fight "in Abe Lincoln's d—— nigher war" would never return.[80]

One perceptive Republican thought his party accused political opponents of disloyalty too often. Taylor county Republicans, said J. W. Hewes, often called individual Democrats "secesh" and reported them to the local home guard purely out of spite. This created nothing but bad feelings. Hewes was certainly more sophisticated than three Iowans who, much later in the war, told Adjutant General Baker that mere suspicion of a man's loyalty was enough to classify him as a traitor.[81] Frank Palmer of the *Iowa State Register* was inclined toward even swifter judgments. When S. P. Yoemans replaced Patrick Robb as editor of the Sioux City *Register,* Palmer called Yoemans a Tory before he had published his first issue. Yoemans, who was anything but a Tory, refused to take the smear lying down and forced Palmer to make a partial retraction.[82] Clark Dunham also engaged in name-calling. And Dunham claimed that he didn't have much difficulty ascertaining who was loyal and who wasn't. As collector of the port at Burlington working under Treasury Department orders, one of his duties for awhile was to inspect freight and baggage going West. Don't worry, he said. "Merchandise for known loyal businessmen . . . is inspected only by an examination of Railroad way-bills. Boxes . . . will not be opened unless well grounded suspicion [exists] that they contain contraband articles for the rebels." But Dunham did not believe in resorting to the courts or to violence against dissenters. Dunham's views on civil liberties were similar to Nathan Brainerd's. It was not treason, he wrote, to oppose the war, to rejoice at federal reverses, to cheer for Jeff Davis or Beauregard, or to villify the Congress, the President, or Northern generals. Those who so acted were as guilty in their hearts as those who acted covertly, he declared. But unless their plotting endangered public safety one should "leave them to popular opinion." In practice, however, throwing oneself upon the mercies of popular opinion could be dangerous as James Thompson of Otter Creek township (Linn county) learned. During his delivery of what unfriendly bystanders called an anti-Lincoln, sympathy-for-treason-and-rebels speech, some cried out to hang him. Pursued by over two score angry war partisans, Thompson ran for his life. He escaped with it by swimming across the Cedar River. Exercising free speech to the extent of "blurting his treason a little too obviously" got the editor of the Cedar Falls *Northwest Democrat* into a fight and earned him no sympathy at all from Palmer. Majority opinion in the Methodist Episcopal church at Montezuma decreed that several presumed Southern sympathizers within the congregation should henceforth worship elsewhere.[83]

In Dubuque the *Herald* complained about certain public school teachers who elicited classroom votes on issues of the day, arraying pupils against each other and bringing censure on some. "It is said," declared the paper, "to have been practiced by some of the female teachers and in reference to the younger pupils who would at the moment be as likely to vote 'South' as 'North' according to the nature and manner of putting the question." The writer suggested that the school board intervene to head off unnecessary excitement. Pressure by Governor Kirkwood over a year's time on the board of trustees finally caused the resignation of President Silas Totten of the University of Iowa, according to the angry *State Democratic Press*. Totten, Virginia born, conservative in politics, and sometimes suspected of voting Democratic, had been called disloyal, a secessionist, and a traitor. Now, queried the *Press,* was the university to be under the gubernatorial thumb, with the trustees to be "abject instruments of a mean and meddlesome bigotry?"[84] Kirkwood, however, was sensitive about charges that he was excessively partisan. In the summer of 1862 when the state encouraged communities and counties to establish home guard units, particularly along the Missouri border, he told organizers that his directive to enlist loyal men only did not necessarily limit membership to Republicans.[85]

Throughout this period Iowa's Republican officeholders and Marshal Hoxie acted as if they feared no serious voter backlash would develop from the way they handled the loyalty issue and its concomitant problem, meeting the state's enlistment quotas. This was partly because they never seemed to doubt that those Iowans who at heart opposed the war were only a small minority, if also a minority that needed to be dealt with sternly when in specific areas or in special cases it appeared to pose a threat to public order. Their confidence was justified. Moreover, the most controversial individuals in that minority, Dennis Mahony and David Sheward being cases in point, were often an embarrassment to members of their own party who did not want to be labeled as Southern sympathizers. The Republicans could also count on a few Democrats like David Richardson to join them at the point of attack on one explosive situation. That was on the willingness of some aliens, most of whom were Democrats, to avoid military service by claiming alienage exemptions. Richardson was as violent in his opposition to such exemptions as any Republican could be—and all the more effective in it because he was not one of them.

In addition, Republicans could always claim federal sanction for steps they took to curb the activities of those they considered dangerous. This sanction included orders from the State Department and, later, the War Department, buttressed by President Lincoln's suspension of the habeas corpus privilege for victims of arbitrary arrests.

Thus, what could have worked to the Republicans' disadvantage, did not. The odds were heavily in their favor.

5

Partisanship and a Divided People: 1862

SAMUEL KIRKWOOD struck a somber note regarding the economy in his message to the state legislature at the opening of the regular session in January. The Governor pointed out that some markets for Iowa products remained closed, resulting in a drop in prices. Citizens must now forego some luxuries to which they had become accustomed. Taxes, of course, would rise to pay for the war effort. And, Kirkwood added, "We must give up the idea of money making to a great extent until the war is over."[1] The Governor was perhaps too pessimistic. The year 1862 was not economically bleak, although it was fall before anyone could say with certainty that the war brought general prosperity. As to giving up the idea of money making, obviously no Iowans were going to make that sacrifice if they could possibly help it. Certainly two of Dubuque's Democratic lawyers were not. They told Charles Mason that they hoped to go into business as pension and bounty-land agents. Nor was the Des Moines barber who charged the city council seven dollars for shaving two dead soldiers, much to the disgust of the *Iowa State Register* which, rather unrealistically, thought he should have performed the service cheerfully and for nothing.[2]

Worry over the circulation of paper money of dubious value and about an absence of specie continued intermittently into the summer. Dubuque merchants struggled through a period when people hoarded metallic currency because they distrusted the bills of eastern banks. Increased circulation of United States treasury notes eased the situation in the fall.[3] Barter was not uncommon. Fairfield's Dr. William Dial, for example, accepted over 50 percent of his fees in the form of goods and services during the years 1861–1862.[4]

The 1861 and 1862 tariffs aroused some objection, although neither they nor the direct tax on the states of 1861 nor the excise taxes of 1862 aroused the ire of Democrats as much as the "nigger question." Nevertheless, they served as springboards for sectionalist attacks on the East, particularly New England. The Iowa *Agricultural Society Report* of 1862 complained that "the young farmer just beginning on our prairies has to pay just as much as the wealthy citizen in his luxurious New England home." Thomas Clagett was even more indignant when he

72

wrote, "Shall the West Be Compelled to Do All the Fighting, While the East Do All the Stealing?" The Dubuque *Herald* saw the 1862 tax as the effort of eastern capitalists to forge "schackles [*sic*] for the West by which they expect to hold the people of this region in subjection," and the Muscatine *Courier* warned of the approach of an army of busybody tax collectors. Two months before the passage of the 1862 tax, Frank Palmer charged that Dubuque was the headquarters of a secret organization designed to resist tax collectors.[5] Less sure was David Richardson who, when the bill became law, declared that if such organizations did exist, they included no Democrats. Democrats, Richardson said, were loyal and would pay it to the last cent. Those who objected to federal taxes raised to fuel the war didn't belong in this country. Clark Dunham agreed, "It is some satisfaction to know that loyal men will not consult their 'pockets' in opposition to the demands of patriotism." That fall Dunham was even more satisfied. The federal tax was a success. Moreover, he wrote,

> We hear none of the oppression and suffering predicted by the opposition. Business never was more prosperous. . . . Farmers are not complaining. . . . There is no tax upon the productive industry of our state. Even people who consume tobacco, cigars, snuff and whiskey, the articles taxed the highest, do not feel the burden. It falls mainly upon luxuries and persons able to bear it.

Edward Thayer remained unpersuaded. New England, he cried, worshipped money and blacks for which the West paid in blood and taxes. One tax Iowans did not have to pay was a state income tax. The state legislature seriously considered such a levy near the end of the regular session of 1862. Though approved by a joint committee, it failed to pass.[6] Potentially more economically harmful and useful as an issue were escalating railroad rates and the fact that federal use of the rails often deprived the lines of rolling stock needed to carry Iowa's farm products eastward. Failure to break the Mississippi blockade caused Frank Palmer to charge that railroad officials swindled the government by convincing authorities that Vicksburg was impregnable. Whether the charge was true or false was less significant than the fact that Palmer was a Republican. Antagonism to railroads was no Democratic monopoly.[7]

Nor could opponents of the war look to general economic discontent in the populous river communities to swell their ranks significantly. Keokuk's pork packers more than doubled their output during the 1862–1863 season over that of 1861–1862. By November the *Gate City* declared that business was better than it had been for several years. Some of the business came from farmhands who earned as high as $1.50 a day during the summer harvest, thanks to a manpower shortage. Much more came from Keokuk's military hospital which opened on April 20. The largest military hospital in the Northwest and one of the largest in the United States, it eventually had 1,350 beds. In its wake came high wages for workers and prosperity for merchants and farmers—and for woodcutters whom the *Gate City* expected to cut from three to four thousand cords that winter costing $15,000–$18,000. Still, Thomas Clagett could grumble about poor ferry service which he believed deprived Keokuk of much profitable trade with Illinois.[8] Burlington experienced less of a business boom than Keokuk in 1862, a condition that persisted throughout the war. Pork packing, unlike that in Keokuk, underwent no major expansion. But retail trade was healthy enough to fill the *Hawk-eye* with advertisements. At the end of October, the paper did urge consumers to economize, to stock up before prices climbed further, and farmers to hold onto their crops so they, rather than speculators, could reap the profits when demand rose.[9]

Davenport area farmers, anticipating the end of the river blockade, planted heavily in the spring despite a heavy carry-over in grain from 1861. A few miles downstream, however, *Courier* editor Thayer, running for Congress, painted a gloomy picture. Prospects for half a crop combined with "enormous taxation" gave farmers little encouragement to work hard. Thayer was too pessimistic. Grain prices did rise in the fall. Even earlier, Davenport's city marshal, who doubled as tax collector, concluded that the city's financial condition was very good since more citizens paid their taxes on time than in any previous year. In the fall three Davenport firms landed contracts to supply a total of 5,570 uniforms for Iowa volunteers. Other contracts for 2,000 and 3,000 went, respectively, to a firm in Lyons and one in Dubuque. Davenport's business community was hardly dismayed by the June arrival of over two hundred immigrants from Holstein, most with "more or less money" to invest in farms and lots, including one man with $5,000 in gold. The *Democrat* reporter naturally assumed that things were looking up in Scott county.[10] Dubuque papers always reported business, commercial, and agriculture news—good or bad—in greater volume than other Iowa papers. Through the first seven months of 1862, shippers had trouble getting enough railroad cars to carry their goods east from Dunleith on the Illinois side of the river. They also complained steadily about the Illinois Central's rate structure and about the government's failure to open the Mississippi. In January the *Times* worried about surpluses and poor markets, and spoke of a "general feeling of political and financial uncertainty. We were never more in need of a great and decisive military success than at present," said the paper. The victory at Fort Donelson stimulated some improvement. But not until September did commodity prices rise markedly. Poor weather damaged the 1862 wheat crop throughout Iowa, but since many farmers had held onto much of their 1861 crop, they made money as demand increased. While 1862 damaged wheat sold low, the corn crop was excellent, and oats and hay better than average. Dubuque anticipated a real spring real-estate boom, but nothing happened. The *Times* blamed the *Herald* and its followers for giving the city a bad name, causing immigrants to settle elsewhere. Meanwhile Dubuque beer found customers as far south as Memphis when traffic below St. Louis expanded.[11]

Des Moines was a growing city. Toward the end of 1862 the *Iowa State Register* observed that while the residents worried about rising prices, most farmers no longer complained about hard times. Des Moines pork prices in December were $2 to $2.50 cwt., 15¢ to 25¢ below the price at Dubuque in February, a price Dubuquers had described as the lowest in years. Yet the Des Moines hog business was brisk. Most slaughtering establishments were small, half a dozen being located in the heart of the city. Too late the citizens began to rebel against the smell, especially after expansion of the A. W. Rollins works on Second Street and the rise of a new Tuttle and Company building, one block west of the Savery hotel.[12] In the northwest, Sioux City shook off the slump. By late May, there was plenty of money for business purposes, and merchants reported making large sales for cash. All mechanics and laborers were busy. Realtors also reported many cash sales "at fair prices," a development that surprised and pleased the *Register* editor. No railroads yet existed in northwest Iowa, but the paper proposed that the uncompleted Dubuque and Sioux City line should eventually link with the also uncompleted Pacific railroad at Council Bluffs. That city witnessed a resurgence in 1862 also, but the *Nonpareil,* remembering 1857, was cautious. The editor hoped to see "good times in earnest, and not that temporary, artificial fluctuating prosperity which we are too apt to construe into a reality. . . ."[13] Along the southern border, Appanoose county enjoyed a prosperous year according to the *Iowa Homestead,* doing especially well on sales of hogs, sheep, horses, and cattle.[14]

Obviously the period from late 1861 into the winter of 1862–1863 was not a period one can cover with a swift generalization. In the middle of the period, the *Homestead* made a try when it declared that while the war hurt Iowa finance, commerce, and industry, it helped the farmers. But western Iowa farmers without railroad access, or farmers who had sold most of their 1861 wheat crop to pay debts, only to have the poor weather ruin that of 1862, had little cause to view the year as profitable. On the other hand, workers at Sam Perry's garment-making firm in Davenport with its big contract for uniforms (3,570 of them) could count themselves fortunate, as could the many Keokuk residents and outlying farmers who found that the army hospital needed their labor and their produce.

There were new directions in agriculture, notably a move toward sheep raising in the expectation that wool prices would advance with cotton supplies cut off. The year 1862 saw the importation of flocks of sheep from Ohio, Indiana, and Pennsylvania in great numbers. This trend peaked in 1864. (By 1866, Iowa exported to the East ten times what it imported, the reverse of 1864.) With sheep came a problem—dogs; so, Iowa legislators felt increasing pressure to protect sheep raisers. Editors in affected areas, as did everybody else, approached the problem seriously, but with no clear idea of what to do. There were some good, well-fed, useful dogs, declared the *State Democratic Press,* but the people needed better legislation to control the rest. Sheep production did not, of course, loom large in 1862. The primary indices for measuring Iowa's economic health remained wheat, corn, hogs, and cattle. The first three, after standing still or declining for about six months, began to nose upward to meet military and European demands in the third quarter. Cattle prices followed in the fourth. Some cattle, a small percentage, went west to Denver. Farmers, even if most were beginning to make money, had to worry about help as well as about poor weather. In the Waterloo area, farmers with sons in the army allowed that they were "awful tired." Ironically, farmers around Monticello got help from a source which evoked mixed feelings. Wrote Samuel Farwell to his brother, "There are still plenty of men left among the Secesh around Cascade and in Dubuque and Jackson counties and they came out this way and helped us do the harvesting.'"15 One other factor worked to Iowa's economic benefit in the latter part of 1862. Railroads were at last becoming more efficient in moving goods on a large scale over longer distances. And greater competition between roads and lake carriers led to better rates for shippers.16

Lysander Babbitt, however, was hardly prepared to concede that 1862 was a year of improvement. It was, on the contrary, a bad year, especially for farmers. Compared with 1860, he said, they had to raise six times as much corn in 1862 to pay the same tax as in 1860, eight times as much pork and twelve times as much corn to buy a pound of coffee as in 1860.17 Babbitt's figures are as suspect as those of any other angry partisan who tried to prove a point. Most farmers, it appears, perceived their condition in a better light than did Babbitt. It would have been strange had they not done so. None regarded the depression of the late 1850s, its carryover into 1860, and the uncertainty over markets and prices in the first year of the war with nostalgic affection. Certainly if they had been as unhappy as Babbitt thought they were, the commitment of the Republicans and the Democrats among them who supported the war might have been sorely tested.

A tougher test was always the race issue and abolition. Able to capitalize on prevailing racist conceptions about black inferiority and on white laborers' fears of competition from free blacks, antiwar Democrats made the most of their opportunity. In the river cities Repubicans had to respond constantly to claims that they were "nigger lovers" who were determined to reverse nature by elevating blacks over whites. James Howell of the *Gate City* had one of the most tenacious of all opposition editors to deal with on this matter. Two factors made the task especially difficult. First, opponent Thomas Clagett was a War Democrat; hence he was much less vulnerable to standard charges that he was a traitor. Second, Keokuk's location made it a handy stopping place for many migrant blacks displaced by the war in the lower Mississippi Valley.

On April 30, 1862, Howell printed an extended defense of his position on the black issue in response to Clagett's charge that he was a hypocrite for not favoring black suffrage, other black political rights, and black equality in general. Howell's editorial is worth quoting because it so well reflects the reasoned but wearied explanations most Republican leaders had to make throughout the war to assure their constituents that they were not dangerously radical on the subject of race.

[W]hen we insist that every human being has an equal right to liberty, to seek his own welfare and to enjoy the fruits of his own labor with ourself, it don't follow that we therefore bind ourself to vote with, sleep with, or eat with every such human being. It does not follow because we believe it is wrong to hold certain human beings in slavery, that we should therefore hold it right that such human beings should marry into our family, or into the families of our friends. Equality of natural, inherent God-given rights, does not imply equality in physical and mental capacities and endowments, nor political and social rights or position.[18]

Howell's feelings were in tune with Senator James Harlan's whose reservations about the place of the foreign born in American society were more than equalled by his beliefs that blacks were naturally inferior and that racial intermarriage was "loathsome." House Republicans in the regular session of the Iowa legislature, held in the first four months of 1862, did solidly oppose a bill to regulate settlement of blacks in Iowa. Later, however, 9 out of 59 present to vote, voted for a resolution which looked to the possibility of some day passing a constitutional amendment which would ban black entry into the state altogether. Nor were many House Republicans interested in ratifying a Senate resolution favoring citizenship privileges for blacks in the federal service. The House also turned down a resolution asking that the legislature request federal action against slavery, accepting a Republican-authored committee report which declared that Congress had no power to so act. During the 1862 extra session in September, the black-exclusion issue arose again. The House Republican speaker appointed three Democrats as the only members of a committee to deal with petitions calling for an exclusion law. Predictably, the three, Christian Denlinger of Dubuque county, George Schramm of Van Buren, and Harvey Dunlavy of Davis, reported a resolution and a bill for exclusion. All Republicans joined by 6 Democrats rejected both, 58 to 19.[19] The Democratic convention in July predictably announced that black equality had no place in a government established by and for whites exclusively.[20]

The social issue seen in Harlan's remark on intermarriage was one which Democrats exploited when they could. Under the headline "Disgraceful and Beastly Criminality" the Dubuque *Herald* told all it thought fit to tell of recently discovered liaisons between two of the city's black barbers and two white hired girls. It recommended the heaviest penalty the law allowed if authorities could prove that the two males had promoted the "unnatural" association. The final paragraph of the story, obviously a last minute addition, revealed that the two black men had "absconded." The paper's coverage was not entirely demeaning toward blacks, however. Its first sentence had a strangely mid-twentieth century ring: "Dubuque undoubtedly has many respectable colored people, but. . . ." As to the flight of the black men, one who has read the wartime *Herald* and become aware of the occasionally volatile nature of the Dubuque citizenry of that era, might justifiably speculate that the city's Marshal Hewitt assisted their departure in order to avoid a potentially ugly incident.[21] In Burlington, the *Hawk-eye* angrily objected to Democratic papers' exploiting news of a black male's attack on an Ohio woman and pronouncing it a result of abolition doctrines. What about the fact, the writer asked, that a leading Democrat,

> one who has been several times before Democratic conventions of Des Moines county as a candidate for office now lies in the county jail awaiting trail for a similar outrage upon a child? Is not this just as good; is it not a better item than that from the Ohio paper? Neither item has the least political bearing and the man who would outrage decency and propriety by parading in print, for the purpose of catching votes, such an indecent story, would suffer by comparison with an average contraband.[22]

When possible, Democrats tried to build soldier resentment against blacks, including blacks in uniform. David Richardson reprinted a Boston *Post* story which charged that white troops under General David Hunter's command received less than half rations while his black regiment drew fresh bread from the bakery every day. Certainly the disdainful attitude toward blacks held by future Governor Cyrus Carpenter was not exceptional among Iowa soldiers, regardless of party. While on active duty in the South, Carpenter wrote his fiancee that all blacks were cowardly and did not enjoy freedom when they got it. Not only that, those assigned to work for him stuck it out only three days before begging for passes to return to their Alabama plantation forty miles away. "I told them," he wrote, "that if they went they better stay and never show me their faces again." Major William Thompson was more charitable. He found many of them willing and able to work, and "just as sharp as their masters and much more cunning." But Thompson told his wife that, unlike most officers, he would not employ them to do menial labor for him. He explained that "although I wish the negro to have his freedom . . . I can not have them around me unless I can't get a white. . . ." Thompson, unlike Carpenter, believed blacks enjoyed freedom and wanted to be near the army to earn money. Though he didn't want any black women to work for him, he judged their ability objectively: "And many of them are good cooks and clean, yet others are worthless. It is with them like all others, some good others bad."[23] Thompson was relatively kind. Whether his attitude toward blacks was more representative than Carpenter's among Republicans, in or out of the service in 1862, is impossible to say. It was, however, more positive than that possessed by Thomas Clagett and by one of his paper's subscribers. When Surgeon General Hughes of the Keokuk Medical College debarked from the northbound steamer *John Warner* in charge of seventeen blacks, Clagett sneered that the college ought to find them useful for dissection. Or they could be guinea pigs for the study of smallpox and measles; one, he wrote, might be starved to show the effects of starvation on the body. A resident of nearby Vernon responded immediately to the arrival of Surgeon Hughes's wards.

> I see you are having an abundant supply of "contrabands" in and about Keokuk. You had better send some up this way for the "gratification" of

their "bosom friends" hereabouts, as they desire some "respectable negro families" to settle in this place. If any are sent here, have them sent to the care of the Postmaster. The longer their heels and the thicker their lips, the better they will be appreciated. Stand back, "poor white trash," you ain't no whar.

ANTI NIG[24]

Anti Nig's furious conclusion reflected what Howell had noted earlier that year when he tried to portray violent antiblack feeling as a sign of opposition to free labor in general. What was wrong with free labor, he had demanded? Would not the end of slavery bring a rush of Northern capital to the South which would infuse energy into the economy? Ultimately would this not increase the demand for all labor there and draw back to the South those freedmen who had come North? Who really believed that freed blacks, protected in their rights, would voluntarily choose to live in a colder climate? The Dubuque *Times,* always sensitive to this issue, suggested that freed blacks, working on confiscated rebel estates under government overseers until a loyal population arrived to occupy the land, would prefer to stay in the South; moreover, Northern free blacks would return to take advantage of the new economic order.[25]

Republicans sometimes sounded off from disjunctive positions on the black movement north. The *Hawk-eye* berated "The dirty dogs who edit Secesh papers and make secesh speeches throughout the country [who] are . . . trying to convince themselves—for they can convince nobody else—that a huge army of negroes are about to invade the North, and become the competitors of white men in our field of labor." But Howell, who acknowledged that there was a definite movement of black labor up the river, put a good face on it when he argued that "a liberal minded and intelligent people demand the right of employing whatever laborers they choose, coming within their reach.[26] Judge Caleb Baldwin approved this laissez-faire approach. He wanted to get a black maidservant who had no children, who was too old to want a man, but "not too old to be good." So he wrote his friend General Grenville Dodge to send him one, or to tell him how to get such a worker on his own.[27]

Early in 1862 the Washington *Democrat* advocated a drastic solution to the black question which coincided with the aborted exclusion proposal advanced in the legislature. To avert black-white competition for jobs and to preserve white man's government, citizens should circulate petitions in every school district in the state asking the legislature

> to enact a law so stringent in its provisions as to totally prohibit any negroes from emigrating into, settling or holding property in Iowa. And if not in conflict with the Constitution, that you [the legislature] also cause those now in Iowa to be removed in as reasonable a time as your judgment may suggest, and that you make it a duty of the trustees of the several townships to see that said law be faithfully enforced.[28]

News about the possible loss of jobs to blacks on riverboats spread quickly down the river when the St. Paul *Pioneer* reported a rumor that the president of the Minnesota Packet Company planned to hire "intelligent contrabands" from St. Louis to break a deckhands' strike. However, there was no urgency in any newspaper coverage after the first day's report, and the strike ended a week later.[29] Nevertheless, the river cities remained alert to every sign that blacks were moving North. And Richardson complained that those who came didn't go to work in the rural areas which could use them. Rather, they crowded into the towns where they made only a precarious living. Clagett claimed Keokuk would suffer more than other Iowa communities. He argued that unless citizens took steps to exclude blacks the city would soon become a "negro colony," and whites would find themselves competing with blacks for the benefit of wealthy capitalists.[30]

During the fall election campaign the issue loomed larger and larger, with Republicans increasingly fighting claims that emancipation would produce a torrent of blacks which would inundate the state. The Dubuque *Times* responded with stories about the possibility of black colonization outside the United States. When the Democratic Des Moines *Times* and other papers appealed to mechanics, farmers, and laborers to help keep Iowa white by voting against Republican congressional candidates James Wilson, Josiah Grinnell, and John Kasson, Senator Grimes came to their aid by repeating his favorite theme: when freed, blacks would remain in the South.[31] Abolitionist Grinnell, especially, was a favorite target. The Washington *Democrat* claimed that he was a land shark who held mortgages on his neighbors' small farms, and that he employed contrabands only on his own much larger holdings. "How do the farmers of Iowa," cried the editor, "who do their own work expect to compete with this prairie King and his contrabands? It makes no difference to him how many white men want work, or how many children cry for bread. . . ."[32] On the eve of the election such appeals became more frequent in the Democratic organs in Dubuque, Davenport, Muscatine, and Keokuk as they reported regular movements of blacks going North. Clagett said half a dozen a day passed through Keokuk. He and his fellow editors predicted that white servant girls, workingmen and returning soldiers would find themselves replaced by blacks. Then when abolitionists ceased to employ them, the taxpayers would have to assume their welfare costs. In Iowa City a critic reported that blacks had indeed found work there. Employing them in the place of "white trash," he remarked sarcastically, was a "foolish and fashionable novelty"—if also cheaper.[33] Equally sarcastic was another who, writing on "How to Get Employment," advised job seekers to black themselves with burnt cork since "Ebony is all the go now and who would not prefer a black skin to an empty stomach?—Try it white trash."[34] The *Constitution* told of a Van Buren county farmer who came to Keokuk searching for black laborers because he could get them more cheaply.[35]

Infrequently one might profess concern for blacks. Stilson Hutchins declared that a "poor miserable lot of unfortunate negroes" which passed through Dubuque to Cedar Falls where the "tender mercies of abolition charity" awaited them, had made a bad trade. Better, he said, for them to have remained in the South under people "who understand and practice the first great principle of

Christianity 'to love thy neighbor' " rather than a group of people "whose entire creed is wrapped up in the base sordid desire for money making."[36] It remained for the Dubuque *Times* to state a three-pronged rationale for importing blacks which mixed expediency, charity, and wishful thinking with a dash of chivalry. One adult black male plus fifteen women and children had settled in Iowa Falls (Hardin county), with families who could get no other help and who would care for them while the war lasted, the paper reported. They would probably return to a warmer climate thereafter. In the meantime they would alleviate the labor shortage which forced thousands of women to work in the fields. Better to have a contraband plow the land than a woman, declared the writer.[37]

Republicans felt they were on firmer ground when they opposed slavery. Democrats did not usually care to be labelled defenders of the institution. John Gharkey in West Union, like Dennis Mahony, declared that if he had to vote for or against slavery he would vote against it. Slavery was clearly a great sin, a great evil; but, he added, it was constitutional. More dangerous than perpetuating such sin or evil would be its destruction by a higher-law majority.[38] Some, like Clagett and Charles Mason, preferred to sidestep the moral question by maintaining that a slave South was a profitable market for western farmers and that no true conflict existed between slave and free labor.[39] Lysander Babbitt believed that federal efforts at Port Royal in the South Carolina sea islands, showed that freed blacks were uneducable and unable to become useful members of society. Whether Babbitt regretted this alleged failure is not clear.[40]

What is clear, even though they felt it relatively safe to oppose slavery, is that some Republicans early in 1862 preferred not to have to address the issue. Samuel Kirkwood was one of these. He complained to Charles S. Clark of Fairfield about "that infernal fascination [with slavery] as a too preoccupying subject of those in power in Washington." Clark agreed but suggested that since slavery was the cause of the war, it must be destroyed. On the other hand, the Governor's message to the legislature on January 15 sounded a slightly different note. "It may be said," he remarked, "that if we proclaim freedom to the slaves of rebel masters, slavery must suffer and be extinguished. I reply: So be it." Kirkwood at times seems to have wanted to put distance between himself and what he might have called sentimentalists. He regarded himself as a practical man and wanted to get on with the war which was the business at hand.[41] More pragmatic, and at least as common a Republican position, was that abolition was perfectly acceptable as a war measure. If the government couldn't suppress rebellion without abolishing slavery, go ahead and abolish it, urged the Dubuque *Times*.[42] Major Thompson, observing slavery in Missouri, found other reasons. "[I]t needs no great for sight," he wrote, "to tell where slavery exists, for in all cases, you will see neglect, dirt and most unchristian slovenliness prevail & that too where Yankee thrift would make the land teem with golden harvest & the Orchards bend with splendid fruit." *Der Demokrat*'s similar view was that slavery created extremes of wealth and poverty as well as contempt for the working class.[43] Though the editorial of the June 18, 1862, Waterloo *Courier* did not deal with slavery, it defended Southern blacks so extravagantly that it is almost certain that the editor wanted them freed. The black man, he wrote, "has nowhere exhibited those traits of character which have been attributed to him. He has not murdered innocent women and children—he has not even murdered his oppressor. . . . If there is anywhere in all rebeldom any thing resembling honesty, honor, christianity and civilization . . . it is to be found no where except in the 'wooly headed,' 'long-heeled,' 'gizzard footed' African slave. . . . If there is any loyalty left there, the negro has it."

Frank Palmer of the *Iowa State Register,* unlike Kirkwood, was one who saw no reason to avoid the issue. Palmer viewed the North as a party to the evil of slavery. When the North was sufficiently punished for its blindness to the "sin of the age," he wrote, slavery would end, the Union be restored, and the government of the Founders once again administered to their spirit and intent.[44] One who never feared to discuss slavery as a moral issue and as an institution worth destroying was Clark Dunham. He called for the timid to join him.

> The terror of being called "Abolitionist" still makes liars and hypocrites out of very good men—preachers of the Gospel and politicians—statesmen and men of letters. But . . . [in] the more intelligent and enlightened portion of the free States, a man may now assert, even from the house-top, "I am opposed to slavery" without danger to his person or property, and he can add, "break the shackles, unloose the bonds and make all the slaves free," provided he puts in a plea that the niggers must be turned loose as a political necessity, and the speaker takes a solemn oath that his bowels of compassion never yearned and never shall yearn towards the African race. Here is progress—We are thankful for it. And we look upon it as an indication that before many years more of sacrifice and heroic effort, we shall so strengthen our loins and develop our courage, as to be able to speak our honest feelings and sentiments upon this slavery question, at all proper times and places. The time will come, and soon, when every man who feels that slavery is a national evil, a national crime, and at the bottom of all our divisions and strife and of the civil war which devastates our fair country will speak and act his true sentiments. . . .[45]

Still, some Republicans believed that emancipation sentiment should not rush ahead of events. Better to have more victories in the field first, wrote James Howell in March. By July, delegates to the state Republican convention felt it safe to endorse congressional antislavery action if necessary to preserve the Union. *Der Demokrat* went even further. Looking beyond emancipation it declared that the German radical press would solidly oppose deportation of freed blacks. Human rights, the editor declared, should not depend upon color. But Muscatine Congregational minister Alden B. Robbins found that not all of his parishioners were as radical as he. His diary for September 9 carried the entry, "Preached in favor of emancipation of slaves. Full house—some excitement."[46]

Lincoln's Emancipation Proclamation met with clear Republican approval throughout the state. The Democratic Sioux City *Register,* whose editors plowed an independent course throughout the war, also approved emancipation if it would help beat the rebels, a position similar to the Republican Council Bluffs *Nonpareil*, farther down the Missouri.[47] More positive were the Iowa City *Republican* and *Der Demokrat*. The *Republican* exclaimed, "Now we have a policy . . . it is to humiliate and annihilate treason and despotism by the exaltation of four million things to the rights and dignity of manhood . . ." *Der Demokrat* wanted the Proclamation to be delivered to the South with fire and sword.[48]

How soldiers would react concerned Republicans. An Ottumwa doctor with the Thirteenth Iowa in Tennessee wrote his wife that a large majority approved emancipation, but as a military expedient, not because the men favored freedom for blacks. Sgt. Cyrus Boyd, writing from Memphis, reported that many men of the Fifteenth Iowa objected to a move to put them on record as supporting some officer-written resolutions which approved the Proclamation. Twenty-eight of them had the temerity to argue with regimental commander Col. Hugh Reid. "Some thought themselves better than a 'nigger,' " wrote Boyd, who personally favored emancipation. Unsigned letters, purportedly from soldiers, which appeared in Democratic papers nearly always reported even more negative soldier responses to emancipation.[49]

Months before Lincoln issued the Proclamation, the Council Bluffs *Nonpareil* gave an accurate assessment of Democratic responses to suggestions that the war might be related to slavery and that its demise might be a national benefit.

> [S]ome of our Democratic contemporaries, rational enough upon other subjects, no sooner hear of a proposition to quell rebellion by striking at the root of the evil, to take away from the rebellion's "masters" the power to injure us by taking away their slaves—no sooner, we say, is this plan mentioned, than your over nice Pro-anti-Slavery-Democratic-Union-man smell nigger, and howl; talk of perverting the power of the nation to sectional purposes, and repeats the old stereotyped cry of "abolition war!"[50]

For awhile in 1862, Democratic editors regarded Lincoln as a conservative holding the line against those who wanted to add emancipation to the war aims of the North. Strangely, the Dubuque *Herald*, although adamantly against government-sponsored emancipation, complimented the President for proposing compensated emancipation. The scheme was impractical, too expensive, and questionable social policy, although patriotic, said Mahony. To concede that it was "patriotic" was probably less of a slip than it appears. Mahony always believed that a healthy concern for Southern slaveholder property rights was truly patriotic in contrast to uncompensated abolition "robbery."

Thomas Clagett's position exemplified the *Nonpareil* editor's evaluation of Democratic resistance to the idea that slavery had anything to do with the war and to congressional or presidential action to abolish it. However, Clagett did not reject its destruction as a by-product of military action against rebellious masters. As he put it, "[If] the slaves become worthless as property or even make their escape altogether no Northern Democrat will ever say ought against it." Clagett exaggerated the unanimity of Northern Democrats, although he had a valid point. A majority of Northern Democrats were not unalterably against the death of slavery—but they were concerned about the means of execution. David Richardson held essentially the same view.[51]

By the summer of 1862, the *Herald,* always more suspicious of the Lincoln administration than Richardson and Clagett, judged that the war was "degenerating into an enlarged John Brown raid." Richardson believed that congressional meddling with slavery was giving the South proof that the main object of the war was to free blacks, not preserve the Constitution. Clagett too thought he saw a shift.[52] When Lincoln finally did issue the Emancipation Proclamation, most leading Democrats responded angrily. Charles Mason was enraged. Lincoln, he wrote privately, was a despot whose power was "subject like that of all tyrants to the limits fixed by revolution or private assassination."[53] The *Herald* was bitter, and Stilson Hutchins, temporarily in the editor's chair, claimed emancipation and black equality, not restoration of the Union, were the objects of the war. Richardson at first, however, saw no difference between the Proclamation and the confiscation acts, and refused to get excited. But two days later he was nearly as angry as Mason, now convinced by the Chicago *Journal* that Lincoln was "a dupe of his black republican abolition, negro worshipping friends who . . . believe that a Union with slavery is not worth preserving. . . ." The Davenport editor's outburst inspired some opponents to question his loyalty. He found a defender in Republican C. M. Hollis of the *Cedar Valley Times.* Richardson was just mistaken, not disloyal, said Hollis. Emancipation was simply a necessary war measure.[54] The Keokuk *Constitution* reacted less wrathfully than might have been expected, possibly because Charles Smith, a Clagett associate, wrote the editorials for a period while his chief recovered from being kicked by a horse.[55] In Muscatine Edward Thayer warned that emancipation might "foment insurrection and encourage the indiscriminate murder of men, women and children by the slaves of rebels." Foreign intervention to halt such barbarism was a possibility, Thayer thought. Less apocalyptic but no less bitter was the Washington *Democrat* which charged that no Republican could now claim to be anything other than an abolitionist and a revolutionary. The Burlington *Argus* announced that after January 1, because of the Proclamation, it would "protest against a further continuance of the war."[56]

The Dubuque *Times* surveyed some of its Democratic competitors at the end of the year and concluded that the Emancipation Proclamation made a difference regarding support of the war to the *Courier,* the *Argus,* the *Democrat,* and the *Constitution.* They were now no longer loyal. The last two, it is true, saw less purpose in continuing the conflict than before, but Richardson and Clagett, though depressed, did not become peace proponents. They only became increasingly vitriolic about abolition, violation of civil liberties, and the war's mounting death toll.[57]

Charles Mason was still sputtering with rage at the turn of the year when emancipation became official. It was illegal, he wrote. The government could not do just anything to win a war. Then, without skipping a beat, Mason denied that the government had any power to continue to enforce a regulation once the necessity from which it arose in the first place no longer existed. Thus, according to Mason, even if emancipation were a legal war measure, which it was not, it would provide temporary emancipation only. When the war ended, freed blacks should be reenslaved.[58]

Throughout the year the Democratic peace and war factions contended for party leadership, the exclusive right to enunciate a stern party orthodoxy, and to choose candidates reflecting that orthodoxy. There was little tendency to accommodate different points of view. The *Herald,* which always demanded that the Lincoln administration do nothing to inhibit the exercise of free speech and a free press (except by abolitionists),[59] was pleased when it heard that the Davenport *Democrat* was about to cease publication. "[N]either fish nor fowl politically . . . [it] has been drifting before the wind of public opinion," declared Mahony. Davenporters should now read the *Herald.* This angered Richardson who retorted that his organ was very much alive and that, in any case, the *Herald* would be unacceptable in Davenport.[60] David Sheward, like Mahony, had no use for "War Hawks" among the Democratic press. Clagett in turn judged Sheward to be disloyal for opposing Lincoln's appointment of Andrew Johnson as military governor of Tennessee. The ousted Harris government was secessionist, and it was, Clagett added, unthinkable that anyone claiming to be a Democrat and a loyal man should write and publish sentiments like Sheward's.[61] The Sioux City *Register* and *Cass County Gazette* also attacked the peace men regularly and warned against Vallandigham-Jones factions, Breckinridge elements, and "northern traitors seeking public office."[62] The *Herald*'s business practices as well as its presumption to speak for all Democrats irritated the Lansing *Argus.* The *Herald*'s low rate subscription clubs, said the *Argus,* hurt local papers which best represented local interests and upheld "true Democracy."[63]

Republicans, however, couldn't capitalize enough on Democratic discord to prevent Democratic victories in spring city elections in Dubuque, Davenport, Iowa City, Des Moines, McGregor, and LeClaire. Democrats, recalling the disastrous factionalism of 1861, were united enough at the state convention in June to write a platform which won unanimous approval and to select candidates for state office with a minimum of open controversy. Richard Sylvester, Iowa City newspaperman, headed the ticket as nominee for secretary of state, the top state position at stake. Most of those who favored the war claimed to be satisfied with a declaration that the government should suppress the rebellion by employment of "constitutional means, not merely by force of arms." The delegates rejected emancipation, with or without compensation; opposed elevation of blacks to social, political, or economic equality with whites; denounced both secession and abolition; and excoriated federal tariff and taxation policies as "favorable to the few and injurious to the many."[64]

Unanimity soon disappeared, however. Chester C. Cole, a convention speaker and long a party regular, announced his rejection of both platform and party. Cole's defection was only one among several during the summer and fall of 1862. Other defectors included George Tichenor, a former secretary of the party's state central committee, and Adj. Gen. N. B. Baker. Not all defectors turned Republican immediately. Tichenor professed to remain a Democrat even while announcing his resignation. Cole officially turned Republican only in January, 1863. Others who quit the party at this time were James A. Williamson and H. H. Heath. Enoch Eastman announced his resignation earlier, but excited speculation that he was opportunistic when he let it be known that he would like to run for Congress as a Republican. Cole won election to the state supreme court in 1864, running on the Republican ticket.[65]

Even more destructive to the fragile accord among Democrats was a development which relegated the state contests to secondary importance in the campaign. That was the nomination of Dennis Mahony as the party's candidate for Congress from the Third District in northeastern Iowa. When a razor-thin 52⅔ to 51⅓ majority of aroused Mahony friends and antiwar men beat down the bid of moderate George W. Gray of Allamakee county for the nomination in district convention on August 20, they handed the Republicans their best campaign issue. Traitors and disunionists, Republicans trumpeted, controlled the Democratic party. Probably a majority of Iowa Democrats regretted the nomination. Of the Democratic papers in the state, only Mahony's *Herald* immediately approved his nomination. Some announced that should Mahony clear himself in court, they would back him. An occasional Mahony critic, Patrick Robb of the Sioux City *Register,* ignored both Mahony's arrest and nomination. The Chicago *Times* assumed that where there was smoke there was fire. "His arrest," said the *Times,* "must be supposed to have been by competent authority, and while he remains in custody, it is contempt of that authority to place him in . . . nomination. . . ." Despite external and internal pressure, Third District Democrats refused to retract the nomination. From Old Capitol Prison in Washington, Mahony campaigned as best he could by letter, aided by *Herald* assistant editor, Stilson Hutchins. Before his arrest Mahony had expected to get the nomination if he wanted it. In June he wrote Charles Mason asking for help from Ben Wood, Clement Vallandigham, and other eastern Democrats. He wanted speeches and documents from them which he could circulate throughout the district. Mahony told Mason that a recent trip throughout Dubuque county showed him that the people were ready to resort to force to reverse government policy. But he believed they were educable; documents heavy on facts would "effect a change, radical and thorough in this state." Editorial associate Stilson Hutchins was less optimistic. Mahony would do well in the general election in Dubuque county, he wrote Mason. But elsewhere there was much opposition to the nomination which might inhibit the Irish editor's supporters. "Men mean well enough," he declared, "but they are timorous and do not dare to do their duty."[66]

Other Democratic congressional candidates as well as state office candidates found the Mahony nomination no help. It placed them on the defensive from the outset and allowed their opponents to be more aggressive than they might otherwise have been. It may also have been a contributing factor to the Republicans' taking a strong stand in support of the Emancipation Proclamation. Senator Grimes wrote Salmon Chase after the election, "We took the bull by the horns and made the proclamation an issue. . . . I traveled the state for four weeks . . . and the more radical I was, the more acceptable I was. The fact is we carried the state by bringing the radical element to the polls."[67]

The Republicans won easily in all but the Fourth Congressional District. There Republican Josiah Grinnell profited from the soldier-vote law. Grinnell, running in a district where Southern-born voters were numerous and abolitionist sentiment weak, beat Henry M. Martin only because he won heavy soldier support. Mahony, who received the lowest soldier vote of any congressional candidate, 125, lost to William B. Allison, 12,112 to 8,452. In the top state race Sylvester lost to James Wright 66,014 to 50,889. Republicans captured other state posts by similar margins.

TABLE 5.1[68]
REPUBLICAN AND DEMOCRATIC STATE ELECTION PERCENTAGES, 1860–62

Year	Republican	Democrat
1860	56.2	43.8
1861	59.4	40.6
1862	56.5 (Total)	43.5 (Total)
	52.2 (Civilian)	47.8 (Civilian)
	78.3 (Soldier)	21.7 (Soldier)

On its face at least, there seemed to be something to the Democratic charge that officers influenced the way enlisted men voted. But Republican ability to capitalize on the "vote as you shoot" theme was a factor. There was no doubt that Republicans were entirely unambiguous in their desire to whip Southern rebels soundly. And those rebels at bottom were responsible for nearly all Iowa soldiers being in the army in the first place. It required no more than an ordinary state of awareness to know that a few very controversial and very vocal Democrats were not so enthusiastic about whipping rebels at all—much less, soundly. Even so, Republican officer pressure was no doubt a factor, as it was to be in 1863 and 1864. Richard Sylvester recognized the possibility for fraud in soldier voting. But Sylvester, after touring army camps containing Iowa units, wrote that both enlisted men and officers disapproved getting the vote and saw it negatively as "politics," sound in principle but faulty in policy and practice. The editor-candidate may have been whistling in the dark. Col. James Williamson of the Fourth Iowa and a recent Democratic dropout said he didn't like the idea either, especially since it made electioneering possible. However, Williamson said nobody in his unit would be coerced into voting for a choice not his own if he could prevent it.[69] Earnest private soldier Jacob Hunter, who left a young family to fight in a war he believed in, was not capable of coercing anybody. But Hunter proudly told his wife that he helped get five or six votes for Grinnell in his largely Democratic Fortieth Iowa Infantry regiment.[70] Col. Cyrus Bussey had more power than Private Hunter, and he was inclined to use it. His regiment at Helena, Arkansas, was largely Democratic, he said. Fortunately it voted Republican. Had he not been in St. Louis for two weeks prior to the election, it would have returned an even larger Republican majority than it did, he told Governor Kirkwood.[71] As for Grenville M. Dodge, his left hand may not have known what his right hand was doing. Lt. William Tracy of the Fourth Iowa wrote Dodge that he was complying with Dodge's request to get a Republican vote out of C Company. But Dodge wrote his wife in response to charges about his influencing votes, "I could scarcely tell you the political affiliations of any of my officers, much less of my men. We never think of these things."[72]

How much coercion there was to vote Republican in Iowa units is difficult to tell. Some angry soldier letters in Iowa newspapers affirmed that there was a lot. Others, equally angry, claimed that specific stories about coerced votes, burned Democratic ballots, or soldiers being put in the guardhouse for being too ardently Democratic on election day, were lies. Others told of fouled up vote-taking which resulted primarily from poor organization, or from the fact that some units were in the field beyond reach of the civilian voting commissioners on election day. Some signed letters including one from Captain James Seevers of the Fifteenth Iowa and enlisted man Seth Wheaton of the Twenty-Seventh Iowa did tell of a shortage of Democratic ballots and a surfeit of Republican ones. Seevers admitted he didn't know why this was the case. Some counties probably neglected to send Democratic ballots, or if they did they were "suppressed," he surmised. But Seevers also noted that there were Democratic ballots from Lee and Mahaska counties. M. V. B. Sheafor of the Fourth Iowa Cavalry told his brother that his outfit had enough "Wooly" (Black Republican) ballots for two regiments, but no Democratic ballots. The Dubuque *Times* went against interest when it printed a soldier's letter that reported and approved the burning of "Mahony" ballots at a camp near Rolla, Missouri.[73]

The Keokuk *Gate City* was not generous toward Democratic soldier votes in its report on election results. It called them "Tory." This angered the Lee county board of supervisors whose ten Democrats, joined by one Republican (three Republicans abstained), voted 11 to 0 to rebuke the paper. The Dubuque *Times* was more charitable toward thirty-four Irish soldiers in one company, all of whom voted for Mahony. Their choice was understandable, said the paper. They were not Tories. Their enlistment proved that. They were only "deceived patriots" who would "curse the demagogues who have deceived them" after they got some combat experience.[74] Wapello county's board of supervisors, also Democratic by an 8 to 6 margin, was less friendly to soldier votes than the Lee county board. It set aside the state canvass board's certificate attesting to the validity of the county's soldier vote total. This unseated the newly elected Republican county clerk whose 27 vote majority stemmed from a 267 vote lead in soldier ballots.[75]

The *Gate City* and the Fairfield *Ledger* drew identical conclusions from the Iowa vote that fall, bolstered as it was by the soldiers' participation. Had all soldiers in the loyal states been able to vote, like those from Wisconsin and Iowa, they said, the Democratic victory elsewhere would have been transformed into an overwhelming Republican triumph.[76]

Dennis Mahony's imprisonment temporarily caused Stilson Hutchins to soften the *Herald*'s strident tone. But in mid-September the paper was back to form. Hutchins told Charles Mason, "I only regret that I took his [Mahony's] advice . . . and ceased for even the short term I did to give to the people sentiments which they hungered for and which they needed." Nevertheless, Hutchins was discouraged. "I am tired," he said, "of dealing blows for a people which they do not care to deal for themselves. It is dangerous service with little recompense." Hutchins contemplated selling the paper after the election. From prison Mahony grew more and more anxious also. He speculated that if he agreed to sell the *Herald* he might win his release. At least he wanted a parole so he could settle the paper's financial problems. The main problem was a $2,000 mortgage. J. B. Dorr, the *Herald*'s owner prior to Mahony, had promised to pay off the debt himself when he sold out to Mahony in 1860. Since then Dorr, a strong War Democrat, and Mahony had become bitter enemies. Now Dorr failed to discharge the debt, perhaps in collusion with creditors who disliked the paper's editorial policy. Hutchins met the crisis by buying the old Dubuque *North-West* office just as the Republican sheriff took over the *Herald*'s plant. Without missing an issue, Hutchins got out the *Democratic Herald* just as Mahony returned from prison. (The paper reverted to its original name within a few months.)[77]

In contrast to Hutchins, Mrs. David Sheward was exhilarated by the task of publishing the Fairfield *Constitution and Union* during her husband's enforced absence. She had not believed she could work so hard; her husband would be proud of her, she exclaimed. The paper had gained new subscribers, and their friends were sticking by them, including banker-lawyer Charles Negus who helped her keep the paper alive. "Your arrest," she told Sheward, "is the greatest honor they could confer on you."[78]

During the election campaign the *Times* did its best to show that the *Herald* was a traitorous organ under Mahony's leadership. On October 8 it reprinted three columns of excerpts from *Herald* editorials extending from late May until August 14, the day preceding his arrest. With the exception of a July 17 declaration on the Conscription Act that "No citizen is bound to respect or obey this usurped power," none of them came close to advocating resistance to the laws, much less treason. They did reveal Mahony's hatred for abolitionists, how deeply he despised the President, certain members of the cabinet, war partisans, and those he believed to be leading the country to ruin. They also revealed that he blamed Northern fanatics for forcing the South into rebellion in defense of its constitutional rights. One editorial seared Northern war proponents as people who had descended "to the lowest depths of savage barbarity" in waging war on their fellow citizens, and one suggested that foreign intervention designed to prevent the conflict from becoming even more barbarous might lie ahead. More vehement than Mahony was the editor of the Cedar Falls *North-West Democrat* who, like John Jennings, hoped to see Southern warriors fight valiantly. He also hoped that they would conquer the North into recognizing the Confederacy. The Lincoln administration proposed to establish a "revolutionary military despotism," he maintained. Therefore, "Usurpation must be met by equally violent usurpation. No half-mad 'higher law' dictator must be allowed to reign. . . . The people must rise in their might before they are bound and enslaved." The *Times* reprinted this editorial also in an attempt to demonstrate the true character of the Democratic opposition that fall.[79]

On the other hand, as Jacque Voegli has noted, the *Times* played down antislavery as a weapon against Democrats. If it wasn't effective in Dubuque, neither was it in Burlington. The Democrats there won, the *Hawk-eye* believed, on the strength of a last minute campaign among the city's Irish. "An Irish woman," the paper reported, "expressed great concern yesterday about the 'nagurs.' Eleven 'Conservative' gentlemen had been to see her husband and post him up. He wasn't afraid of the 'tame nagurs' who live in Burlington. But he didn't like the '4000 wild nagurs' which the Black Republicans were bringing here to do all the 'wurk.' " According to the reporter, the efforts of "These 'Conservative' gentlemen" on Sunday before the election, "visiting our working men and ventilating this negro story [caused] one hundred and fifty honest and loyal laboring men [to be] cheated into voting the secession ticket." Two days later the paper bitterly noted that "Part of the promised invoice of '4000 niggers' came in yesterday—3,999 are supposed to be on the way."[80]

Thomas Clagett, however, believed that most Iowa laboring people had failed to vote their best interests that fall. "How long," he complained, "will white laborers of Iowa continue to vote the negro loving abolition ticket." Conversely, his *Gate City* opponent believed that was precisely what the laborers did *not* do. They listened to Democratic lies, James Howell wrote. They believed in a massive migration of blacks northward, they feared for their jobs, and they voted Democratic. Republicans, he declared, favored no such migration, but their denials did no good.[81]

The Chicago *Tribune* saw the Democrats' midwestern successes in the October elections resulting from low farm produce prices, doubled or quadrupled prices on goods farmers bought, skyrocketing wages of farm labor, and higher taxes. The *Tribune* saw these conditions existing in Iowa also, but neglected to explain why the state voted Republican. The fact is that economic conditions were improving by election time. The *Herald* business reporter noted on election day that "Business is generally good." Farmers were getting better prices for old wheat, other grains, butter, and eggs.[82] It is doubtful anyway that economic conditions had much to do with how Iowans voted. Those who had always assumed as a matter of course that their best material interests lay with one party or the other did not change their minds with the rise and fall of commodity prices, the disruption of Mississippi River trade, the fluctuation of the currency—or the yet small influx of freed blacks. In fact there was so little change in the Iowa Democratic and Republican vote percentages, 1860–1862, that it is reasonable to suggest that all the fall electioneering did was to keep the habit-prone faithful in line.

Iowa Democrats had nothing to cheer about in the state results. So they took pleasure in Democratic victories elsewhere. Edward Thayer saw them as a prelude to peace and reunion. Charles Mason, always an elitist, acknowledged that he had judged "the people" too hastily. "They have come off victorious," he wrote. Mason would reverse that judgment eventually, but now he and Iowa's beleaguered Democrats took their satisfaction where they could get it. One satisfaction in Dubuque was the demise of the *Iowa Staats Zeitung,* a beaten competitor of the *National-Demokrat.* The price of the paper was too high and its abolitionism too unpopular, declared the *Herald.* One Democrat who had nothing to cheer about was John H. Wallace, Secretary of the State Agricultural Board. The Board fired him in January, 1863, by a vote of 14 to 13 and replaced him with Dr. J. M. Shaffer of Jefferson County. The secretary's ouster, claimed the Keokuk *Gate City,* resulted from his "disloyal position in the present crisis of the country." The board eased the pain by complimenting Wallace on his years of service. It also offered him the chance to get in the last word. He took it and said, "He was happy to know that it was not for any lack of ability or devotion to the welfare and success of the Society that had severed his connection with it, but a cause that was unworthy to be introduced . . . and that time would demonstrate not only impolitic but unjust."[83]

How much satisfaction did Iowa Democrats take in the rare Union victories in 1862? With some exceptions, such as Mason, Jennings, and the Cedar Falls editor, they were as pleased as Republicans, both groups taking special note of developments in the West. Mason hoped for Union defeats in Arkansas where Iowa Gen. S. R. Curtis, whom he hated, enjoyed success. And he yearned for foreign intervention which would force a peace favorable to Southern interests.[84]

The Fort Donelson victory was a shot in the arm for nearly all Iowans. It promptly affected the Dubuque market as buyers paid more for wheat and pork. The *Herald* as usual drew different conclusions than others from the win. Whereas other papers saw Fort Donelson as a prelude to more and more Northern military successes, the *Herald* and a Charles Mason "X" letter called for the North to offer magnanimous terms to the South which would cause it to return to the Union with its "rights" intact. Mahony added another reason, which displayed, depending on how one interpreted it, a streak of cynicism, psychological insight, cool rationality, or all three. The North now could afford to act magnanimously, he declared, since the victory proved that it could whip the South and demonstrated the uselessness of Southern resistance and Southern attempts to dismember the Union.[85] David Richardson did hope that victories like that at Island Number Ten would cause Southern unionist sentiment to develop, but he saw no reason for the North to quit fighting. Nor did Thomas Clagett. Clagett did hope that men on both sides could meet to work for compromise even as the war continued. But there should be no compromise with disunion, he warned. If the South had to be forced back into the Union by military action, so be it.[86]

Republicans like Clark Dunham remained suspicious of Democratic reactions to Northern victories. He thought there was a difference. "The difference," he wrote, "between the semi-secession papers and the *Hawk-eye* is this: We desire all our Generals shall succeed." Democrats, he was sure, applauded only those victories achieved by Democratic generals.[87] The Council Bluffs *Nonpareil* believed that city's "secesh" element (not specifically defined as Democratic) rejoiced at Union setbacks. The following may be overdrawn, but apparently some so-called "secesh" in Council Bluffs did favor Southern success.

> The "Secesh" of this city were happy—jubilant—exultant—on Wednesday and Thursday—over the supposed defeat of the Union forces before Richmond. They congratulated one another—they smiled—they got drunk—they taunted Union men—they manifested the utmost joy in repeating: "What did I tell you? Didn't I tell you *our* side would whip you out before Richmond?" "The South can take care of itself yet!" exclaimed a rebel, who claims to be an F.F.V.; but in fact was never nearer Virginia than Posey County, Indiana.[88]

However, Lincoln-hater, abolitionist-baiter Lysander Babbitt of the *Bugle* was not one of these. Babbitt was always pleased with Northern victories in 1862. And he was sure the Twenty-Ninth Iowa Infantry, drawn largely from western Iowa, would give a good account of itself when it got to "Dixie."[89]

6

Calls for Peace and the Iowa Response: 1863

ON many subjects, the depravity of abolitionists and war profiteers, black subordination, iniquitous war taxes, the unfair nature of the draft, civil liberties violations, and the growth of federal power, Iowa's Democrats could usually agree. But they could not unite behind a peace policy. Early in 1863, however, shocked that the Emancipation Proclamation was allowed to become official policy, and heartened by Democratic electoral success in the rest of the Midwest, the peace forces appeared to gather strength at the expense of those who favored the war no matter how angry they were at emancipation.[1] What followed looks like grass-roots democracy at work. No centralized planning by the Democratic state central committee lay behind the sudden appearance of scores of township, city, and county peace meetings which sparked controversy across the state, particularly during the period January through April[2]

Jefferson county witnessed a flurry of such meetings from December 31, 1862, through January, 1863. Two occurred in Fairfield and Abingdon, the others in rural schoolhouses or churches. By far the greatest concentration through June was in southeastern Iowa counties, including (besides Jefferson) Wayne, Wapello, Davis (Bloomfield), Van Buren (Keosauqua), Lee (Fort Madison), Des Moines (Danville), Henry (New London), Monroe (Albia), Lucas (Chariton), Warren (Palmyra and Indianola), Mahaska (Oskaloosa), Keokuk (Sigourney), and Louisa (Wapello). East central and northeastern Iowa counties where peace meetings occurred were Cedar (Tipton), Floyd (Charles City), Johnson (Iowa City), Linn (Marion), Dubuque (Dubuque), Jones, Jackson, Clayton, and Allamakee. In central and western Iowa, peace partisans promoted meetings in Polk (Des Moines), Madison, Decatur (Leon), and Clarke counties. Two of the largest peace rallies featured Henry Clay Dean. Dean, who possessed physical stamina as well as remarkable oratorical powers, spoke for seven hours with one brief intermission at Oskaloosa on January 31, before an estimated 6,000 to 8,000 people. He spoke three weeks later at Dubuque. In both places Dean argued for a negotiated peace. Neither he nor his listeners explicitly resolved that permanent separation might ever be necessary, although at Dubuque Dean employed language which contained the germ of the idea when he said, "It is folly that we cannot make treaty, truce or look to peace, with men in revolution. This was done by George III with our Fathers in 1783."[3]

It is worth noting that some larger communities—Burlington, Davenport, and Council Bluffs—apparently hosted no peace meetings, or none beyond a handful of people at a precinct level as in Keokuk. Even more significant is that if all the participants in Iowa's peace meetings could have gathered in one giant conclave they could not have agreed on a common posture on the peace question. They opposed a war for emancipation; but many also proclaimed they would accept no separation or assumed that the result of any national peace convention would inevitably result in reunion. Only in Madison county did the peace forces call for peaceful separation if a national convention failed to agree on terms for reunion. Representing a polar position to Madison was Decatur where Democrats at Leon favored continuing the war to achieve reunion but eliminating "unconstitutional abolition" as a war objective. The Leon and Fairfield Democrats, in fact, sounded very little like true peace partisans. Moreover, one must recognize that they may have better represented what might be called a disgruntled but often silent majority of the party—disgruntled about emancipation and other issues, but not disgruntled enough to take a radical step like calling for a peace conference while Southern rebels yet successfully resisted reunion. Nor would they take another radical step which some peace partisans did: proclaim that they would physically resist a draft and arbitrary arrests as did Davis county peace men.[4]

Clark Dunham recognized real divisions among the Democrats, particularly between party leaders and "patriotic masses." So did W. W. Junkin who attacked Fairfield peace exponents, Charles Negus, James Thompson, M. M. Bleakmore, and David Sheward, while leaving the rest of the community's Democrats unscathed. David Rorer believed that the great majority of Burlington's Democrats were loyal. In fact, Copperheads allowed the loyal men to be the front men at rallies in order to conceal their role in them, Rorer told a friend.[5] Nevertheless, Governor Kirkwood and many other Republicans viewed the peace rallies with concern. "Disloyalty," he wrote Grimes, Harlan, and J. S. Wilson, "is becoming more bold and defiant in Iowa. More are saying openly and daily what no man dared say a year ago and really many of our people are afraid of an outbreak at home. Can't something be done? I am disheartened and discouraged and I find the same feeling almost universal." Stephen Van Benthusen, writing from Wayne county, asked Kirkwood if there was any way to squelch secession sympathizers who openly cheered for Jefferson Davis and rejoiced over Confederate victories. E. A. Crockett wanted Adjutant General Baker to do something about Wilton Junction peace advocates. Two men in particular needed Baker's attention. "I have to report one James Kelason and one Charles Crofford," he wrote, "for going around in this section advocating secas principles and their by corrupting the morils of the Egnorant class and forming clubs caled the Democratick Union Club but in fact they are the Knights of the Golden Circle." In Dubuque, Deputy United States Marshal, P. H. Conger, observing the call for Dubuque's peace rally, felt beleaguered. "We are surrounded by traitors," he wrote Baker. What Dubuque's union men needed was a regiment of loyal soldiers. Marion's Jane Thompson was furious at local peace men. They were worse then rebels. She suggested that her husband resign his commission and come home to fight them, adding unhappily, "I can do nothing but scold."[6]

Yet Republicans in general were as belligerent as Mrs. Thompson. In Jefferson county they responded to the peace men's challenges with equally partisan union meetings of their own, usually in places where Democrats earlier had made their appeal. Nor were War Democrats silent. If they dominated a meeting, they made certain that if they went on record against an abolition war, they also went on record in support of war to suppress rebellion. If they found themselves outnumbered, they sometimes took to print to disavow both peace resolutions and "disloyal" peace partisans. Louisa county Democrats didn't like emancipation, and they disapproved conscription in principle, but they supported war against secession and agreed not to resist a draft if officials handled it fairly. This conditional support for the draft, voiced at Wapello on May 9, was significant because by this time peace men were scoring some successes in getting rallies to approve resolutions which declared that Democrats should resist the draft forcefully regardless of the circumstances.[7]

After mid-year 1863, the number of peace rallies declined markedly. Two of them, however, one in late 1863 and the other in 1864, were major productions. The Iowa City meeting on October 5, 1863, doubled as an election rally and attracted an estimated 12,000 to 15,000 persons. Scheduled to appear were some of the leaders of the peace movement in the Midwest and the East including Fernando Wood, Charles Mason, Samuel S. Cox, Daniel Voorhees, and William A. Richardson, none of whom showed up. Edward Thayer plus William Gaston and Ira Mitchell of Iowa City orated in their stead. Dubuque peace partisans relied on Iowa talent exclusively to lure 15,000 Democrats to a peace rally in August, 1864.[8]

As Democratic peace sentiment appeared to coalesce suddenly early in 1863, more of Iowa's leading Democratic papers also began to preach the peace gospel. One, certainly, had long been in the peace camp. Stilson Hutchins reminded *Herald* readers that as early as April 26, 1861, the Dubuque paper had advocated peace and warned against the consequences of civil war. And Dennis Mahony thought that the *Herald* had at last won its long battle to reshape Iowa Democratic thinking. "We know that we speak for the party in Iowa," he declared emphatically, "when we say that a slave-emancipating labor-degrading war is not their war nor will it in any particular command their support." That the *Herald* spoke for the party was surely debatable, but there was no doubt that peace sentiment was stronger than it ever had been. Mahony wanted to keep it that way. He tried to build a strong constitutional case for the peace forces, never relying exclusively on war-weariness to shape opinion. His recent distasteful experience with oath-taking behind him, he lectured on the proper relationship between oath-taking and duty in wartime. When one took an oath to support the Constitution,

Mahony said, it meant only that one agreed to obey the will of the sovereign states which gave birth to the Constitution in the first place, not the will of the federal government. Logically, then, since no power could ever become greater than its creator, the federal government could not legally use force to coerce the states. Those federal officials who attempted to use force for that purpose were revolutionaries. Citizens who supported such revolutionaries were traitors, Mahony concluded.[9]

The Dubuque editor was more sophisticated in his arguments than most of his fellow Democratic newsmen. Edward Thayer of the Muscatine *Courier,* who shifted into the peace camp for a time after the fall elections of 1862, stressed two simpler points. First, it was apparent that military force would never subdue the South; second, emancipation was so abominable that the Northern public would not support a war to achieve it.[10] Richard Sylvester of the *State Democratic Press* believed that emancipation had changed the character of the war. No longer a war for Union, the war was only "an instrument in the hands of treacherous leaders, to build up and perpetuate a corrupt and lecherous dynasty. . . ." Sylvester even speculated that peace sentiment was so strong that most Northerners might welcome foreign intervention to end the conflict. Reunion, however, would come only through "peaceful counsels."[11] Stop the war now, demanded Lysander Babbitt of the Council Bluffs *Bugle.* Only by respecting Southern rights could the Union be restored. A War Democrat, Babbitt declared, was "a degenerate villain who will sacrifice all for his selfish purposes regardless of friendship, right, patriotism or honor."[12] Simple war-weariness compelled the editor of the Bloomfield *Democratic Clarion* to write, "The time to quit has arrived. . . . It is useless to go any further. . . . Today the rebellion is stronger than at any previous time." The Burlington *Argus* and *Des Moines News* (Keosauqua) also came out for peace.[13] Most prominent among the smaller peace papers was the Fairfield *Constitution and Union* under David Sheward, which stood for peace before as well as after Sheward's arrest in August, 1862.

But when William Merritt started up the Des Moines *Statesman* in July after the demise of the prowar Des Moines *Times,* any hope that peace forces might be gaining an outlet in the state capital disappeared with Merritt's first editorial. Merritt was clearly in the middle of the road. "[C]onciliation unaided by the sword, or war unsubdued by a disposition to compromise would never restore the Union," he wrote.[14] Nor did Thomas Clagett in Keokuk or David Richardson in Davenport become peace men. Richardson did waver somewhat for a six-month period after the 1862 elections, but he never consistently called for a halt to the war and for negotiations with rebels. In early spring he began to warn Democrats not to accept peace at the expense of Union. The Dubuque *Times* monitored Richardson's views closely and soon announced that he was once more acceptable to loyal men. The *Times* watched Thayer also. The day after clearing Richardson of disloyalty, editor G. T. Stewart announced that Thayer too was again promoting loyal doctrine: restoration of the Union and no recognition of the Confederacy.[15]

Other Democratic papers also refused to promote peace. As W. W. Junkin put it in a somewhat confusing headline, "Not All Copperheads in the Democratic Party." Junkin meant that most of the Democratic "masses" were loyal and for war. So were some Democratic papers, particularly the Sioux City *Register,* the McGregor *North Iowa Times,* the Bellevue *Argus,* and the Des Moines *Times,* which was then (March) still struggling to survive. Junkin especially approved a *Times* declaration that "The North has advanced so far toward peace as she can with safety . . . further clamor for peace must have a demoralizing effect upon our armies and upon the friends of the Union."[16] When Edward Russell, editor of the Davenport *Gazette,* wrote that no man could remain a Democrat without also being a traitor, a rebel, and a murderer, he went too far for his coproprietors of the *Gazette.* The next day Russell admitted that the Dubuque *Herald*'s course and "appeals for civil war" by Ohio Copperhead Clement Vallandigham prompted his exaggeration of Democratic wickedness.[17]

Most of the editors of the foregoing Democratic papers promoted the war even at the height of the peace movement in the first half of 1863. Richardson constantly berated Union generals for botching the job on the battlefield as did John Gharkey of the *Fayette County Pioneer.* They pined for Union victories. But whether the Union armies won or lost was irrelevant to a true peace paper like the *Herald* which held that the war was needless to begin with.[18]

One could anticipate growing peace sentiment among some disaffected Democratic civilians and Democratic papers. More disappointing to Iowa war partisans was evidence of disenchantment with the war among the state's soldiers. There was some, but how much was clearly distinct from normal civilian-soldier complaints about army life is hard to tell. What there was, stemming from whatever source, Democratic papers readily printed, whether they were war or peace papers. Rarely were the letters signed, leading to speculation by the Fairfield *Ledger* that civilians, not soldiers, wrote nine out of every ten. Editor Junkin observed that signed letters and petitions from soldiers in support of the war and administration policy flooded Iowa Republican papers in March while none supporting the peace cause appeared in Democratic papers. The ordinarily astute Junkin might more wisely have concluded that for active duty soldiers to sign letters or draw up petitions attacking the administration and the army was unrealistic.[19]

Two such letters appeared in the *Herald,* however. An alert staff man looking over the *Herald*'s exchange papers gleaned one from the *North Iowa Times.* George Wood of the Twenty-Seventh Iowa, then in Tennessee, told the *Times* that nothing was going well. Soldiers went unpaid for four to six months, their families were destitute, speculators and swindlers ran rampant in every military department, food was scarce, and the troops believed that rebel army morale was high. Peace must come soon, Wood thought, or there would be trouble in the ranks. B. D. Everingham of the Thirty-Second Iowa at New Madrid, Missouri, wrote a friend in a letter given to the *Herald* that half the regiment was antiwar and anti-Republican. Furthermore, many soldiers who were formerly abolitionists and had favored enlistment of black regiments now hated blacks and said they'd shoot any black soldier placed beside them in the field.[20]

For a time the *Herald* thought it had a third signed soldier letter. Sgt. J. R. Menkler of Company F of the Twenty-Seventh Iowa was disgruntled about fighting for emancipation, about blacks, about officers, and about short rations. "If it was not for the sake of a few hungry officers who haven't got their haversacks quite full yet, the war might have been closed a long time ago," Menkler declared. The only trouble was that there was no such trooper as J. R. Menkler in the company. An outraged and very real F Company Sergeant, C. S. Taylor, so informed the Dubuque *Times,* adding for good measure that his company was entirely loyal.[21] But W. M. Kelsey of the Second Iowa Cavalry in Tennessee told Laurel Summers not to put any stock in officer-written resolutions attacking traitors and supporting the war. Only one-fourth of the regiment really approved them, he claimed.[22]

The Keokuk *Gate City* to a degree inadvertently verified some of Kelsey's charges. On March 25, 1863, the *Gate City* carried a glowing account of the manner in which soldiers in the regiments of the famous Crocker's Brigade responded to a series of officer-written resolutions approving the federal government's war aims and the Emancipation Proclamation. "Nearly all" officers signed, wrote the paper's correspondent. In the Fifteenth regiment "all but 28 men" responded enthusiastically. The twenty-eight men said they'd be "loyal and good soldiers," the writer added. The Eleventh and Thirteenth regiments approved by "unanimous shout" and "without a dissenting voice," respectively. The Sixteenth hedged, however, and the correspondent explained: "Owing to a variety of circumstances of a peculiar nature they [men of the Sixteenth] declined taking any general action upon the question—all of them, however, expressing loyalty and a determination to obey orders and faithfully support the government." One of Iowa's most colorful soldier letter-writers, Sgt. Cyrus Boyd, described the plight of one of the Eleventh regiment's "unanimous" soldiers. During that same month, March of 1863, this soldier untactfully "cussed" President Lincoln, called him a black abolitionist, and swore he would shoot him if he could. Now, reported Boyd, he carried a 20-pound ball around two hours a day. A disgruntled Brigade officer wrote the Muscatine *Courier* that the unenthusiastic Fifteenth regiment soldiers were marched up and down in front of their tents for a spell and that the Sixteenth regiment actually roared a unanimous "no" to a resolution in support of the Emancipation Proclamation. Sergeant Boyd, probably a more accurate reporter than the officer, said the Fifteenth's nonconformists got off more easily than that. When their Colonel attempted to straighten their thinking, he wound up second best while arguing with a group of anti-black, anti-abolitionist troopers. Intercession by a popular officer, Lt. Col. William Belknap, who proposed three cheers for the Union, got the Colonel, Hugh Reid, off the hook, and the men out of trouble.[23]

One letter, purportedly from an officer (unsigned) with the Thirty-Fourth at St. Louis, condemned army leadership and battlefield failures. "[T]he more thinking ones of us," he added, "have made up our minds that to conquer and subjugate the South will take at least 150 years. The thing can't be did—never." Moreover, former abolitionists were now becoming "the most bitter, sarcastic Democrats." There were probably less than twenty-five Republicans in the whole regiment, he guessed. There was, however, an incongruous note in his letter. Most of the regiment, reported the officer, were "exhilarated" with the task of guarding several thousand prisoners taken in Arkansas.[24] Other unsigned letters were equally bitter against blacks, abolitionists, officers, emancipation, and political resolutions. Some urged readers to work for peace. A few proclaimed that a man would be foolish to enlist. They came from so many different regiments that it must have seemed to hopeful peace men as well as anxious war men that half the army was ready to quit the war. Among the regiments represented besides those mentioned already were the Twenty-First, Twenty-Sixth, Twenty-Ninth, Thirty-First, Thirty-Third, and Thirty-Fifth.[25]

None of these letters should have caused any wonder. The first few months of 1863 were the low point for the Union during the war. But, as with most army units anywere at any time, morale rose with certain basic changes in their situation. For the Twenty-Eighth Iowa, warmer weather, drying ground, improving health, and the arrival of the paymaster made a big difference. So did a better diet, caused less by army efficiency than by enhanced soldier skill at foraging. W. J. H. told the *State Democratic Press* that a quick trip to the "tall timber" always brought satisfactory results like fresh pork, beef, sweet potatoes, onions, and corn dodgers.[26]

Soldier dislike for blacks could diminish as a result of new experiences. Sergeant Boyd had no antiblack animus to begin with, but it is unlikely that he was alone in his anger at seeing small black children and very old decrepit slaves abandoned by a "cruel and barbarous" master who took his ablebodied slaves with him as he fled from Northern troops approaching his plantation. Boyd's diary for that day, February 10, 1863, also reveals how one Iowa soldier in Boyd's unit suddenly arrived at a new perception of slavery. It was a case wherein the eye and the ear of the beholder created an impact which no amount of abolition lecturing on the evils of the peculiar institution could create. Wrote Boyd:

> Among a band of contrabands that came in today was a bright little girl whose hair hung to her shoulders and was just a little *wavy*. Her features were not like a Negro but were sharp and clear while her eye was *dark blue* and yet she was a *slave*. Her mother was along and looked a little like she had African blood. She said this was her little girl and that she had *two* more daughters grown up and the *father* of all three was her *Master* who classed them all as his *slaves*. A soldier who stood by and heard the Mother tell this story exclaimed in the fervent patriotism of his feeling. *"By G——d I'll fight till hell freezes over* and then I'll cut the ice and fight on."[27]

The year 1863 saw the word Copperhead achieve first rank as a derogatory term in Iowa. Why Copperhead became so popular with Republicans and so unpopular with Democrats is not clear. Those smear words which preceded it like traitor, tory, secesh, sympathizer, Butternut, and even Mahonyite were at least as bitter in connotation as Copperhead. Democrats themselves stuck the traitor label on abolitionists and those they accused of undermining the "Union as it was and the Constitution as it is." Sometimes editors made a serious attempt to be accurate in describing their foes without resorting to acknowledged smears. Thomas Clagett exerted himself once to speak well of "liberal-minded conservative Republicans" as opposed to "radical abolitionist Republicans."[28] An intraparty foe once described Dennis Mahony as a "radical Democrat, *but* . . . honest and principle[d]."[29] Charles Mason, on the other hand, used the term "loyal people," usually without quotation marks, as a private expression of scorn for those who approved the war and Republican policy.[30]

But Copperhead, which stung most Democrats to the quick, was the most effective of the code words which attained wide currency during the war. Nevertheless, it was a late arrival, attaining common usage long after it won favor east of the Mississippi. As noted earlier, the Mount Pleasant *Home Journal* of October 11, 1862, was the first to apply it in a general sense to Democrats ("journals of the defunct copperheads") during the last days before the fall elections. On January 24, 1863, the Burlington *Hawk-eye* pinned it on eastern free-state Democrats. Within ten days the paper began to apply it to local Democrats.[31] Still, it required constant use by Frank Palmer of the *Iowa State Register* to popularize Copperhead as the best word to sting Democrats, particularly Democrats believed to err on the side of sympathy for the South. S. P. Yoemans of the Sioux City *Register,* a War Democrat, tried hard to force Republican organs, especially Palmer's *Register,* to draw sharp distinctions between Democratic factions. Yoemans wanted Palmer to acknowledge that Democrats who favored a military solution to the war but who also opposed abolition were loyalists, not Copperheads. He pressed his case so vigorously that Palmer eventually admitted that the Sioux City paper was the "ablest Democratic paper in the state." This was not enough. Palmer never did completely satisfy the scrappy Yoemans. In June the Des Moines editor probably came close, however, to establishing the difference between Copperheads and other Democrats as Republicans saw it. Copperheads were "rebel-sympathizers" in contrast to the "scores of Democrats in this city who rejoice with us over Federal triumphs and who mourn with us over the defeat of our arms." Palmer also believed that those who viewed Clement Vallandigham's arrest as evidence of military despotism were Copperheads. The Dubuque *Times* and the *Iowa State Register* occasionally contrasted War Democrats with Peace Traitors and War Hypocrites. War Hypocrites were worse than Peace Traitors said the *Register* because Peace Traitors were honest and open in their opposition to the war. War Hypocrites, on the other hand, pretended to favor the war but opposed all measures to carry it out. Neither term attained popularity.[32]

James Howell castigated the Lee county community of West Point as a Copperhead place marked by "declining barbarism." And a Montrose resident informed the *Gate City* that in Montrose it was "pretty well established . . . *as*

CALLS FOR PEACE AND THE IOWA RESPONSE

sound copperhead doctrine that a man may whip his wife when he pleases.''[33] One of the very young in politically conscious Dubuque also had some firm notions about Copperheads according to an amused Dubuque *Times* reporter. He wrote:

> *An Astonished Child*—A few days ago a little four year old son of a Union man, in this city, happened to look out of the parlor window and see a neighbor whom he knew to be strongly for the Union, shaking hands with a Copperhead. It astonished him.—He ran to his mother crying out ''Momma! Momma! I just seed a genelman shake hands with a Copperhead! Ain't he wicked, Momma!'' The child still persists in calling Mr. Blank a ''wicked man.''[34]

Hardly any more sophisticated was Clark Dunham of the *Hawk-eye* the next year when he proclaimed that there no longer existed a Democratic party, only a Copperhead party. Its leaders were dishonest and probably its masses also. Even if they were merely ignorant, not dishonest, that was inexcusable. Enough had occurred in three years of war, said Dunham, to make clear ''the righteousness of their country's cause. . . .''[35]

Long since, however, many Democrats had accepted the Copperhead label, sometimes ruefully, sometimes defiantly, occasionally matter-of-factly. The latter was more or less the case with the Muscatine *Courier* where by early March, 1863, Edward Thayer headlined an election results story with the line ''Copperheads Ahead.'' By April the Washington *Democrat* was blasé enough to use the terms Copperhead and Democrat interchangeably in meeting notices and reports, as, ''Pursuant to notice the Copperheads of Dutch Creek met at Middleton's School House, March 28th, and organized by the election of A. Maxwell, Esq., Chairman, and J. M. English, Secretary.'' Dutch Creek's Democrat-Copperheads hardly stirred out of the Democratic mainstream as they condemned both secession and abolition and resolved to support no candidate for office who was less than an ''unconditional Union man.''[36] The Oskaloosa *Times* also accepted the label and called participants at a peace meeting Copperheads. The Burlington *Argus* defended those who wore Copperhead breastpins. Yet in Burlington not all Democrats or friends of Democrats felt totally at ease with the word or at being seen in the presence of self-styled Copperheads. ''Called at Rorer's,'' wrote Charles Mason. ''All pleasant. He afterwards passed me without turning his head. I was standing with several other Copperheads.''[37] David Richardson decided to define Copperhead as he wished and not worry too much about it. Copperheads, he said, favored prosecution of the war even more vigorously than anyone else, but ''for the *sole purpose of restoring the Union,*'' or for ''unconditional Union and the Constitution,'' as he said on another occasion.[38] Later on, Richardson, by omission, backed away from this description as Copperhead came to mean less than a full commitment to a war policy.

Stilson Hutchins was ambivalent about it all. If Republicans insisted upon calling Democrats Copperheads, then Democrats should call Republicans African Vipers, "until they shall become tired of calling names." Copperhead snakes, after all, were harmless in comparison. Soon Hutchins shifted gears. A Copperhead, he recalled, adorned the Revolutionary War flag with the bold inscription "Don't Tread on Me." But by 1864 a different editor, Patrick Robb, was much less willing to see the *Herald* described as a Copperhead paper. Robb was the only one of a succession of four *Herald* senior editors during the war who was a War Democrat. This, however, didn't immunize him against the Copperhead smear. The *Times* believed that Robb's *Herald* exhibited Copperheadism by pervasive and consistent opposition to all measures which promoted the war, soldier and soldier families' welfare, and Northern morale.[39] Nor could G. M. Todd at the Burlington *Argus* deny that Copperhead was a harmless term, even if he could defend those who wore Copperhead pins. After the presidential election of 1864 he angrily headlined an editorial, "Democratic Soldiers Are Not 'Copperheads.' "[40]

Two Des Moines residents learned that it was useless to sue Frank Palmer for libel when he called them Copperheads. The grand jury examined charges brought by B. N. Kinyon and J. C. Turk but dismissed them, to the displeasure of the Des Moines *Statesman* which warned that if the courts refused to do their duty, citizens might have to find other means to protect themselves.[41] In Keokuk, as in most of Iowa, that meant not protection but satisfaction after the fact, if one were tough enough to win it. As the *Constitution* drily reported, ". . . one man called another a copperhead, and had his frontispiece disfigured."[42]

Being in the service was no guarantee that a soldier or his unit would escape the Copperhead tag. The Fortieth Iowa, the last organized of the state's three-year enlistment regiments, was occasionally called the Copperhead regiment. This happened partly because the unit contained a large number of Democrats. One Republican soldier of the Fortieth who defended the unit against the taint of Copperheadism acknowledged that charges about Democrats failing to enlist in proportion to their numbers contributed heavily to Democratic enlistments in the regiment during the great recruiting drive in the summer of 1862. One Iowa writer in defending the Fortieth, said that it always returned at least a small Republican majority in wartime elections. Lurton Ingersoll had good intentions, but he was wrong. The unit cast a small majority for Democratic Gen. James B. Tuttle when he ran unsuccessfully for governor in 1863. More accurately, Ingersoll claimed that Capt. M. V. B. Bennett, commander of A company, was mainly responsible for the Fortieth's reputation. Formerly a state representative from Marion county and "an enthusiastic partisan of the most straightest sect of Democracy," Bennett was outspoken both in and out of the service. When Bennett raised his supposedly all-Democratic A company, he applied to Governor Kirkwood for a commission. Kirkwood appeared reluctant to grant it, and Bennett derisively threatened to report him to higher authorities for discouraging enlistments. A year later Charles Mason heard Bennett speak at a Democratic campaign rally while he was yet in the army. Mason predicted that the Captain's bitter indictment of the Lincoln administration might lead to his expulsion from service. Bennett did resign before the unit saw action.[43]

At least one member of the regiment agreed with critics that the nine-hundred-man body was not overly committed to the war. After five months' service Private Jacob Hunter of E company voiced his concern to his wife. Hunter had especially grave doubts about Captain Bennett's troopers.

> One third of the 40th ridgement is no better than jefs [Jefferson Davis's] hounds I fear if ever it should be called to fight   I could not have believed their was men in Iowa so Degraded as company A is   they are close to us so I can know their corruption   there is but one or two loyal men in the company   they do nothing but curse abe lincoln and the abolutionists   this was their dayley business and at night they hold mock meetings in their tents till the cornel stoped them and one of their own loyal men told them if they did not stop secesh talk he would have them arrested   they have been very still since but they are yet the same   this is democracy.[44]

Two other units briefly acquired a Copperhead stigma. One was the Sixteenth, caused by the news that the men resisted attempts to put them on record in favor of the Emancipation Proclamation. The other was the Sixth Cavalry whose troops had no desire to fight "for niggers" according to a Chicago *Times* correspondent, a charge the unit's officers hotly denied. The Sixth, they claimed, favored all administration measures designed to put down the rebellion.[45]

Sons of noted Copperheads attracted attention from observers who wondered if their offspring would follow in their father's steps. Not young Jeff Durham, son of Marion's Samuel Durham, Jane Thompson happily reported to her husband. "Jeff Durham," she wrote, "has enlisted and gone into the army very much against the wishes of his Father . . . he has been going to school at Mt. Vernon but he said it was no use for him to go to school, for his mind was on going to war, and go he did, and may God bless him."[46] James Dunlavy, son of Harvey Dunlavy, state representative from Davis county, won plaudits for combat performance in Arkansas from the *Gate City* and the *Hawk-eye*. Both papers refrained from comment on the father's political course.[47]

To some extent soldier conduct, apart from the issue of fidelity to the cause of Union, was of some concern to Iowans. They, like the rest of the country, had not been accustomed to the presence of large bodies of military forces in their midst. Inevitably this presence led to incidents which sorely tried civilian goodwill and created feelings on which opponents of the war could capitalize. Or it created situations which Republicans could use to show how unpatriotic Democrats allegedly were. This happened when Democratic members of the Marion county board of supervisors tried unsuccessfully to block appropriations to clothe and equip Company E of the Eighth Iowa. Their opponents rejected the Democrats' reasoning, that the recruits, like those of another company a year earlier, would simply trade the clothes for whiskey.[48] Davenport at one time or another was the site of five army camps, the biggest of which was Camp McClellan, a training center established in August, 1861. When soldiers got out of hand, drinking, fighting, stealing, and committing acts of vandalism, they put war partisans in a difficult spot. The Thirty-Nineth Iowa, recruited from central Iowa and commanded by Col. H. J. B. Cummings, was something of a cross for the community to bear. To criticize the Thirty-Ninth's behavior, however, as did the *Democrat,* caused Frank Palmer to call the paper a tory sheet and a secesh establishment, which it most decidedly was not. Unintimidated, the *Democrat* blasted Colonel Cummings as "a contemptible puppy . . . a natural born ass" when the regiment left for the South in December, 1862. Even the Republican *Gazette* correspondent condemned the unit as "a regiment of sneaks and thieves."[49] The Republican *Journal* in Muscatine had enough of the Thirty-Seventh Iowa also and recommended that local saloons accede to the request of that regiment's officers that they not sell to soldiers.[50] When the Sixth Iowa Cavalry departed for Northwest frontier duty, the *Democrat* praised the unit, adding, "Let the Indians beware." But many Davenporters probably breathed a sigh of relief, especially local chicken raisers and a German saloon proprietor whose establishment the Sixth's soldiers twice wrecked. Ironically, the wreckers, including one group of officers, were trying to put Aschermann's saloon out of business because they deemed it a public nuisance which threatened the discipline and order of Camp McClellan. A year later soldiers in Davenport were still a problem. Some, although a minority, the *Democrat* said, were inclined "to beat up old men who are unable to defend themselves, and negroes. . . ."[51]

Soldier conduct in the South was more a topic of concern to the Dubuque *Herald* which never hesitated to print stories about soldier misdeeds and failures. The following headlines give some idea of the nature of the *Herald*'s coverage.

The Outrages Committed by Federal Troops
Destruction of All Kinds of Property
Instances of Vandalism

[Dec. 23, 1862]

The Men and Officers of the Twenty-First
The Total Inefficiency of the Latter
The Incompetence of the Medical Staff

[Dec. 27, 1862]

Outrages Perpetrated upon Southern Women and Children
[Dec. 28, 1862]

Outrages Perpetrated by Federal Soldiers upon the Southern People
[Feb. 8, 1863]

Fiendish Conduct of Union Soldiers in Missouri
[Mar. 7, 1863]

No other Iowa Democratic papers so consistently featured such stories or used such alarmist headlines to describe their contents. These papers did not ignore them completely, but they accented them less.

There is evidence, certainly, that Iowa troops, like others, could act like locusts on the land. Col. James Williamson, commander of the Fourth Iowa, wrote Gen. G. M. Dodge after a troop movement in Arkansas that the march "ended in nothing save acts by the soldiers which would disgrace any army of half civilized men on earth. Theft and rape were the chief results of the expedition." Williamson said, however, that he kept his own troops under control by "paying close attention to my business." Frank Thorn of the Thirtieth Iowa wrote his parents that although officers always detached guards to protect Southern property while on march, "most always there are some [men] that get to the house and take what they want, and sometimes destroy a good deal of property such as cotton gins or something of that kind."[52]

Stilson Hutchins believed the worst, aided by the reporting of "Zeta" who regularly sent letters to the *Herald* denouncing Northern troops and commanders. Wrote Hutchins in February, 1863, of the troops:

They have robbed private houses, stores and *churches;* they have stolen family plate and heirlooms, destroyed sacred relics, murdered or brutally maltreated helpless infancy and old age. They have in thousands of instances—great Heaven that it should be told—ravished wives, mothers and daughters before the eyes of husbands, sons and parents—and yet we talk in flippancy of this restoration of the Union?

Hutchins maintained that the destruction of state capital buildings at Baton Rouge, Louisiana, and Jackson, Mississippi, would justify Lee's burning the Pennsylvania capital, Harrisburg, when the Confederates marched into the Keystone state in June.[53]

Just before the battle of Gettysburg, Hutchins became so enraged that he wrote a diatribe entitled "Barbarism and Civilization" which described the difference between Northern and Southern people as he saw it.

Northern civilization plunders Southern homes, insults and outrages women, robs and impoverishes children, destroys wantonly all species of property down to agricultural implements, burns and lays waste fine buildings and grounds, while Southern barbarism respects private property, studiously avoids offence to women or cruelty to children; even foregoes public advantage which shall involve personal loss, and threatens summary punishment to all who shall overstep the lines of rigid propriety. Northern papers congratulate Northern troops on the amount of wanton damage done. Gen. Lee and Gen. Early impress upon Southern troops the fact that the war has its limits and restrictions—and that women and children and private property are secure from visitations.[54]

But Hutchins never reported the kind of behavior Peter Wilson described to his parents on July 4, 1863. Wilson told how the Fourteenth Iowa acted under provocation during that holiday at Columbus, Kentucky. Officers marched the unit three miles under a hot sun to hear patriotic speeches. The men had nothing to eat except what they could purchase from civilian vendors who were prepared to make a killing (lemonade at 10¢ a glass, for example). The incensed and thirsty troops were about to "clean out" the vendors, stall by stall, when Col. William T. Shaw called them to attention and marched them back to camp to the usual fare of hard tack and pork. "There was plenty of beer, whiskey, wine and c.," Wilson wrote, "and we had both the will and the power to take it. The Col. touched us on the only weak place we had when he told us we will show them that western men are too well disciplined to raise a row even when we have been provoked."[55]

The *Herald*'s reporting naturally attracted unfriendly attention. The *Gate City* said it grossly exaggerated Union losses at the battle of Murfreesboro.[56] When Hutchins extolled Stonewall Jackson as the "bravest American of the 19th century," the *Times* asked when had he ever praised the Union dead. When Joseph Hooker retreated before Lee in late June, the *Herald* attacked his generalship, although the tone of the paper hardly suggested that it would welcome his success. It prominently displayed a Chicago *Times* dispatch from Washington which maintained that Lee suffered no defeat at Gettysburg. Gettysburg, in fact, was no Northern victory, Hutchins editorialized, "unless it be a victory to have succeeded in successfully resisting the shock of the Confederate army." Lee, he added, with half as many troops had moved at will against the Union forces when he wished, and away from them when he wished, without interference, when he wanted to accomplish something elsewhere. Victory claims were simply another administration deception.[57] On June 27 Hutchins predicted that the capture of Vicksburg lay in the distant future. When the city fell a week later, one headline read, "The Garrison of Vicksburg, after a Gallant and Unexampled Resistance of Several Weeks, Surrendered to the Federal Forces." This hardly sounded as if the *Herald* appreciated the victory, observed the *Hawk-eye*. The *Herald* also objected when celebrants heralded Vicksburg's fall by ringing the bell at Dubuque's city hall; it was enough to cause everyone to believe that something was on fire, the paper grumped. The *Times* too, during this period, pointed out that the Democratic organ seemed to take no pleasure in any Union victories, nor the quelling of New York's draft riot, nor the federal attack on Charleston.[58] That fall the *Times* called attention to its rival's position again. The *Herald*, now anticipating the fall of Fort Sumter and Charleston, decided that victories there would only contract rebel lines, release more troops for the rebel defenses, and require more federal occupation troops.[59]

Hutchins and his staff weren't the only Democrats whose attitudes toward Union successes were considered suspect. Under the headline, "Those Who Didn't," W. W. Junkin printed the names of eight Fairfield Democrats who failed to illuminate their houses on the night Fairfield citizens were asked to do so to celebrate the Gettysburg victory.[60] But in Davenport, David Richardson was elated. Edward Thayer was pleased also, although he noted that speakers at a Muscatine victory celebration had more to say about the editor of the *Courier* and Copperheads than about the victories.[61] In Burlington the *Hawk-eye* discerned that everybody was delighted about Vicksburg including "Copperheads who have been laboring for a year to turn the Democratic masses against this 'Aboliton War' . . . who have sworn the Union never could be saved by fighting—that war was disunion . . . and 'peace' was the only panacea for our national troubles. . . ."[62] The *State Democratic Press* acclaimed the victories also. Only two out of several speeches at a big celebration on July 8 insulted Democrats, the editor reported. In Des Moines, *Statesman* editor William Merritt also rejoiced in the Union successes. He noted, however, that all but one of the celebration speeches at the Savery House villified the Democrats.[63] The *Iowa State Register* claimed that Democratic state conventioneers reacted coolly to the Vicksburg triumph. "Not a thrill of joy nor an emotion of patriotism moved on their frigid, rebel-sympathizing spirits!" said the paper.[64] The *Register* was hardly a neutral observer. But it would be difficult to maintain that the Dubuque *Herald* in 1863 ever had much positive to say about the federal armies and its commander-in-chief—or much that was negative about their opponents. Hutchins judged that Jefferson Davis' year-end message to the Confederate congress was "an honest appeal to the judgement of the civilized world and one which cannot be abused out of influence." In contrast Lincoln's proclamation of conditional amnesty was "absurd . . . no people alive to self-respect could accept such an offer. . . ." If they did, they deserved "not only to lose the slaves they have but to become bound to them in the bonds of the most galling servitude."[65] Nearly all other Iowa Democratic papers might be equally hard on Lincoln; but they appreciated Northern victories even if they favored peace, gave the benefit of the doubt to Union troops if not their officers, and the back of the hand to rebels.

Dennis Mahony was a bitter man after his release from Old Capital Prison in November, 1862. He wanted vindication. And more than ever he wanted to influence the people's course so they would end the war and repudiate the Lincoln administration. Mahony did not reassume the editorial reins of the *Herald* until the first of January. But he had free use of its space to vent his spleen. He attacked Governor Kirkwood for "outrages" he "suffered to be committed" on Iowa's sovereignty and upon its citizens, and scorned him as a "faithless public servant." In a more temperate tone he wrote President Lincoln. He proposed a national convention at which North and South would meet on equal terms to draw up a new Constitution which would reunify the country. He summarized his views which he believed led to his arrest, criticized the President's liberal interpretation of his executive authority, and signed off as "another of the victims of your exercise of arbitrary power." He also wrote Horace Greeley, accused Greeley of stigmatizing him as a traitor in the *Tribune* and hinted that he would seek legal redress unless Greeley made "due reparation." Neither Kirkwood nor Lincoln answered him.

But the New York editor did in no uncertain manner. So far as he could tell, Greeley declared, Mahony hoped for Confederate success "in defying the authority and destroying the integrity of the United States," expected and worked for a "disunion Peace," and wanted the West to split from the East, thence to join the South under the Montgomery Constitution. Whether this made Mahony a traitor in the legal sense, Greeley said, he did not know. But so far as he was concerned Mahony was one in a moral sense, and he, Greeley, had no intention of suppressing that opinion.[66] Mahony also tried to get the United States Senate to investigate the way the War Department extracted oaths from arbitrary arrest victims, oaths which forestalled suits against arresting officers or those initiating arrests. Senator Lazarus Powell of Kentucky made the fight for him in the Senate. The Senate requested Secretary Stanton to submit all documents pertaining to the subject, which Stanton did on January 5. After several unsuccessful attempts, Powell succeeded in bringing the matter before the entire upper house. What started out as a request for a resolution to have one thousand copies of Stanton's report printed for the Senate to study, turned into a discussion of Mahony's loyalty, with Powell on one side crossing swords with Henry Wilson of Massachusetts and Senators Grimes and Harlan on the other. The two Iowans were leery of a direct assault on Mahony's loyalty; but they did not wish to see him escape with a clean bill of health. Ultimately the Senate approved Wilson's move to postpone the Powell resolutions indefinitely by a straight party vote, 21 to 19. This effectively scuttled Mahony's attempt to chastise the War Department and to sustain his political course.[67]

By this time Mahony was once again in the East, having left Dubuque on January 23 to write a book on his prison experiences. Before he returned to the *Herald* on May 19, he had written not only the book, *Prisoner of State,* but also two pamphlets, *The Four Acts of Despotism* and *Reconstruction of the Union,* plus numerous provocative letters back to Dubuque expounding his views. He also conferred with national Democratic figures in the East, addressed the Young Men's Democratic Association of New York City, and became an honorary member of the Anti-Aboliton States Rights Association. He also accepted the editorship of the Philadelphia *Journal,* arranging for Hutchins to join him. This plan collapsed when his Dubuque supporters objected to his proposal to sell the *Herald* to Patrick Robb. They believed Robb's commitment to peace was less clear cut than Mahony's.[68]

Mahony's writings delighted friends and infuriated his enemies more than ever. From Pittsburg he told readers that public feeling in the East was such that "You may be prepared to hear that the blood of revolution flows at any moment, for unless the people have become entirely lost to their rights as freemen, and the danger which threatens their liberties, they will not much longer tolerate the usurpations of power which are so common in Washington and so alarming throughout the country." He advised Iowans "to prepare for the work. . . . One rash act of the Administration will light the fire of civil war in the North . . . by preparation I mean organize yourselves, in such a manner and act when the time for your action will have to come as it soon must; unless reason and common sense shall resume their legitimate influence in the councils of the Government." From New York he wrote that "For every man assaulted by an Abolitionist for the expression of his opinion there should be ten subjected to retaliatory punishment. For every Democratic newspaper mobbed by Abolitionism there should be ten destroyed by freemen." He seconded a proposal by Philadelphia's Charles Ingersoll "that if any one were arrested in that city contrary to law or if any one were subjected to harsh treatment on account of his political opinions by the administration, the person of the President should be seized in retaliation, to be held as a hostage for safe-keeping. . . ." This, he added, somewhat disingenuously, was no call for mob violence; rather, it was a course of action to prevent mob violence. In *Prisoner of State* Mahony warned that submission to despotism would enslave the citizenry; and he charged the Lincoln administration with rebellion against the Constitution. In the *Four Acts of Despotism* (tax, finance, conscription, and indemnity acts), he declared that "no four acts ever passed by any legislative body equalled these in despotic exaction in tyrannic oppression. . . ." And in *Reconstruction of the Union* he proposed that a national convention meet to amend the Constitution in order to guarantee that the slave states would have equal power in perpetuity to the free states.[69]

Mahony's outpouring attracted increasing animosity. Finally on July 18, *Times* editor G. T. Stewart got tough. Stewart charged that New York mayor Fernando Wood suggested to Mahony that he write the *Four Acts* pamphlet. Mahony consented, then deliberately produced a polemic designed to incite New York's Irish to violence in case federal officials attempted to implement the conscription act in the city. The result, claimed Stewart, who never submitted any evidence to support the idea of a Wood-Mahony conspiracy, was the bloody July draft riot. Furthermore, he added, Mahony's Pittsburg letter printed in the *Herald* on February 6 was a clear incitement for Dubuque citizens to revolt.[70] Within four days, Mahony again sued Stewart for libel. The *Times* man repeated his charges, using most of his editorial page to cite over thirty Mahony passages from his book, pamphlets, letters, and editorials to show that the Irish editor was disloyal and advocated violence against the government. Again Mahony lost. "The grand jury," wrote a laconic *Times* reporter, "found too much truth in the article complained of."[71]

The grand jury action was anticlimactic since Mahony had retired from active participation on the *Herald* a few days earlier. A month later Dubuque county Democrats unanimously nominated him to run for county sheriff. He won the election handily by 879 votes out of a total of 4,260. Yet it was obvious that his course and the fervor with which he pursued it during the war had alienated many within his own bailiwick. He scored heavily in the rural townships but lost the Julien township vote which included most of the city of Dubuque; and his majority was considerably less than the 1,266 amassed in the county by the party's gubernatorial candidate.[72]

Mahony's retirement from the *Herald* was the act of a man weary of the battle, not only the political battle but also the battle for economic survival. He was not alone. Economic pressure on editors and other businessmen who espoused unpopular ideas was common throughout the war. Said the *Iowa State Register* of one Des Moines entrepreneur, "This man depends on the public for support. He insults Union men and then expects Union men to buy his goods. We refrain at this time from publishing his name; but we tell him here and now, that he has either to stop his foul utterances of treason or take the consequences of a public and thorough exposure of his villainy." W. W. Sweetser, who had the post concession at Camp Franklin in Dubuque, faced strong competition from an unnamed Dubuque jeweler. The jeweler, Sweetser complained, had always called the war "a damned Black Republican war," had sneered at the flag, and accused men of joining the army merely for pay. Now he was eager to fill his pockets with soldier greenbacks. When the Wentworth Hall Hotel of Clinton let it be known that Copperheads were unwelcome there, an Illinois editor suggested that all Democrats should avoid the Wentworth. Consequently, the Dubuque *Times* urged all loyal men to patronize the Clinton establishment. Thomas Clagett threatened to print the names of Keokuk businessmen who discriminated against him and called him a traitor. Democratic shoppers, he warned, would take their business elsewhere.[73]

The Burlington weekly *Argus*, established in 1862, had a difficult time getting advertiser contracts. Through January and February, 1863, it had only ten column inches of ads, which increased to only one full column by summer. But a drive to get $1-a-year subscribers in the winter of 1863–1864 helped as circulation doubled in less than three months from 1,600 to 3,000.[74] Many smaller Democratic papers (and some Republican ones) were not so fortunate, although many newly dead or allegedly dying papers somehow survived, or established themselves in more congenial surroundings, to the chagrin of partisans who sometimes saw opposition newspapers as blots on the good name of their town.

Many Iowans hoped to see the *Herald* go broke. Under both Mahony and Hutchins it had problems similar to those of lesser papers, and it too mounted periodic campaigns to win new subscribers and advertisers. When Hutchins eulogized Stonewall Jackson, the angry Waterloo *Courier* proposed that Waterloo merchants boycott Dubuque suppliers. That was going too far for the Dubuque *Times*. Dubuque's wholesalers, the paper said, were a patriotic group who never advertised in the *Herald* anyway. They deserved both business and praise, rather than a boycott.[75] The *Herald* survived, although in late 1863 it still complained that its enemies harassed subscribers in outlying communities, bullied *Herald* men attempting to collect money owed to the paper, and threatened prospective subscribers and advertisers.[76] Hutchins's vituperative editorials contributed at least as much as Mahony's writings toward the antagonism which many Iowans felt toward the *Herald* in 1863, although readers often mistakenly credited them to Mahony, particularly when the senior editor was in the East. Hutchins, besides denouncing the war and proclaiming the inevitability of separation, veered close to inciting men to desert from the army. Soldiers could be used as tools to free slaves and help adventurers win plunder. But, he asked, were they "bound by patriotism, duty or loyalty" to do so? If not, he said, answering his own question, let them follow the dictates of their conscience. His invective stung like a whip. Unfortunately for him, one of his readers had a long memory. Cedar Falls' Fitzroy Sessions, adjutant of the Third Iowa, recalled that early in the war Hutchins libeled him as one of a class of men who were "brutal as gorillas, but as destitute of courage as jackals." When Hutchins unwisely ventured into Cedar Falls, Sessions beat him up. John Hodnett, an associate editor of the *Herald*, fared better during a business trip to the same community until he indiscreetly uttered a Hutchins-type opinion. Instead of a beating, a self-appointed committee of citizens gave him twenty minutes to get out of town. Hodnett quickly departed for Manchester.[77] After Hutchins advised *Herald* subscribers to purchase arms for their protection, Dubuque postal officials alerted J. B. Henion, collector of customs, to an incoming shipment. Henion refused to turn eight Colt revolvers over to purchasers, citing a Treasury Department regulation prohibiting importation of powder or weapons across state lines except those destined for military posts or government stores. Hutchins angrily declared that Democrats needed the weapons for defense against Union Leaguers and warned that they would contrive to get them by other means.[78] The *Herald* and its patrons were not the only targets in the city. Davenport's *Der Demokrat* believed that patriots should send the *National-Demokrat* readers South where they belonged.[79]

Generally Republican leaders did not advocate violence against opposition editors and papers, although some believed the government had the right to act against them. John Mahin of the Muscatine *Journal* thought that opponent Edward Thayer deserved arrest as much as Mahony. The government's failure to try Mahony, much less to punish him, deeply irritated Congressman John Kasson, Samuel Kirkwood, and others. Gen. Grenville Dodge and his officers proclaimed that the *Herald*, Keokuk *Constitution*, Davenport *Democrat*, and unnamed lesser papers were "disloyal and revolutionary in their tendencies." When Dodge grumbled about their influence among the troops, Kasson told him that he could simply exclude them from his command.[80]

The Iowa City *Republican* argued that "Newspapers . . . addicted to defaming the government and to the habitual uttering of base falsehoods concerning individuals should receive the severest penalty of the law and an undivided public reprobation." Clark Dunham was more tolerant. Simply leave such papers to public opinion, he said, except "where their plottings endangered public safety."[81] Dunham's view, voiced in the first half of 1862, was not one which appealed to impatient citizens in 1863. There were enough of those on February 19 among Keokuk's large convalescent soldier population to march on Thomas Clagett's *Constitution,* smash the presses, and toss much of the equipment into the Mississippi before surprised local and federal officials could intervene. Democrats throughout the state were incensed, but the soldiers defiantly announced that they had only done their duty in ridding the community of the *Constitution*'s "treasonable influence." The apparent trigger was an editorial,

"Politics in the Army," printed the day of the mob action, which reacted angrily to reports that Indiana (not Iowa) officers subjected their regiments at Corinth, Mississippi, to political pressure. "Partizan officers in the army are the pliant tools of . . . partizan bigots at home," Clagett had declared in words hardly as sulphurous as those which he often used to chastise Republicans, abolitionists, and occasional radical peace Democrats. Not until September did the *Constitution* resume publication.

Brig. Gen. B. S. Roberts, commander of the Iowa Military District, investigated the incident. He found no officer complicity behind the mob action, which Clagett believed existed. But he condemned the rioters and promised to punish those who committed similar breaches of military discipline in the future. Roberts appended a gratuitous if indirect slap at Clagett in the conclusion to his report by appealing to Iowa citizens "to discourage such license of newspapers as are calculated to inflame the resentments and passions of suffering and wounded soldiers." Samuel Kirkwood was only slightly more sympathetic when the Keokuk editor asked him for protection and redress against such acts. Kirkwood said he regretted the occurrence, but asked, "Is it strange that men enduring what soldiers are enduring should give such expression of their feelings towards the men in the North they believe are aiding the enemy? . . ." Three months after the incident Clagett wrote a public letter listing his troubles at the hands of Keokuk's soldiers. He claimed that soldiers, egged on by officers, mobbed him three times, caused him $10,000 in property damage, ransacked his home while searching for Henry Clay Dean, stole food and personal possessions, and fired a cannon in his front yard.[82]

John Gharkey, editor of the West Union *Fayette County Pioneer,* was Clagett's equal as a pungent political commentator. West Union, he untactfully trumpeted, was a "stinking hole of Abolitionism." Men who came to town holding unpopular opinions were in danger of bodily assault. The night of May 23, a mob invaded the *Pioneer* office and did enough damage to force the paper to suspend publicaton for three weeks. Indignant Democrats, several hundred strong, publicly met and collected enough money to put Gharkey back in business. Even this did not significantly improve Gharkey's opinion of the general run of West Union's populace. Nor did the arrival of a former friend, printer and ex-soldier Andrew J. Felt, who returned to head the opposition *Public Record.* Felt exceeded the limits of decency, even by the loose standards of the day, when he called the *Pioneer* editor the "offspring of a bawdyhouse." Gharkey eventually tired of the battle in West Union and moved to Missouri in search of a more congenial political climate.[83]

David Sheward's Fairfield *Constitution and Union* also suffered harassment in 1863. Sheward, who was an embarrassment to middle-road Democrats, persisted in printing the Butternut emblem in his paper at a time when it signified treason to most Fairfield and Jefferson county citizens. Under duress, Sheward handed the printing emblem over to a company of the Eighth Iowa Cavalry. W. W. Junkin, who always maintained that Sheward wanted to be a martyr, condemned the soldiers' pressure. He could understand their resentment, he said, but the troopers had to endure Sheward for only one month whereas Fairfield had to put up with him all the time. In 1879 the Iowa legislature denied Joseph Shollenbarger's petition for reimbursement for destruction of his newspaper, the *Keokuk County News* (Sigourney), during the Tally War of early August, 1863. Shollenbarger claimed the *News* was a prowar paper. He said that soldiers brought in to quiet the county were temporarily quartered in his office. While Shollenbarger was out, they and some civilians who didn't like his editorial policies tore up his plant. When he couldn't reestablish the paper, Shollenbarger, a Union veteran, reenlisted. The petitioner resided in a soldiers' home in Milwaukee at the time he submitted his request. He said he was partly disabled as a result of illness that afflicted him during the war. His petition is the only source the writer could find which tells of the alleged incident.[84]

Violence, threatened or actual, against Democratic editors and their papers, was a sign that the tolerance level of war partisans was on the decline in 1863. This decline coincided with popular use of the term Copperhead. Altercations between Republican-designated or self-designated Copperheads and others increased noticeably. These altercations often resulted merely from a defiant Copperhead's wearing a Copperhead breastpin cut out of a penny, or a Butternut pin which symbolized the same set of attitudes, attitudes distinct from those held by other Democrats. This distinction appeared in newspaper stories about the meaning and danger of wearing Copperhead pins in Bradford, a small town in Chickasaw county. A group of war partisans there forcibly deprived one local Copperhead of his supply of Copperhead pins and destroyed them. The group further warned Bradford's Copperheads to cease wearing such pins or else suffer a ducking in the Cedar River. Stilson Hutchins learned of the incident. He had never advocated the wearing of such pins, he said, since they caused too much trouble in feverish times. However, people had a right to wear them. Hutchins then offered unsolicited commentary and advice.

> All Democrats without distinction being called Copperheads, accepted the appellation and made it respectable. . . . [I]f the Democrats of Bradford were to club together and shoot the first man who attempts to interfere with their right to wear Copperhead badges or butternut ornaments, there would be a speedy end to such intolerance.

Bradford's War Democrats would have none of that. Meeting in the town square, they affirmed their support for the administration, for the war, and their opposition to "secesh"—and they burned Hutchins in effigy.[85]

Mahony had another view about wearing such pins. He approved expulsion of a pin wearer from the University of Iowa. "Schools and colleges," he wrote, "are not the places in which partisan feelings or sentiment should be manifested." Still, wearing Copperhead pins was no disgrace, and communities which harassed those who did deserved contempt. Cedar Falls was such a community, said the *Herald.* So intolerant were the citizens that it was "a Sodom in comparison with other towns in Iowa."[86] A young man and a young woman who wore Copperhead pins in Mount Vernon during Cornell College's commencement day festivities got into trouble. War partisans forcibly removed the pins. Flushed with success, they forced several Mount Vernon Copperheads to cheer for the Union. The affair did not end there. The pin wearers haled their tormenters into court where they stood trial for assault and for inciting and participating in a riot. The plaintiffs lost when the jury accepted the defense argument that wearing Copperhead emblems was a sign of disloyalty; hence removing them from one's person constituted no crime.[87] But in Dubuque a justice of the peace levied a $10 fine and costs on a soldier who assaulted a pin wearer who flaunted the badge in his face.[88] Home guards in Van Buren county pounced on a suspected Copperhead and demanded that he take a loyalty oath. They also insisted that he remove a Copperhead pin from his wife's dress. When he proved obstinate on both counts, they delivered him to their startled captain. More tolerant than his excited guardsmen, the officer apologized for their behavior and released their stubborn captive at once. Scuffles went on all day in a Fairfield park between Jefferson county Democrats on one side and home guardsmen and their friends on the other. Most of the trouble arose when the latter tried to tear Butternut badges off the Democrats' clothes. One Mahaska county Copperhead suffered the loss of pins twice in one day on the streets of Ottumwa. The second encounter nearly led to a shooting as he and his wife tried to ward off their foes with a pistol.[89] A German-born blacksmith in Farmington whose son, without his knowledge, made Copperhead pin fasteners for occasional customers, paid for his ignorance. Guardsmen took him to Keokuk where authorities required him to recite the oath of allegiance and to post a $500 bond to insure that no one performed such a service in his shop again.[90] In August, 1863, a confrontation between soldiers and a badge wearer near Peoria (Mahaska county) led to the death of one of the soldier-assailants. Farmer Mart Myers went on trial for murder twice, once in Ottumwa and once in Albia. Both trials resulted in hung juries.[91] Iowa's newspapers reported many other brawls between political partisans that summer and fall, including a knife fight at the state fair.[92]

The most serious incident was the one known thereafter as the Tally War, or the Skunk River War, which occurred in early August in Keokuk county. Following a Peace Democrat rally outside South English on August 1, the Democrats rode back through the heart of the town, a Republican stronghold. There, led by the Reverend Cyphert Tally, the rally's chief speaker, they exchanged hot words with opponents. Both sides were armed. An accidental discharge of one weapon led to a burst of gunfire. Tally fell dead. Tally's friends vowed vengeance on South English and assembled at the Skunk River 16 miles south. The town's citizens sent urgent messages to Kirkwood for help against the Skunk River "army" which they wildly estimated at 500 to 4,000 men in size, the lower figure probably being considerably in excess of the actual number. Cooler heads prevailed and the "army" largely melted away before the six militia companies called out by the Governor ever reached the area. Kirkwood himself came to Sigourney, the county seat, and vowed that he would use whatever force the situation required to quell any similar disorders in Iowa. Lawmen arrested twelve men suspected of involvement in Tally's death, but the grand jury returned no indictments. This enraged Democrats throughout the state, prompting allegations that one of the twelve had bragged in open court that he killed Tally, only to be pardoned on the spot by the Governor. Another member of the twelve, Ed Cabler, an army veteran, actually fired the fatal bullet, but he and the few men who knew it kept his secret until they died. Kirkwood requested standby federal help late in the Tally War from Secretary of War Stanton and of General Roberts in Davenport. Stanton approved. What is interesting is the shared opinion of Roberts and his commander, Gen. John Pope, head of Union troops in the Northwest. Both men did not believe that civilians should threaten to call out federal troops to clamp down on free speech or on those who threatened to resist the laws. This only invited trouble which would probably blow over otherwise, said Pope.[93] In a speech at a mass Union meeting later that month in Dubuque, Kirkwood told a cheering crowd that he would act just as forcefully in that city as he had in Keokuk county if necessary. The *Herald* was unimpressed. "His bluster doesn't intimidate," wrote Mahony.[94]

Acts of intimidation and harassment committed by Copperheads against those who supported the war have never received much scholarly attention. But there were persons, who if the local climate was safe, were callous enough to make life more difficult for the wives and children of men who were off to war. Monroe's Jacob Hunter believed neighbors who opposed the war deliberately tormented Mary Hunter by telling her lies about the situation in the army, by causing her to worry about loss of army pay, and by cheating her. Hunter vowed vengeance on Monroe's Copperheads, but died before he had the opportunity to carry it out, leaving his wife and four young children with a dreary immediate future in a somewhat hostile community.[95] One soldier's wife felt so unhappy at her treatment in Shueyville (Johnson county) while her husband was in the army that she wrote a poignant letter asking Governor Kirkwood for help.

July 2th

    Governer Kirkwood   honerd ser
I am under the painful necesity of Calling on you for protecktion from the Coperheads   my Husban is in the airmy   he be longs to the Iowa fourteenth   my boys tho only 12 and 9 yerrs old is not a loud to sing Union Songs without being Club   yesterd tha was siting In the wood yard whar tha had bin Cuting stove wood while tha was sitten tha Commenced singing hang Jeff Davis on a sour aple tree   Cas shueys wife Came down and Clubed them and said if tha ever sung that a gane whar she was she would kill them   she all so a bused me or more properly [word illegible] and threten me what she would do if I dident make them boys stop singing Jeff Davis   she hoped my boys would be hung befour Jeff Davis
    hopen for protecktion and the puting Dow of tresen   I am for the Union

[Mrs.] E. J. Runyon[96]

A Cuba (Monroe county) widow whose husband and brother-in-law died in the trenches before Vicksburg woke up one morning to see an effigy of a black man stationed before her door. The Eddyville *Star* could only fulminate against the "contemptible, cowardly, unfeeling, villainous wretches" who pulled the stunt.[97] Mrs. Grenville M. Dodge was unhappy with some people in Council Bluffs, not for what they did to her, but for what they felt about her husband. "Your enemies sneer at you," she wrote. "You might as well be dead as far as they are concerned." Mrs. Dodge was, however, a chronic complainer. Her situation was in no way comparable to that of Mary Hunter or of Mrs. Runyon.[98]

One cannot take at face value, however, all the charges of evil doings attributed to Copperheads by Republican papers. The Fairfield *Ledger* may have been correct when it blamed Copperheads for a series of fires and other acts of vandalism against outspoken Union men in Jefferson and Van Buren counties during the winter of 1863. Maybe Copperheads in Monroe county burned veteran Nathan English's house and tried to shoot him in the bargain, as the Albia *Union* charged. And there may have been Copperheads in Cedar Falls "mean enough to steal vegetables out of gardens belonging to war widows," as the *Iowa State Register* believed. Whether these acts were Copperhead acts can't be proved. On the other hand, it is unlikely that Republicans were behind the unsuccessful attempt to disrupt the work of two young Lansing women who ran the local Freedman's Aid Society.[99]

Dubuque's Republicans sometimes felt they were in need of protection from the county's bellicose Copperheads. Still, they were not so worried but what they told state officials specifically what they would and would not do when it came to organizing themselves for that purpose. They would form a home guard for protection of their homes and the interests of the government. They could use government arms, but they could also supply their own. So armed they could put down any outbreak before it could spread. But they would not serve outside Dubuque or subject themselves to the call of the Dubuque Provost Marshal or his deputies because (a) they did not want to "serve as material to feed the ambition of a few adventurous, inconsiderate and speculative individuals aspiring to office . . ."; and because (b) they shouldn't be needed elsewhere since Dubuque was the only place in Iowa where one could expect real trouble.[100]

Soon after, Adj. Gen. N. B. Baker issued General Order No. 117 which promoted the voluntary organization of home guard units. Baker stipulated that such units would be subject to the calls of Provost Marshals, the last thing Dubuque's imperious but not-so-stupid loyalists wanted.[101]

DENNIS MAHONY, editor, Dubuque *Herald.* (State Historical Society of Iowa)

HENRY CLAY DEAN, minister-lawyer, Mount Pleasant.

CHARLES MASON, lawyer, Burlington and Washington, D.C.

DAVID N. RICHARDSON, editor, Davenport *Democrat.*

GEORGE W. JONES, former United
States senator and diplomat, Dubuque.

SAMUEL KIRKWOOD, governor,
1859–1863, Iowa City.

HERBERT M. HOXIE, United States
marshal for Iowa, Des Moines.

WILLIAM M. STONE, governor, 1863–
1867, Knoxville.

JOHN DUNCOMBE, lawyer, Fort Dodge.

JAMES B. HOWELL, editor,
Keokuk *Gate City*.

JAMES HARLAN, United States senator,
Mount Pleasant.

JOSIAH B. GRINNELL, United States
representative, Grinnell.

NATHANIEL B. BAKER, Iowa
adjutant general, Clinton.

JAMES GRIMES, United States senator, Burlington.

STILSON HUTCHINS, associate editor, Dubuque *Herald*. (Washington *Post*)

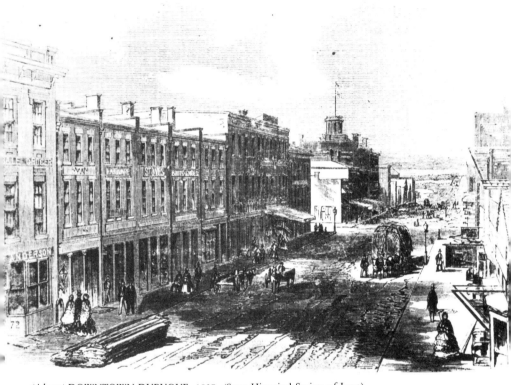

(Above) DOWNTOWN DUBUQUE, 1857. (State Historical Society of Iowa)

(Left) UPTOWN DUBUQUE, 1857. (State Historical Society of Iowa)

CITY OF DAVENPORT, IOWA.

DES MOINES, from Capital Hill, 1857

7

Holding the Line for Order and Union: 1863

NEVER far from the minds of state and federal officials was the troubled situation in the southern tier counties. State militia units there, dubbed the Iowa Border Brigade, always received more materiel support than others on the sensible assumption that they needed it more. Missourians seeking to escape harassment at the hands of both "loyalist" and "secesh" bushwhackers continued to move into Iowa as they had been doing since the start of the war, carrying their grudges with them. Though their numbers included every type from respectable merchants to thieves, they all had one common characteristic, a Decatur county man told Kirkwood. None of them joined the army, which meant that Decatur could not fill its enlistment quota. Moreover, this made the county even more pro-Southern than it already was.[1] War men also complained that some commanders were careless about whom they let into the Border Brigade. Some Davis county petitioners, on the other hand, charged that the guard served no useful purpose except as a haven from the draft. Guard Captain Hosea Horn disagreed. Twelve of the twenty petitioners, he said, were his personal enemies, seventeen were bitter political enemies. Besides, they preferred that persons of "doubtful loyalty" control his company. Davis county's board of supervisors agreed with the petitioners.[2] But the guard remained intact. State officials weren't taking any chances with doubtful Davis. The question just how doubtful Taylor county was revealed a difference of opinion between two Taylor citizens. The county had only one disloyal man and he bothered no one, wrote J. A. Hewes to Kirkwood. But Taylor county wasn't all that loyal according to Capt. John Flick. Southern sympathizers paraded their sentiments openly in Platteville. Nevertheless, Flick did agree that the county's guard unit was a focal point of discontent. He suggested that Platteville's guard activity be restricted to periods of emergency in order to avoid a local explosion.[3]

J. M. Hiatt, provost marshal for the border region, and W. D. Gallagher, special agent from the Treasury Department, gave a gloomy assessment of the border in early 1863. Gallagher predicted social convulsion if the army didn't take Vicksburg soon. Hiatt claimed widespread disloyal sentiment existed and wanted the Border Brigade mobilized and better armed. Capt. F. W. Johnson of the

Clarke county guard added nothing to Hiatt's peace of mind by telling him that the KGC was alive and threatening to clean up abolitionist Osceola. Clarke county, said the captain, was a good Union county, but with patriots joining the army the "secesh" had become insolent. In addition, Clarke's KGCs bragged that they could count on the assistance of two hundred helpers from Decatur county and five hundred from Madison to do the job on Osceola.[4]

Madison again! Obviously Herbert Hoxie's raids the previous summer had done no good. Winterset's loyal populace needed arms, wrote worried J. M. Holiday to Kirkwood. Kirkwood agreed, and ordered Adjutant General Baker to supply them. Hoxie, figuring he would have to make another sweep, asked Kirkwood and Congressman John Kasson to pressure the War Department into giving him weapons and manpower, possibly the Border Brigade. Thus prepared, he could disarm Winterset's Copperheads who, days earlier, had freely roamed the streets and ordered a Fourth Iowa recruiter out of town.[5] Further cries of alarm came from Horace Everett, Fifth Congressional District collector of customs. Warren, Lucas, and Wayne county secessionists threatened to resist the government, he wrote. Secessionist Missourians, driven out of Missouri, added to the problem. So did disloyal public officials. Cowed unionists wanted help. They wanted the Governor to declare martial law, Marshal Hiatt to remove the errant officials, secessionists disarmed, and the Missourians arrested and sent back where they belonged. Kirkwood again took notice. Everett asked too much. To suspend the writ of habeas corpus and remove public officials would be unwise, the Governor told Stanton, but the marshals and the United States District Attorney should receive clear instructions to get rid of the Missourians. He asked for more arms and for authority to organize two or three regiments to function as a state guard. That same day, March 23, Kirkwood issued a proclamation to the people of Iowa. He warned them against Missouri intruders, particularly the guerillas and former rebels among them. He asked the citizens to report their presence to the district attorney, the marshals, or to him. Send names and affidavits, he said, "showing their criminality before coming to this State and their conduct since, to the end that our State may be relieved of the danger of their presence."[6] No wholesale deportation of Missourians occurred, but Corydon in Wayne county still simmered. In July a band of Missourians invaded the town. They beat up a few Democrats including William Morret, editor of the *South-Tier Democrat,* and Sheriff James Carter before riding off. Why this incident occurred is not clear. The Democrats saw its genesis in guard Capt. E. F. Esteb's following through on the Kirkwood call to expel troublesome Missourians. Esteb took Kirkwood at his word, arrested Dr. H. M. Bowman, an "active and fearless Democrat," and thrust him into Missouri. When Bowman's friends talked about filing kidnapping charges against Esteb, he called on the Missourians for help, according to the Democrats.[7] In the most serious border trouble of 1863, Provost Marshal Felix Van Eaton lost his life in a Fremont county ambush. Van Eaton became suspicious of five or six strangers he observed passing through Sidney. Wanting to determine their "real character," he and his assistants tracked them through the countryside and into disaster. The assailants escaped. Within two weeks an explosion and fire destroyed Sidney's courthouse. Although both incidents apparently resulted from unsettled border conditions and the war, most observers didn't lay the blame on the Democrats. They knew that bushwhackers and guerillas came in all political colorations.[8]

As to the KGC, the belief persisted that it or similar secret groups flourished and that it intended to resist the draft, resist payment of war taxes, impede enlistments, and in other ways sabotage the effort to defeat the South.[9] W. W. Junkin, no more of an alarmist than most, believed that the KGC was alive and well in Jefferson county in the winter of 1863. That a Copperhead farmer in the northwest part of the county had ordered members of his family to blow no horn after nightfall constituted Junkin's evidence. Blowing a horn, Junkin explained, obviously served as a signal "to draw [knights] together, in case their treasonable designs are discovered and an attempt made to frusrate them."[10] Brighton postmaster L. B. Fleak, always alert to smell out Democratic conspiracies, told Kirkwood that some loyal men joined a secret society in Washington to act as informers. Why shouldn't Brighton Republicans reverse the process, he asked, by organizing a disloyal society to trap local Copperheads?[11] Senator Grimes believed a society known as the Sons of '76 existed in Iowa and that its members intended to resist federal laws and to "effect a rising."[12]

A series of worried letters from Hoxie and Kirkwood to Washington in February and March described increasing unrest in several southern Iowa counties, supposedly sparked by secret armed societies. These included Clarke, Decatur, and Madison. Both men urgently requested arms for loyal citizens and assignment of a provost guard of 100 mounted cavalry to the region to cope with expected trouble.[13] New London harbored a Sons of '76 lodge according to two men, Richard Root, a recruiter for the Eighteenth Iowa, and J. T. F. Carr. They submitted depositions detailing what they had learned about the organization's supposedly pro-Confederate objectives, methods, and secrets from an evening spent spying on one of its meetings.[14] In Keokuk the port collector confiscated what observers called an arsenal of weapons presumably destined for KGC lodges and Copperhead communities in the interior of the state.[15] From the Oskaloosa *Herald* came a lurid story relating the confessions of a dying soldier who said he joined the army to organize the KGC lodges among the troops. The state KGC headquarters, he said, operated out of Dubuque. Among its leaders were Dennis Mahony and Stilson Hutchins. A fellow soldier claimed he verified the two editors' connection. This may, however, have been a tale too tall for even a true believer to swallow. The *Times* gave it front page space, but in very small type, and editorialized in general terms only about secret organizations existing in Dubuque. The Dubuque *Herald,* contrary to its usual style, ignored the story altogether.[16]

During the last half of the year, reports of secret society activities diminished markedly. But the Tally War promoted one more deposition, this from H. B. Rogers, who claimed that Cyphert Tally had been a leader of the subversive Order of the Star in Keokuk county. Rogers declared that he had been an Order member who underwent a change of heart when his northwest Keokuk county lodge was ordered to join the Skunk River Army after Tally's death. Instead he rode off to Davenport to join the Eighth Iowa Cavalry, stopping overnight in Iowa City to give his deposition before a notary public.[17] Hoxie, Congressman Grinnell, and the new state Governor, William M. Stone, continued into 1864 to believe that secret societies were strong in the state, although the names were sometimes different. Hoxie believed the Union Relief Society had replaced the old KGC. Stone was sure the Sons of Liberty had penetrated Iowa from strongholds in other states.[18]

Democrats viewed Hoxie's periodic bursts of activity with increasing concern. And even as Hoxie talked about the need to smash Democratic secret societies, they observed the emergence of secret societies among their opponents, the Union Leagues, or Loyal Leagues. Yet there was no concerted Democratic move to follow suit, certainly not on the statewide scale Hoxie believed. When the Dubuque *Herald* reluctantly concluded in mid-March that Democrats should organize "to defend . . . against midnight conspirators and would-be assassins," nothing happened. The *Herald* repeated its suggestion several times through late summer, meeting opposition from Dubuque's Bishop Clement Smyth who warned Catholics to stay out of secret societies or face excommunication. The *Herald* never called for organization of secret societies. Bishop Smyth, however, assumed such protective societies inevitably would be secret. He also believed several of Dubuque's Catholics were members. Specifically addressing the county's foreign-born, he asked them to do nothing to decrease their loyalty to their adopted country.[19] In Louisa county, Democrats took a stand against secret societies.[20] By October, 1863, cautious Charles Mason believed that Democrats might have to form secret groups to counteract Republican organizations.[21] *Statesman* editor William Merritt wrote Mason in February of 1864 that he too saw no alternative to the formation of secret societies if the party were to save the nation from ruin.[22]

Civil War historians now generally agree that Democratic secret societies such as the KGC, the Sons of Liberty, the Sons of '76, the Order of American Knights, and others never achieved the vast organizational structure or effectiveness with which excited Republicans credited them, or that they even existed at all in most areas of the North. Certainly Iowa's leading Democratic figures had no more substantive knowledge of them than the average Republican newspaper reader. At the very time when Hoxie and Kirkwood professed deepest concern with such groups, Charles Negus wrote Mason in some wonder, "The Republicans charge the democrats with being member of the KGC . . . if they know of such an order with us they are better informed than I am." On the other hand, it seems clear that if Iowa's leading Democrats had ever organized in such a manner, which they didn't, Iowa's Republicans caused them to think about it. Negus' letter to Mason continued: "I have always opposed secret political organizations. But some claim the exigencies of the times demand them. What is your opinion?"[23] Recall that it was the next month before the *Herald* openly proposed formation of secret groups and that it was nearly a year later before Merritt favored them "if necessary."

Evidence of secret Copperhead societies in Iowa's archives leaves much to be desired. There are no captured membership rolls or official records of meetings. But there are several notarized statements, records of interviews, "spy" reports, and "code" messages relating to secret organizations. What the first three types of evidence seem to reveal—and inconclusively at best—is that: (1) In 1862, Confederate agents or secret society organizers from Missouri or farther south may have tried to establish contact with opponents of the war in southern Iowa to promote what are generally recognized as the aims of antiwar secret societies. (2) Some secret organizations probably existed, but they, most likely, were entirely home grown. Located in southern Iowa counties, their members talked among themselves against the war and against federal and state activities designed to implement the war effort in Iowa. (3) Some groups employed elaborate secret passwords and ritualistic identification procedures. (4) The members talked earnestly about using violence if necessary to protect themselves from the draft, arbitrary arrests, and the real or presumed aggressiveness of war-supporting neighbors and groups, and to avoid paying war taxes. (5) The memories of individuals who recalled for interviewers the activities of secret societies long after the fact (as late as 1927 in one case) were fallible on specific details, but they did recall and understand some activities and tensions which divided their communities during the war.[24]

Much less convincing are two "intercepted documents" of the KGC. One dated March 9, 1863, at Dubuque purports to be a letter from: "W. A. Chief of [convenient ink blot]d division, Western Department of the K.G.C." to "My Dear Brother of the X + X Order of the K.G.C." This communication, supposedly from the division commander to a district chieftan, discusses organizational plans and membership drives, and refers knowingly to various codes, "books," oaths, and KGC "police policy." It also hints that the organization contemplates acting against its enemies.

The second and third "documents" are "Order No. 198" and "Order No. 199," ostensibly KGC code messages. Number 198 is a hodgepodge of letters, numbers, and signs filling in line after line except when interspersed with English text ranging from one to 14 words in length. Number 198's first paragraph reads:

> ls x v.i.c. 1863. A:44-L - P33 cc the extent I 18cc N.P.T. the Institution of Slavery according to the old constitution with important alterations sufficient to xi or + kG. to cc - F
>
> Rule this continent - X
>
> sway the world xxc 1900.

Number 199 is similar to 198 except that it possesses more (but also less intelligible) text and less code.[25]

What Governor Kirkwood or Adjutant General Baker thought of these, they did not say. On some of the many letters received by these two men which told about alleged traitors and their organizations, they wrote special notes or instructions to each other or to their subordinates if they thought the letters were particularly important. There are no such notes on these three. At least one Republican was suspicious of such proof. S. S. Daniels, editor of the Tipton *Advertizer*, reluctantly passed to Kirkwood an anonymous but persistent Tipton citizen's "secret revelations." Daniels suggested that the Governor file the material for awhile.[26]

Most run-of-the-mill Iowa county histories which mentioned secret Copperhead societies claimed they did indeed exist during the war. But they rarely supplied evidence to justify their claims. Two of the better histories express different views. Frank Hickenlooper's account of Monroe county life during the conflict deprecated the charge that Monroe had KGC lodges. Hickenlooper asserted that had such groups existed, loyal citizens would have apprehended the members.[27] Less certain was a Mahaska county writer. He reported in 1878 that longtime county residents differed on the existence of the KGC. Some claimed they were well organized and corresponded with other lodges in neighboring counties. Others flatly denied this and maintained that "in any cases of companies of men visiting the county seat or elsewhere, they were banded simply by community or sentiment." Even so, the Mahaska writer wrote, men whose veracity no one questioned on ordinary subjects had declared under oath that they attended KGC meetings in disguise.[28]

Iowa's Republican newspapers frequently charged that KGC lodges promoted discord and violence in the state. But they were no more successful than Marshal Hoxie in finding proof which linked the lodges, if any, to specific illegal acts, much less in finding concrete evidence of a communications network between Iowa groups or with groups in other states. Yet Hickenlooper's belief that no secret groups existed is probably erroneous. Monroe county was in the midst of southern Iowa's Copperhead country. Some of Monroe's angry Democrats very likely did congregate secretly because of "community or sentiment" or what the Mahaska writer called "mutual understanding" in opposition to the activities of eager war partisans. The same was probably true of many other southern Iowa counties where Democrats had long enjoyed political influence and were not ready to acquiesce silently in the aims of their equally partisan and aggressive political opponents.

The various depositions in the Des Moines archives may all have some basis in fact. It would be strange if angry Democrats had not met both formally or informally and secretly to talk politics, vent anti-Republican steam, and devise plans to keep Marshal Hoxie and other Republican zealots off their backs. That they might talk about resisting draft officials or home guards, who were often more than a little obnoxious as they sought to enforce their will on outspoken Democrats, is not strange either. That they had weapons and talked about using them was hardly unusual in a day when many Iowans supplemented their diet with the wild turkey, deer, and squirrels which abounded in the countryside. If they rode together into town when feelings between war and peace factions ran high, that was not only neighborly but also good sense—call it "sentiment" and "mutual understanding."

Much of the deposition of Hoxie's "detective" George Rose about Madison county's KGC members has to be suspect on the grounds of self-interest. Rose preferred not to be prosecuted for smuggling arms across the Missouri border. Lt. Richard Root was a recruiter, but even in staunchly Republican Henry county, recruiters did not always have an easy job. He and J. T. F. Carr doubtless heard something as they hid one night in a New London building spying on some local citizens who appeared to act secretively. However, listening through a wall and looking through a fissure as they did, probably provided them with much less information than turned up in Root's very explicit and detailed report. Imagination, hearsay, and conjecture—perhaps honest, but certainly fallible—played a role. There may have been an Order of the Star group in northwest Keokuk county. Whether there was or not, this was Cyphert Tally's stomping ground, and there were enough enraged Democrats around who on the spur of the moment could have decided they were going to band together, ride off, and avenge his death. H. B. Rogers could well have decided, however, that this was not his kind of fight for any number of reasons, including honest and sensible ones— and that to put a good face on them wouldn't hurt anything.

Finally, there were likely some groups similar to the one at Tipton, organized on July 28, 1863, calling itself the "Independent Military Company of Mounted Riflemen." The Riflemen asserted that they had "organized for the purpose of assisting the proper authorities in enforcing the laws of the government, upholding the Constitution of the United States and the State of Iowa, and for the further purpose of protecting the rights of citizens, preserving order and quietness in the community." The purpose sounds clear enough, and it made sense to the Riflemen. But the writer of this portion of the county history identifies the group and its eighty-odd signers as an organization to resist tax collectors, the draft, and military arrests. Some of the signers had not paid their taxes for 1861 as of September, 1862, and may have been protestors against the war at an early date.[29]

As they did in 1862, Marshal Herbert Hoxie and his deputies resorted to arbitrary arrests to break up the supposed secret societies. Hoxie kept Grenville Dodge apprised of his activities. He told Dodge in early July that he hoped to win "some" convictions in court. Copperheads feared him everywhere except at Des Moines, his headquarters; and they "skipped out" when he arrived in other communities, he bragged.[30] In the period June-August, 1863, he concentrated on Henry, Decatur, Clarke, Wapello, and Mahaska counties. Arrests there, plus others over the state, became so common that summer that the *Iowa State Register* for a time employed two standing headlines, "Arbitrary Arrests" and "More Arbitrary Arrests." It was not always wise to intercede for arrest victims. Four Decatur men who came to Des Moines in behalf of the Decatur arrestees landed in jail also, thanks to Hoxie's caprice.[31] Aided by troops from the Border Brigade, Hoxie, in one late July raid, arrested twelve men, nine from Wapello county and three from Mahaska. A grand jury indicted the men for "conspiracy against the Government." Among those in the Wapello group was J. H. D. Street, editor of the Ottumwa *Mercury*. A Street associate on the *Mercury* maintained that to be so arrested was an honor rather than a shame.[32] Nevertheless, most arrestees acted as if it were an honor they could do without. They made strenuous efforts to regain their freedom. Some won release almost immediately without being charged. Some won release on bail and never underwent further prosecution. Some received paroles after periods of detention. Others, out on bail, traveled to district court as many as four times expecting to be tried, only to find that for one reason or another their cases were continued to another term of court. For a few men this process dragged on over a year and a half before they got off the hook, usually when the prosecutors dropped the charges.[33]

Hoxie did not order the arrest of contentious Copperhead orator-minister Henry Clay Dean. But he was not displeased when an impulsive group of Keokuk's convalescent soldiers arrested Dean on what could best be described as general principles. They turned him over to Provost Marshal Hiatt. Hiatt hoped to come up with evidence that would justify sending Dean to his superiors at St. Louis so they could deport him to the Confederacy as President Lincoln had done with Ohio's Clement Vallandigham. But he could not; he reluctantly let Dean go on July 11 after holding him nearly a month.[34] Although Dean was not universally popular among Iowa's Democrats, his arrest sparked considerable anger. Dean claimed to have suffered "savage treatment" at the hands of his captors. But it is apparent that he got off more easily than most other political arrestees in Iowa in 1863. Not only did Dean get out sooner, but he also struck up a friendship with E. M. Amsden, the deputy provost marshal who had developed two field-piece weapons for military use which he and Dean hoped to promote for their mutual profit. Two of the many sides of Dean's extraordinary character are so sharply etched in a letter he wrote to Charles Mason from jail that part of it is reproduced below. Dean wrote that he feared no foe but would:

> abide by the determination of the powers and of course submit—I have no power to do anything. . . . It would be folly for me to undertake to make a mulish war in my Physical Person against a million of Bayonets if I desire to. I shall of course maintain my principles and convictions unchanged and my integrity as a man and my manhood as a Citizen though I perish with my life or suffer ten thousand deaths. I have always been honest and shall be true to myself.
>
> Now the principle object of this letter is of a purely business character and is this:
>
> Mr. E. M. *Amsden* the Deputy Provost Marshal of this Post under Mr. J. M. Hiatt is the inventor of two most extraordinary Field Pieces a description of which he will send you. . . . I regard one of them as the most extraordinary in its power, practicability for use on the field of battle, and availability in every kind of action.
>
> My honest convictions are that there is in these two guns an independent fortune only second to the pistols of Colt. . . . I think that there is money in it—a heavy pile.

But there was a problem, Dean told Mason. Amsden had no money; and no successful weapons contractors and manufacturers already making money from their own products would help him manufacture and market his inventions. Therefore, he and Dean believed it best to test them in Europe. Success there would lead to general adoption in the United States. Accordingly, he commended the matter to Mason's attention and suggested that Mason observe the weapons in operation. "They have been fired many times," Dean continued, "and are said to operate at a most decided success having many elements of destruction unknown to modern guns." Mason, he suggested, might be able to interest American investors. Then Dean concluded, "It may be that I shall go to Europe if I am released. Be kind enough to say to the gentlemen who assail me that *it requires but* little courage to attack a prisoner surrounded by bayonets."[35] For one uncowed Copperhead, the war, and temporary incarceration, were both a curse and an opportunity.

There were times when the regional provost marshal clashed with local judges in arrest cases. Marshal Snow at Ottumwa refused to obey a writ of habeas corpus issued by Judge H. H. Trimble. Judge H. B. Hendershott, also of Ottumwa, clashed with Snow in a similar case.[36] Although most Republicans, and probably some War Democrats, approved the arrests of political dissenters, a few had qualms. Mrs. Seneca B. Thrall, whose doctor husband was serving with the Thirteenth Iowa, asked him: If conscience compelled one to freely disapprove of the acts of the administration, was one a traitor? Dr. Thrall gave a serious response to a serious question.

> Difference of opinion, discussion and opposition to certain measures and opinions of government may be and *is* tolerated. But the fact of the *existence* of *revolution* of civil war makes an ill defined boundary beyond which serious opposition should not be tolerated. . . . If conscience approves it [secession-revolution] it is not because of *right* but because of a clouded mind and Misguided reason.[37]

Over a year later Republican John Miller of Iowa City seemed reconciled like Dr. Thrall to the necessity for political arrests, but he still had a concern for the rule of law. Miller wrote Adjutant General Baker that he had heard that Baker had threatened to make political arrests with or without recourse to required legal processes. Miller hoped this was not true and that Baker would clarify his position. What Baker wrote in reply, or if he wrote at all, is unknown.[38]

Dean's arrest and the Wapello and Mahaska county arrests attracted much attention, but more common were arrests of deserters and those who supposedly aided them. Throughout the first part of 1863 these constituted the bulk of arbitrary arrest stories in Iowa papers, chronicled more thoroughly in the *Iowa State Register* than elsewhere. Then with the passage of the conscription act, men accused of resisting enrollment appeared more and more frequently on the arrest lists. Sometimes the arrests assumed the air of a spectacular. Marshal Hoxie used over thirty armed guardsmen to make his biggest score when he swooped down on Story county to round up twenty-two Irish railroad workers charged with "driving off the Enrolling Officers with clubs and pick-axes."[39] Neither Hoxie nor state officials ever underestimated the size and strength of their opponents. They fed each others' fears; these in turn stemmed from the fears of "loyalists" who kept them informed about trouble spots, suspected secret society members, and about those believed to be stirring up antiwar sentiment among soldiers. Recruiters who had trouble filling quotas also reported those persons and those communities hindering their efforts. One recruiter complained that two fast-talking peace men in the Richland area persuaded eight prospects to change their minds about enlisting. Winterset gave recruiter Lt. G. A. Henry such a hard time that J. M. Holiday, editor of the local *Hawk-eye Flag,* circulated a petition asking Kirkwood to bring a company of recruits from Davenport to do their training in Winterset. Their presence might bolster the town's jittery Union men, Holiday believed.[40] Kirkwood thought the situation across the state was so serious that a draft would lead to violence unless the War Department supplied loyal citizens with 5,000 guns and ammunition.[41]

Meanwhile the Governor also became increasingly worried about reports that some Iowans were writing letters to soldiers which tried to undermine their morale and cause them to desert. Some evidence came from Brighton postmaster L. B. Fleak. Fleak was not one to let regulations interfere with duty. When a Brighton Copperhead neglected to seal a letter to his soldier son, Fleak summoned a witness, read the letter, copied it, sent the copy to Kirkwood, then sent the original on its way. If Fleak's work was accurate, one soldier in the Thirtieth Iowa did indeed receive a letter telling him to desert and to return home to help resist the draft. Fleak also told Kirkwood that many such letters left Brighton and that he had asked Lt. James Smith of the Thirtieth Iowa to try to get hold of some. Other Kirkwood informants told him the same thing. Peter Wilson didn't write the Governor. But he told his folks that "Sometimes I see letters to the boys in this Regiment [the Fourteenth] so full of Secesh notions that if the writers were exposed they would be severly punished, letters encouraging desertion & c."[42]

Finally Kirkwood acted. On March 28, 1863, he issued a proclamation to Iowa soldiers urging them to send him any letters that counseled them to desert. Hoxie followed suit and asked Grenville Dodge to have someone collect such letters for him. He would use them to try to get indictments against the writers in the May term of the United States Circuit Court in Des Moines.[43] Whether the proclamation choked off such letters or whether there were many in the first place, soldiers did not flood the Governor's office with incriminating mail.

During this period officials continued to anticipate violence stemming from attempts to enforce the conscription act. The New York draft riots did nothing to alleviate their fears. Nor, presumably, did a Dubuque *Herald* editorial declaring that eastern Democrats need not heed a call to arms to resist Lee's impending invasion. Let Lincoln and his "traitorous Administration" defend themselves; in fact, said the paper, Democrats had a duty to withhold service until they were certain they would be used to defend the laws and the Constitution, not to "carry into effect partisan theories and projects. . . ."[44] As to the riots, the *Herald* claimed that they stemmed from the fact that the draft act was unconstitutional and discriminatory. Edward Thayer argued that revoking the Emancipation Proclamation would end both rioting and the need for a draft. But David Richardson had no sympathy for the rioters. A law is a law, he said, and the government should bring lawbreakers to justice. Richardson did suggest, however, that tax money go to poor draftees so they could buy exemptions like the rich.[45]

General John Pope, who three weeks later was much more relaxed about the Tally affair, accepted Republican fears and Copperhead rhetoric at face value. He believed veteran federal troops might be needed to maintain order in Iowa during the actual drafting process.[46] The government sent no troops, but two incidents in the northeastern part of the state demonstrated that a tense situation existed there. In July, Deputy United States Marshal P. H. Conger and assistants arrested two Clayton county men for violation of the conscription act. Lodged in jail in Dubuque, they won release on a writ of habeas corpus signed by Stephen Hempstead, county judge. The men quickly filed kidnapping charges against Conger and his men. When the Marshal and his deputies appeared before C. J. Chapline in justice court, they secured their release on $5,000 bail. Here the confrontation ended, and nothing further happened to either the Clayton men or to the marshals; but the incident provoked acid comment throughout Iowa about Copperhead justice in Dubuque.[47] Then in August, Wendel Jacobi of Peru township, Dubuque county, died at his home from gunshot wounds when provost marshal officers botched their attempt to arrest him for desertion. Jacobi's brother Adam suffered serious wounds at the same time but survived. The coroner's jury found that Jacobi died at the hand of an unknown person "wilfully." But the grand jury, which did learn who fired the fatal shots, namely, William Hungerford, deputy provost marshal from Allamakee county, failed to resolve conflicting testimony on the sequence of events given by the participants. Accordingly, it returned no indictments, a development which infuriated Dubuque county Democrats.[48] At Davenport the provost marshal confiscated a shipment of rifles which he believed to be destined for draft resisters in Poweshiek county. And from Burlington came reports that numerous armed men, who were preparing to resist federal officers, skulked on islands in the Mississippi.[49]

The strongest blast against the draft came from John Gharkey of the *Fayette County Pioneer*. Wrote Gharkey, "You should resist the conscription with your rifles, your shotguns, or whatever weapons you get hold of. If you, young men, do not resist conscription you are unworthy to be called American citizens. . . ."[50] Others were more prudent. Dennis Mahony employed arguments based on his reading of the Constitution to build a case against conscription. Mahony claimed that the draft was legal only when it operated through requisitions by the federal government on state authorities. To an extent this evaded the central question whether any draft was acceptable. But he soon took care of that. "The rights of the people to life," he wrote, "are superior to that of the Government for existence"; if the people didn't want to preserve the government, the government couldn't force them to do so. Like most critics he hit hardest at the discriminatory nature of the $300 exemption clause. And Stilson Hutchins bluntly asked if the rich would have accepted the conscription law if it had been "so drawn up as to place the burden upon men in proportion to their ability to pay it. . . ."[51] W. W. Junkin, however, remained skeptical of Democrats who said they opposed the draft because of the $300 exemption provision. They would likely resist a draft call even if there were no such exemption, he guessed. But the $300 clause was not popular either with the abolitionist German language paper in Davenport. The editor favored formation of private associations to buy exemptions for men whose families needed them.[52]

When it became apparent that draft machinery was going to move into gear, the *Herald* printed a two column story explaining what physical problems would win a man exemption from service. It also printed information on other ways to secure an exemption.[53] There were enough ablebodied enlistees, however, to fill the state's quota. On October 6 the War Department informed Governor Kirkwood that Iowa's total enlistments from 1861 on gave the state an excess of 1,281 men. The excess, happily, could be applied to Iowa's account in future calls.[54]

Adjutant General Baker deserves some credit for insuring that those Iowans who went into the service in 1863 were a useful lot. In August he visited the Eighth Iowa Cavalry, then being formed in Davenport. Baker weeded out between 80 and 100 young boys and old men, mainly the former. They were, he said, "subject to be habeas corpused, to fill the first hospital the regiment might encounter, or line a long road with sick on the first forced march." The skeptical Adjutant General returned soon and winnowed 12 more recruits out of the unit. They might make good soldiers in five or six years, he declared, but now they would have to go back to their mothers since the government had not "completed its nursery department as yet."[55]

Baker, not unexpectedly, was unhappy with aliens who sought exemptions in 1863. He published the numbers and names of aliens in each of the six congressional districts who sought alienage exemptions, listing also their country of origin. David Richardson went a step further. In the *Democrat* he published the names of Scott county's claimants under the inflammatory heading "Sneak List." To no one's surprise the Irish topped the state list in 1863 with 235 names out of 508, coming primarily from Dubuque and other river counties. Aliens from Denmark, Norway, and Sweden followed with 116. Those from the German states numbered 83. Surprisingly, Winneshiek, a Scandinavian stronghold, led all Iowa counties including Dubuque by a wide margin with 144. Dubuque had 95, Clinton 61, Scott 54, and Johnson 32. When a partial list of alienage exemptions came out at the end of 1864 revealing a similar pattern, Baker waxed indignant. But his indignation was selective. He said nothing about the great number of Scandinavian alienage claimants, while heaping scorn upon Germans who could "crawl away from duty under the protection of some little German principality. . . ." Irish received equally short shrift from the Adjutant General. They sought liberty in the United States, he complained, but were unwilling to protect it.[56]

Iowa's escape from the draft in 1863 did not, of course, end the debate over who should serve, who should not, or whether anybody should at all. Ira C. Mitchell of the *State Democratic Press* took a position common among Copperhead Democrats when he wrote that "Men who think it is their duty to strengthen the already mighty arm of the Washington despotism, owe it to their conscience and their country to volunteer. . . ." Thomas Clagett contributed a different view after reporting how three other Iowa papers looked at the draft and military service. The Burlington *Hawk-eye* declared that the October election results revealed that Republicans joined the army while Democrats did not. The authorities should, therefore, conscript Democrats in the next draft. Absolutely not, retorted the Burlington *Argus* and the Dubuque *Herald*. Republican abolitionists brought on the war; Democrats should have no part of it. Clagett rejected both positions. In a war "constitutionally declared by legally constituted authorities," he wrote, all men should share equally in the fight. Demonstrating a talent for reverse logic, the Keokuk maverick argued that the worse the government managed public affairs, the more the people should support it to save it from self-destruction.[57]

For those who rejected Clagett's or any other rationale for going to war, there was the possibility of escaping the draft through membership in a private association which would put up the necessary money to hire substitutes for members called to serve; or one might use public funds voted by cities or counties to pay the $300 exemption for those who desired it. LeGrand Byington, state Democratic central committee chairman for 1863, promoted the latter scheme. Ultimately the method most commonly employed was to use public money, often supplemented by private funds, to pay bounties to those enlisting to the credit of the county. Purist Stilson Hutchins opposed a bounty system in February, 1863, on the ground that the war was a bad war in the first place, this despite the fact that Dubuque county had spurred enlistments for a short period during the summer of 1862 by offering $50 to volunteers enlisting to Dubuque's credit.[58] Less of a purist in the fall of 1863, Hutchins called for reelection of Democrats to the county board of supervisors who had fought successfully to get the board to consider selling bonds to raise money to pay the $300 exemption for those who wanted it. Keokuk's Democratic-dominated city council, however, voted down a resolution to levy a special tax to pay the exemption for Keokuk citizens who didn't want to be drafted. Boone county's supervisors, supposedly Copperhead controlled, also refused to pay enlistment bounties.[59]

Whether Democratic enlistments lagged proportionally behind Republican enlistments at this point in the war is yet a matter of conjecture. Whatever the case, in Harrison county, even when Democrats did enlist, "scores" of Republicans who stayed out of the army professed doubt about the enlistees' sincerity, claimed Harrison's articulate historian Joe H. Smith. Smith, in rhetoric common to that era, but uncommon in a county history written for sale in a Republican state, declared those Republicans to be "cowards and political tricksters . . . guilty of contemptible depravity."[60]

Whether Union forces should enlist black soldiers was a subject of spirited debate on many different grounds. Democrats almost always opposed such enlistments. So did many Republicans until black troops performed successfully in the field. Democrat David Richardson felt white men alone should shoulder the burden of preserving the white man's country. Republican G. T. Stewart of the Dubuque *Times* opposed black service on the grounds that if the white man with his "intelligence and bravery" could not save the nation, the "poor, subservient ignorant negro slave" never could either. But the Iowa City *Republican* believed the Union should use any help it could get including armed blacks. So did *Der Demokrat* which suggested that President Lincoln had suspiciously Democratic tendencies on the subject.[61]

In the summer of 1862, Alexander Clark, a Muscatine black, wrote Kirkwood asking that the state organize black companies to serve in Iowa's regiments. In Kirkwood's absence, his secretary, Nathan H. Brainerd, sent Clark a thoughtful but negative reply. "You know better than I," he wrote, "the prejudices of our people for you have felt them more severely and you know your color would not be tolerated in one of our regiments. However wrong this may be we cannot ignore the fact." Kirkwood and Senators Grimes and Harlan did favor black enlistments in principle, Grimes and Kirkwood being more blunt as to the reason. Grimes told Dubuque citizens that he would rather "see a Negro shot down in battle than the son of a Dubuquer." And Kirkwood wrote Henry Halleck that he would not regret it if at the end of the war "that a part of the dead are niggers and that not all are whites."[62] But many Iowa soldiers well into 1863 often expressed violent dislike toward blacks and opposed their enlistment, particularly after the Emancipation Proclamation.[63] Finally, from June on, a few soldiers began to report otherwise and commented favorably upon black enlistments and black valor in battle.[64]

In late July, Kirkwood, with some reluctance, proposed to Stanton that Iowa be allowed to enlist a regiment of black soldiers. Stanton quickly agreed and authorized the raising of a three-year regiment, each enlistee to be paid $10 a month, $3 of it in clothes, and one daily ration. The blacks were to receive no enlistment bounty. Six companies recruited in Iowa soon joined with four more companies from other states to make up the First Iowa African Infantry. The Iowa black enlistees, coming from a total black populace estimated variously from less than 1,500 to 2,000, may have included nearly all the pool of eligible black males in the state. The unit saw no combat, but performed guard and garrison duty in St. Louis and in other parts of the lower Mississippi Valley. Kirkwood's reluctance stemmed from his belief that there weren't enough available blacks in Iowa and because he had heard that some self-styled loyal Missourians might prowl around the regimental camp and try to claim some of the enlistees as fugitive slaves.[65]

Sarcastic encouragement for black recruitment came from Iowa City where the *State Democratic Press* hoped that the recruiters would take every "buck nigger out of our city." Ignoring the small number of available blacks, the Dubuque *Herald* proclaimed the recruiting drive a failure when recruiters came up four companies short of a full regiment of Iowans.[66] Abusive stories about black troops remained a distinguishing feature of some Democratic organs to the end of the war.[67] On the other side of the coin, beginning in late 1863 with an *Iowa State Register* story praising Iowa's black troops, Republican journals began to defend Union black units and to flay those who scorned them.[68] Thomas Clagett, long an opponent of black enlistments, finally began to complain about substitute brokers from Quincy, Illinois, paying Keokuk blacks $400 to enlist to the credit of Quincy and Hancock county. Black enlistments to the credit of Lee county were now quite acceptable to the mercurial Keokuk editor.[69] Charles Mason, who scorned Northern black troops as cowards and barbarians, began to hope the Confederates would enlist blacks to help stem the Union tide late in the war. "The Confederates are about to call 200,000 negroes into their armies," he wrote. "Captain Lockwood thinks they make the best kind of troops. If so, they may trouble us yet."[70]

Coincident with a rise in racist rhetoric in 1863, some Iowans began to defend slavery once more, although such defenses probably represented a minority view even among the most conservative Democrats. In Dubuque, Thomas Monroe defended the system on biblical grounds before the Dubuque Catholic Institute and the city Democratic club. Monroe also employed statistics from the 1850 census purporting to show that criminality and pauperism ran rampant in New England's free states but not in the slave states. A letter in the Burlington *Argus* signed "Blank" defended bondage as "a moral reform institution founded and conducted on a magnificent scale. . . ." The *Herald* claimed that the Northern people had not abolished slavery out of principle. Consequently they would reinstitute it when they rediscovered how profitable it was. The paper also quoted a Dubuque black woman who supposedly found life so hard in the North that she longed to go back to her old master in Virginia. All other Dubuque blacks agreed with her, she said. David Richardson, no great defender of slavery, was sorely troubled about what would happen to blacks in freedom. Sending them back to Africa, he wrote, to "the darkness of barbarism [would be] an act of grossest inhumanity, by the side of which the worst form of slavery would be spotless white." Richardson doubted that black apprenticeship under white masters in a free economy would be any better than slavery. It would, in fact, be worse, since masters, freed from ownership responsibilities, would abuse their charges more than slaveowners ever had. He concluded that blacks probably would be better off in slavery for two hundred more years.[71]

Generally, however, antiblack rhetoric did not signal any rise in proslavery sentiment. It simply portrayed blacks as vicious, indolent, and unfit to live among whites; and it labeled their white friends as fools and hypocrites. Any time Democratic editors believed they had evidence of black males' alleged lust for white women they printed it. The *Times* perversely professed to believe that the *Herald*'s antiblack torrent stemmed from a lack of confidence "in the abilities of its supporters to resist the attraction of darkies. . . ." When the *Democrat* found what it thought was nativist sentiment among Davenport blacks it told the city's German and Irish to take note of these " 'American born citizens of African descent,' these kinky heads, who think themselves better than any foreign white man. . . ."[72] Thomas Clagett, who in 1862 appeared to be more abusive toward blacks than most other editors, seemed less so in the fall of 1863, at least compared with Stilson Hutchins. He reported news of alleged atrocities by black soldiers, but more often merely poked fun at blacks and questioned their intellectual capacity. When white youngsters, some of whom were supposedly sons of Republicans, scrapped with black youngsters, he lectured the young whites, saying, "That is all wrong boys. You should know better; especially you whose parents were instrumental in getting them here, that is if your fathers are honest in their principles, and practice that kindness at home which they preach about."[73]

Some Polk county Democrats tried to force implementation of the exclusion act of 1851 against Archie Webb, a farm worker in Delaware township who had escaped his Arkansas master. They failed when Fifth District Judge John Henry Grant ruled the law unconstitutional.[74] Davis county men had more success getting rid of a black laborer. Fifty-four of them seized him on February 9 and carried him off to Missouri. Two days later an opposite minded group of Bloomfield citizens thwarted efforts of three Missourians to abduct a black man working at a local hotel. The hotel worker soon fled Bloomfield. Captain Hosea Horn of the Border Brigade wrote N. B. Baker that there was little chance for successful legal action in the county against those who kidnapped blacks.[75]

Rumors that large numbers of blacks were en route to a community often excited angry citizen responses, including threats to keep them out by force. When less than six out of a rumored sixty contrabands came to Fairfield, W. W. Junkin had a laugh at the expense of "secesh Democrats."[76] But blacks did come, and at Keokuk they did enter the labor force at very low wages as their antagonists feared. One group of men, women, and children arrived unannounced on the *Jennie Dean* one evening from Arkansas and spent the night in the care of the Provost Marshal. Word of their arrival spread, and by nine the next morning, according to the *Gate City*, there were more applicants for their services than there were numbers. The men went to work for $8–$12 a month and the women for about $4. When two groups of eleven and thirteen blacks arrived at Dubuque, heading for Delaware and Hardin counties respectively, the *Herald* claimed they came by invitation. The paper also thought it had proof that the government was deliberately furnishing job competitors for poor whites. It cited a letter from an officer of the Thirty-Seventh Iowa at Schofield Barracks in St. Louis, which said that if Iowans wanted any contrabands he could send a lot, many of whom preferred to settle in Iowa. When over a score of blacks, mostly female and described as "hideous looking creatures," arrived at McGregor, many citizens were furious. Presumably they went to work for abolitionist households. "Some of our female philanthropists," stormed a townsman, "have advised the Norwegian, German and Irish girls to emigrate to the region of the Rocky Mountains and thus make room for the new order of things.'' He also speculated that fathers, brothers, and lovers of the allegedly fired white girls might even be serving under army officers who promoted ''such vile traffic.'' After a perceptible increase in the black population in July, some Dubuquers took direct action. They seized six new arrivals and set them adrift on the Mississippi. The *Herald* disapproved. The blacks were not at fault; treat them kindly, said the paper. Those to blame were men who persisted in forcing them on a white populace which didn't want them. In a classic understatement which obliquely answered the journalistic who and why, the *Herald* said, ''The hostility of a certain portion of the Caucasian race was excited by the state of things. . . .''[77] In Van Buren County's Chequist township, John Swiers refused to fire his black helper despite threats to burn him out and to shoot both him and the helper.[78]

Finally David Richardson unburdened himself in an extended discourse on Davenport's experience with its growing black populace. On first arrival, he wrote, they ''are not at all troublesome or vicious. They mind their own business, are respectful to their superiors, lazy but accommodating, and can be tolerated as a necessary evil.'' But after a while they became impossible. The first to disown them were their ''loud mouthed philanthropists.'' Then, if they were saved from trouble, if they were saved at all, their saviors were those who were supposed to be their worst enemies. Elaborating on the same theme, Richardson described the life of Davenport's blacks.

> Many of these Negroes are industrious, worthy characters, who have earned reputations for honesty and fidelity by faithful service and uniformly good conduct. They are respected by our citizens, and every right the law guarantees to the white man is guaranteed to them. Others of the race are exceedingly vicious and troublesome. Frequenting low negro gambling houses and saloons, they acquire villainous habits of intemperance and crime, and sooner or later wind up in the county prison or State Penitentiary.

Northerners were charitable, Richardson concluded. But if the troublesome blacks continued to act up, the legislature would pass removal laws, laws which would not discriminate between the desirable and the undesirable; therefore, they should ''render their presence in our midst as little obnoxious to the people as possible.''[79]

Edward Thayer sympathized with a group of contrabands temporarily staying in a Muscatine warehouse. Families faced separation, and the old ones were crying in despair. ''Though some of them may have been slaves for sixty-five years, yet they are just beginning to know what slavery is,'' Thayer wrote. ''God in his mercy stand between these poor creatures and their new masters.'' They would have less freedom than on Southern plantations; there would be no close associates to mingle with, no dances, songfests or holidays. Farmers, he believed, would find them unprofitable, and they would end up drifting into the towns, there to be supported by the taxpayers.[80] Peter Wilson doubtless reflected the attitude of most soldiers as well as that of most Iowa civilians when he wrote of contrabands he saw at Memphis, "They are a kind of people I would not like to have for neighbors." Frank Palmer also believed that blacks belonged to a "degraded race," but added that those who abused them were worse. Republicans sometimes catered to pervasive antiblack sentiment by arguing that even if blacks fought for the Union, owned their own labor and voted, they would remain unequal, their status still "just what God made it, in the scale of humanity." In the scale of humanity that was never much above the buffoon stage for the Council Bluffs *Nonpareil,* which was not exceptional among other Republican papers in attitude.[81] Most Mount Pleasant citizens may not have viewed blacks much differently, but some of them began to raise money to purchase or build a structure to serve as both school and church for the town's growing black population. The local Freedman's Aid Society not only sent aid to Southern blacks but also to destitute local blacks. The Society was embarrassed when it discovered that some sickly Mount Pleasant blacks had escaped their notice and died during the winter. Occasional reports on contrabands in the papers reveal that some of the migrants were elderly. One notable act of good will toward blacks occurred in Keosauqua where some citizens paid a young woman to run a school for twenty-two black students. Amy Sheppard's school, said the *Iowa State Register,* angered Keosauqua Copperheads who preferred that blacks remain as ignorant as themselves.[82]

If the general attitude of Iowans toward blacks was callous, or simply that they were a species apart and slightly less than fully human, it was the same toward Indians. Camp McClellan housed several hundred Indian prisoners taken when the army quelled the 1862 uprising in southern Minnesota. By March of 1864 only 250 remained. Small pox, reported the *Democrat* dispassionately, was "thinning them out rapidly. About twenty have been sent to the pest house within a week. This disease will probably have them much reduced in numbers."[83]

Despite early summer drought and unexpected frosts in August and September, Iowa's corn-hog economy did well in 1863 because of expanding markets in both the United States and in Great Britain. Estimates that the corn crop would reach only 34 million bushels proved to be far off the mark as the total hit nearly 64 million. Corn sold at 32¢ a bushel in August, then vaulted to 48¢ by October, and 55¢ by December.[84] Cattle sales eastward increased, and the Davenport *Democrat* suggested that cattle raising ought to be expanded, not only because of high profits but also because cattle raising supposedly required less labor than tilling the soil. And by the fall of 1863, impressed by the demand for onions in the army, the paper began to tout onions as a crop that brought in the most money for the least work and trouble, a good way to get $500–$600 yield per acre.[85]

Again, however, a broad-brushed picture of the Iowa economy does not tell enough about the state's condition at mid-year. In Burlington by November, the city's business leaders noted sagging mercantile employment while talking hopefully about industrial growth, without seeming to know what to do to stimulate either. Some still blamed the 1857 depression for the city's problems.[86] Keokuk, on the other hand, wasn't looking back at all. The military hospital was a continuing stimulus to trade. Pork packing boomed and several new industries arose, turning out cigars and other tobacco products, ladies hosiery, woolen garments, rope, brushes, stoves, and railroad cars—both passenger and freight. Aiding all this was the extension of the Illinois and Southern Railroad to the east bank of the Mississippi across from the city. The railroad provided accelerated connections to the Lakes, to the East, and to the South as far as Cairo.[87] Davenport did well also, enjoying population and building growth. Wages were high and farmers paid their debts; merchants expressed astonishment that fall about how much money people carried and about how much they bought. The city's merchants appeared a bit avaricious so far as a *Democrat* reporter was concerned. Dry goods which sold at 10¢ a yard a few weeks earlier had climbed to nearly 50¢ a yard in March. Prices would go higher so long as the war lasted it seemed. People had better buy now, advised the reporter, even though the merchants were not anxious to sell "as they consider it no favor to let their goods go at the present rates. . . ."[88]

Dubuque and its trading area also had a good year. One figure shows how prices could jump to a producer's advantage. Early in January, 1863, live hogs brought only $2.90–$3.25 cwt. But by the end of the month one Prairie Creek farmer sold 22 hogs averaging 400 pounds each for $4.35 cwt. Being a pork center had some disadvantages. Too many hogs roamed freely over the levee getting into sacked oats. They also wandered throughout the city, some dying of disease on the streets. Matter-of-factly the *Herald* remarked that if this kept up, the city would soon need another soap factory. Dubuque ice cutters took advantage of the cold weather to harvest 40,000 tons of ice before spring arrived.[89] The rise in commodity prices was no unmixed blessing as the *Herald* observed. The poor, especially soldiers' families, were hard hit by increases which saw flour move up to $5.50 cwt., wood to $5.50 a cord, butter to 20¢ a pound, and potatoes to 40¢ a bushel. With hay from $12 to $18 a ton, the paper complained, one might as well butcher a cow rather than feed her. She could never produce enough butter or milk to pay expenses.[90] The *Herald* often sounded pessimistic, even if most people seemed to be making money. Prepare for a panic and depression which might well come when the war ended, a reporter warned. Pay all debts; don't mortgage one's comfortable home to modernize it. Creditors should get their debts well secured and put the payments on the longest time schedule possible. He might be wrong, he admitted, but the 1857 experience was worth recalling.[91]

Farther up the river McGregor was doing well. A Democratic stronghold after the spring elections, one citizen wrote that ". . . our city is indomitable; her copperheadism keeps pace with her business prosperity and that is the very best encomium I could pass on . . . [her] . . . patriotism. . . ."[92] Similar tendencies among farmers around Dubuque provoked the *Times* beyond endurance:

The Hypocrites—The Copperhead farmers of this county, who bring their grain and other products here to sell, heap the foulest abuse on the administration and all connected with it. . . . When they receive their pay they won't take anything but the "Dirty Greenbacks," as they call them, to carry home. This is a fair sample of the shameless hypocrisy of the party which controls the politics of the county.

In Council Bluffs also, Copperhead farmers who refused Uncle Sam's draft were never known to refuse his notes, fumed the *Nonpareil.*[93]

All this farmer prosperity was only imaginary said the Washington *Democrat,* which published figures purporting to show that farm commodity prices lagged far behind escalating prices farmers paid for goods they purchased. "When," demanded the editor, "will the people cease running after negroes, and look a little to their own interests and welfare."[94] But hog raisers around Des Moines probably did not see it that way. At least the *Statesman* didn't. In November it claimed that $3.50 to 4.00 per cwt. was a good hog price even accounting for inflation, recalling that the price a year earlier had been $2.25–$2.75.[95] Council Bluffs business, good in the spring, remained so. Citizens there saw more good times coming after the city shipped its first 1,000 bushels of wheat ever to Chicago on a route that went down the Missouri to St. Joseph, thence east by rail.[96] Land prices climbed steadily in the spring in Iowa City, and all Johnson county witnessed an influx of people into both urban and rural areas which helped nullify the effect of a larger than usual out-migration of families leaving for Nevada and California.[97]

Reopening of the Mississippi was a relief to Iowans and added greatly to the general expectation that the state would somehow be economically secure once again. But the great markets which were the source of Iowa's prosperity were still to the east, as they had been for years, although some citizens seemed unwilling to admit it. The *Herald*'s editors sounded the sectionalist theme more vigorously than others—although they could always count on help from Henry Clay Dean, whose antieastern bias once caused W. W. Junkin to accuse him of following rebel instructions to create antagonism between East and West.[98] They contended that economic interests naturally linked West and South. Since the South would win its independence eventually, the West should look there rather than eastward. Ultimately South and West would unite, Hutchins believed. Writing from the East, Mahony envisioned reunion after a period of peace, without specifically indicating whether New England should be excluded or included. He spoke only of two sections, North and South.[99] H. B. Hendershott of the Ottumwa *Democratic Mercury* linked slavery with continued western prosperity and recommended separate negotiations to keep the upper and lower Mississippi Valley together if "constitutional" means failed to restore the Union. Democrats at Pleasant Ridge (Wapello county) believed that the Emancipation Proclamation had destroyed all hope of reunion and that a new republic composed of the middle, northwestern, and southern states, firmly excluding New England, was a desirable replacement.[100]

Most complaints about the East, particularly New England, reaping economic benefit from the war at the expense of the West prompted no demands for separation. David Richardson, reflecting Davenport's ever-alert business community, only suggested that the West should promote industry as well as agriculture. Westerners, thus, would be independent of the East economically while the East would yet remain dependent on them. All this, Richardson enthused, would be to Davenport's particular advantage. The city would be the center of everything.[101] Rarely did any Iowans defend the East. But two men did, early in 1863, James Howell and Clark Dunham. Dunham's defense especially was extended, specific and articulate, and cited numerous examples of New England charity to the prewar South, New England support of western churches and schools, and New England contributions toward wartime soldiers' relief drives. Furthermore, New England businessmen had always dealt honestly with the South, Dunham declared, whereas Southern merchants had a deserved reputation for defalcation on debts. Dunham, whose words could sting as much as Mahony's and Hutchins' when he stirred himself, had little use for Southern civilization. Its chivalry was fraudulent. It was a society at once arrogant, haughty, aristocratic, violent, selfish, and marked by extremes of wealth and poverty.[102] Dunham's blast was singular in its length and its heat, but it is likely that many thousands of Iowans agreed with him, not all of them abolitionists. Many had New England ties; moreover, alleged Southern virtues appeared less and less admirable as it became clear that the rebels were totally disinterested in reunion despite earnest Copperhead contentions to the contrary.

Dunham's defense of New England did not mean that he was happy about "railroad monopolists" who, he claimed, swindled western producers. Others echoed his complaint. Dubuquers refused to believe that the Illinois Central couldn't do a better job finding cars to carry goods east. The *Times* suggested that the railroad was in league with grain speculators, while Illinois Central representatives maintained that federal use of its rolling stock was still the true source of the difficulty. At any rate, discontent with railroads was not a partisan political issue in 1863. High freight rates and irregular rail service hurt all producers and sellers, regardless of their politics.[103]

Wartime inflation and military manpower requirements brought in their wake a more assertive labor force in Iowa. In January, Keokuk blacksmiths and those who built carriages and wagons formed a mechanics union. They invited neighboring mechanics to join them. Also in January, a carpenter's strike caused Dubuque contractors to raise wages from 75¢ to $1 a day. Soon other Dubuque laborers, citing the "extraordinary" high prices of provisions, were demanding $1.25 for a ten-hour day. Ice cutter wages rose from 80¢ to $1 a day which the *Herald* believed was "little enough considering the expenses of living." Gravel workers demanded $1.25 a day, having previously asked for $1 a day and gotten it. But the gravel firm now offered only $1.15 and vowed to hold the line. Then all twenty-five tailors at Becker's Clothing House struck for a $1 increase for making coats and 50¢ more for pants, vests, and other apparel. Becker offered to pay two-thirds of the demand, but the tailors rejected his offer. With that Becker sent for others to take the places of those who walked out.[104]

Then came a printers' strike at both the *Times* and the *Herald*. Foremen wanted a jump from $12 to $15 a week, journeymen asked for $12, and composers asked for 5¢ raises for 1,000 ems of type, up from 25¢ for work before 10 P.M., and up from 30¢ after 10 P.M. The *Herald* heretofore had maintained a general neutrality toward wage demands, except in the case of the ice cutters. Now, however, the paper, which still viewed itself as the friend of the laboring classes in contrast to monied black abolitionist Republicans, became enraged. The strikers quickly lost. Strikes to remedy a wrong were acceptable, Hutchins piously declaimed, but those "dictated by a spirit of malevolence and a desire to extort, we do not hesitate to oppose." Ever one to rub it in, Hutchins termed the affair "a mortifying and disastrous failure" for those "designing men" who brought it on. The union men were beaten, he crowed, but "the most penitent ones" had returned to work. The departed strike leaders and those who returned now hated each other, he added with ill-disguised pleasure. Much less violent in its language was the *Times* which simply explained that the wage demands were beyond its capacity to pay if it wished to remain in business.[105] With the printers, particularly at the *Herald*, put firmly in their place, Dubuque's labor problems diminished. But saloon keepers had one of their own. They decided to hold out for lower prices for the lager beer they purchased. With lager jumping from $6 to $10 a barrel in a year's time, their profit was too thin. Especially hurt if prices weren't rolled back, said the saloon men, would be the "2 glasses for five cent drinkers."[106]

In Des Moines the *Statesman* sympathized with laborers who worked for the city when city officials cut their wages. The same officials still drew their own pay, observed the paper, while they refused to pay workers enough to support their families.[107] Farmhand wages naturally jumped in 1863, with hands sometimes asking as much as $2.50 a day. That seemed too steep for Edward Thayer who observed men standing around in Muscatine doing nothing.[108] When coal miners struck for higher wages in central Iowa, both the *Iowa State Register* and the *Statesman* felt they were trying to scalp the public. The *Statesman* believed that miner demands for 20¢ a bushel, up from 15¢, were unjust and heartless. The poor would suffer. Laborers earning only $25–30 a month would have nothing left for food or clothing. The *Statesman* even sympathized with state legislators for whom the $6–10 a week which landlords charged for board and room was "pretty thick."[109]

After the Democratic successes elsewhere in the fall of 1862, Iowa's Democrats hoped for a revival of their fortunes. Nothing of the sort occurred. Copperheadism, perceived both by Republicans and War Democrats as a too friendly attitude toward the Confederacy and as a force which undermined the Union war effort, made the party more vulnerable than ever. Peace and war partisans tangled acrimoniously. Dennis Mahony's speeches and writings particularly angered those who felt that the Democrats could ill afford the disloyal label. Mahony deserved sympathy for his arrest, said the *North Iowa Times*, but "as the advocate of a dishonorable peace, and a new Union which shall leave out the Middle and New England States, he deserves contempt; as the mouthpiece of the Northwest he justly earns ridicule." Montrose Democratic club members expelled their president from office and from the club altogether when he joined the Loyal League. Oskaloosa Democrats argued over the wearing of Copperhead pins at a party meeting. Those who opposed the emblems won, and they escorted a recalcitrant loser out of the building.[110] Reflecting a classic case of political schizophrenia, the Burlington *Argus* suggested that the party might unite behind one of seven men as candidate for governor in the coming fall elections. They were peace men LeGrand Byington, Henry Clay Dean, and Mahony; Charles Mason, equally a peace man but less open about it; George W. Gray of Allamakee county, a moderate who supported the war; and Col. William Belknap and Gen. James Tuttle, War Democrats on active duty.[111]

The state Democratic convention in July was rife with controversy. The peace faction fought bitterly to put its stamp on the results. However, the War Democrats successfully resisted efforts to repudiate the war outright, including what they saw as an effort to lay primary blame for the conflict on abolitionists rather than secessionists—the only consolation, incidentally, that abolitionists ever could win at any Democratic assembly of any size in Iowa during the war. The delegates were more united on planks opposing a war for emancipation and opposing the application of martial law in noncombat areas, as well as on planks defending civil liberties and the right to voice dissent during wartime. But the section of the document which attracted the most fire was a plank nailed in by the peace forces. It said that Democrats would "hail with pleasure and delight any manifestation of a desire on the part of the seceded states to return to their allegiance to the government of the Union, and in such event . . . would cordially and earnestly cooperate with them in the restoration of peace and the procurement of their interests and rights."[112]

H. C. Rippey, prominent Democratic lawyer from Dallas county, liked neither this nor most of the rest of the planks. They were, he cried, "a disgrace to those adopting them and an insult to every loyal Democrat in the state. . . . On reading them, one would suppose that the administration was trying to destroy the Government, and establish a monarchy instead of Jeff. Davis and his clan." S. P. Yoemans of the Sioux City *Register* condemned the peace faction leaders and the resolutions for "seeking to place the Democracy in a false position to the Government." LeGrand Byington, new state party chairman and short-time editor of the *State Democratic Press,* who favored an even stronger stand for peace, lost control of the paper after the convention when his editorial stance caused rebellion among its stockholders.[113]

All this was nothing compared with the storm over selection of the party's gubernatorial candidate. The peace men were determined to nominate one of their own. They placed five men in the running: Byington, the most vociferous antiwar man in the state; Mason; former governor Stephen Hempstead; Col. Isaac Preston of Marion; and John Duncombe, all determined to block the war partisans' choice, Gen. James Tuttle. On the second formal ballot the peace forces coalesced around Byington, but he emerged second to Tuttle, 231 to 228. When David Richardson, convention secretary, requested time to check the accuracy of his count, the peace men refused. They bulled through a proposal to take a third formal ballot. Richardson proceeded to recount the votes anyway and soon announced triumphantly that his first count was entirely accurate. The delegates, however, were in no mood to listen, the two factions being hotly engaged in an exhausting battle for supremacy. Eventually the peace proponents rallied behind an acceptable moderate, Maturin L. Fisher, Clayton county farmer and lieutenant governor nominee of the 1861 Mahony convention. Fisher won, 245 to 214, over Tuttle, and the tired delegates voted to make his choice unanimous. They quickly settled on Copperheads Duncombe and Mason for the two remaining positions, lieutenant governor and supreme court judge.

Tuttle backers were furious. Their outraged cries troubled Fisher. On July 20, as had Mason in 1861, he wrote Richardson declining the nomination. A reading of the convention proceedings, Fisher wrote, convinced him that his nomination was "not fairly made." Fisher also revealed that "prominent and reliable Democrats" across the state, in addition to his own county delegation, recommended his withdrawal. Richardson praised Fisher's candor and immediately demanded that the central committee call a new convention to select another candidate. Instead, Byington, now the chairman of the central committee, called a meeting of the five-man group to select the candidate. Meanwhile Fisher had second thoughts; he regretted his withdrawal; and he wrote Byington that if the committee wished, it could nominate him and he would accept. Armed with this news, Byington and fellow committee member Frank Plum believed they could persuade the other three members, Phineas Casady, A. F. Seeberger, and A. W. Carpenter, to accept Fisher. To their chagrin they could not. Now it was Byington, along with Plum, who pressed for a new nominating convention. The other three rejected that idea and voted for Tuttle. The two angry and frustrated peace men refused to make the vote unanimous.[114]

Tuttle accepted the nomination, surprising his Democratic and Republican friends in the army, as well as the state Republican leadership. They knew he was interested in running for governor, but assumed that he would reject what they called a "Copperhead nomination." When he accepted it, they turned against him regretfully. Kirkwood wrote a friend, "Tuttle will I think be badly beaten. I am very sorry he has taken the course he has. He is too good a man to be sacrificed by such a damned hard lot of scurvy politicians." The Burlington *Hawk-eye* praised Tuttle for dealing the rebels many hard blows as a soldier but "never . . . half as severely as he has the Iowa Copperheads."[115] What earned Tuttle this unexpected accolade was his letter accepting the Democratic nomination which indeed did nothing to endear him to the Copperhead wing. The General bluntly stated that he stood for Union "without an *if* and regardless of whether slavery stands or falls by its restoration.'' A Chicago observer pointed out that Tuttle's statement amounted to a refutation of a key plank in the party platform, the one opposing a war for emancipation.[116] Tuttle had much support even so. He quickly won editorial backing in Keokuk, Burlington, Davenport, Des Moines, Sioux City, and West Union. Papers in Fort Madison, Keosauqua, and one in Dubuque *(Der National-Demokrat)* soon followed suit, as did almost all other Democratic organs including the Council Bluffs *Bugle*.

Democrats had some reason to hope that Tuttle might prove popular enough with the electorate to overcome what was beginning to appear like a permanent Republican majority in the state. This hope sprang in part from the man whom the Republicans put at the head of their ticket, Col. William M. Stone of Knoxville. Although Stone had a reasonably good service record (he was wounded during the Vicksburg campaign), many Republicans regarded him without enthusiasm. They always had a surplus of candidates for high public office in the 1860s, spurred by the prospect of nearly certain victory. When dark horse Stone won the nomination by shrewd preconvention and in-convention politicking, many important Republicans and their followers felt cheated. Some contrasted his image unfavorably with Tuttle's. Tuttle was one of Iowa's legitimate combat heroes, and men from both parties took pride in his record.[117] Some Republicans feared that soldiers would support him rather than Stone. But soldiers who believed they understood soldier attitudes didn't think so. "I presume he is just as good as Stone," wrote Peter Wilson, "but being in bad company is what we don't like." Cyrus Carpenter gave an insightful explanation to his brother on why Stone would win the soldier vote. He wrote:

> Everybody in the army says it is a pity that Stone was nominated but since he is the candidate we must elect him. The soldiers will vote on the principal [*sic*], regardless of the man and everything else. The soldiers believe in putting down the rebellion and they argue everything from the anti-slavery standpoint, not because they have any feeling on the moral question of slavery but because they think it a good joke on the rebels to strike them through the institution they cherish.[118]

Carpenter had put his finger inadvertently (and in quite a different context) on one major issue of the 1863 campaign in Iowa, the black question. Stone, ordinarily noted for felicitous political expression, told a Keokuk audience in early July that he would rather "eat, drink, live and sleep with a nigger than a Copperhead." From then on, Iowa Democrats made capital of Stone's alleged social and sexual preferences. The campaign against Stone was frequently dirty. The Dubuque *Herald* and other Democratic papers charged that Stone had been a coward in battle and that he once had seduced a servant girl in his home. Republicans reacted hotly, and the Burlington *Hawk-eye* offered to pay $500 to the *Herald* if that paper could find one responsible citizen of Stone's home county (Marion), who could verify the accusation. Democrats at a parade and mass rally at

Monroe in October dramatized their sentiments. Reported the approving Burlington *Argus*, "We must not omit . . . the delegation from Vandalia which consisted of 34 young ladies in a large wagon drawn by six horses. These young ladies were dressed in red, white, and blue, and bore a splendid banner, with the inspired inscription 'White Men or none'."[119] Charles Mason's 1863 campaign pamphlet, *The Election in Iowa*, published by the New York-based antiwar organization, the Society for the Diffusion of Political Knowledge, made no direct attack on Stone's Keokuk remark. But it played heavily on the black issue. Mason emphasized the black threat to white labor. And he questioned the wisdom of an administration that continued to wage war "for the single purpose of suddenly turning loose four million semi-barbarians, to prey upon mankind and in the end to be exterminated themselves."

After Stone's faux pas, Republicans took no chances on the black issue, especially in Dubuque. When Senator Lyman Trumball spoke there in August, he told listeners that the Republican party was a white man's party and that emancipation was a boon to whites because it made white labor respectable by eliminating slave-labor competition. The *Times* also claimed that the best way to protect white labor's interests was to proceed with emancipation. Blacks would then choose to remain in the South.[120] The paper reported opposition to slavery among Catholic church leaders. It also listed Catholic generals appointed to important posts in the Union armies and denounced Confederate leaders as "Protestant Infidels" who, if victorious, would use Catholic voters for their own purposes while granting them nothing in return.

In Davenport David Richardson seemed reconciled to the idea that Davenport's Germans, whatever their religion, were too solidly Republican to be moved. Keokuk's Republicans complained, on the other hand, that the September naturalization of several Germans and Irish by a Democratic circuit court judge was a move to increase Democratic votes pure and simple. Thomas Clagett happily pointed out that this was unlikely unless one were to believe that a Republican judge who also naturalized nearly two score Germans and Irish in Keokuk had hoped thereby to create Democratic votes. But Muscatine Democrats did believe their newly naturalized citizens would support them. They helped the community's alien residents to acquire naturalization papers in time to vote. After the election, the *Iowa State Register* charged that last minute "naturalization of 120 Copperhead Wooden Shoes" kept Pella in the Democratic ranks. But the Burlington *Hawk-eye* credited the city's Germans with providing the Republicans with their victory margin.[121] Late naturalization of county voters made no difference in Lee and Muscatine counties for the Democrats. Republicans in both won—by fraud, claimed editors Clagett and Thayer.[122]

Allegations that there was fraud in soldier voting may have contained some substance. In Keokuk, Democrats charged that the city's large soldier populace intimidated Democratic voters and destroyed Democratic ballots. From the field came reports of officer exhortations to vote Republican, of an absence of or destruction of Democratic tickets, and of underage soldiers voting. Some time earlier Republican state chairman Herbert Hoxie had told General Grenville Dodge that he hoped Dodge and his officers would see to it that the soldiers did their duty and voted Republican. But Dr. Seneca Thrall told his wife he saw nothing illegal at the polls of the six to eight regiments he visited on election day. "[I] . . . never saw an election more *fairly* conducted," he wrote, "and can testify that no means were used to influence the voters, even ½ so much as always occurred at any and all elections I have ever seen." Thrall was an honest man and probably did see nothing untoward. But it seemed not to cross his mind that this was Vicksburg, General Tuttle's station, and that the General's tent was there in the field. Thrall added that soldiers liked Tuttle but would not vote for him, implying that they would not vote Democratic in any great numbers.[123]

Stone never worried about losing. He confidently predicted that he would win an overwhelming victory if civilian voters did half as well in proportion as he claimed the army would do. He was correct. Whatever hope the Democrats had for a comeback under a war hero disappeared under a deluge of Republican ballots. Stone won 60.5 percent of the total vote, defeating Tuttle 85,896 to 56,169. He won 85 percent of the soldier vote and 56.4 percent of the civilian vote.[124]

The way the Democrats analyzed their dismal showing revealed a lot about the thinking of the two opposing factions. On the War Democrat side stood Thomas Clagett. Claggett blamed "peace radicals" for the party's defeat.

> In their bitterness of mere partisan spirit . . . [t]hey befogged and bewildered the public mind by metaphysical disquisitions between allegiance to the government and allegiance to the party instead of meeting the real questions involved in the war in an open, distinct, straightforward manner. . . . [They hold] the preposterous idea of saving the Union by a vigorous prosecution of peace, which mean[s] nothing more than the disbanding of our armies and acknowledging the *right* of secession under the delusive expectation that the Southern States would form a union with the North, upon peaceful terms satisfactory to themselves and us.[125]

Stilson Hutchins spoke for the peace men. Tuttle's nomination put the Democrats in an anomalous position since the official platform was a peace platform; he declared: "We are anti war or we are nothing. We cannot support all the measures they [the Republicans] support and endeavor to divide votes with them on technicalities."[126]

By April James Tuttle was once again in the good graces of Iowa Republicans. He commanded the Union forces at Natchez where an admiring correspondent reported that he was "very stringent" with rebels. "He is," the writer elaborated, "in favor of Confiscation, nigger soldiers, and ever [sic] other measure for which the Republicans and the administration have contended. Wendel Phillips with all his Abolition principles could not go farther than General Tuttle." This was not quite accurate. Tuttle indeed favored the measures named. But he was callous toward freed blacks in a way few abolitionists ever would have been. He backed a draconian measure instituted by A. W. Kelly, his chief health officer, which expelled from Natchez all freed blacks not employed by "some responsible white person in some legitimate business." Blacks could no longer secure rental quarters. They could not work for themselves. Nor could whites employ them without Kelly's approval. Tuttle backed his subordinate to the hilt. He scorned Northern missionaries and school teachers who protested Kelly's decrees, and he threatened action against them. Kelly's measures split black families, evicted black soldiers' wives and children from their Natchez homes, and left many destitute. Tuttle's black soldiers became enraged. They threatened vengeance on those who treated their families so brutally. Higher authorities soon forced the health officer to soften his system. Not long after, the army transferred both men out of Natchez. The Iowan resigned his commission later that spring.[127]

8

Copperheadism at Bay: 1864

AFTER the fall 1863 elections, Charles Negus wrote Charles Mason that the Democratic party was "powerless and dead." "It no longer wields," he said, "that benign influence that it was once accustomed to do. To now be a democrat is considered disloyal, a traitor to our country. . . ." The Southern confederacy, Negus added, was a "fixed fact."[1]

Besides rejecting James Tuttle decisively, the voters elected only four Democrats to the Iowa senate and six to the house. Six of the ten came from Dubuque county (two senators and four representatives). Allamakee county voters chose one of the senators and one representative while Lee county chose one senator and Van Buren one representative.[2] Governor Stone's inaugural address gave them no comfort at all. Stone was explicit:

> There is [he said] no longer any middle ground where loyal men can stand, and find refuge from the stern and positive obligations of the hour. . . . Those who hesitate now to yield an unreserved support to the Federal Government, or fail to sustain its constituted authorities, unmistakably array themselves on the side of its enemies and will be so recorded in the history of the times. If treason is a crime, to sympathize with traitors is also clearly criminal.[3]

The minuscule representation of Democrats was bound to disagree with Stone's definition of either loyalty or criminal behavior. But they could hardly change his mind. Nor could they block anything the Republicans really wanted to do—not that they were really obstructionists anyway. Only one Democrat voted against the bill that required county boards of supervisors to levy a tax to provide relief for soldiers' families.[4] And three Democrat senators plus one house Democrat voted with the Republicans to repeal Iowa's black exclusion law. On the other hand, they did unite against a resolution instructing Iowa congressmen to promote a federal amendment ending slavery, a resolution which passed overwhelmingly.[5] House Democrats fought a resolution that proposed confiscation of Confederate-owned property in Iowa and property owned by Iowans who supposedly aided and abetted Rebels. But so did some house Republicans. The proposal died in the senate.[6] The Democrats exhibited no antirailroad tendencies in their votes. In the senate they voted with the majority in a successful move to table a bill raising taxes on railroads. And they approved an act designed to aid railroad corporations who wanted to issue construction and equipment bonds.[7]

The relief law of 1863 mandating aid for soldiers' families stemmed from the Republican belief that Democratic-dominated county boards of supervisors refused to appropriate money for that purpose as the state allowed them to do under the act of 1861. Stone spoke directly to this point in his inaugural. In most counties where Unionists were in the majority, soldier families got aid, he claimed. Where the "opposite party" prevailed, they did not.[8] How widespread this denial of aid was is not clear. The Fairfield *Ledger* supported the 1864 law on the grounds that soldier families in Jefferson county received county assistance until Democrats won half the seats on the board. Thereafter, charged editor Junkin, Union men had to support soldiers' wives via private funds. Where Democratic-run boards did give aid, they equated the service with pauper relief, charged the *Iowa State Register*.[9] Public indignation among Wayne county citizens in June, 1863, forced reversal of such a demeaning policy just before it was to take effect. But Boone county's board resisted pressure that August to supply any relief funds at all.[10] As usual many Republicans took a keen interest in what Dubuque city and county did regarding relief of soldiers' families and returned but destitute soldiers. As early as August, 1862, the Dubuque *Times* claimed that because Dubuque's supervisors failed to act Dubuque was the only large county in the state to deny aid to soldier families. Should it continue to evade its duty, the paper warned prophetically, the state would eventually require county support. From time to time in 1863 the *Herald* and the *Times* quarreled over the amount and the quality of care Dubuque soldiers' families received. The *Herald* occasionally claimed that private charity groups discriminated against families of foreign born and/or Catholic soldiers.[11] That fall the county board, by a 15 to 4 vote, voted to deny a request that it help support a privately sponsored soldiers' home, a way station for returned sick, wounded, and needy soldiers. Instead, the board directed the Superintendent of the Poor to look after the soldiers in ways he deemed expedient. It also directed him to prevent "persons from becoming a public charge to this county who probably belong elsewhere." The *Herald* defended the board's action, arguing that to accede to one private charity's request (the Women's Sanitary Society) would lead to a deluge of requests from other private charities. Dubuque's city council responded angrily by a 6 to 5 vote, Democratic mayor John Thedinga casting the deciding vote. The council denounced the board as "ungenerous, ungrateful and unjust" as well as callous and unpatriotic. It also voted to pay some support to the home.

The *Herald* and the supervisors remained vigilant over relief money spent on soldiers and their families. In January, 1864, the board claimed that Dubuque county recruiters appeared to be enlisting persons who would be credited to other counties but whose families might choose to claim support from Dubuque.

Accordingly, the board directed the Superintendent of the Poor to make sure that only bona fide Dubuque county soldiers' families received aid. Then in January, 1865, the Dubuque supervisors voted to rescind an action taken during the October, 1864, recruiting drive. At that time the county paid bounties to men enlisting to the credit of the county. It also agreed to provide aid to their families. But in January it halted the aid, reasoning that the bounty was sufficient for soldier family needs.[12]

In Dubuque's defense, and in defense of other counties which moved slowly on such relief programs, is the fact that most Iowa counties, regardless of political complexion, labored under difficult financial burdens during the war. While the state government ultimately managed to pass the great bulk of its war expenses onto the federal government, Iowa's city and county governments provided almost all the relief given to destitute returned soldiers and soldiers' families as well as all the bounty money given to volunteers. The relief monies totaled $1,122,247 and the bounties $1,083,901.[13]

Wartime prosperity, emergent in Iowa late in 1862, became full-blown throughout most of the state in 1864. Those who previously counseled caution still did so occasionally. But it was plain to them as well as to everybody else that good times had arrived. Nobody forgot that there was a war on, of course. The casualty lists, the periodic and frantic drives to recruit soldiers in order to avert the draft, and the dashed hopes for the final success of Grant's armies in the East were sufficient reminders. Also, prices moved up annoyingly.

Still, it was difficult to be excessively gloomy while agriculture and business prospered. The river cities, as always, were alert to all the possibilities for making what was good even better. Keokuk was so busy that a *Constitution* writer suggested that the community needed more housing, another dry goods store, and a wholesale hardware store. The winter ice on the Mississippi was solid early in the year, and the enthusiastic *Gate City* invited Illinois farmers to bring their business across, saying, "The road is smooth, the sleighing is excellent and the ice strong enough to bear a team of elephants." It was stronger than that at Clinton. There, enterprising railroad men laid track across the ice and up the banks to connect with rails on each side. Then they would send one loaded car, or as many as three empties, down the sloping bank and watch it coast half a mile to the other side. A waiting locomotive would hook up the load and pull it onto the main track. Burlington, like Keokuk, did good business with Illinois so long as the ice remained solid, and even that city enjoyed better times for awhile.[14]

In the West, Council Bluffs pork packing quadrupled during the 1863–1864 season over the 1862–1863 total. The *Bugle* reported that the hogs packed were larger and "better class." Council Bluffs merchants, however, were too lazy, complained the *Nonpareil*. They weren't advertising enough to attract all the spring emigrant trade heading to the gold fields. If they didn't do better, the paper warned, Ottumwa merchants might persuade travelers that they could sell goods more cheaply.[15]

On a broader scale the *Iowa Homestead* saw the prosperity heralding a new and more profitable sectional realignment. "Southern Trade—What Is It Worth?" headlined an article whose text, in effect, answered, "not much." The writer painted a picture of high mutual regard between East and West which, if overly saccharine, nevertheless pointed to an undeniably closer tie between the two sections. "The distrust and jealousy which once existed . . . have disappeared," he wrote, "and given place to that perfect harmony and good feeling which will exercise a powerful influence in promoting their respective interests." As the Dubuque *Times* put it, "Bridging the river may incommode to some degree the commerce up and down the stream, but we believe it is a settled fact that the commerce which crosses the river is far greater. . . . As this country develops this east and west trade must be largely increased." That fall the paper observed the tremendous shipment of butter from Dubuque to the East and commented, "If all the butter made in the Dubuque region were consumed at home, the price would be less than 10¢ a lb."[16] Dubuque hosted a May convention of persons interested in developing a canal to the Lakes via the Wisconsin and Fox rivers. *Herald* editor, Patrick Robb, who recently had bought out Stilson Hutchins and Dennis Mahony, believed such a canal would not only be enormously profitable but also a force for Union solidarity.[17] As for the immediate future, one writer saw a need for farmers to produce all they could, both for the country and for their own pocketbooks. "A thriftless do-nothing farmer who permits his broad acres to remain unplowed, unsown, and unplanted," he declared, "is as great an enemy to the material interests of the country as the leading Copperhead who puts in his time on the corner of streets discouraging enlistments. . . ."[18]

For consumers the inflationary rise in prices was not welcome. When egg prices hit 50¢ a dozen in Chicago, eggs climbed briefly to 25¢-35¢ a dozen along the river. When speculative activity ceased, the price dropped to 15¢, threatening a glut.[19] As meat prices climbed, Dubuquers became apprehensive. When the *Herald* noted an increase in cattle receipts, it suggested that butchers lower their prices. This was on June 29. Not until a buyers' strike hit the butchers in late July did they come around. Those at the city's Central Market quickly cut the price from 20¢ to 15¢ a pound for "good beef." (Sirloin cuts cost 20¢ a pound as early as mid-May.) The *Herald* was more sympathetic with local saloon keepers. With lager beer up $2 a barrel, they had to use smaller glasses which gave a drinker only two swallows for five cents compared with two glasses for five cents a year earlier. "Nobody grumbles, saloons must keep up with expenses as well as other institutions," said the writer.[20]

Thomas Clagett, who rarely commented on economic matters, complained that high prices hurt farmers as well as mechanics and other laborers. Bondholders, office holders, shoddy manufacturers, and thieves were the only ones getting rich off the war. But David Richardson believed farmers complained too much. Two to three years earlier they got 15¢-16¢ a bushel for corn and dreamed of getting 40¢. They wanted nothing better. "Now," he declared, "they are getting 80¢, and think it an outrage that they cannot get a dollar. Such is human nature—farmers are no exception." The *Iowa State Register* was less calm about it. Twenty-cent butter was "extortion." Other prices were bad too. It had heard, the paper said, that farmers were deliberately keeping goods off the market in the hope that prices would rise even higher. Moreover, Des Moines rents were "enormous," and the cost of dry goods "simply awful."[21] By July corn at Burlington was over a dollar a bushel. The *Hawk-eye* believed that such a price, plus high prices also for wheat ($2), cattle ($4–$6), and hogs ($7–$8), would generate enough prosperity for all Iowans that they would be able to pay the high costs for groceries and dry goods. The Eddyville *Star* noted the great number of sales for reapers and mowers, most for cash, in that small community. Richardson, always a believer in getting "out from under," thought that farmers around Davenport who left town with pocketsful of greenbacks must be paying off their debts.[22] Farmhands wanted some of those greenbacks for themselves. According to the *Democrat* they got a good share of them, $5 worth a day for awhile in July. Thus, the paper welcomed an influx of five hundred emigrants, mostly Germans ("with considerable capital"), whom it expected would work for $3 a day for help-starved farmers and mechanics. Davenport's city council took an unusual step designed to benefit the farmers. The council resolved to forego street improvements between July 1 and September 1 except for essential work so that the street crews would be available to help with the harvest. At the same time farmers around Lyons offered $3 a day with no takers.[23]

Urban editors believed farmers had little reason to be dissatisfied. When Appanoose county farmers called for a convention of farmers and laboring men to meet in Centerville to consider raising their prices unless they could get Centerville and Keokuk merchants, doctors, and druggists to lower theirs, the *Gate City* was unsympathetic. Farm prices had kept pace with all other prices, the paper maintained. The *Hawk-eye* believed that it was foolish for Democrats to talk of hard times to farmers during the election campaign of 1864. Only a farmer blinded by political prejudice would deny that he was prospering despite higher taxes and higher merchandise prices. But Richardson, who had the temerity to suggest that farmers increase their working hours and their crops in order to reduce prices, got a quick reply. That was easier said than done, a Pleasant Valley farmer rejoined. There weren't enough hours in the day. Besides, farmer prices weren't too high, all things considered, like prices and wages they paid and the type of currency they received in payment for their crops.[24] Average prices received by farmers in Iowa for their major products did jump well over those of 1863. Table 8.1 demonstrates this increase.[25]

Interior communities were prosperous and optimistic in 1864. The *Iowa State*

TABLE 8.1

AVERAGE PRICES FOR SELECTED AGRICULTURAL PRODUCTS IN IOWA

Year	Butter	Eggs	Barley	Wheat	Oats	Corn	Beef	Hogs
	lb	*doz*		*bu*			*cwt*	
1863	.13	.09	.84	.79	.43	.34	2.41	3.57
1864	.22	.14	1.14	1.18	.53	.70	4.22	...

Register called attention to the coal and water power available in Des Moines and suggested that the city could eventually acquire the same reputation for manufacturing as New England. Foundries already existed there as well as a machine shop. Other producers turned out furniture, woolens, steam engines, plows, and other agricultural equipment. Iowa City should go the same route, proclaimed the *State Democratic Press,* which believed the town was suited for the production of cotton and woolen goods, paper, and agricultural implements. Even the state penitentiary at Fort Madison had a farm implement manufacturing plant, run by a private contractor. The prisoners turned out superior products according to officials who boasted of sales in Nebraska, Kansas, Missouri, and Illinois besides Iowa.[26]

Dubuque knew that it was enjoying a good year economically. And the *Times* was amused when John Mahin of the Muscatine *Journal* professed astonishment at his city's prosperity. Dubuquers, said the *Times,* would be astonished if their city was not prosperous. One new Dubuque establishment, a distillery located on the levee, encountered opposition from the Dubuque *Religious News Letter.* Distilleries, Patrick Robb responded firmly, were the "most loyal institutions in the county. . . ." They paid a larger tax to the government than any other enterprise in the city. Then he got to the main point: "We look to the agricultural and manufacturing welfare of Dubuque and Iowa." In Civil War Iowa, Republican or Democrat, urban or rural, business was business, and the more of it the better.[27]

Well, almost. Better to have more of it in one sector than another, said the Council Bluffs *Nonpareil.* Western Iowa had changed drastically in the last six to eight years, the paper observed. Substantial frame and brick homes replaced cabins. Towns grew, but no faster than the rural districts. Exhibiting a bias for the countryside, the paper concluded: "We regard this as a better sign of the times than the building up of cities; in the improvement of our broad and fertile acres is our hope of the future."[28] The countryside had its problems in 1864. There was a bad frost and drought in June which affected parts of the state. Chinch bugs destroyed much grain in the northeast. Lee, Decatur, Wayne, Taylor, and Madison counties in the south suffered badly from dry weather. And Franklin county in the north central part of the state hoped for extension of the Dubuque and Sioux City Railroad within the next year to Iowa Falls. Franklin's farmers profited too little from their wheat, because of an expensive 50-mile haul to the nearest railhead, Cedar Falls.[29]

Even so, it was a good year, although Dr. J. M. Shaffer, secretary of the state agricultural society, had some sobering admonitions, faintly related to the thinking of the *Nonpareil* writer. Shaffer was not notably antiurban. But in a speech to the wool growers of southeastern Iowa he objected to the extravagant ways Iowans exhibited their new-found prosperity. There was, after all, a war going on, he told his listeners. It was ruinously expensive in both lives and dollars. American foodstuffs and raw materials, sold overseas, could not alone pay the cost, especially since the people had developed an inordinate liking for European luxuries which drained the country of gold. Shaffer called for a rededication to self-sufficiency, "to the simplicity of habits and economy and frugality of life which characterized the fathers of the Republic. . . . The tinkle of the ubiquitous piano is well enough, but it is an unwarranted luxury if indulged in at the expense of cramped creditors; a crime if at the cost of Union and Nationality; and madness, if it banish the music of the spinning wheel and clothes a man in shoddy."[30]

One other Iowan, not particularly a music lover either, looked with apprehension at Iowa's prosperity. But his reasons differed from Dr. Shaffer's. "Saw Senator Grimes," wrote Charles Mason in Washington on December 14. "He says everything is prosperous in Iowa. The hay crop will bring $25,000,000 [sic] into the State. The price is $9.50 per hundred gross weight. There will be no peace while war brings such results."[31] Doing well himself through investments and his patent law practice, Mason was not about to practice what Shaffer preached, although he occasionally mused about the virtues of the simple life. Mason implicitly believed that economic self-interest ruled all men; all men, that is, except for the small minority who, like himself, possessed superior intellect and morals. The war would cease only when it hit the "masses" where it hurt most—in the pocketbook. Mason was not altogether mistaken. But he never knew such men of the masses as Indianola's sturdy sergeant, Cyrus Boyd, or Monroe's doomed patriot and father of four, Pvt. Jacob Hunter.

Workers in the river cities felt the inflationary pinch. They often struck for higher wages; frequently they won. Sometimes they didn't have to strike. In labor-short Keokuk, journeymen shoemakers presented employers with a wage list averaging 20 percent over the existing rates and saw it accepted immediately. Steamer deckhands asked and got $60 a month, but some captains couldn't get enough hands even at that figure.[32] Journeymen saddle and harness makers in Davenport struck for $2-$2.50 a day, up from the prevailing $1.75-$2 rate. Several sought employment elsewhere when only a few employers agreed to accept their demands. Davenport typesetters struck for a 25 percent increase, a story notable by its absence in the *Democrat*, with the exception of an advertisement for a "good steady boy" with some printing experience to work for the paper "at good wages."[33]

Dubuque's working class, as in 1863, did not hesitate to push for wage hikes. Deckhands on the *War Eagle* successfully struck for a boost from $60 to $75 a month plus board, an increase which the *Times* believed was too steep. This position was not common for the paper. It usually favored wage increases. The *Times* readily granted a request by its eight carrier boys for an increase of 75¢ a week.[34] Carpenters and joiners asked for and got a $2.50 minimum for a ten-hour day. Shoemakers won a two-day strike for a 20 percent increase. Other skilled workers asked for increases at the same time, and the *Times* backed them editorially. In late July, Dubuque's mechanics and laborers met to form an association which would work to maintain "living wages" for all classes of city workers. The assembly resolved that "until we will be free—divided we are the slaves of capital." The *Times* supported the journeymen wagon and carriage makers and blacksmiths in their demands for 25 percent average increases, from $2.50 to

$3.25 a day. The paper described the workers as "some of the best" in their trades. A majority of employers agreed in advance to the workers' proposals. Two employers resisted, however, and their workers drew strike benefits from their labor association treasury. The most notable coverage of labor problems in the *Herald* was an April tirade against American typographical unions, proving that the paper under Patrick Robb, as it had been under Mahony and Hutchins, was most friendly, when it was friendly at all, to organized labor that worked *outside* the newspaper industry. Robb complained about a second round of wage demands. And he applauded several large papers in the East which resisted such demands and fired their strikers. Robb approved the establishment of schools to recruit and train women replacements for male printers. Newspapers made too little money to meet men's wage demands, he asserted.[35] Late in the year the steamer *Muscatine* overcame a walkout of angry Irish deckhands who quit the vessel at Burlington. The captain simply used a party of soldiers sailing with him to round them up and force them to return to work.[36]

War profiteers took sound thrashings from both Democrats and Republican papers in 1864. Republican organs in particular enjoyed describing Davenport's allegedly rampant materialism. The *Hawk-eye* attacked its contractors who supplied pork "unfit to eat" and unground, poor quality, adulterated coffee to the troops in training there. The Muscatine *Journal* complained that "The principal occupation of the inhabitants [of Davenport and Scott county], engrossing all their time and attention, is money making. They care nothing for the bountiful hand that has so liberally fed them, so long as the crumbs continue to fall." The *Journal* contended that Davenport, despite governmental favors bestowed upon it, like army camps and business contracts, lagged far behind less favored areas in meeting its recruiting quotas. The Dubuque *Times* echoed the *Journal* and claimed that Dubuque had largely redeemed itself from the odium of Copperheadism and deserved better treatment at the hands of the state's Union men than did Davenport's greedy populace. The paper waxed sarcastic at the expense of Davenporters on another occasion, this during the spring of 1864 when the midwestern states recruited several "hundred-days" regiments. These regiments were enlisted for short term garrison and guard duty in order to release the veteran three-year regiments for combat service. While recruiting was underway, the *Gazette* extolled one Davenport employer who agreed to pay the salary of one of his workers throughout the man's enlistment. Scores of Dubuque employers did the same, declared the *Times,* many of whom sought no publicity for their generosity.[37] One other clear act of generosity, or something related to it, did occur in Dubuque, and it was unusual for its day—or for any other. A farmer who borrowed $600 in gold from a Dubuque capitalist in 1861 paid back the loan in specie in 1864, not in greenbacks, to the surprise of the lender. One good turn led to another. The lender refused to accept any interest.[38]

David Richardson worried sometimes about the economic future of the country. He feared a "financial whirlwind" after the war. Richardson favored higher federal taxes in order to put the government and the war on a "pay as we go" basis and to prevent national financial ruin. Such taxes would force the upper classes to dip into their surplus funds and, in the bargain, cut their "reckless extravagance." But he wanted local taxes held down. Thomas Clagett and Lysander Babbitt also complained about current federal financial policies which, they believed, benefited too much the interests of capital. Clagett also fretted about the rise in the price of gold. As it rose, he said, so would the prices of cotton, coffee, sugar, and tea. After buying essentials, citizens had to spend what was left in taxes to pay off a few millionaires who held all the government bonds. Nevertheless, editorial concern about these matters was limited; people seemed to be able to pay taxes, buy essentials and, contrary to Clagett's assertion, still have something left over.[39]

Some people remained watchful of the railroads, believing that their best interests did not necessarily coincide with those of the roads. Still, there was no continuing clamor about railroad rate extortion. The *Herald* and the *State Democratic Press* defended rate increases on the grounds that railroads like every other business had to pay more for materials and wages. The *Press* pointed out to the *Iowa City Republican,* which did occasionally cry extortion, that while rates were indeed high, shippers could get their produce to the Mississippi far more cheaply than they had before the railroads arrived.[40] Of more concern to shippers were the periodic difficulties they experienced in getting enough cars to haul freight east, or, at Dubuque, getting freight across the river in either direction on the railroad-owned ferry. Illinois Central officials made efforts to overcome the bottleneck, but achieved only temporary successes.[41]

If Iowa Democrats could not effectively play on economic discontent among the electorate in 1864, neither does it appear that they could or did ride the race issue quite so much as they had earlier. Charles Mason, publicly and privately, still liked to cite what he believed was conclusive evidence that blacks lived better in slavery than under Northern liberators. He also proclaimed that blacks had no "finer" feelings, no need for liberty, no past worth knowing, and no future except under white dominion. But even he conceded that blacks were undergoing an "infant" stage of development on their way to freedom—though that freedom lay in the distant future.[42] Thomas Clagett also continued to denigrate blacks. Hannibal, he said, was no black, but rather "a pure blooded red (copper colored), man, a race to which the North American Indians belong, and one which . . . have ever conquered and held the negro race under subjection whenever the two have come into contact with each other." Clagett especially wanted to put to rest any notion that blacks had any superior fighting qualities. But Clagett, or some other writer on the *Constitution,* could deal with Keokuk's growing black populace almost evenhandedly. When the city's blacks celebrated the anniversary of West Indies emancipation with a parade, the paper noted that the paraders, mostly women and children, conducted themselves in an "unexceptionable" manner "and presented a very neat and geneteel appearance."

Moreover some of the women could easily have passed for white.[43] The Dubuque *Herald* respected black abilities occasionally. When three whites assaulted a black man who was minding his own business on the levee, he whipped all three. The paper applauded his skill and, by inference, the result. Dubuque's justice court could deal fairly with blacks. When white John Seymour assaulted an unoffending black in a case of mistaken identity, the court fined Seymour $10 and costs and lodged him in jail.[44] Republican editors reported good news about blacks when they could. When a group of women and children from the South landed at Burlington seeking work, most, "having been tutored to labor," found jobs. Employers soon pronounced them "faithful and industrious." To appear too pro-black, however, could bring scorn on one's head, as John Mahin of the Muscatine *Journal* found out when Clagett declared that Mahin should have been born black.[45]

Miscegenation quickly acquired status as a scare word, and Iowans of all political persuasions constantly sought to show that they approved none of it. If there was a Democratic inference that abolitionist women at the Sea Islands of South Carolina were becoming mothers with the assistance of black men, a Republican journal would remind readers that race-mixing had been a "favorite diversion" of the First Families of Virginia. W. W. Junkin reacted hotly when Clagett charged that a Keokuk mixed couple had gotten married in Fairfield. It was a lie, he wrote, "a slander on our city," but if true would be more moral an arrangement than "the illicit intercourse which white men, claiming to be Democrats, have with Negro wenches." The *Nonpareil* maintained that one Pottawattamie county Democratic activist had been "peaceably miscegenating" with a black woman for years, that everybody knew it, but that no one questioned the propriety of the arrangement because "Copperheads and niggers have a perfect right to mix. . . ." The writer declared, however, that it was never proper for loyal men and women to mix [sexually] with blacks. When William Merritt in Des Moines complained that it was not uncommon "to see a white lass hanging upon the arm of a gentleman of color," the *Gate City* declared that Copperhead ladies and Southern slaveholders might engage in such "unseemly conduct," but Republican ladies never. Dubuque had a black residence on Clay near Fourth street where white girls were seen "to enter at all hours of the night to meet the sable sons of Africa, or those of lighter hue." The *Herald* accepted the place wryly, adding, "The house has an excellent run of custom[ers] judging from appearances, and should declare a dividend before long." But Thomas Clagett saw no humor whatever in what he thought was an increasing amount of race mixing in Keokuk, particularly black-white marriages and the birth of mulatto children to black women.[46]

Iowa whites didn't usually want black children in public schools next to their own. When one Dubuque citizen asked if there were no way to expel black children attending the first ward school, T. Hardee, secretary to the board of education, assured him that there were no such children, including mulattoes, in the school system. Soon after, however, a Dubuque woman opened a small school for the city's black youngsters. Then on June 3 the board decided to follow the recommendation of its select committee on the education of colored children that it contribute $10 a month to the school's teachers retroactive to May 1 and thereafter at the discretion of the board. The committee stated that the school had at most thirteen students out of some potential twenty in the district. While these numbers were not reason enough to provide public support, the members believed that Dubuque's blacks deserved some educational aid.[47]

One would like to know more about the life of Iowa's black population during this period. How, for instance, did those fare who came up the river, moved inland, settled with or near abolitionist sponsors, and worked as domestics or farm hands? How many places actually provided some education for black children? Where blacks and whites had daily and casual contact as in the river cities there was always some tension. The *Constitution* observed that when a few blacks got together, a crowd of whites would cluster and "pitch into" them. Newspapers often printed stories about drunkenness or other unseemly behavior by blacks. How the papers handled such stories varied with their political predilections. When one Dubuque black woman acted in an aggressive manner toward a white man on the levee, the *Times* concluded that she had been "made shameless by habits contracted on a southern plantation in the days of slaveholders' power." The *Hawk-eye* and the Muscatine *Journal* repeated the *Times* story verbatim. But when a writer for the *Constitution* saw a black woman drinking freely and enjoying herself in a Keokuk saloon, he sermonized differently, judging that "Such is the effect of Lincoln's philanthropy for the negro—take them from good masters and comfortable homes to visit the miseries of drunkenness and taste of its bitterness."[48]

Some Iowans could not abide gratuitous violence visited upon blacks and their enterprises. When rowdies of the "Copperhead stripe" demolished a black barber's shop in Cedar Rapids, sympathetic citizens quickly collected enough money to make up his loss.[49] Nor could Davenporters ignore the wanton murder of George Frame, a "peaceable, quiet," married black veteran. William Knapp, a drunken soldier of the Fifth Iowa, shot Frame in the back. Knapp and his attorney were uncertain enough about his chances before a Davenport jury that they secured a change of venue to Clinton county. There a jury failed to arrive at a verdict. The War Department then requested that Knapp be returned to military jurisdiction for court martial. Governor Stone agreed. A military court found him guilty, but not of felonious intent. Knapp served a three month sentence in the military prison at Alton, Illinois, before being mustered out of the service on November 10, 1864, ten and one-half months after the killing. The *Democrat* declared that he was fortunate to get off so lightly for such a serious offense. A similar case involving the unprovoked murder of a Des Moines mulatto by a drunken soldier resulted in sympathy for the dead man, not for his killer, a reenlistee of the Tenth Iowa.[50] But a black accused of a sex crime was in a very dangerous position. In Muscatine a mob tried to lynch a black man accused of attempted rape of a fourteen-year old Muscatine white girl. After beating him senseless and nearly strangling him with a rope while dragging him down the street, they left him for dead. The man, J. English, survived and stood trial. When convicted, the judge sentenced him to ten years in the penitentiary. (Pat Murphy, also found guilty of the same offense at the same session of court, received an eighteen-month sentence.)[51]

Reports of black soldiers' battle performance commanded attention in all Iowa papers. Republican journals emphasized their success and Democratic journals their failures, especially alleged cases of cowardice. The Dubuque *Herald*'s May 1 coverage of combat action involving black troops was standard for Democratic organs. Of eight banks of headlines, the third read: "The Nigger Troops Throw Down Their Arms and Make for the Rear." Only the last two sentences in the long text of the story dealt with the black soldiers. The first of the two repeated the essence of the headline. But the second read, "It is doubtless a canard." Coverage of the Fort Pillow massacre varied according to a paper's politics also. At the surrender of Fort Pillow, Tennessee, April 12, 1864, to Gen. N. B. Forrest, the victorious Confederates slaughtered an undetermined number of Union captives, both black and white. But black troopers bore the brunt of the victors' rage. The most extreme Democratic reaction may have been that coming from West Union's John Gharkey:

> Instead of shrieking for vengeance, we would admonish our Government to profit from past sad experience and put stolen niggers in their proper places. That the cowardly, deceptious, black sons of bitches ran and secreted themselves, and left the whites to fight the battle, there can be no doubt, and according to our mode of thinking, death administered by the proper authorities was their just desserts.[52]

Democratic editors had nothing good to say about Lincoln's and Grant's refusal to exchange prisoners so long as the South threatened to return the former slaves among the black POWs to their masters.[53] And at a great peace rally at Dubuque in August, Democrats approved a resolution which, if taken literally, called for the enslavement of *all* blacks, including freed and free blacks. The peace men declared in part that, "the liberty of the descendants of Africa in the United States is incompatible with the safety and liberty of the European descendants;— their slavery forms an exception, an exception resulting from a stern and inexorable necessity to the general liberty of the United States. . . ."[54]

On this subject, by that time, those Democrats who generally accepted the Copperhead label, were at odds with such men as Thomas Clagget who did not. This is not to say that Copperheads and War Democrats in Iowa or elsewhere in 1864, or at any other time, were primarily distinct from one another on the slavery issue and the position of blacks in America. But War Democrats did not insist that slavery be regarded as sacrosanct. They did not whine that slavery was a full-fledged Southern right which was essential to the restoration of the Union and an essential condition to the maintenance of white freedom in the future of that Union.

Clagett, too much scorned by Copperheads, and falsely accused of pro-Southern sympathy by Republicans, opposed the Emancipation Proclamation, not because he liked slavery, but because he saw the Proclamation as a dangerous assumption of presidential power which would lead to the assumption of more powers and the end of civil liberties. Nevertheless, slavery was doomed from the start of the war; no Northern man, Democrats included, he added inaccurately, would regret its natural death. Clagett saw no reason why Lincoln and the North should not insist that the South "consent" to abolition of its slave property as a penalty for acts of "rebellion and treason." This would entail no arbitrary emancipation since in return for Southern consent the North should not demand that the loss take place all at once. The South had only to make provision for gradual emancipation "so that there . . . be a final end of slavery within a reasonable time."[55] Clagett's approach was his own. His specific solution was hardly one most men had considered. But in a sense he addressed himself more to the existing dilemma of war over Union *and* slavery than did the Copperheads who remained intransigent on all fronts: on the war—stop it; on slavery—restore Southern rights "full-fledged"; on reunion—it *would* come since the South did not mean what it said about independence.

From the Republican side came two penetrating critiques of the Copperhead arguments on the fixedness of slavery and the total subordination of blacks in the United States. Clark Dunham's was the most thorough and the longest. Dunham posed a series of questions: (1) Why place so much emphasis on whiteness in determining who should have power or who should be enslaved? (2) Who was, after all, white, or half-white, or black? Why were some dark whites acceptable but lighter blacks not? (3) Were only Europeans to be considered white? Were not many of them half-white? (4) If only Africans were fit for slavery, which Africans? Many Africans were as white as half of Europe. (5) Why were "Negroes" alone selected for slavery? Dunham believed that Africa-descended blacks were less barbarous than American Indians, South Sea Islanders, or Australian aborigines. Then he got to the nub of his argument. It dealt ultimately with the preservation of freedom:

There is no possibility of giving a sensible reason for talking about the rights of white men being superior to those of blacks or any intermediate shade. The simple fact is that white men had the *power* to make slaves of black men and they *did it*. It was wrong then, wrong now, and will be wrong to all eternity. We are now paying the penalty of that wrong. The civil war grew out of that wrong. The blood and treasure and cares and anxieties attending the war is our punishment for the outrage we have committed against the laws of reason, justice and humanity. And one of the worst penalties we are suffering under is that insane hate of the Negro, who is hated *because* he is wronged, which so blinds the madmen that they cannot see that freedom to *all,* is the only possible security for freedom to *any.* To admit that *any* man should be a slave is an admission that *all* should be. Nothing but force makes slaves. It makes the law of *might,* not of right.[56]

The editor of the Corydon *Monitor* was also interested in the Copperhead Democrat insistence upon hard and fast distinctions among men being the sine qua non for the maintenance of popular government and freedom. He wrote:

> If we make distinctions at all, where shall we stop? and if we make distinctions in color, why shall we not in size? and if in size, why not in intellect, in education? And one who appreciates the true spirit of republicanism, knows that a step in that direction is a blow to popular government and a bitter sarcasm on the people who boast of freedom and whose motto is "equal rights to all men."[57]

The effect such editorial excursions into the implications of black slavery in an otherwise free society had upon readers was probably small. More germane to the average man were news or speculation about an influx of blacks into the labor force. During 1863 that prospect loomed larger than it did in 1864. The year 1864 was generally a year of labor shortage. The sight of black deckhands on the *Pembina* twice provoked a fight between crewmen and Dubuque "wharf rats." But city officials and the *Herald* sided with the crew. The *Herald* firmly asserted that men who wouldn't work for $50 a month should not interfere with those who would.[58] Thomas Clagett remained alert to the possibility that blacks would oust whites from jobs. He reported a rumor that some Keokuk merchants were discharging white men and hiring female blacks in their stead at wages too low for family men to survive. If true, he declared, this was "mean [and] despicable" and harmful to "Honest and industrious Europeans." But Clagett never followed up the rumor and never throughout 1864 labored this theme as he had in 1863.[59]

Getting enough recruits to fill Iowa's quotas for the army remained a serious problem through 1864. The Muscatine *Courier* had no doubt as to who should enlist, namely, Muscatine Loyal Leaguers. Wrote editor Thayer, "Come now, WM. F. DAVIS—unloose your hold of the government teat—and become a 'bold soldier boy.' Follow suit, JOHN MAHIN, and leave the Post Office that you may respond to your country's call. PLINY FAY, Can't you stop chawing government pap, and 'rally round the flag, boy'? . . ."[60] David Richardson scorned Scott county Republicans who, he said, excelled in "theoretical patriotism," which did not include joining the army.[61]

Governor Stone tried hard to ensure that the state would meet its quota under Lincoln's call for 500,000 men, to be met by a March 10 draft if necessary. Bothered by reports that numerous military-age males were preparing to head West in the dead of winter to find their fortune in the gold fields, the Governor issued a proclamation forbidding the citizenry to depart the state before the draft date without proper authorization. He requested militia unit commanders along the Missouri River to guard all crossings between Sioux City and Leavenworth. He instructed them to turn back any persons not bearing passes issued by the provost marshals of their home districts. Gen. S. R. Curtis wrote Stone from Leavenworth that while he approved the Governor's objective, he had too few troops to carry it out.[62] How many men actually departed before or after Stone's proclamation no one knows. But those who did surely inspired those who had not to think about it. Delaware county's John Kenyon wrote, "I have not had the fever [to go West] much yet, but I think I should if Uncle Sam makes another call for half a million or less." In May the *Gate City,* although located several hundred miles east of the Missouri River, concluded after weeks of observation that there were indeed many Iowans heading West and that they were all Copperheads, not Republicans. Those who sought other ways to avoid the service irritated David Richardson. "The prevailing elements complained of by those who aspire to exemption," he declared, "are rheumatism and hernia, although almost all, especially those who have a bogus claim upon disability, present a catalogue that would startle their nearest relatives." Lysander Babbitt was also dubious about the sudden appearance of a host of infirmities among the draft eligibles in Council Bluffs.[63]

There were enough recruits to keep Iowa free of the draft that spring. But it was a different story that fall. At that time the government conscripted 1,862 men from wards and townships who could not raise sufficient commutation or bounty money to get men to enlist to their credit.[64] Many Copperheads, and nearly everybody else, did their best to render a draft unnecessary in their own subdistricts. Both the *Nonpareil* and the *Bugle* in Council Bluffs approved a city bounty of $20 a month to all married and $10 a month to all single enlistees in December of 1863. When Polk county's board of supervisors refused to vote a bounty, the Des Moines city council came through with one of $50, better than none, though still too small, judged the *Statesman.*[65] Fremont county's supervisors turned down a bounty by a 5 to 2 vote, but not those in Blackhawk who voted enough money to entice enlistees from Chicakasaw and other nearby counties to enlist to Blackhawk's credit.[66] George Williams, superintendent of the Keokuk, Fort Des Moines, and Minnesota Railroad, told one of his enlisting employees that if he could round up four men to go with him, he, Williams, would give each man $50. The inducement worked. Keokuk's A. Hine likewise gave $50 to each of two enlistees. Keokuk could use such generosity that winter because the city council failed by a 5 to 4 vote to approve a city bounty.[67] The *Gate City* sympathized with Marion township. Marion, it said, was strong for the Union, but too poor to offer a bounty, whereas "intensely Copperhead" West Point [50 percent German born] could offer liberal bounties which enticed enlistees from Marion.[68]

With Lincoln's July, 1864, call for 500,000 men acting as a spur, pressure to raise bounty money increased more than ever. Keokuk did produce such money this time and escaped a draft once again. Clagett claimed this occurred at the expense of poorer rural townships who previously supplied more men proportionately than Keokuk to the army, but who could not match Keokuk's wealth. Clagett also noted the $700 going price for substitutes in Muscatine and the $900–$1000 supposedly offered in Davenport. Poor men in both places, he reported quite superfluously, could not pay such prices.[69]

Poor men in Dubuque county who didn't want to go to the army didn't have to because a belated massive effort to raise bounty money succeeded handsomely. On September 22, officials held a public drawing of names for the draft for that portion of Julien township which lay outside the boundary of Dubuque city. Michael Carney won what most felt was the dubious honor of being number one among forty-six names drawn. By this time some of Dubuque's leading Democrats were moving swiftly to head off a further drawing. These included Dennis Mahony and Col. John F. Bates who urged the county supervisors to meet immediately in order to vote public funds to pay bounties. The *Times,* which preferred that the drawing proceed on schedule, was sarcastic about the role Mahony and Bates played. "We are pleased," said the editor, "to see these distinguished advocates of an immediate cessation of hostilities engaged in a vigorous effort to secure volunteers to prosecute this 'unnatural and unjustifiable War,' and hope they will be eminently successful." He also objected to using public money to pay bounties. Hundreds of Dubuquers had enlisted without such an inducement. Furthermore, their property would be taxed to benefit those who set up a "fire in the rear" in their absence. Let the "peace sneaks" raise bounty money from private sources, he concluded. Meanwhile, committees in each ward and township in the county began to solicit funds to add to the anticipated county bounty. On October 1, the county board agreed to raise the necessary money by issuing $125,000 in coupon warrants at 6 percent interest annually payable in ten years. The board made its rationale and its sentiments clear when it said, "There is reason to believe that the peace of the County would be disturbed, its prosperity impaired, its business in the various walks of life suspended and the better portions of its able bodied population driven to exile to avoid compulsory conscription. . . . ." The results were immediate and gratifying. As word of Dubuque's munificence spread, scores of men from western counties flocked in to enlist for the $400 the county offered. Some fortunate recruits collected up to $700 by enlisting to the credit of wards and townships which made certain that they filled their quota by adding between $200 and $300 to the county bounty. Substitute brokers had a field day. When the frantic bidding for recruits ended, Dubuque county had issued warrants totaling $129,050 and staved off the draft once more.[70]

Irish laborers in Jackson county's Butler township also hoped desperately to avoid a draft. They received a late reprieve when local farmers raised substitute money. Some draft evaders fled Jefferson county, a few of them teachers. Oran Faville, Republican state superintendent of public instruction, warned them to return or else he would invalidate their teaching certificates. When some did not, Faville carried out his threat.[71] There was a draft in Iowa City. Local officials and the provost marshal handled the drawing fairly, the *State Democrat Press* admitted. But the editor was angry anyway. Loyal Leaguers brought on the war, bought themselves out of it, then left Democrats to do the fighting.[72] The draft especially embittered Council Bluffs *Bugle* editor Lysander Babbitt whose son Charles Babbitt was one of Pottawattamie county's conscripts. "Ghouls like these intensely loyal stay-at-home patriots," wrote the anguished senior Babbitt, ". . . seem to revel in the misery and suffering which has been thus brought upon two households by the 'Lottery of Death'. . . . We trust, however, that this fiendish feeling will not be satiated to its full extent, and that Charlie will soon return to wife, parents and friends. . . .'' Babbitt vented his rage upon opposition editor W. S. Burke of the *Nonpareil*. Those who promoted the war but never went were "cowardly hypocrites." Or if they did go, they ran away under fire. Burke, he claimed, did exactly that at the battle of Corinth, a charge he had repeated often over the previous two years.[73]

Jesse Macy described a carload of draftees leaving central Iowa for the army. Macy, a Quaker, who enlisted to do noncombatant service with the freedmen or as a medic, wrote:

> They generally seemed composed. Not a tear was shed, either by soldier or bystander. A veteran who was standing by remarked that "crying was about played out." I observed however one lad perhaps eighteen who was not so thoroughly trained in the "stoical" school. He took from his pocket a memorandum book to write. His face flushed with pure emotion.

Macy, after becoming acquainted with several veteran soldiers, was not inclined to believe that army experience would corrupt those who underwent it. "They [the veterans] were rough and profane in their habits," he observed, "yet one could see that they loved to talk to civil and religious men. Hence I would say do not turn the cold shoulder to the returning soldiers. Many of them may yet make usefull [sic] and agreeable Christian men."[74]

After the draft threat disappeared, some old faces, "recently returned from Canada," reappeared in Dubuque, according to the *Times*. And in Story county, reported one writer, a sudden outbreak of sickness among draft-age men, including home guardsmen, vanished as rapidly as it had come once the county fulfilled its quota.[75] Army demands for manpower had limits so far as Gen. Grenville M. Dodge was concerned. While he was away, he wanted his brother to stay home in Council Bluffs to attend to their mutual business problems. "If drafted," he advised Nathan, "get a substitute."[76] There was a possibility of one more draft, that scheduled for March 15, 1865. But the worst was over. Enough Iowans enlisted to make it unnecessary.[77]

Exemption for aliens was still a sore point with some citizens during the last year and a half of the war, especially David Richardson. Richardson, as he had in 1863, published the names and nationalities of those Scott county aliens who claimed exemptions. This angered *Der Demokrat*. Why not name the men applying for disability exemptions? asked the German paper. Since a reasonable doubt existed that all those who claimed to be physically disabled were truly unfit for service, there was some merit in *Der Demokrat*'s point, if not its suggestion for exposure. Richardson was not impressed. All who thought they might be incapacitated had a duty to find out if they really were, he answered. Aliens who simply wanted to avoid service to their chosen country in its hour of need were a different category altogether.[78]

One major act of violence connected with the draft occurred in Iowa. That was the ambush-murder, September 30, 1864, of two United States deputy marshals in Poweshiek county while they were en route to arrest several draft evaders. Two of the three assailants escaped. State officials quickly ordered two militia companies to the scene to preserve order. Public feeling ran high and the furious authorities arrested several other suspects. The affair culminated in forcible disbandment of one home guard unit, the "Democratic Rangers," and a life sentence for the captive, Pat Gleason. Republicans quickly made capital out of the event, calling it an inevitable result of Copperhead teachings. One Democratic paper desperately maintained that it had evidence that the three attackers were Republicans.[79] Few Iowans took the claim seriously.

There was always less difficulty getting Iowans to join home guard and militia units during the war. Trouble often arose, however, over granting officer commissions to those units. Sometimes officials faced a dilemma over whether to accept a proffered unit in the first place. The loyalty issue was usually at root in both kinds of cases. Loyalty was less an issue earlier in the war. But when official pressure increased in 1863 to establish home guard units to deal with the alleged Copperhead menace, loyal men came more and more to mean Republicans. Between July and November, Adjutant General Baker received eight letters from would-be officers who applied the Copperhead label to competing applicants and warned that they alone represented true Unionists in their counties or townships. The same situation developed again in the summer of 1864 when the compulsory militia enrollment law went into effect. Baker this time received over seventy-five different letters between the middle of July and the end of the year warning him not to recognize or arm alleged Copperhead guard units. The great majority came in the period between July 18 and August 15. Political partisanship frequently resulted in attempts to establish separate companies in the same locality. Men who found themselves in units apparently dominated by Copperheads wanted out and requested transfers to "loyal" companies.[80] One self-styled "loyal Democrat" militia captain in Washington wanted the Adjutant General to remove his two supposedly Copperhead lieutenants.[81] One anonymous informant told Baker that disloyal Copperheads and "Dutch [German] Catholics" comprised the unit raised in Lee county's West Point township. A different problem arose in the pietistic Amana colonies located between Iowa City and Marengo. Amana society members claimed exemption from the militia law. Angry William Springer wrote Baker that the Amanaites asked too much. "If they would be as neutral in voting against the country as in bearing arms in favor of it," he said, "there would be some consistency in them. . . . [instead] They ask special exclusive protection and favor from the government and vote *en masse* against it." Baker wrote on the back of Springer's letter, "No one will be exempted unless the laws exempt and if they don't do like other citizens I will try the effect of the law"—a solution which missed a relevant point that if the Amana people were to organize a guard company, the unit might be one which Baker would find politically unacceptable anyway.[82] Nathan Brainerd informed the Adjutant General that Johnson county's

Cedar township couldn't raise a full unit because several prospects refused to join, preferring to enter a Copperhead company being recruited in Big Grove township.[83] Audubon county had two rival groups. J. Lyman Frost, described as a Republican zealot by an Audubon county writer, headed one, and B. F. Thomas the other. Thomas's unit, the same writer reported, had a total of 61 Democrats out of a 71-man membership, some of whom were "emphatic anti-war men." Frost, a postmaster, solved the problem to his satisfaction by refusing to deliver the state-issued officers' commissions to the Thomas group.[84]

The oath prescribed for prospective militia officers was a stumbling block for some Democrats. It was a strong political statement pledging the taker, in effect, to support the Lincoln administration's war policies and to use his influence "to sustain those in power." Even the Republican Davenport *Gazette* said that considering the service the state intended the militia to perform, such an oath was "entirely unnecessary and wholly unwise." Stone wrote Baker that he never dreamed that anyone would object to the oath since the units would have a vital role, particularly in the southern counties where they would guard against guerillas and bushwhackers. Under pressure he changed the oath slightly so that it read that the oath-taker would sustain those "in authority" rather than those "in power." David Richardson correctly observed that this was no real change. In Winneshiek county some men elected to officer posts refused to take the original oath. In Union county some balked at Stone's new oath; they made up their own and swore to it. This was not good enough, a Union county man wrote Baker. The state should refuse to recognize the unit. Despite all the publicity about the guards' organization, oath, and purpose, some prospective enlisted men still didn't know much about it. One puzzled captain reported that three persons refused to enlist unless the unit's purpose was to resist the draft.[85]

By late August, Adjutant General Baker had grown weary of dealing with the flood of denunciations and complaints.[86] Not Stone. He believed reports that 33,000 members of secret Copperhead societies were yet active, particularly on the southern border. He judged that two-thirds of all Iowa Democrats were disloyal and told Baker, "I do not deign to be caught with chaff of any kind either Copperhead or pretended 'Union Democrat.' They must be Simon pure, or I shall not trust them." Eventually, however, even he tired of the interminable task of weeding out "traitors." By January, 1865, the two men had delegated the responsibility for determining officer and unit loyalty to local committees.[87] Before his enthusiasm flagged, the Governor also worried about the loyalty of those who applied for notary public commissions. In the spring of 1864, he had instructed his secretary to make certain that all applicant endorsements came from loyal people. Apparently Stone had granted notary commissions to some persons deemed unworthy by local patriots. Their complaints led to his demand for tighter loyalty checks.[88]

Though Baker and Stone in their more anxious moments may have thought to employ a military solution to the Copperhead problem, they turned down such a proposal by a Greene county man. Shortly after Stone's inauguration in 1864,

William Anderson wrote the new chief executive seeking permission to organize a 500-man anti-Copperhead regiment to squelch "traitors" anywhere in the state. Anderson desired weapons and a colonel's commission for himself. He confided that he had already picked his own lieutenant colonel and major. Stone's military secretary, George North, informed Anderson that the Governor found his spirit commendable, but added that no equipment was available for that purpose.[89]

State officials overreacted on the loyalty issue. Thomas Clagett believed they took southern border problems too seriously also. The Border Brigade was useless, he declared early in 1864. The state never had needed such a force. Its only defenders were Republicans to the north of the southern counties themselves. Many Brigade officers, Clagett charged, were men who "constantly manifested a disposition to intermeddle with the political privileges of the citizen for the benefit of the Republican party."[90]

Stone and Baker saw the border region differently. At the height of the militia enrollment drive in August, the Governor issued a proclamation similar to Kirkwood's of 1863. This one forbade Iowans to give asylum to any Missourians who had warred against the Missouri state government. He believed that Missourians were responsible for arson, robbery, and other crimes in the southern counties. He also made certain that over half of all the state's supply of arms went to the Border Brigade.[91] Baker issued "shoot to kill" orders to the Brigade in September. He would require no reports of prisoners taken, he said, and further promised that "any officer who takes as a prisoner any guerilla, murderer, thief or marauder of such armed band, will at once be dismissed from the state service." Baker also prohibited the use of blank cartridges and threatened to dismiss any officer who employed them "for preserving public peace."[92] Such orders, fortunately, did not apply to homegrown Copperheads. Capt. Samuel Glenn of a Clarke county company used 20 men in a bloodless raid which netted 12 of them plus seven rifles, five revolvers, one shotgun and a supply of ammunition.[93] Not so fortunate were two persons who, some thought, died because of Baker's order. One, Richard P. Dunn, alleged horse stealer and murderer, a former member of the Fifth Missouri Cavalry, was killed at Hamburg in Fremont county on November 1. The second victim was an unnamed "highwayman," thought to be guilty of horse stealing and robbery. Council Bluffs citizens found him hanging one morning from a willow tree at the rear of Hagg's block. No great hue and cry arose from either incident. What is interesting is that while two Democratic editors thought they might have stemmed from Baker's draconian directive, they didn't complain much about either one. William Merritt reported that Dunn had murdered a Thomas Rodes on October 16 and that "The murder was malicious and without the least provocation." Lysander Babbitt regretted that there had been no trial for the Council Bluffs victim, but added, "The man no doubt got his just desserts. . . ." Babbitt was at least as much concerned with using the incident to prod the Pottawattamie county supervisors to erect a better jail as he was with using it to remind the people that they should take the delegated powers back into their own hands "and the execution of criminals in their own way."[94]

There was one bloody guerilla foray into southern Iowa in the fall of 1864 which seemed, paradoxically, to demonstrate the need for well armed guard units *and* their ultimate ineffectiveness in coping with a real guerilla problem. On October 12, a group of marauders disguised in Union army apparel swept into Davis county from Missouri. They robbed nearly a score of persons, destroyed household weapons, kidnapped several individuals, and murdered three men, two of them soldiers. They terrorized the countryside for over twelve hours before releasing the rest of their captives and vanishing across the border. Frustrated militiamen, five hours behind the invaders, couldn't trace them in Missouri. State officials set up active border patrols for a time thereafter. The patrols engaged in several shooting affrays with border crossers which resulted in one more Iowa death and jail for 13 Missourians. Iowa eventually turned all 13 over to Missouri authorities.[95]

The October 12 raid also worried Provost Marshal J. M. Hiatt. He sent an urgent message to Gen. John Pope, commander of the Department of the Northwest, calling for application of "military law" in southern Iowa to keep the guerillas at bay. Hiatt also claimed to be credibly informed that Keokuk stood in danger of imminent attack. Pope sent two observers, Brig. Gen. T. C. H. Smith and Maj. E. P. Ten Broeck, to Keokuk to see how serious the Keokuk and southern border problems were. Both men concluded that a reorganized militia could handle anything else that might arise. Pope was generally skeptical in 1863 and 1864 that Iowans ever had much to fear from either internal disorders (draft resistance) or external ones (trouble from Missouri). He wrote Smith that the government should send no federal troops to the region. Citizens would demand that they stay long after they were no longer needed.[96]

Except for the border troubles, violence against persons seemed to decline in Iowa during the last year and a half of the war. Still, there were some notable incidents. One Dutch schoolgirl at Pella refused to remove a Copperhead pin from her dress. She employed a poker to ward off assailants who tried to take it by force. Told by her principal to discard the pin and apologize, she refused. She said she would sooner leave the "abolition institution" which she promptly did. Veteran soldiers of the Fourth Iowa, home on leave in April, forced several Winterset Copperheads to take the oath of allegiance. A squad of recruits at Adel compelled some Adel Democrats to do likewise. But they failed to cow one Adel lawyer, a two-year army veteran, into following suit. At Mount Vernon three soldiers who extracted oaths from some unhappy citizens found themselves before a local magistrate who fined them $10 each for their fun. The angry soldiers then compelled the local zealots, who had egged them on in the first place, to pay their fines and costs.[97]

Soldiers vandalized several Cedar Rapids businesses and threatened others, all of them allegedly run by Copperheads. The *Cedar Valley Times* was ambivalent about the destruction visited upon dentist A. K. Minor's shop. The

Times deplored the act, but had no sympathy for Minor, whom it called "a most violent Copperhead." William Merritt noted that one opposition paper, the Iowa City *Republican,* had a respect for law and order and civil liberties. The *Republican* condemned the soldiers. Smashing the businesses of men holding different political opinions changed no minds and led to anarchy, the editor said.[98] In one Dubuque county community, Cascade, different political opinions sorely tried William H. Francis. Francis was still trying vainly to organize a home guard unit as late as February, 1865. Copperheads there threatened him with a ducking in the river if he didn't desist. "This is the most treasonable place I ever set my foot in," he sputtered angrily to Adjutant General Baker. He blamed his troubles on the *Herald*'s teachings.[99]

Democratic editors in Iowa during 1864 were more often on the receiving end of trouble than on the other. Even the *Herald* in Democratic territory was not entirely immune. In mid-March, 1864, Sheriff Mahony, his deputies, Provost Marshal Shubael Adams, Deputy United States Marshal P. H. Conger, and officers of the Ninth Iowa Infantry got wind of an attempt to incite members of the regiment, then on its way South, to mob the paper. They reacted quickly and nipped the plot in the bud. A local citizen learned that what might go unpunished elsewhere, was not treated so lightly in Dubuque. Authorities bound him over to district court under $500 bond to face a charge of inciting to riot.[100] Such was the initiation of Patrick Robb, F. M. Ziebach, and M. M. Ham who had just bought out Mahony, Hutchins, and John Hodnett. Robb as senior editor pursued a moderate course compared with his predecessors. What trouble he usually had thereafter came from other Democrats who thought he was a warmonger. The *Times* noted this development and analyzed the situation. The plight of Dubuque's Democrats was similar to that of Democrats across the country, said the paper. There was a large group of "ultras" devoted to slavery, to meeting Southern demands, and to peace at any price. There was also a second and larger group of "peace sneaks" who favored the war to a point, or who at least deemed it unsafe to be openly against it. Out for spoils, they had no clearly defined policy. If Union armies were successful before the fall election, they would more strongly support the war. If the armies met disaster, they would cry "peace." There was a third group, continued the *Times.* Robb belonged to it. This group consisted of third-rate politicians who scrambled for crumbs left by the other two groups. It published the bitter broadsides the "ultras" and the "peace sneaks" fired at each other with nary a comment on either. "[L]ike a kindhearted and impartial nurse," wrote the *Times,* "[it] endeavors to care for the wounded of both the belligerents." Pejorative language aside, the *Times* saw Robb's stance more clearly than the *Iowa State Register* which erroneously insisted that Robb was as much a peace man and opponent of Northern victory as was Hutchins. Robb did object strongly to Grant's expenditure of men. But what he wanted from Grant was decisive victory to justify the cost. More shrewdly than the defeatists, Robb refused to believe that no news from Sherman in December spelled disaster. If the news was bad for the Union, the Richmond papers would let everybody know about it, he declared. Then on January 14, 1865, Robb retired because of ill health. New senior editor Ham quickly indicated that there would be an editorial shift in the *Herald*. The *Herald* would now stand for peace, exactly where it thought the party stood.[101]

In Republican Burlington, the *Argus* had worse problems than the *Herald*. At the start of 1864 its weekly edition remained alive, but the daily died of anemic circulation. The death evoked no sympathy from the *Hawk-eye*. On the other hand, Keokuk's Thomas Clagett viewed it as an opportunity to increase the readership of his own struggling *Constitution*. The *Argus* weekly nearly met its end in April when some antagonists tried to persuade the men of the Fourth Iowa Cavalry to put it out of business. However, three Republicans, two of them marshals, spoke firmly to the soldiers who then left it alone.[102] Also in April, soldiers publicly humiliated Muscatine *Courier* editor Edward Thayer. They surrounded his house, some of them brandishing weapons, and ordered him out to take the oath of allegiance. Marched to the mayor's office for the ceremony, Thayer expected local Democrats to come to his aid. When he encountered only "several hundred Abolitionists, but no Democrats," the furious editor took the oath. Thayer blamed local abolitionists and the Muscatine *Journal* for inciting the soldiers. He vowed vengeance on the *Journal* and called for Muscatine Democrats to organize and arm themselves for their own protection. The Iowa City *Republican*, as it had following the vandalism in Cedar Rapids, condemned the soldiers and their allies.[103]

Nobody tried to wreck Lysander Babbitt's *Bugle* in Council Bluffs. But the Republican-dominated city council gave the town marshal the right to award printing of the city's delinquent tax list to whatever responsible printer he chose, regardless of who was the low bidder. The marshal gave it to the *Nonpareil*, which charged nearly twice as much as the *Bugle*, according to the disgruntled Babbitt. Babbitt professed to be unworried, however, since he had a lot of well-paying job work. What really angered him was a *Nonpareil* charge that he had been an abolitionist lecturer in Illinois years earlier. That *was* going too far! His furious denials had no effect on the *Nonpareil* which gravely asserted that "more than a thousand eye and ear witnesses" could verify Babbitt's unsuspected past.[104] The editor of the *State Democratic Press* in Iowa City never suffered the indignity of being called an ex-abolitionist. But his paper was not the money-maker Babbitt's was. Hence, he called for increased private support so he and other Democratic editors like him could stand up to the opposition, "fed from the public trough . . . obese and gorged" as it was.[105] The opposition usually was economically healthier. After the November elections, several Democratic papers folded temporarily or permanently, or like the *Statesman*, ceased to publish a daily but carried on with a weekly edition.[106]

Republicans charged that Copperheads tried to burn the Fort Madison *Plain Dealer* in March, a charge that remained unproved. Other than that, Republicans remained physically unscathed, unless one counts the bruises a *Nonpareil* writer suffered in June of 1865 at the hands of Joe Foreman, described as a Copperhead seller of dry goods and whiskey. Foreman objected to the way the paper handled a story, not to its description of his politics or his business.[107]

There were three cases of violence against Democratic papers in 1864, all of them occurring early in the year. Thomas Clagett ran into trouble with a gang of soldiers from the military hospital who tried once again to put the *Constitution* out of business. Intending to smash his press, they succeeded only in breaking several windows.[108] Less fortunate was David Sheward of the Fairfield *Constitution and Union.* Soldiers of Company E, Second Iowa, partially destroyed Sheward's shop and tried to set it afire in February. Civilians quickly rushed to his rescue and put out the blaze. Sheward never revived the paper. Instead, he crossed the state to work as a typesetter for the *Bugle.* Sheward's competitor, W. W. Junkin of the *Ledger,* along with Frank Palmer of the *Iowa State Register,* condemned the soldiers. "We are an advocate of free speech, and we're in favor of Sheward using it," wrote Junkin pithily.[109] In Oskaloosa, A. W. Wheelock's Oskaloosa *Times* met a similar fate. Wheelock's trouble stemmed from the aftermath of an 1863 political altercation which left one Mahaska County man dead. The victim was a soldier on furlough whom Wheelock editorially deprecated as a "Lincoln hireling." When the *Times* issue containing the offensive judgment reached the dead man's unit (Company H, Third Iowa) in Missisippi, the members vowed to get a retraction from the editor. On their next furlough several soldiers asked Wheelock for an apology. He refused. Shortly after, they pied his type and tossed the cases into the street. Wheelock left the county shortly.[110]

Most Democratic editors were more careful than Wheelock. This is not to say that as a rule they were antisoldier or opposed to Union army successes. Rather it means that those who had doubts about the rightness of the war did as the *State Democratic Press* did in the latter part of 1864. The *Press* applauded Union victories and the valor of Union soldiers even as it warned that "in the subjugation of the South is involved the surrender of our liberties, the erection of an odious monarchy on the ruins of the Republic."[111] Clagett's misgivings about the results of Northern victory were fewer. But in soldier-filled Keokuk those questions he did raise won him more enemies among "true Unionists" than he deserved. More perceptive about him than those who periodically tried to destroy his paper was the Burlington *Hawk-eye.* The *Constitution,* said its upstream rival, was inconsistent and made a fool of itself; but the *Hawk-eye* inferred nothing traitorous about either characteristic. Clagett's idiosyncrasy, it argued, lay in his complaining about Lincoln's repeated call for vast numbers of enlistments even while he praised Grant and eagerly anticipated the fall of Richmond.[112] David Richardson expressed doubts similar to Clagett's, but like the stormy Keokuk editor, he always approved Union successes and Union soldier performance in battle. Richardson even admired the way Sherman waged war. And in typical Richardson prose, he lauded one of the General's presumed tactics. It was a passage which must have caused apoplexy among what Peace-Democratic readership he had— although upon reflection they might have recalled that the editor always was a "pay-as-you-go" man. Wrote the Davenporter approvingly: "The Sherman expedition made expenses, and something over, out of this trip, if the report as to the quantity of cotton he has taken in Savannah is correct. It is a good thing to make an enterprise pay."[113] Smaller papers also, though unbending Lincoln critics, could, like the Independence *Conservative*, praise Union military successes and hope they would lead to the fall of the Confederacy.[114]

There were a few Iowans like Charles Mason who wanted the North to lose the war, but they did not trumpet that fact in public, although Mason's letters, signed "X" in the Dubuque *Herald*, could hardly be said to have welcomed Northern victories or praised Grant, Sherman, and their troops.[115] Nor did a letter from a Dubuque woman to her brother serving in the Confederate army, a letter which appeared first in the Mobile *Advertiser and Register*, then in the Atlanta *Appeal*, and finally in the Dubuque *Times*. The scornful *Times* omitted the writer's name but printed her letter in full. She said if she were a man she would fight with her brother and the "noble soldiers" of the South against the "worthless scum of the North."[116] Some Dubuque Copperheads got taken in during the fall of 1864 by a man who turned up calling himself Captain Sullivan and claiming to be a rebel escapee from a Northern prison camp in Ohio. They wined and dined him and collected $100 for his use when he said he needed money to get back to Georgia to rejoin the Confederate forces. When "Captain Sullivan" next appeared, he was an army recruit flashing bounty money (plus $100) in a camp at Davenport, having been one of the numerous enlistees who poured into Dubuque in the fall of 1864 to take advantage of the county's free-spending policy aimed at avoiding a draft.[117] One entire family, the Prettymans in Davenport, found themselves in a worse predicament. In an obvious case of entrapment, they befriended two supposedly "escaping" rebel soldiers trying to make their way to Canada. When the fugitives turned out to be undercover agents, the Prettymans had to post a $5,000 bond and take an "ironclad oath" guaranteeing their future loyal conduct. The *Democrat* ignored the conclusion of the episode. But the Dubuque *Herald* defended Prettyman, the packet agent for the Northern Line, maintaining that he had only acted like any other Good Samaritan.[118]

The war cooled relations between some who formerly had been friends and professional associates. Before he went off to the army, Major William Thompson was the partner of Col. Isaac M. Preston in the Marion law firm of Preston and Thompson. Preston was a peace man who viewed his ex-partner's course with dismay. "Col. Preston says," Jane Thompson wrote her husband, "[that] if you live to get home, you will find that you have not as many friends in this country as you used to have." Mrs. Thompson remained unworried. Preston was wrong, she thought. The Major would still have both the friends and the influence he formerly enjoyed. She was correct. After getting out of the army, Thompson served both elective and appointive posts for many years including district attorney, federal district court judge, congressman, and chief justice of the Idaho Territory.[119]

The year 1864 was a year of bitter dissension among Iowa's Democrats. They agreed on only one point: Lincoln and the Republicans had to be defeated in order to save the country from ruin. Neither the war nor the peace faction, however, had the remotest confidence in each other's means nor the principles behind the means to achieve that end. Very early in the year David Sheward called for peace men to organize so they could dominate county conventions, the state convention, and, ultimately, with peace men from other states, the national convention, there to choose a peace candidate who would surely win the presidency.[120] Two who agreed with this general approach were D. Baugh, Clayton county party chairman, and Nathan Sales of Anamosa. Both also believed Confederate military victories would help the Democrats, especially if they nominated a peace candidate to run on a peace platform.[121] There were some who agreed with Sheward's approach without being so optimistic as he about the outcome. Thomas Clagett neither agreed with the approach nor with the wisdom of the anticipated result, much less with Baugh's and Sales's hope for helpful Confederate successes along the way. A peace president could not restore the Union, he said; and the only possible peace was a peace based on Union.[122]

Generally agreeing with Clagett were William Merritt, Patrick Robb, David Richardson, Edward Thayer, G. M. Todd of the Burlington *Argus* and, to a lesser degree, Ira Mitchell and John P. Irish of the *State Democratic Press*. The peace forces had fewer big name editors. Lysander Babbitt was the only sure one. On the other hand, the 1863–1864 state party chairman LeGrand Byington and the 1864–1865 chairman, Laurel Summers, were peace men. So were Mahony, Hutchins, Sales, Henry Clay Dean, Charles Mason, Charles Negus of Fairfield, most but not all of Dubuque's Democratic leaders, A. C. Dodge of Burlington, and John Wallace, recently deposed head of the state agricultural society. There were factions within the factions, particularly in the peace group where Byington was determined to force the more pragmatic among them as well as the rest of the party, to stand unequivocally for an immediate armistice, peace negotiations, and a return to the status quo antebellum.[123] Cooler voices than his made some of Byington's supporting points better than he. One was Samuel Durham who wrote Laurel Summers that since the United States could not constitutionally make war against a sovereign state, there was no use arguing whether the Lincoln administration conducted the war in a constitutional manner. Pottawattamie County Democrats did not deal with the constitutional question. But they made a serious statement about the war and those who fought in it which was one of the few truly forthright yet nonabrasive statements made by any political group in Iowa during the war. They simply said, ". . . while we accord to soldiers in the field mede [*sic*] of praise for deeds or daring and courage, we are nevertheless opposed to a further prosecution of the war."[124]

Byington temporarily held the upper hand in the state party by virtue of his position. He used it, as had Dennis Mahony in 1861, to enunciate his own version of party policy when he and his committee issued a formal call for the state convention. Byington called for a restoration "as far as may be possible [of] the *status quo ante bellum*," for selection of delegates who favored "speedy termination of the existing war; maintenance of the Union by strict observance of the Constitution; and punishment of guilty leaders of sectional parties, North and South."

Such leaders were men "tending to bankrupt, brutalize and Africanize the nation."[125] Byington's efforts were in vain. Enough war men attended the convention to turn aside all efforts to write any state platform at all, a War Democrat victory since their objective was to commit Iowa's Democrats to campaign on whatever platform the national convention adopted. Nor did the peace men succeed in electing a solid peace delegation to be sent to Chicago. They even quarreled as to whether some of the peace men in the delegation were really pure in their commitment to peace.[126]

This was intolerable to Byington. Even though Summers was now state chairman, Byington called for a new state convention. He declared that his convention would write a peace platform and choose delegates to go to Chicago who would ensure that Iowa's voice there was a voice for peace. The Iowa City maverick's course caused consternation, even among his friends. He held his combination convention-peace rally in Iowa City on August 24 and made certain that it drew up a platform to his liking. The lengthy declaration judged the war to be unconstitutional, proposed an immediate armistice and convention of sovereign states, affirmed the irredeemable inequality of blacks, and declared allegiance to the Virginia and Kentucky Resolutions (and "interpretations thereof of Jefferson, Madison and Jackson"). Byington's convention decided, however, against sending a competing slate of delegates to Chicago.[127]

Dubuque's peace men also felt disgruntled by the regular convention's refusal to write a platform and to choose unadulterated peace men to go to Chicago. They too decided to do something about it. Their solution was to put on a typical Dubuque production: hold a giant rally; start it with a two-hour parade sparked by six bands; prime the crowd of about 15,000 with two of the best orators in the state, Henry Clay Dean and John Duncombe; get the listeners' vociferous approval to a previously prepared list of aggressive peace resolutions; and listen to more orations until late in the evening. The results were at least cathartic. There was no equivocating about the evils of abolition, Republicanism, and the Lincoln administration, or about the need to end the war immediately.[128]

At Chicago a few days later, Dean gave another oratorical tirade against the war and the President. He cried:

> Such destruction of human life has never been seen since the destruction of Sennacherib by the breath of the Almighty. And still the monster usurper wants more men for his slaughter pens . . . . Ever since the usurper, traitor and tyrant has occupied the presidential chair, the Republican party has shouted "War to the knife, and the knife to the hilt!" Blood has flowed in torrents; and yet the thirst of the old monster is not quenched. His cry is for more blood.

But his Chicago listeners could not afford to be as uncompromising as those at Dubuque. The majority of Iowa's delegates, both peace men and war men, accepted the platform and its so-called peace plank. And they accepted McClellan's nomination, a bitter pill for the peace men. They were even unhappier with the General's partial repudiation of the key plank. Most, including Babbitt and Mahony, eventually supported McClellan because they had no alternative. This was partly due to the efforts of Charles Mason who, after casting about for other possibilities, including Ulysses Grant, came around to McClellan and urged Iowans to accept him as a "practical necessity."[129] LeGrand Byington was not through. So angry was he at the failure of the peace "ultras," as they came to be known, to win control of the party that for a time he contemplated entering the race for Congress from the Fourth District against both the Republican nominee, incumbent Josiah Grinnell, and the regular Democratic nominee, Iowa City rival, Ira Mitchell. Ex-Senator George Jones excitedly warned Summers against this unexpected development. "For God's sake," he wrote, "effect a compromise between our friend LeGrand Byington and Mitchell or both will be defeated and that dog Grinnell . . . re-elected." Byington finally did withdraw, but Grinnell won anyway, 13,914 to 10,217.[130]

Even though he was pleased with McClellan's nomination, realist David Richardson was skeptical about the worth of one-to-one voter appeals in his behalf. Don't engage in street corner politics, he told Democrats.

> Those with whom you talk cannot be converted by any words of yours. They have made up their minds, and desire to proselyte you. In nine cases out of ten all such conversations will end in bitter abuse of one another, and bad feeling. Eschew it then, entirely, and leave street corner politics to loafers and pot house politicians.

Richardson gave Republicans the same advice with one addition. Said he, ". . . if you wish to convince men of their error, do not commence by calling them Copperheads or traitors."[131] Nathan Sales, who had vowed never to support a man connected with war, reversed course. Sales told Summers that many Anamosans spoke openly for McClellan while few did so for Lincoln. Thirty to forty Lincoln voters from 1860 would now go for McClellan, but the Democrats were keeping purposefully quiet about these gains. However, there was confusion in another quarter. John H. Wallace headed the party's ticket as its candidate for secretary of state. Helping Wallace in his campaign was party regular Benton J. Hall. According to Frank Plum, Wallace spoke good party doctrine, but Hall, speaking on the same platform, sounded like an abolitionist.[132]

In Washington, Mason, heading two McClellan committees, believed that if the General won, peace and reunion would result in six months. He had faith, he wrote, that McClellan might actually win, although he could not analyze the sources of that faith.[133] War Democrats found McClellan quite satisfactory. He filled the bill by offering them, however vaguely, the hope of peace and reunion without capitulation to Confederate demands. They hoped he might garner more soldier votes than Lincoln, although their 1863 experience with General James Tuttle was hardly a cause for optimism. There was little reason to anticipate many votes from officers. Republicans expected to get nearly all of those. In 1864, when assessments levied by the party's state central committee on Iowans holding federal office produced insufficient campaign revenues, state chairman Herbert Hoxie wrote General Dodge that the committee wanted each Iowa major general and his staff to contribute $100 to party coffers. Brigadier generals and their staffs should pay $75, while lesser officers and their staffs should send in proportionate sums. There was one officer, not connected with an Iowa unit, who was beyond Hoxie's reach. E. P. Bartlett on the ironclad *Chickasaw* off Mobile happily reported to Summers that Lincoln decisively lost straw votes on the *Chickasaw* and on a nearby vessel. Bartlett, who despised the President, exulted over the fact that enlisted men especially voted heavily against him.[134]

One soldier letter, far different from Bartlett's, tells something about the kind of steadfast, principled opposition faced by Copperhead Democrats like Byington and Mahony who, while claiming to be men of principle themselves, often failed to recognize the same in others, including opponents in their own party. By September, Ben Stevens of Oskaloosa had spent nearly four years in the army. His father had died in the service and his younger brother was missing in action (later found to be captured). In response to his mother's request that he resign and come home, he wrote that he could not for at least six months, by which time the country would be out of danger. If the draft furnished the men Grant and Sherman needed, the war would end in less than nine months. But, Stevens added,

. . . if the Copperheads and Peace men succeed in carrying out their prin- cipals, [*sic*] *we will have war as long as there is a single square foot of land* in the North *that dare call itself a free soil.* Think of this and then thank God that you have children that will support the Government that *your* Father sup- ported.[135]

There was one group of voters among which the Democrats thought they might make some gains. That was the faction of Germans who favored Fremont over Lincoln. So the Democrats looked hopefully at the German-language press. In the end, one German paper, the Lyons *Banner* which had leaned toward Fre- mont, actually did come out for McClellan, joining the Dubuque *National-Demokrat,* about whose choice there never had been any doubt. The *National-Demokrat* complained that the draft operated unfairly on Germans, particularly in Illinois—and probably by design. It also claimed that the stupidity and corrup- tion of the Lincoln administration had prolonged the war and strengthened the rebellion.[136] Opting for Lincoln were the revived Dubuque *Staats Zietung, Die Tribune* (Burlington), and *Der Demokrat* (Davenport). *Der Demokrat* accepted Lincoln reluctantly. Late in October the editor explained why. Lincoln was no real liberator, he wrote, but the President no longer had the power to protect slavery nor to make a ridiculous peace. So it was safe to support him.[137]

Most Iowans thought so too, if not always for the same reasons. The Republican party, on most ballots called Union or Union Republican party, won all contests handily. The Lincoln electors ran slightly behind the state office can-

TABLE 8.2
REPUBLICAN VOTES AND PERCENTAGES, 1863–64

Year	Civilian		Soldier		Total	
1863	68,895	56.4	17,001	85	85,896	60.5
1864	72,183	57.7	16,852	90	89,035	64.2

didates, but their 89,035 to 49,596 margin was convincing evidence that Stone's surprisingly decisive win in 1863 had been no fluke.[138]

With the pressure off, the Burlington *Hawk-eye* could safely ventilate an angry question, "We should like to know how it is and why it is that every Catholic voted the Copperhead ticket in the late election."[139] It was a question that no one bothered to answer, at least in the *Hawk-eye*. The real anger welled up among the losers. John Irish articulated it best when he wrote that the Republicans, "the enemies of the people, the villains, scoundrels and thieves, who have plundered and persecuted us for the last four years," had won by fraud and deception. Charles Negus announced that the great mass of people were insane; that they were committed to abolition. Patrick Robb, more fearful than angry, believed that Lincoln would continue the war solely to end slavery; if he failed to achieve his goal, he would recognize Southern independence in order to preserve Republican ascendancy in the North. Thomas Clagett, however, retained his balance and reminded his readers that the great dilemma from the Democratic standpoint remained unsolved; conquering the South and subjugating its people wouldn't restore the Union; but "extremists" who hoped to achieve reunion by disbanding the armies and relying on peaceable negotiations were wrong also.[140]

Charles Mason told his Washington Democratic Resident Committee that "There has been no honest decision against us—none to which we could be justly required to submit were not the consequences of resistance so momentous. . . . It is better to suffer too long than to exercise resistance too soon." The *Hawk-eye* reacted scornfully but accurately, pointing out that Mason justified revolution for defeated Democrats—if the circumstances were right. Mason repeated the thought a week later in his diary. "Saw Judge Grant of Iowa and Senator Carlisle [John Carlisle, West Virginia] each of whom expressed the opinion that all hope of liberty had fled. We must not succumb to such despondency. Sooner than succumb this way I would organize revolution." But Mason, who ignored Henry Clay Dean's suggestion that he write for Iowa papers under his own name rather than under pseudonyms, was not about to lead any revolution. Nor did he possess all the persuasive powers that Dean attributed to him. A relative with whom he occasionally corresponded, E. G. Gear of Ripley, Minnesota, told him bluntly, "Of course I do not agree with you, that peace would have been the necessary consequence of the election of Gen. McClellan, unless he and his friends were prepared to acknowledge the *independence* of the South."[141] Henry Clay Dean never put much stock in McClellan either, but for a different reason than Gear's, namely, McClellan's participation in the war. "If Lincoln was Odious for policies," he told Summers, "McClellan was not the man to correct them."[142]

9

Rocking Steady on the Homefront: 1862–1865

THROUGHOUT the war, Iowans coped with a normal array of domestic problems, some of them related to the conflict, some not. There was reason to fear outbreaks of diphtheria and measles. There were occasional cases of dreaded hydrophobia. Chinch bugs and hog cholera plagued the farmers now and again. Too many dogs roamed the countryside killing sheep, hogs, and cattle. Delinquent children drank, smoked, and swore like troopers. Pickpockets plied their trade at summer fairs. Burglars troubled urban centers.

Of a different order was the often explosive interaction of politics and religion on the questions of the day. Sometimes this interaction resulted in wholesale condemnation of specific denominations by irritated observers. When 1,700 Dubuque residents petitioned the regular session of the 1862 legislature for passage of a liquor license law, the Reverend G. W. Brendle, pastor of Dubuque's Methodist Episcopal church, charged that the petitioners were all "Romanists, Drunkards and Infidels." The *Herald* and its Des Moines correspondent naturally found this offensive. James Howell also provoked the *Herald*'s anger when Howell told his Keokuk readers that "There are not politicians or presses so earnest in the advocacy of slavery as the Catholic politicians and press, and there is no class of people so fierce in the support of slavery as the masses of the Catholics in this country."[1] When Quakers sought exemption from the draft, many Iowans like David Richardson scorned them in terms as demeaning as those applied to Catholics. Governor Kirkwood was friendly to Quakers and members of the pietistic Amana Society and favored draft exemptions for them, but to no avail.[2] Some Baptists, on the other hand, believed Kirkwood was no friend of theirs. At a Baptist ministers' convention some ministers claimed that the Governor regarded Baptists as disloyal and that he had refused to appoint any army chaplains from that denomination.[3] Lysander Babbitt bore no love for Methodists, and he exulted when the *Christian Advocate* reported that all but six out of forty-eight Methodist annual conferences reported membership losses ranging from 21 to 5,172. Such losses over two decades' time would supposedly kill the church, and Babbitt wrote, "We have no tears to shed in anticipation of its early demise. . . . A

church which leaves the straight and narrow path marked out by the Gospel
. . . to enter the political arena deserves to die. . . ." Instead, he hoped a new
church would then arise whose preachers would "follow the example of their
divine master in teaching obedience to the laws of the country, and submission to
the powers that be." These last words were strange ones for Babbitt who, after the
Emancipation Proclamation and a revival of arbitrary arrests in 1863, increasingly
came to have serious reservations about submission to such powers so long as they
were Republican powers.[4]

Democrats despised what they called "political preachers." Political
preachers, they said, inevitably spouted abolition doctrines. They also promoted
the war and Republicanism while denouncing rebels and their alleged supporters
in the North. Thus, an amused W. W. Junkin reported two southeastern Iowa
ministers' participation in Democratic meetings in early 1863. Two were only a
corporal's guard, however, compared with the legions of clergymen which
Democrats believed to be serving their political enemies. Such religious fanatics
brought on the war, Edward Thayer charged. Thayer wanted ministers well versed
in the "requirements and the compromises of the Constitution." Unfortunately,
they were not. They knew only the Bible.[5] Cedar county Democrats fired a mighty
blast at political preachers when they resolved:

> That as the clergymen of the United States, with a very few honorable excep-
> tions, have apostatized from the principles of the christian religion, and have
> enlisted under the banner of his satanic majesty, and are industriously
> endeavoring to carry out his fiendish designs by first assisting to plunge our
> once happy nation into an unnatural war, then stirring up servile insurrection
> for the indiscriminate butchery of those who, were it not for them would have
> been our brethren and friends, breathing bitterness, spite, malice and ill will
> among those to whom it was their duty to have preached "joyful tidings of
> peace and good will to men," then inciting domestic feuds, encouraging
> mobs and disturbing the peace of the community by prostituting their
> churches to the preaching of negro freedom instead of the gospel of Christ,
> they have forfeited the respect and are unworthy of the support of a virtuous,
> patriotic and moral people.[6]

David Richardson adopted a milder tone when the Methodists admitted several
candidates into the ministry at a Davenport ceremony. "We trust," he wrote,
"[that] these young men who have thus taken authority to labor in their Master's
vineyard will stay there faithfully, and not go climbing over the fence into some
other enclosure and soiling their robes with dirty work that the Master never set
them about or had anything to do with."[7]

Some Catholics complained of political preaching at one Dubuque Catholic
church. But the *Herald* refused to be drawn into the controversy beyond regretting
that any Catholic clergyman would inject partisanship into the church. The
Wapello *Republican* poked fun at the opposition when it "advertised":
"*Wanted*—A preacher who will preach neither politics nor Religion. Such a one

will meet with the hearty approval and everlasting good will of the chief leaders of the Democratic party of the locality.'' The *Iowa State Register* suggested that the Rev. David Sween might fill the bill. Sween, loser in a race for the legislature from Marion county, would "be happy to preach the Gospel of Benedict Arnold to the disciples of Jeff Davis in Eastern Iowa.'' He, like other Tory ministers, the paper added, held that defending slavery and the fitness of Copperheads for political office did not constitute political preaching.[8] William Merritt believed Des Moines needed an independent church free from politics. So did citizens in Plainsville (Warren county). They established a Christian Union church for that purpose.[9] Western Iowa Methodist ministers rejected such thinking. They resolved in convention that they had a responsibility to deal with political questions.[10] Before the year was over, the Iowa Conference of the Evangelical Association, the English Lutheran Synod, the annual conference of the Methodist Protestant church, and the Baptist state convention had taken positions supporting the war and the Emancipation Proclamation. But the *State Democratic Press* doubted the Baptist contention that God had anything to do with the fall election results in Ohio and Pennsylvania.[11]

The Reverend A. B. Robbins of Muscatine's First Congregational church was the unofficial chaplain of the Thirty-Fifth Iowa Infantry. He gave a copy of the Psalms to each of the twenty-three soldiers from his church who joined the unit. At least one bore the inscription, "He teacheth my hands to war and my fingers to fight." The Twenty-Fourth Iowa became known as the Methodist regiment because of the large number of officers and enlisted men in it who came from that denomination. A Cincinnati *Commercial* correspondent noted their fighting prowess at Vicksburg and their impressive religious exercises after battle.[12] Soldier and future governor Cyrus Carpenter learned from his fiancee Susan Burkholder that she had joined the Methodist rather than the Episcopal church in Fort Dodge because the latter had too many "traitors" to suit her. In Story county, proslavery members deserted one Methodist church to join the Episcopalians. Free-Will Baptists and Lutherans there opposed slavery, but one Episcopalian minister jousted publicly with Republicans, claiming that the institution had divine sanction.[13]

Some Democratic church members in the Montezuma Methodist church and in the North River Christian congregation of Greenbush (Warren county) suffered expulsion because of their politics.[14] The Reverend I. C. Curtis of the Methodist Episcopal church at Pella, two-time Marion county representative in the legislature and unsuccessful senate candidate in the fall of 1863, had trouble with his fellow Methodists. Contrary to Copperhead reports, however, the Methodists did not expel him, even though he deserved it, opined some county residents in a letter to the *Iowa State Register*. Mount Pleasant Methodists did get rid of the Rev. Braxton Robinson for voting Democratic and opposing abolition.[15]

Washington's Methodist minister aroused the Washington *Democrat*'s wrath when he asked the Washington Sunday school children, "What's the meanest thing in the world?" He then supplied the answer, "a Copperhead," when the children couldn't muster a satisfactory response. The paper accused him of trying "to instill into their minds a prejudice and hate of their parents."[16] The Reverend Darius E. Jones, general agent of the American Bible Society, announced in 1864 that one out of eight families, 17,797 to be exact, possessed no Bible and judged that where there were fewer Bibles there were more Copperheads.[17] Still, when Jane Thompson learned from the local Bible Society that the household of Marion Copperhead Samuel W. Durham was among the twelve in the community without one, she was astonished. "A man that has lived [in a] civilized community as long as he, with such a family of children and no bible [!]," she exclaimed to her husband. However, after an instant of pious reflection, she added, "I do not wonder at his being a Copperhead. But I hope the Lord will forgive him."[18]

The Reverend Henry Clay Dean, Copperhead, probably felt that he did not stand in need of forgiveness. Dean, who had long since severed his official connection with Methodism, was one of the minority of Iowa's "political preachers" who quoted the Bible to prove that clerical concern with slavery and other temporal matters was misguided. He wrote a pamphlet-length anonymous letter to Methodist Episcopal bishop Matthew Simpson which attacked the church's stand on slavery and cited Biblical justification for noninterference with the institution. Dean hoped to get the Society for the Diffusion of Political Knowledge to publish his work.[19]

Throughout the war, many people took a keen interest in what went on in the public schools. That included discipline as well as what was taught in the classroom. In Iowa City Joseph R. Kettlewell lodged a complaint in justice court against the high school principal for assault and battery on his son. The *State Democratic Press* was unsympathetic. Kettlewell, it noted, didn't like the use of the ferule, "even in its posterior application. . . ." The case was settled out of court with the justice of the peace suggesting that the school board draw up guidelines to govern the administration of disciplinary punishment. The *Press* had more to say.

> We are aware that with the progress of our school systems, corporal punishment to a certain extent has fallen into disrepute, but little good, if any, has been the result. "Spare the rod and spoil the child" is a proverb the truth of which was never more strikingly exemplified than in the lawless, disorderly, uncontrollable character of the present generation of boys. Elect good, responsible, judicious teachers and give them authority, without interference, to exercise parental authority over their scholars during school hours, and a liberal use of the switch for the correction of disobedience or mischief will work more beneficially than a thousand lectures or reprimands. . . . [I]n the classroom . . . the teacher should be literally the master.[20]

Good quality education was important in Dubuque. In the spring of 1863 a *Times* reporter visited the high school which enrolled about thirty students. He observed the mathematics teaching, noting that the geometry class "got into deep water, and did not, as a whole, succeed very well." Algebra students did "middling well" while the arithmetic class was "first rate." The citizens, he believed, did not appreciate the high school enough. The small staff (probably three persons) worked hard. In addition to math, it taught physical sciences, Latin, German, French, and even Greek whenever the students wanted it. Dubuque's fifth ward school attracted attention also. It had about four hundred pupils. Three teachers each ran the two main departments, the secondary and the primary. Said the *Times* man:

> A large per cent.—we should think seventy or eighty—of the scholars in the Fifth Ward School are Germans, a nation noted for large brains and keen thoughts. The man from Germany often seen in our streets with his saw and "buck" on his back, can calculate eclipses of the binomial theorum [*sic*]. He comes from a land of thinkers and his children who attend our schools are among the brightest scholars.

Later that year the Dubuque schools announced that they were switching from the National Readers to McGuffey's, including the McGuffey speller.[21]

In Muscatine the *Courier* recommended that the city's schools follow the pattern of many schools in New England and the Middle states by adopting Willson's Readers. Learning to read from Willson's first and second readers, enthused the reporter, would make "learning to read well be looked upon as a recreation instead of a task." All the other Willson products were good too, he said, especially the fifth which included the natural history of fishes, the history of architecture, physical geography, chemistry, geology, and ancient history.[22] Burlington's schools were crowded, with student enrollment up 25 percent over the previous year. The *Hawk-eye* believed they were in a prosperous, healthy condition, although it suggested that some teachers had too heavy a load to do well by all their charges.[23]

Public education became a political football in 1863. The state teachers association came out firmly in support of the Union. Jasper county teachers resolved that they would try to infuse their pupils with a spirit of patriotism. They also asserted that teachers who failed to properly appreciate soldier efforts to preserve the Union were unworthy members of the profession.[24] In Dubuque it was unwise for educators to teach abolition doctrines or to allow the children to sing inflammatory songs. An irate citizen wrote the *Herald* that a woman teacher at one school ordered her class to sing "Old John Brown" at a regular school exercise. Those students who refused got a black mark by their names. "Are our public schools, for the support of which all are taxed irrespective of party, to become the hot-bed of abolitionism?" the writer demanded to know. Another citizen queried his own children about the matter and learned that students in principal H. H. Belfield's first ward schoolroom regularly sang the offending song. The school directors, he asserted, should take steps "to abate such a nuisance." Belfield responded forcefully. Any charge that he required students to sing "Old John Brown" was false. In September, students sang the song of their own free will at the beginning of the day. Since then "Old John Brown" had gone unsung until one noon in mid-January, 1863. And that occurred only because of the *Herald*'s publicity. Teachers were far too busy to teach abolitionism, Belfield asserted. Students chose their own songs. Now, unfortunately, public interest made "Old John Brown" popular at the school even though teachers considered it "obnoxious." A simple parental request to prohibit its singing, unaccompanied by publicity, would have ended the matter without stimulating student excitement, he declared.[25]

Belfield was not through. "Let me say," he added, "that if the parents of our pupils would visit our schools and show more interest in the progress of their children, not only would hard feelings be avoided, but the efficiency of our schools [be] considerably increased." Dubuque Democrats and the *Herald* did take enough interest to ensure that Democrats won five out of six contested school board seats in the March election. They tossed out board secretary G. S. Grosvenor, a sometime *Herald* target, despite Grosvenor's efforts to persuade voters that he had always been a Democrat, especially a Douglas Union Democrat, not a Republican as the *Herald* charged. The results pleased the paper. Children would hear no more abolitionism. The new board announced that henceforth it would fire any teacher who taught "sectarian or political matter."[26]

In Burlington the labels were different but the situation similar. The *Hawk-eye* backed "Union" candidates for the school board. It explained why.

> The public schools of this city have for years been perverted to party purposes. We do not mean to assert that disloyal teachers have been employed, but we do say that teachers have been employed who have laid themselves out to annoy the loyal people who sent their children to these schools, by little petty tyranny in excluding declamation of a patriotic character, forbidding the use of Union paper, etc., etc. . . . It has been going on long enough. A change is desirable. . . . Those who are drawing their pay from the Government, State or National, ought to be on the side of the law, and ought not to make their loyalty doubtful. The spirit of petty tyranny and spite which has been exhibited by some of the teachers ought to be and will be "dried up."

The Union ticket won, and the satisfied paper told the new members what Burlington citizens expected of them. "Give us good teachers," it said, "—we care not who they are [just] so they know their business and do not employ their time in proselyting for the Copperheads and disseminating treason among the children."[27]

A supposed Copperhead school board slate lost in Farmington where, according to the *Gate City*, voters concluded that "treason is a bad doctrine to instill in young minds." The "war party" won the board election in another politicized race in East Des Moines.[28] In Fairfield the Union ticket won. The board fired two teachers who were persons "with whom the Copperheads sympathize," according to the *Ledger*. Their replacements, said the paper, were known to favor whipping

Southern rebels. The Benton county school superintendent fired a Harrison township teacher accused of "uttering and inculcating disloyal and traitorous sentiments among his pupils, and generally elsewhere."[29] Van Buren county superintendent, D. G. Perkins, fired two "disloyal" teachers. One left without fighting back, but not the other, whose local board refused to recognize Perkins' action. In the summer of 1863, a group of Van Buren parents brought assault and battery charges against a teacher for whipping "loyal scholars." The scholars, said the *Des Moines News,* insisted upon discussing politics in school despite the fact that the teacher had been instructed to allow no such activity. Some citizens faulted her on another count: she refused to eat at the same table with a black man who lived with the same family she did. One holdout on the trial jury saved her from a guilty verdict.[30] Abolitionists largely controlled the Muscatine school board, according to the *Courier.* It was "highly criminal" to allow abolition, which was worse than infidelity or atheism, to poison young minds, the paper declared. Parents ought to remove their children from school if teachers promoted such a doctrine.[31]

Thomas Clagett, who occasionally groaned about "political preaching" in Keokuk, was pleased in early 1864 to report that Keokuk's schools would remain free from "bigoted politicans and religious sectarians," thanks to the defeat of the Union School ticket (the "colored ticket," he called it), by a nonpartisan slate in the city's school board election. In Winterset, however, a Union ticket won a 4 to 1 decision over local Copperheads who for three years, according to the town's Republican paper, had unanimously and successfully voted "against a school house, education and the general advancement of Christianity."[32] One anonymous Marengo citizen was sorely displeased with the state of affairs at the state university.

> [I]t is notorious, that the University, in every department, has become an out and out abolition concern, that persecute, and even *expel,* democrats, for the exercise of private judgment on political questions . . . of course the University suffers from the effects of its negrophobia [*sic*]. It will receive the support of all parties when it ceases to pander to the interests of either—and not before.[33]

The state's teachers were even more politicized in 1864 than in 1863. At their state convention they officially approved a decision by the state superintendent of public instruction affirming the right of county superintendents to withhold teaching certificates "from all persons who show, by act or work, sympathy with the designs of rebels and traitors."[34] On the other hand, a Dubuque teacher attending the convention revealed that teaching in Dubuque required one to exercise political moderation in all things. Reported the *Herald* matter-of-factly,

> Mr. Kretschmer offered a resignation of the position as a member of the committee on 'The State of the Country.' The reason assigned for this resignation was that, as a teacher in the public schools of Dubuque, he did not feel at

liberty to create dissatisfaction among any portion of the citizens of Dubuque, and though he knew of no difference of opinion existing between himself and the other members of the committee, he must nevertheless decline to act.

The committee accepted his resignation.[35]

But in Clinton one student exercised his freedom of speech in an unexpected fashion and got away with it, to the disgust of the Clinton *Herald.* At public school exercises "a young rebel took occasion to deliver a speech reeking with treason." Some hissed his "vile utterances." Others responded with a "murmur of applause." The *Herald* was astounded "that a loyal community like Clinton could tolerate his outburst on such an occasion."[36]

Women ventured forth during the war into activities previously considered beyond their competence or interest. A Mrs. Smith in Oskaloosa ventured too far in 1862. She won the mayoralty election but lost her office to B. F. Ingles when the board of canvassers decided women were ineligible for public office.[37] A year later, however, the Dubuque *Herald* commented favorably upon women's capacity to cope with speeches by Dennis Mahony and state senator B. B. Richards at a political rally in Manchester. Wrote a surprised *Herald* reporter,

> It was highly complimentary to the speakers that the ladies—nearly one third of the audience, listened with the most perfect attention to the discussions of political questions which are generally not interesting subjects to them, and during the entire four and a half hours they manifested not the least degree of uneasiness nor did they appear to be fatigued.[38]

There were limits, nevertheless, to what women should attempt, as adventurous Jane Thompson learned from her officer-husband when she suggested that she come to visit him in the field if he could not come home on furlough to visit her. Major Thompson wrote,

> . . . while it would please me to see you, and I would like to gratify your curiosity in looking at a live camp of soldiers . . . you little know what you wish for. . . . What in [the] world would you do on the march. Not a place for you to ride except on top of some Box on the heaviest kind of lumber wagon with Six mules attached, and a swearing driver. When night comes if it does not rain, no Tents are pitched, and if they are pitched they are little and uncomfortable. In short this is no place for a woman[39]

There were places where women could go in 1862 where few previously had gone, namely, into the fields. With farmers desperate for hands at $2 a day and no takers, editors encouraged women to follow Governor Kirkwood's suggestion to become farm laborers. Some did. The *Herald* believed it would be good for them "to leave behind corsets, belts and cosmetics," to get into fresh air, "to strengthen their frames, to grow robust instead of slender, rosy instead of pallid, brown rather than delicate." Good health for years to come would be their reward. The writer allowed as he might even prefer such a regimen himself. By the summer of 1864, although certainly more common than earlier in the war, urban editors were still intrigued by the thought, and even more by the sight, of women doing farm work. One observer had to look twice to make sure that his eyes weren't deceiving him. They were not, he concluded. Those women in the fields of Buchanan, Blackhawk, Bremer, Butler, and Floyd counties actually were "American" women. Moreover, they were "well educated and refined." The McGregor *News* found the bronzed hands of women farm workers more beautiful than those "of some of their sisters in town, 'who toil not, neither do they spin' and yet are arrayed in the most gorgeous of imported costumes." They would, continued the *News*, stand higher "in the estimation of all men whose opinion [was] worth anything [than] all the Flora McFlimsey's who have ever fluttered in fashionable life since the fall of Babylon."[40]

More women went into retailing also. During the summer 1862 enlistment drive one young Dubuque woman volunteered to replace an enlistee, do his job for half pay, and remit the rest to him. This occurred two weeks after a *Times* story which suggested that women might replace male clerks who might enlist, the women to relinquish the jobs when the men had completed their service. Soon there was a list of twenty young women volunteering to be clerks.[41]

One should not expect or demand too much of women, even so. When a teacher near Winterset lost her job because she refused to walk half a mile in cold weather to build a fire in the school house, an angry *Iowa State Register* writer declared that the school board should fire the district director immediately.[42] Not recorded is what the widow of a deceased Madison county Butternut thought of the demand made on her by her late husband. His will left everything to her— provided that she did not take an abolitionist for her next husband.[43]

Iowans sometimes counted on women's influence to restrain male excesses. At the conclusion of a temperance meeting in DeWitt, all the pretty girls there, said a reporter, signed a resolution that they would "not countenance, or keep company with any young gentleman who use[d] as a beverage ale, beer, or *any* intoxicating liquors." One young man was thought foolish indeed when he crashed through the Mississippi ice seven times while crossing from the Illinois side over to Muscatine—until people learned that he was determined to keep a date to get married at the Ogilvie House.[44] One disturbed soldier who called himself "High Private," fretted about the lack of women's refining influence on soldiers. Camp life, he reported, brought out all latent male vices. Tobacco usage was "common and pernicious," but "more excusable . . . than at home." Liquor, though banned, seemed easy to get, although he admitted that he had yet to observe a drunk. Most disturbing, however, was the widespread obscenity. "It taints the whole character," High Private wrote earnestly, "and speedily leads the young man to the places of prostitution and crime. . . . Obscene language in the form of *double entendre*, vulgar jests, &c., are startlingly common. One can hardly find a group in camp that does not indulge in Bacchanalian songs and jests. All this I attribute to the absence of pure, elevated women.''[45]

Nevertheless, not all women and girls met these expectations in wartime, certainly not in Dubuque. Mrs. George P. Funk was one of their number. She was said to be high strung and passionate, and a considerable problem to her husband. When Funk had had enough, the sympathetic *Herald* reported that he gave his employer one month's notice, paid his debts, got his wife drunk, put her to bed, gathered up the couple's seven-month-old child, and silently departed the city.[46] And there was fourteen-year-old Mary Saunders. Authorities believed that she was enough of a threat to law and order that they put her in jail for want of ability to make $300 bond when they charged her with stealing $25 worth of clothing and jewelry from a Mosalem township farmer. Miss Saunders' confinement was in line with the *Herald*'s remedy:

Danger to Young Girls

Almost daily the police courts have cases brought before them growing out of the depravity, immorality and criminal conduct of some of the degraded men and women and vicious boys and girls who are becoming so numerous here that they are corrupting by their examples, association and otherwise a large number of the youth of both sexes. We believe the remedy to be a more stringent and rigid enforcement of the laws.

The practice of letting off with a small fine the few culprits arrested out of the many who ought to be dealt with, has an encouraging effect on them rather than wholesome fear of the law, for the risk is very slight that they will suffer any legal penalties even if caught in the act of their offences.

The writer also described the experience of another fourteen-year old who escaped the clutches of a man who wanted to set her up in business for $500 and some jewelry. In the same issue the *Herald* contained news of two of the city's problem girls, Mary Ann Daly and Bridget McNamara, both under seventeen. According to the paper, the girls would not work, had no home, and spent their nights on the river bluffs with a host of rowdies. When it rained, they crawled into some available outhouse. They were also petty thieves. Arrested for vagrancy, they were given a choice by the court: leave Dubuque or spend thirty days in jail. Misses Daly and McNamara chose to leave. The *Times* was not entirely unsympathetic. Their prospects were appalling, said a reporter. Both were orphans, homeless, and friendless. Four days later the paper noted their arrest at Center Grove for stealing 12 yards of calico and a dress from a farm house. Justice Chapline sentenced them to a month in jail. At the expiration of their sentences they were back on the streets of Dubuque "with a crowd of boys in their train who should not yet be released from leading strings," judged the worried *Herald*.[47]

In fact, the delinquent and/or obnoxious behavior of Iowa's youth of both sexes was a matter of continuing concern during the war. The Waterloo *Courier* had harsh words for six youths who regularly sat in the back row during Methodist services, whispering and mocking the proceedings. Disgusted worshippers threw them out several times. One such "mean low-lived miserable black guard" eventually found himself arrested and fined for his behavior.[48] Burlington had similar problems. The *Hawk-eye* discussed at length the proper raising of the young, finally concluding that "it is a generally admitted fact . . . that many good citizens of Burlington are raising up idle and worthless children, more particularly boys."[49] The fruits of such faulty nurture were all too visible in Dubuque where worthless boys had grown into equally worthless adult loafers, according to the *Times.* The paper in early 1862 valiantly promoted the "gospel of *work.*" Work made one morally, physically, and mentally a man, promoted virtue, a stout heart, honesty, independence, health, happiness, "and all that women love." But Dubuque's six to eight loafers did nothing, lived with their parents or indulgent relatives and spent their time sleeping, watching card games or billiards, and developing "vicious tastes . . . which promise a harvest of misery and degradation. . . . A hog does even better," concluded the writer, "for he grows and amounts to pork in time, but the loafer, of what earthly use is he? He votes at election, and that is about all."[50]

The situation had not changed much, except maybe for the worse, by the time the war entered its last year. And clearly it was not only the lower classes who filled the ranks of the city's juvenile delinquents. Commenting on some nightly troublemakers, the *Times* said,

. . . these boys are not miserable "brats" from the haunts of vice and iniquity, but the hopeful sons of our bankers, merchants, professional men, christian men, respectable men in every way. In the most aristocratic streets of the city, no decent woman can walk the length of a block without having to force her way through a crowd of insulting, obscene, blasphemous bedlamites, and blessing the city fathers who are so considerate to her blushes as to not flood the streets with gaslight.[51]

Youthful misconduct, according to the *Herald,* was fostered not only by the "political evils of the times," but also by the fact that some citizens thought bad behavior was simply a sign of spunk. Dubuquers also claimed that when Chicago expelled many of its criminal elements, they came to Dubuque where they not only carried on their habitual activities but also entranced local youngsters with "marvelous stories of their doings" in the big city.[52]

Thomas Clagett, who during the summer of 1864 had become convinced that a dearth of police news spoke well for Keokuk morals, was less certain by November. The corrupt times, he wrote, had obviously affected one small boy who pushed over a drunk and robbed him of two dollars. In Des Moines William Merritt had no doubt that "Young America" needed looking after. "Lads scarcely out of the pantelets," he wrote, "can smoke, chew tobacco and swear equal to the most accomplished rowdies in the larger cities."[53]

Toward the end of that winter, the Centerville *Citizen,* perhaps bragging as well as complaining, said, "We will put the boys from six to fifteen years old, of

Centerville, against those of any town twice its size for deviltry, uselessness and loafing." And a few months after the war standards of conduct were not yet up to snuff among the young of both sexes at Albia. At Cedar Creek an encamped emigrant group had a confrontation with a fishing party composed of Albia boys and girls. The Albia boys, to the delight of the Albia girls, but to the displeasure of the emigrants, stripped and went swimming in the raw. When the emigrants objected too vociferously to the exhibition, the girls took on their women in a fight. The Albia justice of the peace crossed up some people's expectations by fining the emigrants, not the swimmers and their girl friends.[54]

Many Iowans judged that alcohol was a source of some of the state's social problems. Catholic Bishop Clement Smyth, more Puritan than many of his Dubuque diocesan flock, was one who so judged. He occasionally expounded on the evils of alcohol, especially whiskey. Its use, he said, destroyed careers and family life, and often led to a life of crime. But alcohol was obviously a part of the good life among some of Dubuque's leading citizens who sent one Captain Washington off to war in grand style. Washington, William B. Allison, Mayor H. L. Stout, Judge S. M. Pollock, Deputy United States Marshal P. H. Conger, a representative of the *Times* (probably Jesse Clement), and assorted military officers feasted one night on stewed oysters, fried oysters, oysters stuffed with quail, oysters straight, coffee, cold meats, sandwiches, ice cream, fresh and preserved fruits, nuts, cake, jellies, "and such" before breaking open "many bottles" of champagne. "Although there was a whole regiment of empty flasks after it was all over," reported the *Times* man, "we can safely say there was not a single one of the party who was perceptibly under the influence of the blood of the grape." If so, this was truly a remarkable performance, highlighted as it was by twenty-eight toasts to such as Captain Washington, George Washington, Colonel Allison, Judge Pollock, Abraham Lincoln, Stephen Douglas, the Iowa Volunteers, "our banks and bankers," the loyal people of Dubuque, the "pulpit, press and women," and the loyal women of the North. Cognac, hot punch, and a songfest ending with "Auld Lang Syne" completed the celebration.[55]

Temperance was more fashionable in Iowa City, or at least some women's groups tried to make it so. One activist disguised herself as a country woman, purchased whiskey at several saloons, and took one seller to court. Found guilty by a jury, he had to pay a $20 fine and costs. The campaign obviously petered out because Philip Zimmerman that fall was freely advertising "Liquor and Wine of all kinds, Pure old Rye and Bourbon Whiskey (from Ohio and Pennsylvania)."[56] Early in 1863 a temperance revival hit Davenport. It was astonishing, wrote a reporter, how many famous drinkers were becoming abstainers. But he remained a skeptic. And well he might. Dubuque's Judge Hamilton thought the state needed a center to deal with problem drinkers, a state Inebriate Asylum. If denied liquor "for a sufficient time they might," he believed, "acquire strength to resist temptation." Waverly might have supplied a few inmates. The town had seven saloons serving about eleven hundred people. Dubuque's fifth ward residents had another alcohol-related problem. They protested the removal of a distillery from the city's outskirts to the Lake Peosta shoreline. The offal, they complained, would pollute the lake and harm the winter ice cutting business.[57]

While Davenport was in the throes of a temperance revival, Council Bluffs Methodists promoted a religious one. The *Nonpareil* couldn't think of a place that needed it more. Davenport might have been a candidate, or nearby Camp Hendershott. Bishop Lee gave the troops there the next best thing, a gloves-off Sunday morning attack on "the various sins incident upon camp life." Much more effective it was "than a thousand . . . doctrinal courses as are usually studied up to place before soldiers," judged a *Democrat* writer. They probably needed all the instruction the Bishop could give them because Davenport had a prostitute problem. Many soldiers were naive ("verdant individuals," said the reporter) and fair game for the ladies, some of whom doubled as expert thieves. Citizens occasionally took direct action. Several of them, "tired of the nuisance," burned down "a house of doubtful purity." A crib, situated near a stone school house, suffered the wrath of a gang of students who vandalized it and roughed up the inhabitants. Still, the *Democrat* could report that crime in the city had been unusually light for a year. Certainly Charles Mason's daughter Molly saw none when she visited Davenport in July. She reported that it was "delightfully situated, much better than Burlington, and, . . . more like a city.''[58]

Iowa City had street walkers whom the sheriff and his marshals periodically tried to remove. Keokuk naturally had similar, and more, ladies—plus one other potential problem which officialdom handled with alacrity. As the *Constitution* reported:

> Four wayward sisters were taken up by the City Marshal on Sunday night, and lodged in the calaboose. Their names are as follows: Mary Stevens, Margaret Ruel, Mary A. Dent and Martha Graham. The latter was enjoying herself in the innocent amusement of parading the streets dressed in men's clothes. Ladies can wear the breeches as often as they are able to at home, but the marshal says he can't allow them to parade the streets in such disguise. Yesterday these four damsels were taken before Recorder Martin, and under the vagrant act, not being able to give bond for future good behavior, were sent up to Ft. Madison.

Dubuquers did not appreciate an innovation introduced by some prostitutes and their keepers. They performed their services in a house on a flatboat anchored at the foot of Seventh Street near the shot tower. The *Herald* suggested that the vessel and its business would be appreciated better downriver. The Marshal thought so too, and the flatboat moved on. Lesser problems than prostitution stirred the *Herald*'s wrath. It asked the Marshal to prevent indecent exposure by certain boys. During the hot summer they took a daily swim in the nude just off the levee by West's warehouse. The public, claimed the paper, was disgusted.[59]

A list of crimes prosecuted in Iowa state district courts for the year ending October 31, 1863, does not include indecent exposure. But out of 523 cases, 258 appeared under the heading "nuisance," the largest category by far. The major crimes prosecuted after that were: larceny, 69; selling liquor, 60; assault, 57; keeping gambling den, 18; and malicious mischief, 8. The warden of the state prison submitted a report on the religious affiliations of the 89 convicts admitted between October 1, 1861, and September 30, 1863. Lysander Babbitt must have been pleased to note that Methodists had a secure lead. In second place were those reporting no affiliation. Methodists numbered 26. The "none" group had 13. Then came: Catholics, 12; Baptists, 10; Presbyterians, 6; United Brethren, 3; Lutherans, Episcopalians, and Campbellites, 2 each; and one each for the Dutch Reformed, Evangelical, Quaker, Seceder, and Universalist.[60]

The years 1864–1865 witnessed no apparent decrease in the kinds of problems which caused many citizens to feel as if society was falling apart. Despite the warning of Bishop Lee, Davenport's red-light houses continued to flourish. A May, 1864 raid on several, if not successful in any permanent sense, enriched the city treasury by about $100 in fines.[61] By mid-November Dubuque's city council had finally hired four night policemen for service on Main Street; and the superintendent of the city gas works had replaced some broken street lamps at important points within the community. In the month before the war ended, new Mayor John Thompson issued an edict "commanding all vagabonds, gamblers and others who have no visible or legitimate means of support to depart forthwith from this city . . . or be subjected to the penalties prescribed by law. . . ." Even before the mayor acted, the city marshal tried his best to do something about the situation. Between November 1, 1864, and April 1, 1865, he ordered thirteen suspicious persons and twenty-two prostitutes to get out of town. Departure of the prostitutes temporarily closed all the city's bawdyhouses.[62]

Across the state, Council Bluffs had all the problems of the Mississippi River towns, though on a smaller scale. The Nonpareil's advice to the city marshal was specific: move the inmates of "houses of ill-shape" outside the city limits; get after noisy saloons and "low doggeries"; quiet the "fast ones" who made loud noises at night; shoot a thousand stray dogs; and "Corrall a few thousand pounds of traveling pork."[63] Eddyville was in trouble too. The editor of the Star called his community a "hard place" and recommended that citizens meet publicly to plan a way "to rid herself of the intolerable iniquities daily enacted in her streets and in her vicinity."[64]

Oskaloosa did its best to overcome such moral laxity by different means. The local Herald reported that as a result of a "general revival of souls" during the winter of 1864–1865, between five hundred and eight hundred persons joined local churches. One was Ira Mitchell, former editor of the State Democratic Press. After his unsuccessful run for Congress, Mitchell was immersed and admitted to communion in Oskaloosa's Christian church. Soon after he began to preach, intending to take it up as his life's work.[65]

Meanwhile, something new was provoking interest as well as astonishment in Dubuque. That was the publication of the income and the income tax paid by Dubuque's citizenry. The interest was natural. The astonishment arose from learning who was *not* on the list since all those who had incomes over $600 had to file, although those who skillfully interpreted the allowable deductions list could escape paying any tax at all. As the *Times* reported in wonderment, some

> can live in large houses, furnish their parlors magnificently, own horses and ride in carriages, give parties and apparently enjoy all the luxuries of the rich and yet not enjoy the ostentation of appearing in the income list. Many may not be able to see *how* the thing is done, yet that people can live thus on incomes of less than $600 is apparent. We wish some of them would set up a school and teach other people the art.

The district assessor suddenly became interested in the art also. He asked citizen help in uncovering fraudulent returns. He announced that those who knew they hadn't made a full statement of their income could come to his office, make an additional return, and save themselves from investigation, a possible $1,000 fine, and even a year in jail.[66]

John and Sara Kenyon didn't have to worry about income taxes at any time during the war. That farm tenant couple one winter had a more pressing problem, namely, hunger. "John has been over to the Beaches," Sara wrote her eastern relatives, "and they gave him a pan of onions and he is eating them raw. It's all the apples westerners have. I made dried squash pies soured with vinegar and call them dried apple pies." One very young Dubuquer also faced an uncertain future. But a notice in the *Herald* suggested that there was hope. Said the paper:

> *Foundling*—a live, healthy male infant, about twenty-four hours old, was found last Friday morning about 6 o'clock at Judge Lovel's front gate, in West Dubuque, and taken in and cared for, where it still remains. The person showed good sense by leaving the child in good hands, and any person willing to adopt it can be accommodated by calling around. The Judge has a family of his own, and can spare this new comer.

At the other end of the economic spectrum, LeGrand Byington angrily surveyed the present and foresaw a future not to his liking. He tried to do something about it, something at once tangible and symbolic. The internal revenue law required that a two-cent stamp be affixed to every check worth more than $20. Byington who was not about to help finance the war if he could possibly avoid it, once drew a large sum out of his account in the state bank, all in $20 checks. When the bank directors heard about it, they ordered the Iowa Citian to take all his money out and do his banking elsewhere. He did—at $20 a clip.[67] Meanwhile people living along the Cedar River had an entirely different problem. But they could do nothing about it. Geese ruined their sleep with "wild and discordant music"; they also devastated the cornfields.[68]

While the war impinged on nearly every aspect of Iowa life, it did not cause any revolutionary change in popular taste or public amusements. For those who still appreciated the sentimental and the traditional in music, mixed with war themes of love and tragedy, the W. G. Gilbert store in Dubuque had what they wanted in the fall of 1862. Gilbert's sheet music offerings included: "Ever Near I Mourn Thine Absence"; "Alice, Where Art Thou?"; "What Is Life of Love Bereft?"; "O Katy My Darling"; "Josiah's Courtship"; "Dream of Love"; "Make Me a Grave in the Dark Blue Sea"; "Weep No More for Willie"; "Emma's Grave"; "Twilight Is Darkening"; "All Forward" (described as "the celebrated Garibaldi hymn"); "The Knights of Alcautara"; "Magdalena"; "Coratina"; and "The Echo Song." The down-to-earth traditional survived also. A farmers' club meeting early in the year, reported thoroughly in one full column in the *Times,* dealt with essential matters such as the best use of corn, what part of the ear was good for what, the merits of grinding, and more. Trap shooting was popular in Council Bluffs where enthusiasts participated in many competitive matches. In December, Lysander Babbitt assumed the presidency of the local club for the coming year.[69]

For entertainment during the winter, river towns could always count on ice-skating. The ice in the lagoon next to the Mississippi at Dubuque was better than that in New York's Central Park, claimed the *Herald.* The ladies loved it and found skating great for their health. Forget crinoline, advised the writer. The bloomer costume with a Polish cap was best. In the summers there were always circuses or carnivals of mixed quality. Dubuquers flocked to one in 1863 which contained, besides snakes, monkeys, and "other articles," a seven-foot giant, a fat woman, and a five-legged dog. Unfortunately, someone poisoned the dog. The show people left in disgust. The dog had been their biggest attraction. B. M. Harger's bookstore supplied the varied tastes of the city's readers. One could purchase, among others: *Freedom and War* by Henry Ward Beecher; *The Life of Victor Hugo; Agassiz's Methods of Study in Natural History; Our Old Home* by Nathaniel Hawthorne; *Social Conditions of the English* by Joseph Kay; *Three Years in Japan* by Sir Rutherford Alcock; George Eliot's *Romola;* and Mrs. Henry Wood's *Castle Heir.*[70]

Possibly entertaining, certainly emphatic, was a lecture offered in April, 1863, at Council Bluffs' Methodist Episcopal church entitled "The Divine Origins of the Scriptures Argued from the Miracles Recorded in the Bible." During October and November an itinerant theater troupe put on twenty-seven performances in that community, "every one of which," exclaimed the *Bugle,* "was a perfect success so far as the acting was concerned." Offerings included "Black Eyed Susan," Shakespeare's "Othello," "Country Cousins," "Uncle Tom's Cabin," "The Maid of Munster," "Kiss in the Dark," and a melodrama, "The Avengers." Keokuk residents who happened to be at the river bank got an unexpected treat one October day. They watched the manager of a departing circus try to persuade four elephants to swim across the Mississippi. After two hours of hard work two made it. One nearly got across, then turned around and came back, despite the storming of his keeper. The fourth would have no part of the river. The two recalcitrants eventually crossed on the ferry. In Des Moines a Mr. Means entertained spectators and won a $50 wager at the same time by running a quarter mile in 57 seconds. But there was no fun to be had in Oskaloosa. At least that's what the sophisticated Dubuque *Times* believed. "In Oskaloosa," wrote an incredulous (or merely bemused) reporter, "it is an impossibility to buy a glass of whiskey; play a game of billiards; or roll at ten-pins. No wonder the Copperheads were beaten there in the last election."[71]

Burlington's winter social season of 1863–1864 included many gala parties. Though the city's "society" remained divided by the war, there was a change from earlier years, former Senator A. C. Dodge wrote Charles Mason. Aside from Judge David Rorer and his family, people who differed with each other on the war were now able to mingle without friction on such occasions. That fall there was a party in Davenport which involved a kind of mingling that neither Dodge nor Mason could have stomached. Nor did it please the Dubuque *Herald*. The guests were military officers from Rock Island, Davenport, Camp McClellan, two pastors, and "other gentlemen." The host identified by the Davenport *Gazette*, from which the *Herald* took the story, was Albert Nuckolls, a black physician.[72]

Council Bluffs was not alone in its appreciation of stage entertainment. In the winter and spring of 1864 "Uncle Tom's Cabin" played successfully before appreciative audiences in Davenport and Dubuque, in the latter place by McFarland's Great Combination Company in six acts. One lover of the stage really appreciated the McFarland players. When they returned to Dubuque a few weeks later with another show, he praised the quality of their offerings. Then he added,

[W]e are tired of the grin and guffaw of the Negro imitators on the stage and in the concert hall. To represent a higher order of civilization, to personify a gentleman or a lady requires education, talent, and refinement which belong to the province of the legitimate drama. . . . Let us encourage a taste for refined, chaste and intellectual amusements, and negro buffoonery will soon disappear from the boards.

Prof. Louis Agassiz drew well in Dubuque when he lectured on the subject "Man's Standing in Nature." Attendance was so good at all three of his appearances that the *Times* said it showed the wisdom of bringing first-class speakers to the city. Iowa City was a different case, in one paper's opinion. People there were "devoid of literary taste and interest in educational enterprises" despite the University's presence, complained the *Republican*. Furthermore, "A circus with a bear, dog, mule and monkey show draws thousands at fifty cents apiece [while] the commencement exercises of the . . . University, free to all, are hardly noticed."[73]

Baseball, "a manly and healthy exercise," caught on in Dubuque during the summer of 1864, but not enough for the *Times* to carry the score of the first two games. The *Herald* did better a year later. At least it reported the score (21 to 12), the fly catches by the winning side (12), by the losers (9), the innings played (9), and the time taken to play the game (2 hours and 15 minutes). But who won remained a mystery, although readers did learn that the Julien Base Ball club had played the best game ever played in the city "if not the best ever played west of the Mississippi."[74]

The *Times*, perhaps, had more serious matters to consider, because the editor worried at length about "Popular Literature and the Increase in Crime." "Americans were a reading people and children learned to read early," he said. "But we do find fault with that taste for impure, indecent literature which is so shamefully on the increase. . . ." It was expected, he continued, that low-class publishers would cater to such tastes, but not respectable publishers. When the higher class fiction they print, he continued, "depend[s] chiefly for their interest upon the intrigues and adventures of adulterers and adulteresses, it is high time for decent and Christian people to enter a vigorous protest." That was not all. Newspapers were even worse. Since everybody read them, they exerted greater power than books or the pulpit. Many city papers were "mere police gazettes, glorying in the privilege of exhibiting to the public the vile scenes that occur in the lowest, darkest hells on earth." Their local columns were often "textbooks in the school of villainy." Religious publications even printed the "most disgusting advertisements of a medical nature, just because it pays to do so." And some heretofore respected New York city papers printed "flaming advertisements of quack nostrums that professional abortionists thus successfully recommend to their numberless victims. . . ." The editor resolved to turn over a new leaf himself. As soon as their advertising contracts expired, he would no longer accept the "vile twaddle of quack doctors," their " 'pills' . . . 'Elixars' . . . and 'Drops,' *etcetera*. . . ."[75]

Soon the *Times* as well as other papers took out after another problem, circuses and circus advertisements. The *Linn County Patriot* (Marion), edited by the Reverend Mr. Lucans, refused to accept circus ads, reported *The Conservative* in Independence. However, the Reverend Mr. Goodenow, editor of the *Buchanan County Guardian*, also of Independence, had no such scruples, declared his competitor. In fact, he even endorsed the circus. But he did have scruples against accepting complimentary tickets for his printers. This stung Goodenow into an explanation. True, he had refused free tickets, but he had given each of his printers 50 cents in lieu of a ticket. He accepted Bailey's circus ads because the copy was tasteful. But he had not endorsed the show. Circuses were not for Christians. He preferred menageries himself. Still, publishers had to allow the public to make its own choices. Some day, hopefully, people would be educated to the point where they no longer demanded circus entertainment. The Mount Pleasant *Home Journal* believed circuses took from the poor what little money they had and wastefully employed men in occupations which benefited no one, or worse, led many persons to their ruin. The *Times* reported on the effects of Dubuque's encounter with Howe's circus. Pickpockets wound up richer by $1,000. The morals of young men and boys suffered from vulgar and obscene exhibtions and despicable side shows. Then, without a blink, the paper concluded,

If, hereafter, our country readers shall see a circus advertisement in the *Times*, let them regard it as a warning to stay out of town on the day of the exhibition. If they would not have their sons ruined, let them by all means keep them at home. If they would not have their daughters put to shame by witnessing the fantastic and indecent performances of the vilest of the fallen women, let them be kept away from the circus.

The *State Democratic Press* seemed less worried about the effect of the circus on the morals of rural youth, although it agreed with the *Times'* inference that the denizens of the towns were a hardened lot. "Bright eyed country lasses and honest farmer lads," said the writer,

> were to be seen in all the glory of unsophisticated enjoyment attracting the amused attention of the *blase* cits [meaning "city dwellers," probably] who see so little of natural sentiment that they come to look upon them with something akin to contempt, where the sons and daughters of honest toil might well look down upon their cremped [*sic*] notions and pity their vitiated taste.[76]

Then there was this man—one suspects that there were others like him in Iowa in those days. He was moral, honest, unsophisticated, given to the expression of natural sentiment. His name was Jacob Hunter, and he sought no glory in the Civil War. He only wanted to help restore the Union and end slavery. So he enlisted in Company E of the Fortieth Iowa Infantry in the summer of 1862, leaving behind his wife Mary and four children, Lewis, 11, John 7, William, 4, and Sarah, 2. Private Hunter was from Monroe, a small town midway between Oskaloosa and Des Moines. There were many "tories" in Monroe, according to Mary Hunter, some of whom were mean to her and abused young Lewis. This frustrated and enraged Hunter, and he vowed to make their tormenters pay someday. He tried to buck up his family's spirits. He told Mary to put her trust in the Lord and to pray that right would prevail. Mary Hunter seemed to worry once that he might change for the worse while he was away. He wrote back, "I am just the same as when I left home. Doe not give yourself no uneasiness about that."

Jacob Hunter did not like the South. He sympathized with the poor blacks he saw. This made him hate slavery all the more, and he wrote his wife that he longed for the day when all men could live in freedom.

Mary Hunter learned from him something about army life, about how some soldiers hated Abraham Lincoln, abolitionists, and blacks, but bedded with black women anyway. He told of some soldiers who abused hungry children and made them cry when they came to their Kentucky camp to fill their bread sacks. But he also told of kindly soldiers who filled the sacks.

Private Hunter was a devout and sensitive man who was appalled at much of what he saw and heard and learned. Mankind was more depraved than he had ever believed, he told his wife. He feared for his country and began to think that God might destroy it for its fall from grace. But he hoped that God instead would punish the wicked and spare the innocent.

Hunter was often sick with cold, fever, and diarrhea. Eventually he died, in a hospital at Paducah on February 24, 1863. A friend, Peter Kline, wrote Mary

Hunter about her husband's suffering in his final days, about his realization that he would never see his family again, about his fears for their future and his hope that they would get along somehow.

"He died trusting in the promises of Christ," Kline wrote, "and I have no doubts he is happy in the Spirit Land." The men of Company E, he added, had lost a friend, a soldier, and a patriot.

After Hunter's death Mary Hunter got a pension of $8 a month. The government paid her $2 a month for each of the children until they reached the age of 16.[77]

10

War's End: Democrats in Disarray, 1865

As the war drew to a close, Thomas Clagett welcomed evidence that some Union sentiment existed, notably in North Carolina. He thought the Lincoln administration should capitalize on it; however, Clagett wanted nothing less than Southern disarmament and submission to "lawful" federal authority. Neither Clagett nor David Richardson had any more sympathy than Republican Clark Dunham for Charleston, South Carolina, or South Carolina in general. All three blamed the state for igniting secession. Dunham wanted Charleston burned to the ground. Clagett hoped that President Lincoln would give its citizens "enough hot shot and hemp to make them remember him to the day of their death." Richardson believed the city was a "nest of traitors." Its people were "boastful, arrogant, and supercillious" and deserved their fate.[1]

The *State Democratic Press* was more sympathetic. Editor John Irish thought the entire South had suffered enough. Still, as late as March 29, he believed that the Confederates would continue to fight so long as they feared that in defeat they would meet "the fate of Poland and Hungary." Irish's solution for ending the war was for the rebels to renounce independence and for the North to renounce abolition.[2] Lysander Babbitt saw no hope for reunion. Babbitt argued that Lincoln should acknowledge Southern independence, then make a treaty of alliance with the Confederacy for mutual protection against foreign powers. Charles Mason believed the war could go on for years. It was February 25 when he hoped that the South would muster blacks into their armies. On March 12, he was dismayed when he learned of Confederate troop desertions. He accused the deserters of selfishly looking out after their own welfare. Mason, like Irish and Babbitt, professed to believe in the possibility of foreign intervention to end the conflict. To him this was more desirable than a peace which would bring the South to its knees. Either foreign intervention, he wrote on April 9, or "some domestic trouble" or successful merger of Johnston's and Lee's troops to form an interior defense line might preserve the Confederacy from destruction.[3]

The Dubuque *Herald* under M. M. Ham in early 1865 was as eager as Mason for the South to keep up the fight. Wrote the noncombatant editor, ". . . we would . . . as soon experience all that the country has gone through during the last four years rather than that any State, much less a number of them, would yield its right to regulate its domestic affairs in its own way.'' The South could and should fight on against the objectives of the Lincoln administration, namely, subjugation, radical changes in the Constitution, centralization of power, and permanent establishment of the abolition party. "Upon such a basis we do not expect, neither do we desire peace,'' he wrote. The South, Ham suggested on February 15, could withdraw from several coastal cities, thence to take the offensive in the interior against Sherman and Thomas. This, he believed, would not damage the Confederacy except for the monetary loss of the abandoned areas. Such views attracted the attention of the Cincinnati *Catholic Telegraph* which charged that the *Herald* was subservient to the "cotton lords" and that it belonged "to that class who impudently prate of the excellence of southern men and customs, and are too cowardly and abject to go South and uphold by acts the cause which they endeavor to sustain in the North . . .'' The unintimidated Ham responded defiantly that

> Even "cotton lords" at a distance are better than tyrants at home and abolition tyrants at that . . . [and] . . . those who attempt to punish secession are avowed disunionists, and at heart worse enemies of the country than any man who ever saw the inside of the Montgomery Convention. In a word, we believe, so far as our experience extends . . . that southern rule is much preferable to odious abolition domination.

When Richmond fell, the *Herald* claimed that Lee could yet prolong the war for a year or two. However, Ham had a better solution. Lincoln should simply proclaim a general amnesty, grant the Southerners all their "rights" including slave property, guarantee them against further federal interference with those rights, and reinstitute all Southern state governments to their prewar position so far as that was possible. Ham continued to give advice right up to the president's assassination. Pleased with the "magnanimous and liberal" surrender conditions Grant offered to Lee he suggested that Grant be empowered to draw up all peace conditions. The South should grant Lee the same power. The result would be a peace all white men wanted. If there was no joy in the *Herald* office over Richmond's fall, or the end of the war a few days later, there was nearly every place else, including the streets of Dubuque. There was rejoicing in both the *Democrat* office and the streets of Davenport, and throughout the rest of the state.[4]

But the Burlington *Hawk-eye* and Keokuk *Gate City* were disinclined to let victory-induced euphoria blot out their political opponents' transgressions. The *Hawk-eye* reported that Burlington's Copperheads wore long faces when they learned of Richmond's fall. The editor was not pleased when the same faces brightened considerably a few days later upon learning Grant's surrender terms. The *Gate City* blasted "Copperhead editors" who

> have become suddenly oblivious to the fact that they ever discouraged enlistments, defamed our soldiers, convened in secret sessions of treasonable

societies, shielded bushwhackers, spouted treason, villified Mr. Lincoln because he was striving to put down the rebellion, threatened resistance to the draft, incited insurrections, and libeled Union officers and soldiers while their only words of commendation were for traitors.[5]

During those last months, even as people eagerly anticipated the end of the war, some looked apprehensively at the economy. There were expectations that it might take a turn for the worse with peace, although the *Democrat* believed that if the federal government used only "ordinary wisdom" the country might emerge from the conflict healthy enough to pay its "colossal" debt. The *Hawkeye* advised farmers and merchants to pay off their own debts in good times to prepare for a "contracting process" it saw coming. The *Democrat* advised the same and pointed out that even as prices fell in March, they were still high enough to provide respectable profits. The Dubuque *Herald* remained determinedly pessimistic. It had no doubt that a financial panic would arrive along with peace and that Treasury Department policies would ensure that the peace would be a rich man's peace as the war had been a rich man's war. Operators of one Dubuque distillery shut down until prices should rise again. Their remaining in business only benefited the tax collectors, they said.[6] As prices dropped, workers found it harder to win wage boosts. When teamsters at one Dubuque firm struck to get a $10 monthly increase, the *Herald* opposed it. The strikers, the *Herald* learned, were to be "paid off, sent adrift and new hands hired in their places." Labor wasn't so scarce, the paper observed, since there was no draft in sight. Adding to teamster unhappiness was the fact that the paper inaccurately reported their pre-strike wages. Instead of $60 a month for driving a 4-horse wagon and $50 for a 2-horse wagon, they got only $50 and $40 a month respectively. When the war finally ended there were many stories in Iowa's papers about declining prices and wages, but few saw them as a sign of hard times. There seemed to be a general assumption that they would naturally decline. The same papers also noted that the economy had adjusted to peace better than expected.[7]

The end of the draft was an enormous relief to Iowans. The *Democrat* correctly gave much credit to Governor Stone and Adjutant General Baker, who wrung every warm body of enlistment credit they could from the War Department's record-keepers. Surprising testimony that the draft, and military service in general, had not been all bad for those who underwent it came from the pen of Charles Babbitt. This was the same Babbitt whose involuntary departure in the fall of 1864 had caused his Copperhead editor-father so many anguished moments. Unlike Charles Mason, who saw the Northern army (but not the Southern army) as potentially revolutionary rabble, Babbitt saw Union soldiers suffering little harm from their military experience. Some of course would turn out badly when they returned to civilian life, but such men had been of no account before they entered the army anyway. On the other hand, he wrote, "[M]any men will go out of the army possessing greater moral integrity and stability of character than when they came in. No true honorable man will receive any injury from the lessons he has learned in the army."[8]

Antagonism to Catholics and/or the foreign born flared briefly in early 1865 in exchanges between the Keokuk *Gate City* and the *Iowa State Register* on one side and the Keokuk *Constitution* on the other. The *Register* attacked the "swarms" of men of foreign birth who had accepted the immunities of American citizenship while rendering "every possible aid and comfort to the enemy" and yet claimed to be "better entitled to the fruits of republican liberty than black soldiers." The *Gate City* lashed out at Irish Copperheads and wondered about ultimate Catholic loyalty to the United States. Clagett furiously defended both the foreign born and Catholics and declared that Republicans believed the "servile black race" was superior to white European emigrants, mentally, morally, and socially.[9] The Dubuque *Herald* in a similar fashion fought with Dubuque Methodists over the relative merits of blacks, Irish, and Catholics.[10] In Marion county the departure, actual and anticipated, of nearly one hundred Pella Hollanders for the West brought no tears from Union men, according to the Knoxville *Republican*.[11] Soon after the war, Adjutant General Baker got into hot water because of a speech in which he excoriated aliens who had sought exemptions from military service. Baker did not retract his views when challenged, but he indignantly denied that he used the terms "damned Dutch" (Germans), and "Irish rabble," and that he ever said they were fit only for catfish bait. The *Herald* discounted Baker's denial, but the Davenport *Democrat* gave him the benefit of the doubt.[12]

There was more good feeling between some editors of opposing parties during 1865 than in earlier years, although not between opposing editors in the same town. The Muscatine *Journal* and the *Democrat* exchanged compliments as well as friendly jibes about their political stands when both papers came out in new formats. The *Iowa State Register,* even as a new election campaign heated up in the late summer, called the *Democrat* "by all odds the most honorable Democratic paper in the Mississippi Valley." The friendly Carthage, Illinois, Republican organ noted accurately that Thomas Clagett was eccentric and independent, going his own way regardless of what other Democrats thought. Clagett proudly agreed.[13]

Abraham Lincoln's assassination evoked shock and anger among thousands of Iowans, including many Democrats. David Richardson blamed the act on the "devilish spirit of secession . . . in the inmost hearts of those who hated the Union," a position which won praise from the *Register.* Two weeks later Richardson told fellow Democrats that even though they had opposed many Lincoln policies they must admit that his administration had been no failure. Rather it was "truly and undeniably a spendid triumph" because he restored the Union. The Dubuque *Herald* could not go so far, but it did report that there was nothing but sorrow in the city over Lincoln's untimely fate. Democratic sorrow, added the paper, was genuine, unlike that expressed by political "parasites" who tried to make capital out of the tragedy.[14] Lysander Babbitt claimed no Democrat desired Lincoln's death and judged that in his last days in office the President had dealt more liberally and humanely with rebel leaders than Andrew Johnson could be expected to do. The *State Democratic Press* regretted the killing and declared that Lincoln's last public position vis-a-vis the South showed him to be a man who favored "forgiveness . . . *conciliation* . . . [and] COMPROMISE."[15]

But there was no generosity for the dead in Charles Mason who wisely wrote his sentiments only in his diary. He believed the assassination was "retributive justice." He had not changed his mind that fall when, pleased with Andrew Johnson's general course, he wrote, "The killing of President Lincoln has been I feel a national benefit. . . ."[16] Iowans who were foolish enough to say openly what Mason said privately got themselves into deep trouble in many communities. Some suffered beatings or duckings. Some lost their jobs. Some were ordered to leave town. Others had to recant publicly. Such incidents, catalogued in both the *Hawk-eye* and the *Register,* occurred in Anamosa, in a rural area east of Burlington, Chillicothe, Comanche, Corydon, Council Bluffs, Davenport, in rural Decatur county, Des Moines, in a rural community east of DeWitt, on a train near Dubuque, in Eddyville, Indianola, Liberty township in Clarke county, Lyons, Mason City, Oskaloosa, Palmyra in Warren county, Pella, Pleasantville in Marion county, Sigourney, Wayne county, and Winterset.[17]

During these weeks, a few more Democrats in addition to Babbitt and John Irish, suddenly discovered much that was praiseworthy in Lincoln's known or presumed plans designed to restore the Union. Ex-Senator George Jones was one of these. Jones wrote a group of Pennsylvanians that he "had reason to know that he [Lincoln] intended to conclude peace with our southern brethren on the most liberal and generous terms. . . ." That was not all. Continued Jones, "His first great desire was the restoration of the Union, next the abolition of slavery; but if the Confederates would have agreed to neither then . . . he would acknowledge their independence and make with them a treaty of alliance, offensive and defensive, for the restoration of the Monroe Doctrine. . . ." The *Iowa State Register* which printed the Jones revelations treated them with scorn.[18]

But what the martyred Lincoln would have done was soon less interesting to Iowa Democrats than what President Johnson was going to do. They even began to hope that Johnson might possibly be a good Democrat. On June 14 Charles Mason had what he described as a "long, satisfactory interview" with Johnson. "He was quite unreserved," Mason wrote, "[and] declared himself an unchanged Democrat. I left him under the impression that all would be well." Conversation with other Washington Democrats convinced Mason that the Iowa party should support Johnson. They told him the new president would rebuff the radical Republicans, pacify the country, and work for a speedy return of the Southern states to the Union. Through George Jones, Mason communicated their views and advice to a number of Iowa Democratic leaders.[19] They liked what they heard. On July 12 they met informally in Davenport and resolved to support administration policy. They also instructed the state central committee to omit the word "Democratic" from its annual call for a state convention. Chairman Laurel Summers, with some misgivings, complied. He invited all persons opposed to removing the prohibition of black suffrage from the state constitution and all persons who favored President Johnson's attitude toward reconstruction to convene in Des Moines on August 24.[20] Despite the hopes of party chiefs, the convention, when finally convened, acquired the name "Democratic."

The reasons for the attempted subterfuge are clear. On June 13, Iowa's Republicans met in their annual convention, and, after a bitter fight, endorsed black suffrage for Iowa by a 513 to 242 vote. The Republicans also renominated William Stone for governor. Stone's leadership was yet only partially satisfactory to those party elements who had opposed him in 1863.[21] These two factors, plus Mason's and others' insistence that the Iowa Democrats eliminate the party label, led to the attempt to promote a "nonpartisan" convention. In Mason's eagerness to devise a strategy for defeating the Republicans he told Jones and Summers that Democrats could properly nominate anyone for governor who was sound on two points: opposition to black suffrage and support for Johnson's reconstruction policy. Mason's strategy was clear. He believed that the Northern Democrats' overriding objective should be restoration of the South to the Union with its privileges "full-fledged." Only then would the party regain a congressional majority and control of national policy, thence to demolish the abolitionist Republicans and all their works except, probably, emancipation. Therefore, Democrats in Iowa as well as elsewhere, should support any ticket, even or especially one with dissident Republicans, which might defeat the regular Republican nominees. That result, he felt, would strengthen Johnson's hand as he attempted to implement his own reconstruction policy. He advised Jones, "I think we should endeavor to adapt means to ends."[22] Jones got similar advice from Montgomery Blair. Blair even suggested that John Kasson, Fifth District Republican congressman, whom Democrats believed to be much less radical than his colleagues, might be persuaded to challenge incumbent Stone in the coming gubernatorial race. Former President James Buchanan was more noncommittal when Jones sought his advice on political strategy. Buchanan simply counseled Iowa's Democrats to stand by "Conservative principles." These, he believed, characterized his and Johnson's positions in late 1860 during the secession crisis.[23]

In the meantime there were political stirrings in Iowa which propelled the state's Democrats into precisely the course suggested by Mason and Blair. The Republican convention's endorsement of black suffrage failed to strike a responsive chord among many rank and file Republicans.[24] For them the move to grant blacks the vote was a move too soon and fraught with political peril. Why they thought so is revealed by any look at Iowa's Democratic newspapers and the correspondence between Democratic politicians. Almost all believed that black suffrage and the future of blacks in Iowa as well as the rest of American society was something they could exploit successfully. Democrats were encouraged, moreover, by signs that soldiers disliked both blacks and the possibility of black suffrage. From the Twelfth Iowa stationed at Selma, Alabama, came reports of a regimental caucus which came out flatly against black voting and against the state Republican convention's nominees. Soldiers dominated two antiblack suffrage meetings in Lee county in July. Lawyer Daniel Miller wrote Charles Mason that fights between blacks and returned soldiers were almost daily occurrences in Keokuk. Oskaloosans witnessed an unprovoked attack on a black boy by several ex-soldiers during a city festival held to honor soldiers.[25] Returning veterans frequently visited the Davenport *Democrat* asking Richardson to tell his readers about soldier antagonism to black suffrage. The soldiers, he wrote, opposed it more than five to one, having "seen too much of Sambo's everyday life" to trust him with the ballot.[26] In addition, some recently discharged Iowa soldiers chafed under what they considered less than adequate recognition by the Republican party. In certain counties, party managers bypassed veterans who desired nominations for county offices. In Story county, for example, disgruntled soldier office seekers were prominent in a separate county soldiers' convention.[27] In early August, Thomas Clagett, displaying his accustomed independence toward the Democratic high command, issued a formal call for a "Soldiers Convention" to be held August 23 in Des Moines, the day preceding the "nonpartisan" but obviously Democratic convention. Seventy-two delegates came, the bulk of them from Lee and Polk counties. Some walked out when it appeared that Democrats were in control. The group which remained constituted itself as the "Union Anti-Negro Suffrage Party." It announced, "We are opposed to Negro suffrage or to striking of the word 'white' out of the article on suffrage in our State Consitution, and will support no candidate for office, either state or national, who is in favor of Negro suffrage or of the equality of the white and black races." The party also endorsed the Monroe Doctrine, President Johnson and his reconstruction policy, a policy of soldier preferral in filling public offices, and the Thirteenth Amendment. To head the ticket in the race for governor, the delegates chose Col. Thomas H. Benton, nephew of the famous Missouri senator. Benton was a former Democrat and state superintendent of public instruction.[28] The next day the not-so-well-disguised Democratic convention, amidst considerable unhappiness on the part of the 1864 "ultras," endorsed the Soldiers convention ticket, as it became popularly known. The Democrats did write their own platform. But its emphasis differed not at all from the Soldiers document. It too scorned black suffrage and praised Johnson's reconstruction policy.[29]

Despite the alacrity with which the August 23 and 24 conventions settled their business, many Democrats harbored strong reservations about the Soldiers ticket. Benton's letter accepting the Soldiers convention nomination didn't help any. "I am a Republican," he declared bluntly, adding, "[The] Democrats have made no overtures to me, nor have I made any to them. They have asked no pledges. I shall give none. Whether they will vote for me, or against me, or not at all, are questions with which I have nothing to do and over which I have no control." Mason, as self-appointed middleman for the Democracy, found the Benton missive highly offensive. He wrote, "Silence in regard to us could have been born but he should have been cautious about using language which . . . [is] positively distasteful to the whole party. If he is elected it must be mainly by our votes. He ought not therefore to have turned up his nose to us quite so ostentatiously." Nevertheless, Benton's stand on issues helped keep the unhappy Democrats in line. Besides favoring "liberal and honorable" terms for the South, he claimed that black suffrage would create racial strife in Iowa. He said Republicans were opportunistic for raising the issue in 1865 after steadfastly ignoring it earlier. Benton also called for fair treatment, protection, and freedom for blacks. The last of these three points caused most Iowa Democrats no pain. For them, as for the rest of the party in the North, the death of slavery removed an embarrassing issue. But the primary reason Democrats supported Benton was a strategic one. Charles Mason kept reminding his friends what it was. Andrew Johnson needed all the help he could get in his efforts to expedite the return of the South to the Union. This accomplished, the Democrats would regain national power. Whatever it took to achieve these goals, Iowa Democrats must do.[30]

LeGrand Byington remained unpersuaded. As in 1864, Byington summoned the party to produce a "true" Democratic platform and ticket. The Iowa City man became convinced early in August that the forthcoming Soldiers and regular party conventions would avoid basic issues and compromise the party. Thus, on August 11, he issued a convention call which clearly expressed the sentiments of the unreconstructed Democrats of the war and postwar years. He called for a convention of persons

> who adhere to the patriotic principles of Jefferson—who are for maintaining the reserved Sovereignty of the States and wish to restore the General Government to its limited Constitutional functions toward States and people—who earnestly oppose the despotic Executive pretensions and corrupt class of Legislation and judicial decrees of the Federal Administration—who are, in a word, in favor of a revival of the Democratic Party as it existed before the late Abolition war.[31]

Byington's convention assembled in Iowa City in mid-September despite the efforts of Mason and others to head it off. The small number of delegates constructed a platform in consonance with the circular. They also nominated a ticket headed by two opponents of the war, Gideon Bailey, former legislator from Van Buren county, and Lysander Babbitt. The Byington ticket received little press support, but the *Iowa State Register* gave it a backhanded compliment. In lieu of voting for the Republicans, the only honest Union candidates, voters should support the Byington faction because, said the editor, "It represents *brains,* and does not add to the crime of disloyalty that of hypocrisy!"[32]

Republicans reserved their heavy fire for Benton. Byington gave him trouble too. When Benton campaigned in Iowa City, Byington challenged him to a debate on states rights. Benton believed the federal government should guarantee the rights of freedmen to life, liberty, and property. He believed, further, that such a guarantee should include federal authority to intervene in the states if necessary to uphold them. But he summarily dismissed Byington's challenge.[33] Congressman Josiah Grinnell was one Republican who attacked Benton forcefully on the issues. Grinnell denied Benton's contention that black suffrage was the only important campaign issue among Iowans. He believed they wanted draft

evaders disenfranchised and traitors punished. Grinnell, who at first opposed
Republican promotion of black suffrage on the grounds that it was politically inex-
pedient, claimed Benton wanted to give the ballot to the "disloyal white South"
while denying it to loyal blacks. He also claimed that blacks, possessing the ballot,
could rely more on their own political weight and less on federal bayonets to protect their interests in a predominantly white society. Grinnell apparently borrowed
his major points directly from General Marcellus Crocker. By September, Crocker
was dead, a victim of consumption. In the preceding four years he had become
one of the party's prized wartime converts, a successful and popular officer, and a
figure whose views Republicans eagerly sought. Crocker, early in July, 1865, made
a strong appeal for black suffrage. In a well-publicized letter to Governor Stone,
Crocker pointed out that under slavery blacks derived some protection in a hostile
society from the master-slave relationship. Now they had only the resources of the
law to protect them. Without a voice in the making of law or implementation of
policy, they were defenseless. Therefore, Crocker argued, freeing them without
the protective ballot would be an injustice.[34]

Generally, however, the Republicans avoided the intricacies of the suffrage
question during the campaign. They relied largely upon the proven effectiveness
of the Unionist versus Copperhead theme. And they added a new word to the
political vocabulary, "Possum," which they applied to the Soldiers ticket.
Republicans divined what basic Democratic aims were and geared their campaign
accordingly. When Senator James Grimes wrote an Iowa friend, "We all know
that the Democratic party desire and intend to coalesce with the returned rebels
from the South," he could have been reading Charles Mason's mind (and
diary).[35]

In the fall of 1865 many independent candidates ran against Republicans in
various counties where Republican leadership, like that in Story county, slighted
returning soldiers or other individuals who believed they deserved nominations for
county posts. These independents reacted hotly to charges that they were Copperheads or Possum, or that they represented traitorous elements. When A. J. Bill
withdrew from a race in Pottawattamie county, his published disclaimer mirrored
the intense feelings in Iowa nearly half a year after Appomatox. In the *Nonpareil*
Bill explained that

> to be elected by the votes of those men whom I now find rallying around me,
> would not be a victory of which I could be proud, for as parties have now
> shaped themselves, my success whould be heralded abroad as a Copperhead
> victory, and there is nothing that I would more deeply deplore than to become
> instrumental in giving aid and comfort to those men whom I have known for
> the past four years as the enemies of my country.

In Mahaska county, George Carson turned down the so-called Possum county convention nomination for sheriff and said he would vote for no one that convention
nominated.[36]

Democrats launched their heaviest attacks against Governor Stone. They again attacked his war record, accused him of cowardice in battle, cruelty to his men, and maladministration of his regiment. They claimed he was thoroughly abolitionist and raised again the charge that he favored blacks to the disadvantage of whites. The *Iowa State Register*, while denying all such accusations as "copperhead falsehoods," admitted that the offensive against Stone was somewhat effective.[37]

In the election Governor Stone did run behind the rest of the state ticket, although he defeated Benton decisively. Top Republican vote-getter was George Wright, candidate for state judge, who defeated Soldier candidate Henry Trimble, 72,069 to 52,018. In contrast, Stone downed Benton 70,445 to 54,070. Dr. Bailey, Byington's gubernatorial candidate, garnered only 350 votes. Iowa election officials still counted some soldier votes, 736 of which went to Stone and 607 to Benton. Two significant aspects of the results were the reduction of the Republican margin and the decline in the total vote from that of 1864. This reduction and decline are shown in Table 10.1. The Soldier ticket of 1865 is included with the sublabel Democratic because the votes it received were essentially Democratic votes, a fact which few Iowans denied. Some Democrats professed optimism about the results. But others viewed their adoption of Benton as a mistake and claimed that the party should henceforth fly under its own colors and principles, regardless of the consequences.[38]

TABLE 10.1
REPUBLICAN AND DEMOCRATIC VOTES AND PERCENTAGES 1864-65

Year	Republican		Democratic		Total
1864	89,035	64.2	49,596	35.8	138,631
1865	70,445	56.4	54,070	43.3	125,865

11

Iowa Vote in Wartime

EXCLUDING soldier votes of 1862 to 1864, 37 of 96 Iowa counties voted Democratic in at least one major fall election (some contests being concurrent) during the period 1861 through 1864. These elections were the gubernatorial elections of 1861 and 1863, a special congressional election in District One in 1861, the regular congressional elections of 1862 and 1864, the elections for secretary of state in 1862 and 1864, and the presidential election of 1864. The special election in District One, a region including all counties in the southern three tiers and those in the fourth tier beginning with Polk and extending west to the Missouri River, is included because the citizens viewed it as something of a referendum on the Lincoln administration policy to that time. Seventeen of the 37 counties voted Democratic 50 percent or more of the time.[1] These were Allamakee, Appanoose, Audubon, Boone, Buena Vista, Calhoun, Carroll, Davis, Decatur, Dubuque, Jackson, Lee, O'Brien, Sac, Sioux, Wapello, and Webster. But among them, Audubon, Buena Vista, Calhoun, Carroll, O'Brien, Sac, and Sioux had such a small number of settlers and potential voters, 10 or less in several cases, that they were negligible in their impact on the state record as a whole.

One can draw few firm generalizations about political behavior on the basis of county returns. Some voter blocks on township levels presented solid fronts on one side or the other of the political fence. But their influence on a county vote was limited if the county at large voted in the opposite fashion to that of the blocs themselves. Therefore, one must turn to township census returns and voting figures to more accurately determine what groups voted in what manner.

Until recent decades Civil War historians tended to assume that persons born in the South, persons born in the border and southern Ohio Valley regions, and Irish voted Democratic. Germans, Scandinavians, and Britishers (non-Irish) presumably voted Republican along with persons born in New England and in the Middle Atlantic states. The Germans benefited most from this assumption; namely, that they fled tyranny before and after the revolutions of 1848 and were, hence, disposed to vote for freedom and the Republican party in the 1860s. The same reasoning was never employed in the case of the Irish who left their homeland for similar reasons.

Iowans of that era, however, were uncertain about the German vote, although few had any doubts about whom the Irish favored. They did believe, though, that Catholicism among both Germans and Irish produced Democratic votes. Democratic Dubuque city in early 1860 had 912 Protestant church members and 6,200 Catholic parishioners according to the *Herald*. Oldt and Quigley's *History of Dubuque County*, which generally treats political developments evenhandedly, praised the settlement of Peosta for its "loyalty" during the war, attributing this to the fact that settlers established Methodist, Presbyterian, and Campbellite churches early in the town's history.[2]

An analysis of township voting in Iowa in the presidential election of 1860 by George Daniels based on numbers of potential voters (adult males twenty-one years of age and older) largely confirms the assumptions of Iowans of that era that the Irish were overwhelmingly Democratic and that the Germans were by no means solidly Republican.[3] Daniels concluded that Iowa Germans were heavily Democratic in those rural townships where they were the numerically dominant voting power. But he noted some tendency of German voters in urban areas to follow the dominant voting pattern of their particular community—a pattern which, however, might better be accounted for by their religious affiliations. In Republican voting communities, townships or wards, the Germans who lived there were, it seems, more Protestant than Catholic—and possibly somewhat less worried about nativist elements in the Republican party. Those Republican editors like James Howell and Clark Dunham who had a nativist tinge directed their barbs at foreign-born Catholics, not foreign-born Protestants. Germans in Dubuque city were largely Democratic and Catholic. Germans in more politically divided but Republican-leaning Davenport were apparently both less Catholic and less Democratic. They did not appear to vote in such a manner as to lessen the Republican vote there. As the *Argus* and *Constitution* surmised, Germans in their cities were not solidly Democratic or Republican. In the fall election of 1862 in Keokuk, for instance, the *Constitution* reported that the Republicans lost because "a large number of American-born citizens, *and some Germans, who have heretofore voted with the Republican party*, . . . [italics added] joined the white man's Democartic party."[4]

The Daniels study also showed that Iowans born in the Middle Atlantic states and in New England largely voted Republican in the 1860 election. Southern-born Iowans mostly voted Democratic along with the Irish and those Germans who settled in predominantly German communities. Iowans born in the Ohio Valley were split in their party allegiance, their ancestral home being a region originally settled by both Northerners and Southerners.

The Daniels work generally answers the question about how the various nativity groups voted in Iowa in 1860. But how did they vote during the war and in the first fall election after the war? Voting records for three or more of the fall elections over the six-year period were found for 41 of the 80 townships which Daniels subjected to analysis. Those 41 had to meet one or the other of two Daniels stipulations, namely, that they exhibit a marked degree of political partisanship (over 65 percent or less than 25 percent Democratic in 1860), or else that they be the most Republican or most Democratic townships in their respective counties.

Table 11.1 which records the voting records of these 41 reveals that they were largely consistent in their political allegiance. Only 6 (14.6 percent) made any shifts at all.[5] One, Republican Harrison township in Benton county, is recorded only because of 6 protest votes which barely denied Governor Kirkwood a majority in the gubernatorial election of 1861. Harrison resumed its strongly Republican stance thereafter. Another township, Taylor, Dubuque county's only markedly Republican township, voted solidly Republican, 1860–1864, then swung decisively Democratic six months after the war ended, its Democratic percentage increasing dramatically from 37.9 percent in 1864 to 56.3 percent in 1865. Clear Creek in Johnson county, which scored a 66.3 percent Democratic vote in 1860, registered steady Republican gains until it became Republican in 1864. Massilon in Cedar county and Collins in Story county changed from Democratic to Republican between their first and last recorded votes. Rockingham in Scott county switched from Democratic to Republican for a two-year period but reentered the Democratic fold in 1865.

In short, what the 1860–1865 figures seem to show is that there was relatively little tendency among voters in townships which showed a marked party preference in 1860 to shift from that party of preference, at least through 1865. It seems also that what in- or out-migration those townships experienced did not significantly change the composition of their nativity groups—or that the in-migrants, whatever their origins, tended to conform to the townships' established voting patterns. They also suggest that Daniels' findings about how specific nativity groups voted in 1860 largely hold true for the next five years, 1861–1865. In the 4 townships in which the Irish were the dominant group and the 6 where Germans dominated, the vote was solidly Democratic. The single township in which New Englanders were dominant was one with a straight Republican record. Six of the 10 townships in which persons of Middle Atlantic states origins were the dominant group remained staunchly Republican. In 1 of the 10 (Auburn of Fayette county) the township voted straight Democratic. In the other 3, the voters switched one or more times. They were Clear Creek of Johnson, Taylor of Dubuque, and Rockingham of Scott. In 2 townships where Middle Atlantic states voters shared dominance with Ohio Valley voters the record was straight Republican. But as Daniels noted, persons from the Upper Ohio Valley were less politically predictable as a group. Six of the townships in which they were numerically the largest group had straight Democratic voting records. But in 9 others the voting pattern was straight Republican. Three Ohio Valley dominated townships which switched one or more times were the previously mentioned Harrison (Benton county), Massilon (Cedar county), and Collins (Story county).

Even in the nonselect townships where parties were more evenly balanced in 1860 this tendency toward stability of township-voting behavior through 1865 existed also. There were 248 of these in the 18 counties from which came the 41

TABLE 11.1

VOTING PERFORMANCE OF SELECTED IOWA TOWNSHIPS, FALL ELECTIONS, 1860–65

County	Township[a]	1860 Nativities	%	Democratic Vote Percentage 1860	1861	1862	1863	1864	1865	av
Jones	Washington	Ireland	78.1	93.4	92.8	98.5	75.2	95.2	90.6	91.0
Dubuque	Iowa	Ireland	46.5	89.2	86.4	88.7	90.3	87.0	95.6	89.5
Benton	Union	Ireland	45.2	86.7	93.5		90.9	96.3	90.3	91.5
		Upper Ohio Valley	29.0							
Dubuque	Liberty	Germany	68.9	86.6	91.9			92.6	98.5	92.8
Johnson	Liberty	Germany	33.1	83.3		94.3	79.1		87.7	83.2
Dubuque	Prairie Creek	Upper Ohio Valley	23.3	83.0	89.0		90.2	93.1	99.2	90.9
		Ireland	68.8							
Dubuque	Mosalem	Germany	47.7	81.9	85.0	90.7	86.1	89.4	82.8	87.7
		Ireland	23.9							
Lee	Jefferson	Upper Ohio Valley	25.3	73.9	100		75.2		81.3	82.6
Des Moines	Augusta	Upper Ohio Valley	31.0	73.1	74.4	67.7	70.3	69.1	59.1	69.0
		Middle Atlantic	24.1							
Henry	Baltimore	Upper Ohio Valley	35.0	70.9	74.2	76.5	68.8	66.7		71.2
		Middle Atlantic	24.5							
Lee	West Point	Germany	49.4	70.0	71.6		70.8		65.2	69.4
		Upper Ohio Valley	24.8							
Des Moines	Pleasant Grove	Upper Ohio Valley	40.5	67.7	66.3	72.6	69.2	56.1	61.4	65.6
		South	26.2							
Des Moines	Benton	Germany	27.5	66.7	62.2	75.6	62.4	62.4	68.1	66.2
		Upper Ohio Valley	24.2							
		South	20.9							
Johnson	Clear Creek	Middle Atlantic	38.3	66.3			53.9	42.9	47.3	52.6
Linn	Buffalo	Upper Ohio Valley	36.2	63.3		61.5		55.9		60.1
Jones	Jackson	Upper Ohio Valley	40.6	60.0	54.7	60.6	62.1	64.4	59.6	60.2
		Middle Atlantic	33.8							
Scott	Rockingham	Middle Atlantic	21.6	57.9	64.3	56.3	42.5	41.2	58.1	53.4
Cedar	Massilon	Upper Ohio Valley	28.9	57.2	50.4	57.5		41.7	30.4	47.4
		Middle Atlantic	23.9							
Fayette	Auburn	Middle Atlantic	42.0	56.4	71.5	63.2	58.4			62.4
Muscatine	Moscow	Germany	32.9	55.8	62.3	71.3	66.5		63.3	63.8
		Upper Ohio Valley	27.2							
Story	Collins	Upper Ohio Valley	58.3	54.2	56.5		53.8	34.6		49.8
		Middle Atlantic	20.8							
Dubuque	Taylor	Middle Atlantic	26.6	35.4	29.9	39.3	35.1	37.9	56.3	38.9
		Ireland	20.5							

TABLE 11.1 (continued)

County	Township[a]	1860 Nativities	%	— Democratic Vote Percentage						
				1860	1861	1862	1863	1864	1865	av
Story	Milford	Upper Ohio Valley	39.4	31.0	31.0	...	37.1	36.1	...	33.8
		Middle Atlantic	27.3							
Fayette	Harlan	Middle Atlantic	29.2	25.0	26.7	...	38.5	...	...	30.0
		Uper Ohio Valley	29.2							
		New England	20.8							
Lee	Cedar	Upper Ohio Valley	40.7	24.8	28.3	...	30.6	...	25.0	27.2
		Middle Atlantic	25.8							
Benton	Harrison	Upper Ohio Valley	40.3	23.6	52.0	...	30.1	25.8	27.3	31.8
		South	28.8							
Muscatine	Fulton	Middle Atlantic	34.3	22.7	37.0	37.5	38.7	...	41.4	37.5
		Upper Ohio Valley	20.4							
Benton	St. Claire	Middle Atlantic	37.5	21.2	35.5	...	39.1	39.2	35.6	34.1
		Upper Ohio Valley	25.0							
Scott	Liberty	Upper Ohio Valley	34.3	20.7	16.5	12.6	14.0	16.3	16.5	16.0
Linn	Brown	Middle Atlantic	41.8	20.7	...	34.2	...	25.4	...	26.8
		Middle Atlantic	30.9							
Benton	Cue (Florence)	Middle Atlantic	29.0	20.0	18.3	...	25.3	28.0	23.4	23.0
		Great Britain	24.7							
Jones	Wayne	Middle Atlantic	45.4	17.8	17.9	30.0	5.0	21.4	14.9	17.8
Cedar	Springdale	Upper Ohio Valley	37.1	17.2	20.9	10.9	...	11.5	5.8	13.2
		Middle Atlantic	20.7							
Des Moines	Yellow Springs	Upper Ohio Valley	38.4	16.9	10.3	18.8	13.9	8.3	10.6	15.7
		Middle Atlantic	24.7							
Washington	Crawford	Upper Ohio Valley	37.0	15.2	13.0	15.2	25.9	14.3	13.1	16.1
		Middle Atlantic	33.2							
Washington	Clay	Upper Ohio Valley	42.0	14.7	13.0	12.7	14.1	11.3	11.7	13.8
		Middle Atlantic	30.1							
Lee	Denmark	New England	34.9	14.0	15.6	...	17.8	...	12.7	15.0
Cedar	Gower	Upper Ohio Valley	27.0	11.3	19.2	25.0	...	4.5	...	15.0
		Upper Ohio Valley	44.0							
Fayette	Putnam	Middle Atlantic	26.5	9.4	14.8	17.8	20.0	...	...	15.5
		Middle Atlantic	48.0							
Benton	Bruce	Middle Atlantic	31.8	7.3	8.7	...	6.1	13.5	12.5	9.6
		Upper Ohio Valley	31.8							
Henry	Wayne	Upper Ohio Valley	34.3	0.8	4.8	3.8	10.7	8.3	...	5.7
		Middle Atlantic	27.9							
		South	25.0							

[a] Township order is based on percentage of Democratic vote in 1860, from highest to lowest.

209

select townships, counties which, incidentally, cast 42 percent to 44 percent of the state's vote in the period 1860–1865. Only 38 (15.5 percent) of this nonselect group of 248 voted differently in their last from their first recorded votes of those which could be located between 1860 and 1865. Four (9.8 percent) of the select 41 townships were voting differently.

Over the whole period the Republicans only scored a net gain of 6 townships in the combined select and nonselect townships. Yet there was clearly a substantial increase in Republican votes. From where did they come? One partial answer lies in the soldier votes which don't show in the township totals—although many soldiers doubtless were voters before they entered the army. Democrats as well as Republicans entered Iowa's regiments. There is no denying, though, that the Republicans reaped the advantage from the soldier vote law of 1862. During the three years in which the soldier vote was an important factor, the Republicans never won less than 78.3 percent of it. That was in 1862. They took 85 percent in 1863 and an even 91 percent in 1864. The soldier vote for those three years was 18,989 in 1862, 20,001 in 1863, and 18,735 in 1864. It is doubtless true that there were more Republicans than Democrats in Iowa's regiments, if only because the state had more Republicans. Yet it is unlikely that they outnumbered the Democrats in the army by as much as their election victories indicated: 3.6 to 1 in 1862, 5.7 to 1 in 1863, and 9 to 1 in 1864. Some Democratic soldiers voted traditionally. But it would be foolish to maintain that exhortations to "vote as you shoot," coupled with the pressure exerted by an officer corps owing appointments to a Republican administration, were ineffectual.

Another explanation for the Republican gain may lie in the fact that some Iowans who entered the state in the migrant flood of the 1850s came of voting age in the 1860s. That flood had contributed heavily to the rise of the Republican party. Most likely it still was. Nor did migration into the state cease during the war. The population increased from 674,913 in 1860 to 756,209 in 1865, bringing more of the same.[6]

By 1860, also, the number of foreign-born Iowa voters, more Democratic than Republican, was probably at the highest level it would ever reach proportionately. The impact of these voters upon the state's total in the war years, then, would likely not have been much, if any, greater than it was in 1860.

The explanation for the increase in the Republican vote rests, accordingly, on the assumption that the potential Democratic voting strength was more stable than potential Republican strength. To some extent the size of the Democratic vote during the period 1859–1866, over a year after the war, bears this out. Table 11.2 reveals that between 1859 and 1866 the Democratic total vote increased by only 2,483. Even more revealing is the fact that the Democratic vote in 1866 was smaller than the combined Northern and Southern Democratic vote of 1860. The Republican vote, on the other hand, increased by 34,695 during the same time span despite two clear declines in 1861 and 1865.

The 1861 election, according to contemporary accounts, attracted less public interest than did the task of preparing the state for its war effort, this despite the

TABLE 11.2
IOWA VOTE AND PERCENTAGES, 1859–66

Year	Republican civilian		Republican soldier		Democrat civilian		Democrat soldier		Other civilian soldier		
1859	56,532	51.5	...	...	53,332	48.5	...	...			
1860	70,316	54.8	...	...	55,091	43.0	...	...	Constitutional Union	1,763	1.4
									Southern Democrat	1,035	0.8
1861	59,853	55.3	...	...	43,245	40.0	...	...	Union	4,492	4.1
									Scattering	663	0.6
1862	51,140	52.2	14,874	78.3	46,784	47.8	4,115	21.7	...	...	...
	[Total: 66,014—56.5%]				[Total: 50,899—43.5%]						
1863	68,895	56.4	17,001	85.0	53,169	43.6	3,000	15.0	...	...	...
	[Total: 85,896—60.5%]				[Total: 56,169—39.5%]						
1864	72,183	60.2	16,852	91.0	47,713	39.9	1,883	9.0	...	...	...
	[Total: 89,035—64.2%]				[Total: 49,596—35.8%]						
1865	69,709	56.4	736	54.8	53,463	43.3	607	45.2	Scattering	350	0.3
	[Total: 70,445—56.4%]				[Total: 54,070—43.3%]						
1866	91,227	62.0	...	...	55,815	38.0	...	...			

Democrats' struggle to find a suitable candidate. In 1865 there was an undercurrent of ill feeling among portions of the electorate against the Republicans and the Stone administration, notably among former soldiers. Those few soldiers who voted while yet in service in the fall of 1865 showed no such overwhelming favoritism toward the party as they had in previous elections. Again, contemporary accounts seem to indicate that the 1865 election took place in an atmosphere similar to that of 1861. There were simply other things to do which attracted the voters' attention. Herbert Hoxie was not alone when in 1865 he gave up the twin toils of politicking and policing for the more lucrative activity of railroad building. But such a mild setback was only temporary for the Republicans.

Excluding the tremendous 1866 postwar jump in Republican votes, the biggest upsurge in the Republican votes came in 1863 in the Stone-Tuttle race for governor. The previous high vote in Iowa history was in 1860 when Iowans cast a total of 128,205 ballots. The 1863 total was 142,065. In this election the Republicans increased their soldier vote by 2,127 while the Democrats lost 1,115. The victors obviously won the votes of most new civilian voters, those Iowans who came of voting age and those who migrated into the state. Republican politicians did run scared in 1863 against the popular General Tuttle. They never ceased to remind the voters that leading Copperheads backed Tuttle's candidacy. They reiterated the charge that Copperheads controlled the Democratic party. And they had most of the elements on their side which contribute to a party's winning an election: money; organization; a favorable press; some coercive power (with soldiers); and the immeasurable but certainly effective appeals to patriotism, loyalty, and duty. Their mild rebuff in 1865 demonstrated that when they did not mesh all of these with foresight and precision, they could lose votes. But such was their reserve of both voter power and prestige with the Iowa electorate that they could win handily against a demoralized and outnumbered foe.

There remains one question: Why did the Iowa Democrats do so poorly in the 1862 elections when their counterparts in Illinois, Indiana, and Ohio scored striking successes in capturing state and congressional offices? There are several explanations. First, the Iowa Republicans were relatively much stronger than the Republican parties in the other three states in 1860. Second, the soldier vote of 1862 which padded the comfortable Republican lead was not a factor in the other three states. Wisconsin, like Iowa, allowed soldiers to vote. Soldier votes from both states favored Republican candidates by an overall margin of nearly 4 to 1. Had soldiers from Illinois, Indiana, and Ohio been allowed to vote, the chances are that the Democrats would have picked up fewer congressional seats than the 34 they did win. In many contests the Democratic margin was narrow enough that a 2 to 1 margin for the Republicans from soldier votes would have resulted in Republican victories.[7]

Projecting Iowa percentages into other states is risky, but one example may serve to illustrate this assumption about a soldier-vote potential. The total vote polled by the Republican congressional candidates in Ohio in 1860 was 218,564. Democratic candidates and others polled 191,199. In 1862 the Democrats won, 188,847 to 174,379. Had Ohio soldiers been allowed to vote and had they voted Republican in the same proportion of 3.6 to 1 that Iowa soldiers did, the Republicans might conceivably have scored a 27,000 victory overall. Ohio soldiers did vote in 1863. Their vote was overwhelmingly Republican, 41,267 to 2,288 in the governor's race. By then, however, their polling power was not of critical importance to the Republicans who scored a 247,194 to 185,274 victory with civilian votes alone. Therefore, it seems reasonable to conclude that in one respect the poor showing of the Iowa Democrats was partly the result of a soldier-vote differential, which, if applied to the other three states in 1862, would have blunted considerably what so long has been regarded as a resounding Democratic triumph and, correspondingly, as a stinging rebuff for the Lincoln administration in 1862.

One should note that the Wisconsin soldier vote in 1862 failed to prevent the election of three Democrats to Congress in that state. All three Democratic winners came from districts containing large numbers of foreign-born voters, particularly Germans.[8] But the soldiers did vote Republican nearly 2 to 1 in the First District which included Milwaukee, and Republican better than 2 to 1 in the other two districts, the Fourth and the Fifth.

A third reason why Iowa's Democrats did so poorly in 1862 is similar to the second in that it minimizes the Democratic victory in the other three states. Henry Clyde Hubbart in *The Older Middle West, 1840–1880*, noted that the Midwest was really divided into a southern region and a lake region. There was a Democratic resurgence in the Midwest as a whole in 1862, but the greatest number of changes to the Democratic side took place in the southern region. This is clearly illustrated by a map in Hubbart's chapter dealing with the election of 1862. This map locates the districts which in Hubbart's words, voted "against Lincoln" and "for Lincoln." What it reveals is that the "against Lincoln" districts were concentrated heavily south of an imaginary projection of Iowa's southern border eastward all the way to Pennsylvania. Twenty-six of the districts above the line voted Republican while only 7 went Democratic. Below the line, 26 went Democratic while only 4 went Republican. Therefore, it seems reasonable to view the Iowa Democratic weakness in 1862 less as an isolated phenomenon than as part of a prevailing pattern existing in the Lake (or northern Midwest) region.

Nor should anyone overemphasize the Democratic "revolt" in the southern portion of the Midwest. Democrats had always been strong there and the region was far from unanimous in support of Abraham Lincoln or Republican congressional candidates in 1860.[9] Persons with Southern or border state backgrounds were numerous, and commercial ties with the Southern states had long been important to the region's economy. Because of this area's proximity to the politically and militarily strategic border states, the federal government and state officials took particular pains to guard against the activities of Southern Sympathizers. Arbitrary arrests of political dissenters and of persons suspected of collaborating with the Confederacy were far more common than in distant Iowa. That the administration should have suffered a sharp, backlash setback there in 1862 should surprise no one.

Iowa's divided Democrats made their case against their opponents as best they could every year at election time. They assumed, as did Republicans, that appeals to self-interest mixed with appeals to principle and emotion would influence voting behavior.

The Democrats claimed that Republicans harbored nativist principles and that they preferred to elevate blacks above white immigrants. They increasingly charged that all their opponents were abolitionists and that emancipation would harm the working classes, immigrant and native-born alike. They claimed that the war was a "rich man's war and a poor man's fight." They railed against arbitrary arrests, suspension of the habeas corpus privilege, and the increasing centralization of power while defending states rights, 'the Constitution as it is' and the status quo ante bellum. These were all standard issues, and probably helped to keep the rank and file in line. But it is doubtful that they won many converts. At best they could make some Republicans uncomfortable, particularly on the black issue and, to some extent, on the violation of civil liberties. But Republicans had them at an even greater disadvantage on what most Iowans of both parties perceived as the greater issue—preservation of the Union—and, for good measure, putting arrogant secessionists in their place. The Democratic task was not made any easier by the fact that some articulate and influential party members, who, while claiming to be for the Union, seemed to oppose every measure designed to keep it intact. These men were often an embarrassment, and their intraparty opponents had to work hard to make certain that they did not dictate party policy or the choice of candidates for office. Democrats, then, had a difficult enough task trying to educate each other, not to speak of the immensely more difficult task of trying to educate a largely united and, to them, obstinately uneducable political opposition.

Was there a significant economic component to the Copperhead movement or to the Democratic appeal in general during the war? Possibly, but Iowa's overall economic condition, ultimately the economic condition of individuals, was not something the Democrats could really capitalize on to win more votes than they already had, nor does it appear that they tried to do so with any consistency. That is because, at least from the last four months of 1862 on, it was apparent that the war brought general prosperity to the state. This is not to say, on the other hand, that any Democrats turned Republican out of gratitude. They didn't, much to the disgust of certain editors who seemed to think they should. There were, of course, some specific economic complaints, about the loss of Southern trade, about the administration's failure to move more rapidly to reopen the Mississippi, and about high railroad rates and high taxes. But Democrats weren't the only ones who voiced them. Republican businessmen and farmers also sounded off, and there were more Republicans among them than Democrats to begin with. Similarly, there were a lot of Republicans who were as economically insecure as a lot of Democrats, particularly those who did not have easy access to good rail transport and river transport systems to facilitate the marketing of their crops. It is also worth recalling that the Dubuque *Herald*'s Copperhead editors and its one War Democratic editor were less sympathetic to Dubuque workers who sought to improve their economic condition by striking for higher wages in inflationary times than were the editors of the Republican *Times*.

Did Democrats come from counties which had poorer soils, and were they, accordingly, less prosperous than Republicans? P.E. Brown's 1936 volume, *Soils of Iowa,* has information on the soil quality of 14 of both the 17 top Republican and the 17 top Democratic counties by voting percentage over the period 1861–1864. In 13 of the 14 Republican counties, Grade 1 (excellent) soil is either the majority grade or the leading grade in terms of acres. Ringgold county's dominant grade is Grade 3 (fair quality). In 7 of the 14 Democratic counties, Grade 1 soil ranked highest in acreage. Grade 3 soil ranked highest in Dubuque, Johnson, and Wapello, while Grade 4 (poor quality) ranked highest in Appanoose, Davis, Decatur, and Lee.[10] However, Robert Rutland, who pointed out that 12 out of 20 counties went Democratic at least once in the elections of 1861, 1863, and 1864, had excellent soil and concluded that there was little correlation between Copperheadism and low-fertility soil.[11]

It may be that a more sophisticated approach to the analysis of economic and voting data of the 1850s and 1860s in Iowa will eventually reveal that rank and file Democrats were significantly less affluent than Republicans[12]—or even that Copperhead Democrats were on a lower economic level than War Democrats. The same kind of approach might verify what more subjective evidence (newspaper observations) indicates, namely, that those Democrats who were members of more theologically conservative religious denominations were more Copperhead than were War Democrats. Paul Kleppner's *The Cross of Culture* indirectly suggests this possibility.[13] This is not to say, however, that religion determined politics for most Iowans. It is true that some persons switched from one church congregation to another or established new ''nonpolitical'' churches after becoming disgruntled with dominant political opinion in their own local churches. But this switching appears to have occurred more between Protestant groups which were not profoundly different from one another in a strictly religious sense. That is, when people moved from one congregation to another or formed a new congregation they usually did not undergo any fundamental theological shift. Rather they were seeking or setting up more congenial local congregations. They simply preferred to be with persons who shared their opinions on the war, who favored one kind of "political preaching" over another, or who professed to favor no such preaching at all.

Finally, whatever future studies may reveal about differences between and among Iowa Republicans and Democrats of the 1850s and 1860s, they are unlikely to show that the state's Democrats were in any position to win many converts, much less change the way most Iowa citizens responded to the demands of the Civil War. That challenge was beyond their strength.

12

Aftermath and Conclusion

THE Civil War left scars which took a long time to heal in Iowa. The state's Republicans for years afterward reminded the electorate that theirs was the party of "Union, Loyalty, and Lincoln." They portrayed their opponents as men who were too evil-minded to support the nation in its hours of trial against the designs of the disloyal South. At election times there was little disposition on their part, nor on the part of their opponents, for that matter, to let bygones be bygones. William Stone's inaugural address in January of 1864 epitomized what was to be the Republican attitude in the years to come when he declared that those who failed to support the federal government without reservation during the war would be recorded in history as enemies of their country.[1]

Some persons believed they had no reason to forget or forgive. Mrs. Cyrus C. Carpenter was one. Shortly after the assassination of President Lincoln she poured out her feelings to her husband who was then in North Carolina with Sherman's army. Describing a Fort Dodge memorial service for the martyred chief executive, Mrs. Carpenter wrote:

> Mr. Boynton wanted us to bury all differences and hard feelings that we may have felt against our *disloyal* neighbors in the grave with Abraham Lincoln. Mr. Griffith said he had sworn eternal hostility to all rebels whether North or South and he believed it was right and Christian like, and I think so too. I can never forget that they killed my brother Barton and now our dear old President. The time to be conciliatory is past. I am bitter, bitter! . . . Some of our Copperheads are trying to be loyal now. Duncombe and Stockdale profess to be very mournful. I really believe Stockdale is, but that low-lived braggart of a Duncombe I cannot believe. . . . They say they fear Andy Johnston will not carry out Lincoln's policy. Well, I hope he won't in one or two things. I hope he will hang traitors when he catches them.[2]

Copperhead LeGrand Byington also forgot nothing and was selective about his forgiving. In October of 1865 he revived his paper, *The Olive Branch*. Byington made clear that his olive branch was extended to Southerners, not Republicans

216

and War Democrats.[3] George W. Jones, Henry Clay Dean, M. M. Ham, and, particularly Charles Mason, were equally solicitous of Southern feelings and aspirations and scornful of their political opponents. Appearing at times to be totally oblivious as to who won the war, they were quite willing to turn the clock as far back toward 1860 as it would go.

There were some who claimed that political antagonists could enjoy friendly personal and business relations. Frank Street of Council Bluffs, a self-styled Republican radical, was one. When Street joined the *Nonpareil*'s staff as associate editor in the fall of 1865, he declared that the Republican party was the only safe and loyal party. But, he added, he would not allow this sentiment to influence his business and social relations. If a Democratic merchant sold cheaper goods than a Republican merchant, he would patronize the Democrat. "What I may have to say therefore of my political opponents, will relate to the politics and not the men," Street concluded optimistically.[4] It was more difficult for most Iowans to separate the politics and the man. W. O. Payne's *History of Story County* told what several other frank Iowa county histories also related, namely, that the residue of wartime bitterness between many politcal opponents was so great that they had little to do with each other in succeeding years.[5]

Burlington editor Clark Dunham was one who believed that sinners deserved no consideration, and certainly not in politics.[6] Nor did wartime peace proponent Charles Mason, who by September, 1866, had not found peace so positive a good after all. He wanted Johnson to use his removal and appointive power even more vigorously. If the President did not, he wrote, "Civil War . . . will have to be resorted to, before we are through."[7] Mason thought Johnson's supporters would be justified in resorting to force if an impeachment crisis arose. However, when he received a letter from a perturbed Iowa Democrat who proposed to raise a brigade to back Johnson, he demurred—but not out of principle. What gave him pause was his belief that the public would not yet approve direct action. Ironically the Iowa Democrat who proposed to raise a brigade was William Merritt who had replaced Mason on the 1861 state Democratic ticket as candidate for governor.[8]

Nor was the bitterness confined to that between parties. Within the Iowa Democracy the wartime divisions were yet apparent. Those who fought to make the party a peace party of "true Democrats" only, and who objected vehemently to endorsement of the Soldier convention nominees of 1865, sought to prevent a repetition in 1866. They failed as the Democratic moderates again swung the party behind a Conservative Republican ticket and platform which endorsed Johnson's reconstruction policies and opposed black suffrage. LeGrand Byington rebelled once more. He promoted a convention and ticket of self-styled Jeffersonian Democrats who complained about the lack of enduring principles among the "Andrew Johnson Democrats."[9]

The regular Republicans won all state and congressional posts with ease that fall. They declined to renominate two congressional incumbents in district convention, however. One change resulted from what contemporary observers took to be a demand for more, rather than less, radicalism by the party's rank and file.

Fifth District Republicans balloted 78 times before they selected General Grenville Dodge in place of John Kasson. Kasson favored admission of those Southern representatives to Congress who would take a prescribed oath of loyalty to the Constitution. The *Iowa State Register* claimed that most Iowa Republicans wanted more, specifically, assurances that the Southerners would be elected by a loyal constituency.[10] Radical Josiah Grinnell fell before equally radical William Loughridge in the Fourth District. In the race for secretary of state, Republican Ed Wright defeated Democrat-backed Conservative Republican S. G. Van Anda, 91,227 to 55,815. General James Tuttle absorbed a 14,296 to 9,898 trouncing from General Dodge in the Fifth District where Tuttle campaigned against radical Republican "treason." The Jeffersonian Democrat ticket was not active during the campaign.

In 1867 the Democrats regained their party identity as the Conservative Republican revolt expired. They nominated Charles Mason for governor. Mason accepted the dubious honor without optimism.[11] The Republicans, with Samuel Merrill as their standard bearer, ran on an aggressively radical platform, which approved congressional reconstruction, votes for blacks, and condemned "traitors and their allies." Mason, who believed free government for Iowa was at stake in the election, received scathing treatment from the Republican press, particularly from the Burlington *Hawk-eye* which somehow acquired a copy of a friendly postwar letter Mason wrote to a classmate of West Point days, a man dubbed "Butcher Robert E. Lee" by the paper.[12] The fall of 1867 saw the Iowa Democrats poll their highest vote ever. But Mason still lost decisively, 90,228 to 62,806. The increase in Democratic votes continued into the 1868 elections when Horatio Seymour polled 74,040 in the presidential race. This, nevertheless, was less than half the Republican gain as Iowans cast 120,265 ballots for Ulysses S. Grant. That same election saw Iowa voters approve black suffrage by 56.5 percent, the culmination of a political, legislative, and referendum process which began with the 1865 state Republican convention's endorsement of the proposition.[13] The electorate displayed no more favoritism toward the Democrats in the next three elections, nor in 1872 when they combined with the Liberal Republicans against the Republican regulars.

During the era of the "farmers revolt" in the Midwest in the 1870s, such merging of diverse elements was common. For the Iowa Democrats this produced very limited success. Mildred Throne in two useful articles attributed this to the party's preoccupation with regaining political power and consequent neglect of the basic issue on which it nominally professed to stand—support for the cause of discontented farmers. The party's leaders continued to espouse states rights, a tariff for revenue only, and a hard money policy, none of which seemed relevant to the disgruntled agrarians. Iowa's Republicans, on the contrary, proved more amenable to farmer demands and subordinated their inclination to favor business interests when political office was at stake.[14]

But some prominent Iowa Copperheads did participate in the Greenback movement of the seventies, notably Dennis Mahony and Henry Clay Dean. Mason and former Senator Augustus C. Dodge were at least fellow travelers. However, John Irish, last wartime editor of the *State Democratic Press* (at most a small "c" Copperhead), was one who fought unsuccessfully to steer the Democrats clear of the Greenback-Democrat coalition of 1878.[15] In fact, those occasions in which the Democrats came closest to achieving political success as a party occurred when they "managed" reform movements without wholeheartedly espousing the principles of the reformers. There were two such occasions during the decade. In 1876, they merged with and then managed in their own interest many but not all of the discontented Grangers in the Anti-Monopoly party. The other occurred in 1878, the fusion with the Greenbackers. In 1873 the Anti-Monopolists actually elected 50 of the 100-member Iowa house. In 1874, Democrat Lucian L. Ainsworth, who had served in the state legislature during the war, ran under the Anti-Monopoly banner and won election to Congress from the Third District. A Republican recaptured the seat in 1876. Not until 1888 did the Democrats elect a state officer. That fall Peter Dey defeated John Mahin in a contest for one of the state railroad commission posts. Mahin was a victim of the railroad interests who reacted strongly to the Republican-dominated General Assembly's passage of a stringent railroad regulation bill of that year.[16] Not since 1857 had any Democrat won a statewide election. In 1889 Horace Boies, a Democratic convert from Republicanism, won the governorship after a campaign in which prohibition was a major issue. Aided by the railroaders, Boies won two terms on platforms which included a pledge to repeal the state's prohibition law. He failed in a bid for a third term as Republicans promised to modify the offending railroad regulation act.[17] Except for Ainsworth and Benton J. Hall, no wartime Democrat of any prominence who remained in the party ever won a congressional or statewide elective office in the postwar years. Hall represented Iowa's First District in Congress, 1885–1887.

Dennis Mahony remained active in politics and journalism. Before he completed a second term as Dubuque county sheriff, he resigned and went to St. Louis with Stilson Hutchins. There he and Hutchins published the *Times*. In 1871, Mahony returned to Dubuque and founded the *Telegraph*. Before his death in 1879, the *Telegraph* became one of the leading Greenback organs in the country.[18] Hutchins eventually left St. Louis after a stormy career in the Missouri legislature and with both the *Times* and the St. Louis *Dispatch*. He was one Copperhead whose past was no hindrance. From St. Louis he went to Washington where he founded the *Post*. One of his associate editors was Richard Sylvester, a wartime editor of the *State Democratic Press*. Hutchins became a power in the city and in Democratic affairs, hobnobbed with presidents, senators, representatives, and the rest of the elite of both parties. He acquired and disposed of other newspaper properties in the capital plus papers in Virginia and New Hampshire, served in the New Hampshire legislature, and eyed that state's gubernatorial office for a time. Hutchins also backed Ottmar Mergenthaler's linotype machine and profited from his foresight. He invested successfully in Washington real estate, industrial and railroad enterprises, became an art collector, and something of a philanthropist. Hutchins also went through three wives, none of whom remained unscathed by the experience. A flamboyant, controversial figure all his life, he died in 1912 leaving an estate valued at $3 million which rose to an estimated $5 million thirteen years later as his heirs struggled over its disposition.[19]

Charles Mason returned to Burlington in the late 1860s and participated in numerous business enterprises and civic affairs. He and his longtime neighbor and political adversary, Senator James Grimes, came to a meeting of minds in early 1871. Grimes, his public career at an end, despaired over the corruption in his party and hoped the Democrats would make "wise nominations" so they could win the election of 1872. To the end, Mason longed for a rejuvenation of the Democratic organization across the country. In 1876 he even pondered the feasibility of the party's nominating a black man as its vice-presidential candidate in order to take the wind out of the Radicals' sails. Mason died in 1882 after several years of failing health, brought on in part, his daughter believed, by the "inevitable discouragements that had come to him politically through the Civil War and Reconstruction days."[20]

George W. Jones never recovered his lofty position in Democratic councils after his release from Fort Lafayette in 1862, although he remained politically active in Dubuque county for several years. After the war, Jones instituted a suit against former Secretary of State William Seward, seeking $50,000 damages for false imprisonment. The Iowan rejected an offer by Seward's lawyer to settle for $5,000. Seward's death in 1872 closed the case at a time when Jones had become confident of victory.[21]

Henry Clay Dean, soured by his wartime treatment and the trend of national and state affairs thereafter, authored a polemic to air his dissatisfaction. In this work he bitterly attacked the new industrial order, the "money power," and centralized government. He bemoaned the passing of "the people's democracy" and the subordination of the West to eastern monopoly. In 1871 Dean left Iowa to settle in Putnam county, Missouri, on a tract of land he named "Rebel's Cove." He vigorously championed the Greenback movement and in 1876 fought to prevent the Democrats from nominating a hard money candidate for president.[22] Lysander Babbitt was another who never swerved from the Jeffersonian path as he saw it. Babbitt served one term in the state legislature after the war. Council Bluffs citizens repeatedly elected him to the city council until he moved to Arkansas in 1881.[23]

LeGrand Byington also remained an "unreconstructed Jeffersonian" to the end of his long life at the age of ninety-one in 1907. Characteristically, Byington led the feeble revolt of "straight out" Democrats in 1872 who refused to merge with the Liberal Republicans in support of Horace Greeley. For Byington, the war and its aftermath were costly. Land sales to satisfy delinquent tax claims, which he would not pay to support an "unconstitutional war," cut into the fortune he acquired from prewar land speculation.[24] John Duncombe, cited in the *History of Fort Dodge and Webster County* as an "inflexible Democrat," always interested in "reform and progress," was not one of those who took part in the antirailroad agitation of the postwar decades. Duncombe came to Fort Dodge in 1855 to practice law, and for thirty-seven years was the attorney for the Iowa division of the Illinois Central. He also served as attorney for other smaller Iowa roads. For nearly two decades he was a member of the state higher education system's Board of Regents.[25] David Richardson served as a Regent also. He, Edward Thayer, and Thomas Clagett continued for many years to publish successful opposition newspapers in Iowa's Republican climate. Laurel Summers took only a limited role in party activities after the war. Venerable Augustus Dodge overcame the Copperhead stigma and Burlington voters elected him mayor in 1874.[26]

The passage of time ultimately diminished much of the lingering antagonism Iowa Republicans felt toward their Civil War opponents. Even so, Robert Rutland discovered that the Des Moines *Register* was still using the term Copperhead as late as 1895.[27] When death came to Iowa's leading Copperheads—Mahony, Mason, Byington, and Dean—Democratic and Republican papers alike lauded them for their courage, honesty, and political consistency, qualities known by other names during the Civil War. Mason's formal obituary in the *Hawk-eye* differed from the others in one interesting aspect. The Republican paper recorded his life in detail except for the period 1860–1870, a decade the writer omitted.

This omission in Mason's life story corresponds with the way Iowa's numerous county histories later treated the Copperhead movement. Most of them appeared between 1878 and 1914. Of the 128 in which one could reasonably expect some mention of Copperheadism, no matter how limited, 86 had none at all. Nineteen of the remainder devoted from one sentence to approximately one page to the subject. Some of these patently overlooked evidence of Copperheadism, or minimized what evidence there was, or, in a few cases, affirmed solemnly but falsely that no Copperheadism existed in their counties. An example is the *Portrait and Biographical Album of Linn County* published in 1887 which stated that "there was no fire in the rear in Linn County." The *Album* writer's statement, "no fire in the rear," implies in context that there was no antiwar sentiment in Linn county. Marion's articulate Jane Thompson, whose letters to her soldier-husband had much to say about Linn county Copperheads, could have told the writer a thing or two.[28]

Twelve county histories cover Copperheadism thoroughly. Eleven others are less detailed, but still helpful to the historian. Thirty-five Iowa counties had enough Copperhead activity to justify some coverage in county histories. But the histories of eight predominantly Democratic counties ignore Copperheadism. These counties are Audubon, Allamakee, Boone, Guthrie, Marion, Shelby, Wapello and Webster. Madison has two county histories, as do many others, but one of them mentions nothing about Madison's numerous and active Copperheads. The other contains only a brief, nonilluminating passage on them.[29] The histories of Appanoose, Jackson, Johnson, and Pottawattamie counties, each of which had many Copperheads, pass lightly over their activities. Among counties which voted Republican but which had significant Copperhead strength, nine failed to mention it. Counties in this category were Des Moines, Iowa, Henry, Linn, Muscatine, Scott, Taylor, Warren, and Washington.

This tendency among some Iowans to ignore the Copperheads as a legitimate part of their past took an interesting twist in Jacob Van Der Zee's *The Hollanders of Iowa*. Van Der Zee, who had great affection for Iowa's early Dutch settlers, obviously felt some pain when a respect for accuracy forced him to reveal that Marion county's Hollanders usually voted heavily Democratic, before, during, and after the war. Van Der Zee stoutly maintained, however, that none of Pella's Copperheads were Hollanders.[30]

Iowa's Copperhead Democrats, like those in other Northern states, became Copperheads when they reached the stage at which they more rather than less consistently opposed a war to force reunion, especially a war conducted by a Republican administration. Some Copperheads, probably a very small number of men like Charles Mason, came to accept the idea that separation, temporary or permanent, was more desirable than any Union dominated by Republicans. The rest continued to engage in wishful thinking, the substance of which was that an armistice and negotiations would result in peace and reunion since the Confederates really didn't mean what they said about independence.

Those Iowa Democrats who did not consider themselves Copperheads reacted furiously against Republicans who applied the stigma to them. To them Copperheads were men who sympathized too much with Southern grievances, who supported the war too little if they supported it at all, and, who, thereby, gave the whole Democratic party a bad name. The non-Copperhead Democrats like Thomas Clagett, David Richardson, and S. P. Yoemans viewed the Union as legally indestructible, the South as illegally rebellious, and the war as a necessary war. They accepted the Lincoln administration as the lawfully constituted national authority, if also an authority which deserved frequent censure for abolitionist tendencies, inept performance, dereliction of duty, and violation of civil liberties.

Copperhead Democrats occasionally spoke of themselves as Copperheads, some of them pridefully. Rank and file Copperheads who wore Copperhead pins or who defiantly "hurrahed for Jeff Davis" in the streets made their feeling clear. When Dennis Mahony, Lysander Babbitt, John Jennings, Stilson Hutchins, John Gharkey, and others called for violent action against the Lincoln administration, or demanded an immediate peace, or wished Southern armies well, or boasted that from the first they had opposed the war, they were voicing positions which non-Copperhead Democrats repudiated.

That these Copperhead leaders and their followers adhered to these positions is not the same as saying that they were traitors who engaged in conspiracy to overthrow the Union or to materially aid the South. In Iowa, certainly, what conspiracies existed, if any, were designed to resist an "unconstitutional draft." Nor was it traitorous to take delight in Southern victories or to laud the real or alleged merits of Southern fighting men and Southern civilization while denigrating Northern victories, Northern soldiers, and Northern civilization.

But there are legitimate questions about the depth of their commitment to the Union. Richard Curry has written that "the vast majority of Northern

Democrats supported a war for Union, if not for Emancipation. . . ."[31] This is true. But the war, despite what many Northern Democrats claimed, was always a war for Union. The question needs to be asked: Was this "vast majority" of Northern Democrats, especially the Copperhead Democrats, committed to the war for Union when it became clear that Emancipation would follow in its wake? This is a crucial question because what the Copperhead Democrats in particular charged was never true, namely: that emancipation was really the objective of the war all along; that Lincoln lied when he, in effect, proclaimed emancipation as a means to end the war, not as an objective; that the Emancipation Proclamation proved that the war was no longer a war to restore the Union, but was rather an abolitionist crusade, hence no longer worthy of support. For some Copperhead Democrats—and how many "some" includes can never be known—the answer is no. They did not want to support the war any more under any conditions—if they ever had in the first place. The Emancipation Proclamation gave them the excuse they needed. For some War Democrats also the Emancipation Proclamation was a shock and it temporarily lessened their commitment to the war. Like the Copperheads they were war weary and angry at the increase in the number of arbitrary arrests or other violations of civil liberties. Nor did they have any love for blacks. Thus, the Proclamation became something more with which to club the administration. Still, these War Democrats had no serious intention of allowing the South to get away with secession. They would swallow emancipation along with victory over the Confederacy. Also, they were simply less concerned with maintaining Southern "rights and privileges," meaning the right and privilege of slave-owning, since the South had done the unthinkable in attempting to destroy the Union.

The question, "Were the Copperheads loyal?" is hard to answer. Revisionist historians have defended them against the charge of disloyalty, arguing that they were primarily conservative unionists, western sectionalists, and extremist political partisans. These are certainly accurate for the most part as descriptions of what Copperheads were—and not too far off the mark, for that matter, as a description of their intraparty opponents who saw themselves as conservatives, unionists, and westerners, although not as extremists. But such a description evades the issue in that it does not directly deal with the question about loyalty. It is a substitute for some necessary speculation about the meaning and thrust of Copperhead writings, orations, and peace rally resolutions.

At the simplest level of meaning during the Civil War "being loyal" in the North meant being loyal to the concept that the Union was indivisible. Functionally that meant that any unilateral attempt to divide it had to be resisted, and that the South, accordingly, had to return or be returned to the fold, sooner not later, voluntarily or under compulsion. A loyal person, it follows, wanted Northern armies to win, Confederate armies to lose, and the Confederacy disbanded. A loyal person believed that "disloyalists" wanted Northern armies to lose and Confederate armies to win enough on the battlefield to topple the elected Lincoln administration, or force it to accept a draw which would result in Confederates dictating terms of reunion, if there were to be reunion at all. The fact that many opportunistic knaves were loyalists and branded other persons as disloyalists who patently were not, does not mean that one has to discard the definition which they, as well as more honest Northerners, believed was a proper one. Charles Mason for one, was disloyal by this standard. Mason wanted Northern armies defeated, which, not so incidentally, meant Iowa soldiers being killed in great enough numbers to lose battles. He wanted Confederate armies to be successful to the point that the South could return to the Union on its own terms if it wished to return. He wanted foreign intervention if necessary to achieve this end. He wanted Southern armies to enlist blacks so they could stave off defeat (enlistment of blacks in Northern armies, however, was unthinkable). He wanted Southern soldiers to hold fast, to stick with their units, and to fight on stubbornly in the last few months of the war. And he once wished that McClellan had deposed Lincoln by a military coup.[32] In 1863, Dennis Mahony, Stilson Hutchins, LeGrand Byington, Henry Clay Dean, and Charles Negus began to claim that secession was an accomplished fact and that the North should not prolong the struggle. They probably preferred a military stalemate rather than Northern *or* Southern military victory—although this writer is not totally convinced that they were really much different from Mason who did want the Confederates to win a convincing edge on the battlefield. By this time it was clear that such a stalemate would result more in meeting the Confederate objective, independence, than it would Lincoln's, restoration of the Union. How many agreed with them cannot be known. These people, whether few or many, were disloyal, then, in the common meaning of the term in those years when a majority of Northerners conceived of "Union" or "the Union" as absolute values and separation as out of the question. If this judgment appears harsh, and if it seems to promote too much—as it probably does—the idea that questions of loyalty or disloyalty can be decided by majority vote, it, nevertheless, is partially in keeping with David Potter's assertion that historians should "appraise the past in the terms which were most relevant to it, rather than in presentist terms. . . ."[33] Holding the Union as an absolute value, loyalty or disloyalty to it were "most relevant" questions to the men who held such a view.

Indeed, Mahony and his fellow Copperheads could not themselves avoid thinking in the context of a loyal-disloyal dichotomy. Time and again they spoke of loyalty to the "Union as it was and the Constitution as it is" and scored Republicans and abolitionists for being "disloyal" to both. At the same time they squirmed on the horns of a dilemma. They increasingly came to view both the legally elected Lincoln administration and its course as revolutionary. Loyalty to either was disloyalty. Vainly did they argue that they were loyal to the "Government," the "Constitution and laws," and to the old Union but that they owed no loyalty to the "administration."

Part of their anger, an anger shared to a considerable degree by some War Democrats, stemmed from their fall from political power in the state before the war. Iowa's Democratic party leaders had enjoyed supremacy in the territorial and state governments until the middle 1850s when the upstart Republicans rudely displaced them. Their egos never recovered. And what was more galling was that the victors posed as defenders of western white men against the parsimonious Southern-dominated Democratic congresses whose concern for western development took a backseat to the protection of slavery and slaveholder rights in the territories. Iowa Republicans had rubbed it in: even if western Democrats in the Congress had pushed western interests more vigorously, their own national leadership was disinclined to help them. Consequently, simple outrage at the Republican takeover permeated the editorials and letters of many Iowa Democrats of the late fifties and the war years. How could such evil-minded, issue-distorting, "nigger loving," immigrant-despising, prohibitionist-meddling, Puritan hypocrites, pretentious pseudodefenders of "freedom" and western interests possibly be fit to govern hard working, liberty-loving Democrats, the rightful heirs of Jefferson and "old Hero!" Were they not even now smearing those heirs as traitors, scoundrels, and blackguards? Were they not the men who had promoted this great national tragedy in the first place? Did they who now controlled the government, an arbitrary government elected by a minority of the voters, really deserve the loyalty they demanded as their due?

The answer of those who became Copperheads was that they did not. The very idea was absurd and abhorrent. Their loyalty was to the "Constitution as it is and the Union as it was," not to this illegitimate abortion. Those who became War Democrats felt somewhat the same way; but the difference was that they felt much less so. To them the Union was more of an absolute value, a transcendent institution upon which, in Potter's words, one's "loyalties . . . converge simply because it does exist."[34]

That said, one must take a final leap of faith and make a judgment that some Copperheads, perhaps a majority, deep in their gut, also saw the Union as an absolute value. Whether and how to support that value without acquiescing completely to the arguments and measures employed by their hated opponents were questions which some could never answer.

Iowa Copperheads suffered the political consequences ever after for the course they had taken during the war. It was their misfortune to be located in one of the most loyal of the loyal states. Had Indiana's Thomas Hendricks and Daniel Voorhees, Ohio's George Pendleton and Allan Thurman, or Illinois' Melville Fuller been Iowans, they would never have climbed higher than the state legislature. The Copperhead albatross was a most disabling burden in the Hawkeye state. It was hardly less so to Iowa Democrats who had never been Copperheads. They knew well the meaning of guilt by association.

What made some men Copperhead Democrats and others War Democrats is a question to which there is no conclusive answer. One might suspect that the Copperhead leadership came largely from the Buchanan wing of the party as opposed to the Douglas wing. But there is no clear one-to-one relationship. Copperheads George Jones, Laurel Summers, Charles Mason, LeGrand Byington, and John Duncombe were Buchanan men. But Copperheads Henry Clay Dean and Thomas S. Wilson belonged to the Douglas faction. P. N. Casady and Dennis Mahony originally were Buchanan men, but by 1860 were supposedly in the Douglas camp, although Mahony's position is uncertain. Pre-1860 Buchanan men who became War Democrats were William Merritt, David Richardson, Hugh W. Sample, and George Paul. Douglas followers Daniel Finch, Lincoln Clark, William Coolbaugh, and Benton Hall appear in the War Democrat ranks after 1860. Robert Rutland has contended that Copperheads came from the strict constructionist wing of the Iowa Democratic party.[35] This, however, is not particularly conclusive since all Democrats including War Democrats considered themselves strict constructionists, which they were for the most part. The Buchanan-Douglas split in Iowa was not clearly along strict constructionist-loose constructionist lines anyway, and, as noted, this split in the 1850s bears an uncertain relationship at best to the split in the 1860s.

As might be expected, Copperhead, War Democrat, and Republican leaders were similar in social and occupational status. They usually were not farmers, although they might be farm owners. They were lawyers, editors, railroad promoters, merchants, bankers, and land speculators. The rank and file of all three groups were much alike also, the great majority being farmers. There was some sense of social superiority among Republicans who linked Catholicism, foreign-born Catholics, and liquor consumption to the Democracy, especially the Copperhead Democracy. But many Democrats (as well as moderate and conservative Republicans) felt superior to abolitionist Republicans.

Why certain leading Democrats became Copperheads is seen to some degree in the pattern of their lives well before the war started. Charles Mason, who left far more material for historians to work with than most, is one of these. Born to a farm family of limited means in New York, Mason worked hard to rise in the world. Despite irregular schooling he secured an appointment to West Point. There he excelled and ranked number one in the graduating class of 1829. While there he became a friend of Robert E. Lee, who finished second, and of Jefferson Davis, and Joseph E. Johnston. After 1837, when Martin Van Buren appointed him United States attorney for the Wisconsin territory which included Iowa, he rose within the Democratic party to a position of eminence. He served four years as head of the United States Patent Office under Franklin Pierce and James Buchanan. He quit the position in mid-1857 in disgust over application of the spoils system to the office by his superiors, expressing distate also for what he saw as the administration's taking "a stand altogether too Southern."[36] Nevertheless, Mason was an establishment man who abhorred abolitionist doctrines and the tensions they created in a civilization and a society which had been good to him.

George Jones had once been a slaveholder and enjoyed particularly good relations with Southerners, including Jefferson Davis, during his one term in the Senate. Henry Clay Dean, born and educated in Pennsylvania, studied both theology and the law. Ordained a Methodist minister, he served a Virginia circuit for several years. The 1844 split in the church over slavery caused him to retire from the regular ministry. His financial ups and downs thereafter in Iowa, to which he migrated in 1850, promoted his antagonism toward "the money powers" whom he came to equate with Republicanism, abolition, and opposition to the common man—even though he had a tremendous yen to make a great deal of money if he could. Friendship with Senator Jones, a Catholic, helped make Dean a staunch opponent of the nativists. Thanks to Jones, Augustus Dodge, Iowa's other senator, and to Governor Henry Wise, whom he aided in a Virginia election campaign by taking the stump against nativism, Dean won election to the chaplaincy of the United States Senate for the first session of the Thirty-Fourth Congress in December of 1855.[37]

Dennis Mahony had no such background of old friendships with leading Southerners. But Mahony, Irish and Catholic, saw himself as a defender of the less fortunate Irish against both the presumed economic threat of freed blacks and nativists in the Republican party. Republican wartime attacks on both his origins and religion only stiffened his resolve to oppose the Republicans and all their works.

In contrast, Thomas Clagett had almost as much reason as any leading Democrat in Iowa during the war to become an angry Copperhead, but he did not. Both Clagett, a former Whig, and David Richardson, a former Buchanan Democrat, operated in a climate where, if the Democracy was relatively strong, it was less completely German or Irish Catholic in composition. Moreover, Keokuk and Davenport had long been centers of opposition to Dubuque's Democrats, who, because of their numbers, wielded an influence which often outweighed that of Democrats in the downriver cities.

For some a sharp change in circumstances or experiences could cause a man to adopt a quite different course from what people had come to expect of him. As noted earlier, Marcellus Crocker was known as a "radical Democrat" just before the war started. In the lexicon of the time in Iowa this meant that Crocker was a strict constructionist and fervent antiabolitionist. Yet Crocker, soon after, secured a military commission, switched parties, and by war's end was more of an advocate of civil rights for blacks than most Iowa radical Republicans. Frank Klement's description of Marcus Pomeroy's conversion from defender of the war to bitter Copperhead is another example. In Pomeroy's case three months spent as a correspondent in St. Louis and Arkansas where he saw firsthand the corruption of war profiteers, civilian and military, as well as the suffering of the common soldier, turned him around.[38]

Iowa's Copperhead Democrats were tied to a vision of the past which caused them to reject the inexorable changes taking place in American life. Thus, they became the cranky radical conservatives of the Civil War period. They did have something worth saying about the perils of increasingly centralized government and about the violation of civil liberties. And they said it. But too often they sounded as if they had nothing to offer except virulent criticism of those who wanted to preserve the Union and those who in the process wanted to deal a death blow to slavery. Their course robbed their party of much of the strength and the moral authority it might have needed in later years to keep the all-powerful Iowa Republicans honest. Fortunately for the state, the Republicans did not perform particularly discreditably, if not always wisely either, despite their secure position. Eventually the Iowa Democrats regained some of the influence they had lost. But the Civil War legacy they left was a hard one to disown in the latter half of the Nineteenth century. And it was well into the Twentieth century before many old stock Iowans could acknowledge that a really respectable person might also be a Democrat.

···❧❦[*Notes*]❦❧···

ABBREVIATIONS

AHR   — *American Historical Review*
AI   — *Annals of Iowa*
CM   — Charles Mason Diary
CWH   — *Civil War History*
DSF   — Disloyal Sentiment File (Adjutant General's Correspondence, "Disloyal Sentiment, 1861–1866," Civil War Miscellaneous, Adj. III, 155, IHD)
IHD   — Iowa State Historical Department, Division of Historical Museum and Archives, Des Moines
IHS   — State Historical Society, Iowa City
IJH   — *Iowa Journal of History*
IJHP — *Iowa Journal of History and Politics*
JAH   — *Journal of American History*
JQ   — *Journalism Quarterly*
MJM   — Mary Jo Mason Diary
MVHR — *Mississippi Valley Historical Review*
ORR   — *The War of the Rebellion: A Compilation of the Official Records of the Union and Confederate Armies* (Washington, 1880–1901)

INTRODUCTION

1. Frank L. Klement, *The Copperheads in the Middle West* (Chicago, 1960), p. 1; Richard O. Curry, "The Union As It Was: A Critique of Recent Interpretations of the 'Copperheads,' " *CWH* 13 (1967): 25, 32; Curry, "Copperheadism and Continuity: The Anatomy of a Stereotype," *Journal of Negro History* 47 (1972): 31. See also his "The Civil War and Reconstruction, 1861–1877: A Critical Overview of Recent Trends and Interpretations," *CWH* 20 (1974): 216–19; William Carleton, "Civil War Dissidence in the North: The Perspective of a Century," *South Atlantic Quarterly* 65 (1966): 392; Wood Gray, *The Hidden Civil War: The Story of the Copperheads* (New York, 1942), p. 222; Irving Katz, *August Belmont: A Political Biography* (New York, 1968), p. 127.
2. *Iowa State Register*, Mar. 18, May 20, 27, 1863; see also Robert Rutland, "The Copperheads of Iowa: A Re-examination," *IJH* 52 (1954): 5. The earliest use of the word Copperhead to designate Democrats in general which the author could find was in the Oct. 11, 1862, Mount Pleasant *Home Journal*. However, the term cropped up on one occasion before the 1860 election, this in the *Marion County Republican* (Knoxville) of Oct. 16. The writer charged that rocks "thrown by some cowardly rowdies, who were 'copper-heads' at heart" injured marchers in a Republican torchlight parade in Knoxville. See folder, "Marion County Copperheads," State Historical Society, Iowa City. Then in the fall of 1861, soldier Cyrus Boyd, en route east to Keokuk with a newly formed company, reported that the proprietor of the Amos House in Eddyville, where the company had quarters for a night, was known as a "violent old 'copper head.' " Mildred Throne, ed., with new Introduction by E. B. Long, *The Civil War Diary of Cyrus F. Boyd, Fifteenth Iowa Infantry, 1861–1863* (Millwood, N.Y., 1977), p. 9.

229

CHAPTER 1

1. See Morton M. Rosenberg, *Iowa on the Eve of the Civil War: a Decade of Frontier Politics* (Norman, Okla., 1972).

2. Charles A. Hawley, "Whittier and Iowa," *IJHP* 34 (1936): 142.

3. David Sparks, "Iowa Republicans and the Railroads, 1856-1860," *IJH* (1955): 276-79.

4. Paul W. Gates, *The Farmer's Age: Agriculture, 1815-1860* (New York, 1960), pp. 92-93; Rosenberg, *Iowa on the Eve of the Civil War*, pp. 31-33, 162-63.

5. Earl S. Beard, "The Background of State Railroad Regulation in Iowa," *IJH* 51 (1953): 8; Leonard Ralston, "Governor Ralph P. Lowe and State Aid to Railroads: Iowa Politics in 1859," *IJH* 58 (1960): 208-18.

6. Erling A. Erickson, *Banking in Frontier Iowa, 1836-1865* (Ames, Iowa, 1971), pp. 85-99.

7. Dan E. Clark, "The History of Liquor Legislation in Iowa, 1846-1861," *IJHP* 6 (1908): 69-87.

8. Sparks, "Birth of the Republican Party in Iowa, 1848-1860," p. 104; William Salter, *The Life of James W. Grimes* (New York, 1876), p. 69.

9. Rosenberg, *Iowa on the Eve of the Civil War*, pp. 183, 185-86, 194; Dubuque *Der National-Demokrat*, May 17, 1859.

10. See Davenport *Gazette*, Feb. 15, 1855, and Burlington *Hawk-eye and Telegraph*, June 18, 1856, on the alleged affinity of immigrants for alcohol. Before the war started the Burlington paper's name was reduced to *Hawk-eye*. For a typical defense of immigrants mixed with an attack on Republicans see Davenport *Democrat & News*, Oct. 11, 1859, hereafter the *Democrat* since that is what Iowans of the time called it.

11. Roland F. Matthias, "The Know Nothing Movement in Iowa," (Ph.D. diss., University of Chicago, 1965), pp. 27-28, 38, 145, 186, 197.

12. Nov. 7, 1859, Jan. 25, 1860.

13. Dec. 3, 1859.

14. In Hildegard Binder Johnson, "German Forty-Eighters in Davenport," *IJHP* 44 (1946): 46, reprinted from Davenport *Democrat and Leader*, Dec. 12, 1920.

15. The 1860 census listed 106,081 foreign born in the Iowa population of 674,913, *Eighth Census of the United States*, 1: 156.

16. Joel H. Silbey, "'Proslavery Sentiment in Iowa, 1838-1861, *IJH* 55 (1957): 298-303; Morton Rosenberg, "Iowa Politics and the Compromise of 1850," *IJH* 56 (1958): 201-2, 206; Roy V. Sherman, "Political Party Platforms in Iowa" (M.A. thesis, University of Iowa, 1926), pp. 116-18; David Sparks, "Decline of the Democratic Party, 1850-1860," *IJH* 53 (1955): 11.

17. Easton Morris, ed., *Reports of Cases Argued and Determined in the Supreme Court of Iowa* (Chicago, 1892), 1: 1-10.

18. Silbey, "Proslavery Sentiment in Iowa," p. 295; Leola N. Bergmann, *The Negro in Iowa* (Iowa City, 1969 [1949]), pp. 12-15; *Iowa State Register*, Jan. 21, 1863. The 1851 law did not expel blacks already living in Iowa, nor did its being on the books prevent a trickle of blacks from entering the state during the remaining years up to the 1863 ruling. By 1860 there were 1,069 free blacks in Iowa. *Eighth Census*, 1860, 1: 595.

19. Sparks, "Birth of the Republican Party in Iowa, 1848-1850," p. 45; U.S., Congress, Senate, *Congressional Globe*, 38th Cong., 1st sess., 1854, 4: 381; Bergmann, *The Negro in Iowa*, pp. 24-25; Hawley, "Whittier and Iowa," p. 116.

20. Silbey, "Proslavery Sentiment in Iowa," pp. 306-7; Sparks, "Birth of the Republican Party in Iowa, 1854-1856," *IJH* 54 (1956): 11-12. On Iowa reaction to the Kansas-Nebraska Act see also James Connor, "The Anti-Slavery Movement in Iowa," pt. 1, *AI* 60 (1970): 371.

21. John A. G. Hull, comp., *Iowa Historical and Comparative Census, 1830-1880* (Des Moines, 1883), pp. 196-99.

22. *CM*, IHD, Feb. 12, 1856.

23. Erik M. Erickson, "William Penn Clarke," *IJHP* 25 (1927): 42; Charles E. Payne, *Josiah Bushnell Grinnell* (Iowa City, 1938), pp. 101-3; Salter, *James Grimes*, pp. 84-86.

24. George Frazee, "The Iowa Fugitive Slave Case," *AI* 4 (1899): 118-37. A few years earlier, in 1850, a federal district judge in Burlington levied a $2,900 fine against a group of Salem, Iowa, abolitionists whom a jury convicted of aiding fugitives to escape a Missouri owner. The judge tried the case under the federal fugitive slave law of 1793. Frazee, "An Iowa Fugitive Slave Case—1850," *AI* 6 (1903): 9-45.

25. "Contemporary Editorial Opinion of the Constitution," *IJH* 60 (1957): 117, 119.

26. Irving B. Richman, "Congregational Life in Muscatine, 1843-1893," *IJHP* 21 (1923): 356,

366. This setback did not deter minister Alden B. Robbins, who ranked *Uncle Tom's Cabin* alongside the *Iliad* and *Pilgrim's Progress* as the greatest of the classics, from steadfastly pursuing the goal of black equality throughout his long pastorate in the river city.

27. Carl H. Erbe, "Constitutional Provisions for the Suffrage in Iowa," *IJHP* 20 (1924): 206.

28. Cited in Eugene H. Berwanger, *The Frontier against Slavery* (Urbana, Ill., 1967), p. 42.

29. Bergmann, *Negro in Iowa*, pp. 19–20. In 1851, black property owners had been exempted from payment of school taxes.

30. Sherman, "Political Party Platforms in Iowa," pp. 146–49, 155–58; Herbert S. Fairall, ed., *Manual of Iowa Politics* (Iowa City, 1881), pp. 31–36.

31. Mildred Throne, *Cyrus Clay Carpenter and Iowa Politics, 1854–1898* (Iowa City, 1974), pp. 36–39. Dubuque's other Democratic organ, the *Daily Express and Herald*, was bitterly anti-Jones, anti-Buchanan, and anti-Lecompton. Editor J. B. Dorr eventually became a leading War Democrat. See Dorr's attack on Jones in the paper of May 2, 1858.

32. Dubuque *Daily Express and Herald* in Dubuque *Weekly Times*, Feb. 24, 1858.

33. Burlington *Daily Iowa State Gazette*, June 30, 1858, in Louis Pelzer, "The History of Political Parties in Iowa from 1857 to 1860," *IJHP* 7 (1909): 199.

34. Dodge to Jones, Sept. 30, 1858, George W. Jones Papers, IHD.

35. Iowa Election Records (Iowa City, Univ. Microfilms); Rosenberg, "Election of 1859," p. 21.

36. Benjamin F. Shambaugh, ed., *The Messages and Proclamations of the Governors of Iowa*, 3 vols. (Iowa City, 1903) 2: 247–51, 380–402; Thomas Teakle, "The Rendition of Barclay Coppoc," *IJHP* 10 (1912): 519–42; Dan E. Clark, *Samuel Jordan Kirkwood* (Iowa City, 1917), pp. 148–52, 155–62.

37. *Eighth Census, 1860*, 1: 156–57; Hull, *Historical and Comparative Census*, pp. 64–67, 76, 179–81, 189.

38. *Fifth Annual Report of the Iowa State Agricultural Society to the Governor for the Year 1858* (Des Moines, 1859), p. 11.

39. *Agricultural Report, 1857*, p. 2.

40. Diary of Solon M. Langworthy, May 1859, Langworthy Collection, IHS.

41. *Agricultural Report, 1859*, p. 6.

42. Burlington *Hawk-eye*, Feb. 18, 1860.

43. *Agricultural Report, 1860*, pp. 5–6.

44. Davenport *Democrat*, Apr. 5, 1861.

45. Dubuque *Herald*, Feb. 21, 1861; Erickson, *Banking in Frontier Iowa*, pp. 99–100, 104, 110–11.

46. Franklin T. Oldt and P. J. Quigley, *History of Dubuque County, Iowa* (Chicago, n.d.), p. 411; *Times*, Jan. 9, 1861; Mildred Throne, ed., "Document: Iowa Farm Letters, 1856–1865," *IJH* 58 (1960): 80.

47. John A. Hopkins, "Economic History of the Production of Beef Cattle in Iowa," *IJHP* 26 (1928): 443; Burlington *Hawk-eye*, Mar. 15, 1860.

48. Dubuque *Herald*, Nov. 24, 1860, Jan. 22, 30, 1861.

49. Ibid., Mar. 15, 19, 21, Apr. 4, 1861; also Dec. 9, 1860.

50. Davenport *Democrat*, Oct. 29, 1859.

51. Ibid., Nov. 15, 1860.

52. Ibid., Feb. 22, Mar. 1, 6, 18, 20, 22, Apr. 2, 1861; Burlington *Hawk-eye*, Mar. 2, 1861.

53. Ibid., Jan. 16, 19, Feb. 27, June 11–12, Aug. 15, 1860.

54. Ibid., Jan. 19, 1860.

55. Ibid., Nov. 5, 1860; Feb. 1, 8, 1861.

56. Gray, *The Hidden Civil War: The Story of Copperheads* (New York, 1942), pp. 20–21; Klement, *The Copperheads in the Middle West* (Chicago, 1960), pp. 3, 11; Gates, *The Farmers' Age: Agriculture, 1815–1860* (New York, 1960), pp. 174–78, 221; *Agriculture and the Civil War* (New York, 1965), pp. 4–5, 9.

57. U.S., Department of the Treasury, *Commerce of the Mississippi and Ohio: Report of the Internal Commerce of the United States*, pt. 2, *Commerce and Navigation* (Washington, D.C., 1888), pp. 210–15, 227.

58. Albert Fishlow, *American Railroads and the Transformation of the Ante-Bellum Economy* (Cambridge, Mass., 1965), p. 296.

59. *Eighth Census, Agriculture*, pp. clvi–clviii.

60. "Antebellum Interregional Trade Reconsidered," *American Economic Review: Papers and Proceedings*, 14 (1964): 356.

61. *Eighth Census, Agriculture*, p. clviii.

62. Dubuque *Herald,* Aug. 24, Sept. 5, 1860.
63. Davenport *Democrat,* Oct. 3, 1860; Burlington *Hawk-eye,* Oct. 24, 1860. Though much less significant in volume, the western slope of Iowa was also exporting its products outside of the state. Woodbury county (Sioux City) sent corn to St. Louis in 1859. In the spring of 1860 the Council Bluffs *Nonpareil* reported other changes in a year's time. Instead of importing flour and potatoes from Missouri, the western counties now exported both to points between Council Bluffs and Kansas City. In 1860, for the first time they sold thousands of pounds of bacon to Pike's Peak emigrants. There always had been some sale of cattle to these travelers by Iowa farmers who lived on the routes to the West. *Agricultural Report, 1859,* p. 414; Council Bluffs *Nonpareil,* Apr. 28, 1860; Hopkins, "Economic History of the Production of Beef Cattle in Iowa," p. 442.
64. "Antebellum Trade," p. 352; *American Railroads,* p. 283.
65. Ibid., pp. 276-77, 282-85, 297. See table 39, p. 284.
66. Davenport *Democrat,* Mar. 25, 1861; *Hawk-eye* in Dubuque *Herald,* Mar. 31, 1861.
67. Burlington *Hawk-eye,* Jan. 22, Feb. 8, 1861; Dubuque *Herald,* Feb. 20, Mar. 23, 28, 1861; White to Mason, Nov. 21, Dec. 11, 1861, Mason Papers, IHD.

CHAPTER 2

1. Parrish to Summers, June 8, 1860, Laurel Summers Papers, IHD.
2. Henn to Dodge, Mar. [?], 1860, forwarded in letter, Dodge to Summers, Mar. 30, 1860, Summers Papers. Nearly all of vol. 1 of the Summers Papers is composed of letters from office seekers and their friends.
3. Jan. 23, 1860, in Kenneth Milsap, "The Election of 1860 in Iowa," *IJH* 48 (1950): 112.
4. Davenport *Democrat,* Mar. 3, 1860.
5. Ibid., June 25-26, 1860; *Iowa State Register,* Aug. 22, 1860; Charles City *Intelligencer,* Aug. 23, 1860. Among the prominent Breckinridge people were W. R. English of Glenwood; P. M. Casady, Des Moines; Ancil Humphrey, Muscatine; Nathan G. Sales, Anamosa; H. H. Heath and Peter Quigley, Dubuque; John Duncombe, Fort Dodge; G. C. R. Mitchell and George H. Parker, Davenport.
6. Ibid., Sept. 3, 1860. John H. Wallace, head of the state agricultural society, was one of the organizers.
7. Davenport *Gazette,* Dec. 29, 1859, *Iowa State Register,* Mar. 30, 1860, in Mildred Throne ed., "Iowa Newspapers Report the 1860 Nomination of Abraham Lincoln," *IJH* 58 (1960): 231, 236, 251-52.
8. Davenport *Democrat,* May 19, 1860. Editor Richardson simply took up where his predecessor Thomas Maguire left off. Shortly before leaving Davenport for good, Maguire complained about Republican "truckling" to the Germans who, he said, had voted Democratic five years earlier. See Jan. 25, 1860.
9. *Die Wochentliche Iowa Post* (Des Moines), Mar. 24, May 26, June 23, 1860.
10. Charles A. Thodt, "Stephen A. Douglas Speaks at Iowa City, 1860," *IJH* 53 (1955), 165.
11. Scholte letters in Burlington *Hawk-eye,* Sept. 19, 26, 1860. Scholte, a Whig-turned-Democrat-turned-Republican could not carry his fellow Hollanders with him on his last switch. They remained Democratic. See Robert P. Swierenga, "The Ethnic Voter and the First Lincoln Election," *CWH* 11 (1965): 27-43, reprinted in Frederick C. Luebke, ed., *Ethnic Voters and the Election of Lincoln* (Lincoln, Nebr., 1971), pp. 129-50.
12. Sept. 1, Nov. 3, 1860; *Bugle,* Sept. 19, Oct. 3, Nov. 7, 1860.
13. Burlington *Hawk-eye,* Aug. 9, 22, 1860; Fairfield *Ledger,* Aug. 10, 24, 1860. The *Hawk-eye* declared that there was evidence that Dean sounded the same proslavery theme at Albia among other places.
14. Council Bluffs *Bugle* in Burlington *Hawk-eye,* Mar. 21, 1860; Osceola *Courier* in *Hawk-eye,* Aug. 2, 1860; Davenport *Democrat,* Feb. 23, 1860.
15. Oct. 25, Nov. 1, 1860.
16. May 12, June 9, Sept. 15, 1860.
17. *Hawk-eye,* Nov. 9, 1860. W. W. White agreed that Burlington Germans voted Republican, being led astray, he said, by Republican promises. White to Mason, Dec. 11, 1860, Mason Papers, IHD; Hawkins Taylor to Kirkwood, Nov. 19, 1860, Samuel J. Kirkwood Correspondence, IHD.
18. Iowa Election Records, 1860 (Iowa City, Univ. Microfilms).
19. Jones to J. S. Black, Attorney General of the United States, Aug. 18, 1860, in Leland L. Sage, *William Boyd Allison: A Study in Practical Politics* (Iowa City, 1956), pp. 39, 342, n. 8.

20. *CM,* Nov. 8, 1860.
21. Davenport *Democrat,* May 10, 1860.
22. May 6, July 3–4, 6, 8, 1860.
23. *Democratic Clarion,* Nov. 14, 1860; *City Advocate,* Nov. 10, 1860, in Milsap, "Election of 1860," p. 120.
24. Nov. 11, 14, 21, 1860.
25. Nov. 13, 1860, in Howard C. Perkins, ed., *Northern Editorials on Secession* (Gloucester, Mass., 1964), 2: 1035–36.
26. Dec. 7, 1860.
27. T. O. Bishop to Summers, Jan. [?], 1861, Summers Papers.
28. Lindley to Summers, Dec. 1, 1860, ibid.
29. Dubuque *Herald,* Jan. 12, 1861.
30. Lowe to Mason, Jan. 21, 1860; Rorer to Mason, Feb. 16, 1861, Mason Papers.
31. Love to C. C. Cole, letter in Davenport *Democrat,* Feb. 7, 1861.
32. Tichenor to Summers, Feb. 26, 1861, Summers Papers; Belknap to Mason, Mar. 11, 1861, Mason Papers.
33. "C" to Burlington *Hawk-eye,* Nov. 21, 1860.
34. Dec. 10, 1860.
35. Dec. 12, 1860.
36. Dec. 19, 1860.
37. Burlington *Hawk-eye,* Dec. 27, 1860.
38. *Gate City* (w), Nov. 16, 1860, Jan. 3, 1861.
39. Langworthy Diary, Dec. 16, 1860, Langworthy Collection, IHS.
40. *CM,* Dec. 4, 1860.
41. *Register,* Dec. 1, 1860; *Democrat,* Jan. 14, 1861; Charles Mason "X" letters in Dubuque *Herald,* Dec. 5, 12, 1860. Mason's letters under this signature appeared frequently in the *Herald* from this point through the end of the war. Mahony's views are in the *Herald,* Dec. 9, 15, 1860, Jan. 4, Apr. 10, 1861.
42. James Grimes in Burlington *Hawk-eye,* Feb. 1, 1861.
43. Dan E. Clark, *Samuel Jordan Kirkwood* (Iowa City, 1917), p. 175; *Iowa State Register* (w), Dec. 12, 1860.
44. Jan. 24, 1861. *Hawk-eye* editorials could be confusing on the subjects of resisting secession and on compromising with rebels. On January 3, the paper suggested that rather than concede anything to the rebels, they should be allowed to depart since conceding anything would violate the principle that the majority ruled at the ballot box. Then on February 6, the paper said that it was "not unwilling that they [secessionists] should prove the beauties of secession by experiment." This would not solve their problems since the rest of the civilized world abhorred slavery also. Having learned this, they would rediscover the virtues of Union, at which time "we shall be willing to extend to them . . . all the guarantees which the Constitution contemplates." And despite earlier avowals to make no compromises with the South, the February 19 editorial spoke of no compromise with traitors *until* treason was put down. Nevertheless, the general position of the paper throughout the pre-Sumter period was that there should be no compromise on the principles of republican government and no acceptance of secession. Part of the disparity between editorial positions may stem from the fact that others besides Editor Clark Dunham wrote *Hawk-eye* editorials during the war years, "with his approval or suggestion." George Frazee, "Clark Dunham," *AI* 4 (1899): 217.
45. Nov. 28, 1860.
46. Dec. 5, 1860, Jan. 9, 1861.
47. Nov. 17, 1860.
48. Dubuque *Herald,* Nov. 11, 1860. See also Mahony's editorial in the *Herald,* Apr. 10, 1861, which restates and elaborates his arguments; Mason's similar views are found in his diary of Nov. 8, 18, Dec. 4, 1860, and in his "X" letter to the Dubuque *Herald,* Feb. 22, 1861.
49. *Herald,* Nov. 27–29, Dec. 2, 15, 1860.
50. *CM:* Nov. 8, 1860; Nov. 18; Dec. 4, 1860. "X" letter in Dubuque *Herald,* Feb. 22, 1861.
51. Mason "X" letter, Dubuque *Herald,* Nov. 14, 1860; *CM,* Dec. 4, 1860; Wilson to Mason, Dec. 21, 1860, Mason Papers.
52. White to Mason, Nov. 21, Dec. 11, 1860, Mason Papers. Mason showed White's letter to Southern friends in Washington. They said, he reported, ". . . that if they were sure that there were 100 men in the north who felt in that way they would have hope. I tell them there are one hundred thousand." *CM,* Nov. 25, 1860.
53. Mar. 16, 1861.

54. Council Bluffs *Bugle,* Dec. 19, 1860, Mar. 6, 1861. Even a *Hawk-eye* writer pondered briefly about a feasible separation. The Potomac would divide North and South. Maryland and Delaware would go with the North by the simple expedient of the federal government's buying all slaves in those states. This, the writer was careful to add, was mere speculation "without an idea that the occasion will occur to put them into practice." Jan. 22, 1861.

55. Apr. 10, 1861.

56. Burlington *Hawk-eye,* Jan. 19, 22, 24, Mar. 30, 1861.

57. Davenport *Democrat,* Jan. 10, 1861, Apr. 11, 1861.

58. Dubuque *Herald,* Jan. 19, Feb. 1, 28, Mar. 16, 1861.

59. *CM,* Nov. 18, Dec. 17, 1860; Dubuque *Herald,* "X" letters, Mar. 13, Apr. 13, 1861.

60. Dubuque *Herald,* Apr. 9, 1861.

61. Burlington *Hawk-eye,* Apr. 17, 1861.

62. Dec. 12, 1860.

63. Jan. 12, 1861.

64. *Iowa State Register* (w), Jan. 23, 1861; Burlington *Hawk-eye,* Feb. 6, 13, 1861.

65. Dubuque *Herald,* Jan. 15, 1861.

66. Ibid., Dec. 14, 1860.

67. Richard B. Latner and Peter Levine, "Perspectives on Antebellum Pietistic Politics," *Reviews in American History* 4 (1976): 23.

CHAPTER 3

1. Marcellus M. Crocker Papers, IHD: Henn to Crocker, Jan. 15, 1861; copies of Henn to Paschal Bequitte, to William Given, to John B. Miller, all of San Francisco, to James W. Denver, Weaverville, and to Joseph Lane, Oregon, Jan. 15, 1861. A. A. Stuart, *Iowa Colonels and Regiments: Being a History of Iowa Regiments in the War of the Rebellion; and Containing a Description of the Battles in Which They Have Fought* (Des Moines, 1865), pp. 255–64; Burlington *Hawk-eye,* July 26, 1861; Charles Negus to Charles Mason, Oct. 28, 1861, Charles Mason Papers, IHD.

2. Kirkwood to Cameron, Apr. 18, 1861, *ORR,* Ser. 3, vol. 1, p. 87.

3. Apr. 20, 1861.

4. White to Mason, May 10, 1861, Mason Papers.

5. Johnson Brigham, *Des Moines Together with the History of Polk County* (Chicago, 1911), 1: 185; Davenport *Democrat,* Oct. 29, 1861.

6. Junkin in his Fairfield *Ledger* took special note of these often irreconcilable Democratic positions and commented wonderingly upon them. *Ledger,* July 6, 18, Aug. 1, Sept. 5, 1861; Ottumwa *Democratic Union,* May 9, 1861; *Des Moines News* (Keosauqua), June 29, 1861; Dubuque *Herald,* July 13, 1861; Council Bluffs *Nonpareil,* July 20, 1861; Burlington *Hawk-eye,* July 26, 1861; *History of Fremont County* (Des Moines, 1881), p. 477; Charles J. Fulton ed., *History of Jefferson County* (Chicago, 1914), 1: 347–49.

7. *Der National-Demokrat,* Apr. 18, 1861; *Des Moines News,* Apr. 20, 1861; *City Advocate,* May 7, 1861; *Democrat,* May 14, 1861; *North Iowa Times,* May 29, 1861; *South-Western Iowan* in Council Bluffs *Nonpareil,* Aug. 17, 1861; *South-Tier Democrat,* Apr. 17, June 5, 26, 1861.

8. The change came in Iowa City when Richard Sylvester replaced John Van Hosen. See Apr. 17, 24, May 4, 21, June 12, 26, Sept. 11, 1861.

9. Davenport *Democrat,* Apr. 15, 17–18, 20, 23, 27, 29, May 4, 9, 13, June 21, Sept. 7, 1861. Richardson was among the few to recognize that any armed conflict would last for years, although, paradoxically, he could quickly turn around to insist on fast action to end it once and for all. The "spread-eagle patriot" label is not too strong for Richardson. See Apr. 18 issue.

10. Council Bluffs *Bugle,* Apr. 17, May 8, June 5, July 3, 1861.

11. Dubuque *Herald,* Apr. 13–14, 22, 26–27, May 3, 7, June 13, July 3, 21, Aug. 3, 1861.

12. Dubuque *Times,* Apr. 30, 1861.

13. *CM,* Apr. 23, 29, May 2, 1861; Fairfield *Ledger,* July 25, 1861.

14. Benjamin F. Shambaugh, ed., *The Messages and Proclamations of the Governors of Iowa,* 7 vols. (Iowa City, 1903), 2: 263.

15. Iowa, General Assembly, House, *Journal,* extra sess., 1861, pp. 3–7, 14–15.

16. Iowa, General Assembly, Senate, *Journal,* extra sess., 1861, p. 18; *House Journal,* extra sess., 1861, p. 15.

17. Senate votes approving three militia bills were 35 to 4, 31 to 4, and 33 to 5. See ibid. (Senate), pp. 38, 54–55, 85. House votes approving the three militia bills respectively were 72 to 0, 81 to 0, and 75 to 1. See ibid. (House), pp. 43–44, 70, 136.

18. *Senate Journal,* extra sess., 1861, pp. 25–26, 68; *House Journal,* extra sess., 1861, pp. 41, 93–94.
19. *Senate Journal,* extra sess., 1861, pp. 25–26, 35–37.
20. *House Journal,* extra sess., 1861, p. 118.
21. Ibid., p. 135; *Senate Journal,* extra sess., 1861, pp. 111–12.
22. *Senate Journal,* extra sess., 1861, pp. 38–40.
23. In Council Bluffs *Nonpareil,* June 8, 1861.
24. *Iowa State Register* in *Hamilton Freeman* (Webster City), July 13, 1861; Benjamin F. Gue, *History of Iowa from the Earliest Times to the Beginning of the Twentieth Century,* 4 vols. (New York, 1903), 2:61.
25. Ivan L. Pollock, "State Finances in Iowa During the Civil War," *IJHP* 16 (1918): 65.
26. Ibid., pp. 83–85; *Iowa State Register* (w), July 17, 31, 1861; Dubuque *Herald,* July 17, 1861; Gue, *History of Iowa,* 2:62.
27. Kirkwood to John Barnette, Sept. 1, 1861, Governor's Department Military Correspondence (Kirkwood), IHD; Earle D. Ross, "Northern Sectionalism in the Civil War Era," *IJHP* 30 (1932): 458.
28. *Report of the Iowa State Agricultural Society, 1861–1862,* pp. 3, 7.
29. Dubuque *Times,* May 14, 1861; Dubuque *Herald,* Apr. 24, June 21, 1861.
30. On the other hand, Dennis Mahony's editorial for the day, "Universal Bankruptcy," was gloomy. Mahony predicted disaster for businessmen and realtors as a result of relief laws likely to be passed by various legislatures if not by Congress. Iowa passed one soon after. May 12, 1861.
31. Keokuk *Gate City,* May 4, 11, 1861; Faye E. Harris, "A Frontier Community: The Economic, Social and Political Development of Keokuk, Iowa from 1820 to 1866" (Ph.D. diss., Univ. of Iowa, 1965), pp. 360–62.
32. Dubuque *Herald,* May 16, 1861; *Democrat,* May 18, June 24, 1861. The *Herald* claimed that the blockade was designed to benefit the metropolitan East perhaps as much as to harm the South.
33. Burlington *Hawk-eye,* June 13, 1861; Dubuque *Herald,* Apr. 28, 1861; Davenport *Democrat,* Nov. 14, Dec. 3, 1861.
34. Apr. 6, 1861.
36. *Fayette County Pioneer* (West Union), May 13, 1861; Gharkey also urged farmers to keep their tools in good repair: "The more one stoops to whet a scythe, the more time lost and the less grain cut." July 31, 1861.
37. *Iowa State Register* (w), May 15, 1861; *Times,* May 3, 1861; see also Sioux City *Register,* June 8, 1861, Waterloo *Courier,* July 31, 1861.
38. June 24, July 8, 15–17, 20, 31, 1861.
39. *Weekly Democratic Union* (Ottumwa), June 6, 1861; *History of Harrison County* (Chicago, 1891), pp. 101–2.
40. *Hamilton Freeman* (Webster City), June 22, 1861; Waterloo *Courier,* Apr. 20, 1861.
41. Fulton, *History of Jefferson County,* 1:339; Keokuk *Gate City,* May 18, 1861; Davenport *Democrat,* Apr. 24, May 24–25, June 5, July 12, 1861.
42. Dubuque *Times,* May 6–7, 1861; Franklin T. Oldt and P. J. Quigley, eds., *History of Dubuque County, Iowa,* p. 138; Dubuque *Herald,* Apr. 28, May 22–23, Nov. 16, 1861.
43. *Hawk-eye,* Dec. 9, 1861; *Democrat,* Dec. 14, 24–25, 1861.
44. Ibid., Dec. 2, 1861.
45. Limmer to Langworthy, Nov. 19, 1861, Langworthy Collection, IHS.
46. Davenport *Democrat,* Sept. 4, 1861.
47. Ben F. Samuels to Mason, Aug. 2, 1861, Mason Papers; Council Bluffs *Bugle,* Sept. 18, Oct. 30, 1861.
48. Davenport *Democrat,* Oct. 15, 1861.
49. *Times,* Jan. 4, 1861; *Herald,* Apr. 23, Dec. 6, 1861; *Hawk-eye,* Apr. 15, 1861.
50. Dubuque *Times,* Apr. 26, May 10, 1861; Dubuque *Herald,* May 11, 1861; Davenport *Democrat,* July 15, 1861; Eliphalet Price to Kirkwood, Aug. 8, 1861, Samuel J. Kirkwood Correspondence IHD; Burlington *Hawk-eye,* Dec. 4, 1861.
51. *Gazette,* Nov. 4, 7, 1861; Davenport *Democrat,* Nov. 6, 1861; Dubuque *Herald,* Nov. 14, 1861; Sioux City *Register,* Nov. 23, 1861.
52. Dubuque *Times,* June 25, 1861; Mildred Throne, "Document: Iowa Farm Letters, 1856–1865," *IJH* 58 (1960): 83.
53. May 29, 1861.
54. Cyrus Bussey, "Cyrus Bussey's Boyhood: An Autobiographical Sketch," *IJHP* 30 (1932): 531.
55. Littleton to W. W. Junkin, Fairfield *Ledger,* Apr. 22, 1861.

56. *Hawk-eye,* Apr. 23-24, 1861.

57. Fairfield *Ledger,* Apr. 25, May 2, 1861; Fulton, *History of Jefferson County,* 1: 340.

58. June 13, 1861.

59. *Herald,* Apr. 24, 26, 28, May 3, July 12, 1861.

60. July 16, 1861.

61. *Der Demokrat,* May 7, 1861; *Democrat,* Apr. 30, May 6, 8, 1861.

62. Aug. 22-23, 1861.

63. Burlington *Hawk-eye,* Sept. 12, 1861; Dubuque *Herald,* Sept. 18, 1861. Years later, however, Mason's daughter, Molly Mason Remey, used the term "southern sympathizers" to describe the family's political position during the Civil War. Charles Mason Remey, ed., *Reminiscences of a Long Life and Letters of Mary Josephine Remey, Wife of Rear Admiral George Collier Remey, Daughter of Chief Justice Charles Mason, 1845-1938,* 12 typescript vols. (Washington, 1939), 10: 155.

64. May 2, 1861.

65. Dubuque *Herald,* Sept. 3, 1861.

66. Clarence R. Aurner, "Historical Survey of Civic Instruction and Training for Citizenship in Iowa," *IJHP* 17 (1919): 148-49.

67. Dubuqe *Herald,* Sept. 17, 21, 1861; Oldt and Quigley, *History of Dubuque County,* pp. 270-71.

68. Allison to Baker, Sept. 17, 1861, DSF.

69. Flint to Kirkwood, Aug. 4, 1862, ibid.

70. Kirkwood to FitzHenry Warren, Aug. 5, 1861, Kirkwood Military Correspondence.

71. *Times,* Apr. 16, 18, May 10, 1861; *Herald,* Apr. 17, 1861.

72. *Times,* July 12, 1861; *Herald,* July 13, Sept. 13, 1861.

73. Dubuque *Herald,* July 18, 1861, Dec. 11, 1861; Mahony to Mason, July 18, 1861, Feb. 27, 1862, Mason Papers; Oldt and Quigley, *History of Dubuque County,* p. 269. For an especially virulent *Times* attack on Mahony see the issue of June 28, 1861, *Buchanan County Guardian* (Independence), June 11, 1861; for calls to boycott the *Herald* see the *Guardian,* cited in the Burlington *Hawk-eye,* July 23, 1861, *Hawk-eye,* Aug. 21, 1861.

74. Duncombe to Mason, Sept. 17, 1861, Mason Papers.

75. June 23, 1861.

76. Gue, *History of Iowa,* 2: 52-54; Dan E. Clark, *Samuel Jordan Kirkwood* (Iowa City, 1917), pp. 181-94. Shambaugh, *Messages and Proclamations,* 2: 252-63.

77. Dubuque *Herald,* Apr. 27, 30, 1861; Oldt and Quigley, *History of Dubuque County,* p. 263.

78. J. W. Lee, *History of Hamilton County* (Chicago, 1912), 1: 112; *History of Audubon County* (Indianapolis, n.d.), pp. 166-67.

79. Hutchins to Mason, July 25, 1861, Mason Papers.

80. June 24, 1861.

81. Burlington *Hawk-eye,* June 29, 1861.

82. Davenport *Democrat,* Aug. 3, 1861; Kirkwood to Capt. A. H. Chapman, Company C., Second Iowa Infantry, Sept. 1, 1861, Kirkwood Military Correspondence; Throne, "Iowa Farm Letters," p. 82.

83. Burlington *Hawk-eye,* Apr. 27, 1861, reporting on Brighton; Council Bluffs *Bugle,* Dec. 11, 1861, reporting on Wapello. *Bugle* editor Lysander Babbitt suggested that Wapello's women patriots might demonstrate real love for the cause by going to war as nurses.

84. Dubuque *Herald,* Sept. 14, 17, 1861.

85. Summers Papers.

86. *CM,* June 18, July 17, Aug. 5, Dec. 10, 13, 1861; Mason to George Yewell, Nov. 4, 1861, in Yewell, "Reminiscences of Charles Mason," *AI* 5 (1901): 174.

87. J. H. Harvey and others to Kirkwood, Jan. 8, 1861, DSF; *History of Fremont County* (Des Moines, 1881), pp. 482-83.

88. Kirkwood Military Correspondence: John E. McDowell, J. W. McKinly, and W. R. Laughlin to Kirkwood, May 6, 1861.

89. W. M. Stone, June 22, and James Matthews, June 24, 1861, to Kirkwood, DSF; J. Place to Kirkwood, June (16 or 26?), 1861, Kirkwood Military Correspondence.

90. Pope to Kirkwood, July 23, 1861, *ORR,* ser. 1, vol. 3, pp. 405-6.

91. Lt. Col. John Edwards to Kirkwood, ibid., pp. 413-14; *History of Taylor County* (Des Moines, 1881), pp. 537-38; *History of Lucas County* (Des Moines, 1881), p. 544; Theodore M. Stuart, *Past and Present of Lucas and Wayne Counties* (Chicago, 1913), pp. 105-7. Stuart wrote a droll account of marching about in confusion from one town to another in the Leon (Decatur county) area in a

vain search for rebel invaders which none of the locals had seen or heard of. Companies, commanders and orders multiplied. The troops began to grumble. Finally commander "Honest John Edwards" took charge and marched everybody off to Pleasant Plains to practice the "art of war."

92. Mount Pleasant *Home Journal*, Aug. 10, 1861; Ben F. Dixon, "Battle on the Border: Athens, Missouri, Aug. 5, 1861," *AI* 36 (1961): 1-15; Cyrus Bussey, "The Battle of Athens, Missouri," ibid., 2 (1901): 81-92.

93. Jones to Summers, May 17, 1861, Summers Papers; Corydon *South-Tier Democrat*, June 5, 1861.

94. Lyons *City Advocate*, Jan. 18, 1861; *South-Tier Democrat*, Jan. 22, 1861.

95. Dubuque *Herald*, June 8, 1861.

96. Ibid., June 29, 1861.

97. For negative reaction to Mahony's action see editorials and/or news stories in the Davenport *Democrat*, June 25, 1861; Dubuque *Herald*, June 14, 21, 1861; Dubuque *Times*, June 21, 1861; Sioux City *Register*, June 15, 1861; *South-Tier Democrat*, June 19, 1861; Clinton *Herald*, July 6, 1861; Lyons *City Advocate*, July 13, 1861. The Bloomfield *Democratic-Clarion*, July 10, 1861, printed Sample's action and accusations against Mahony. For one attack on Sample see the Iowa City *State Democratic Press*, July 10, 1861. The Altman-Mahony exchange is in the *Herald*, Sept. 7, 1861.

98. *Iowa State Register* (w), July 31, 1861.

99. Iowa city and county names can be confusing. Des Moines, the state capital, is in Polk county. Burlington is in Des Moines county. The *Des Moines News* was a Democratic paper published in Keosauqua, a small town on the Des Moines river in Van Buren county. Keokuk is in Lee county, not Keokuk county. Wapello is in Louisa county, not in Wapello county (Ottumwa is the metropolis of Wapello county). Fortunately Dubuque, Clinton, and Muscatine are in Dubuque, Clinton, and Muscatine counties respectively.

100. *Iowa State Register* (w), July 31, 1861; Sioux City *Register*, Aug. 2, 1861.

101. Mahony to Mason, Aug. 1, 1861, Mason Papers.

102. *State Democratic Press*, Aug. 14, 1861; Davenport *Democrat*, Aug. 6-7, 1861.

103. *Iowa State Register* (w), July 31, 1861.

104. Ibid., Sept. 4, 1861.

105. *State Democratic Press*, Sept. 4, 1861.

106. James F. Wilson to Kirkwood, Sept. 6, 1861, and D. C. Bloomer to Kirkwood, Sept. 10, 1861, Kirkwood Correspondence; Charles Negus to Mason, Aug. 5, 1861; Summers to Mason, Sept. 8, 1861, Mason Papers.

107. Mahony to Mason, Aug. 1, 1861, Mason Papers; in Dubuque *Herald*, Sept. 4, 1861.

108. *CM*, July 31, Aug. 5-8, 1861; Dubuque *Herald*, Aug. 11, 1861.

109. Ibid.

110. *CM*, Sept. 20, 1861; Mason to G. M. Todd Sept. 20, 1861, in Albia *Jeffersonian Blade*, Sept. 23, 1861. For evidence of the pressure on Mason see Burlington *Hawk-eye*, Sept. 3, 1861; Mason Papers: G. M. Todd to Mason; Phineas Casady to Mason, Sept. 15, 1861; Frederick M. Irish to Mason; Ben Samuels and Dennis Mahony to Mason, Sept. 19, 1861.

111. Baker to Isaac M. Preston, Sept. 4, 1861, Clinton *Herald*, Sept. 14, 1861; *Jeffersonian Blade*, Sept. 24, 1861.

112. *Iowa State Register* (w), Oct. 2, 1861.

113. Ibid.; *State Democratic Press*, Sept. 27, Oct. 2, 1861.

114. Mason Papers, letters to Mason, Sept. 23-Oct. 3, 1861; *CM*, Sept. 21-22, 1861.

115. Election Records, 1861; Burlington *Hawk-eye*, Sept. 21, 1861.

116. *State Democratic Press*, Sept. 25, 1861; Clark, *Samuel Kirkwood*, p. 203; Merritt to Harvey Dunlavey, Sept. 9, 1861, declining Democratic nomination for lieutenant governor, *Jeffersonian Blade*, Sept. 24, 1861; Kirkwood to Merritt, Nov. 11, 1861, Kirkwood Military Correspondence; Merritt to Kirkwood, Nov. 14-15, 1861, Governor's Letterbook Military Record (Samuel J. Kirkwood), IHD.

CHAPTER   4

1. Ora Williams, "Herbert Melville ('Hub') Hoxie," *AI* 32 (1954): 321-30; L. F. Anderson, "Pioneer Becomes Railway Magnate," *AI* 32 (1954): 331-36; Stanley P. Hirshon, *Grenville M. Dodge: Soldier, Politician, Railroad Pioneer* (Bloomington, Ind., 1967), p. 34.

2. Crocker to Dodge, June 24, 1864, G. M. Dodge Papers, IHD.

3. Sells to Kirkwood, Mar. 22, 1861, Kirkwood Correspondence, IHD.

4. Hoxie to Dodge, Apr. 20, 1861, in Leland L. Sage, *William Boyd Allison: A Study in Practical Politics* (Iowa City, 1956), p. 47; Hoxie to Dodge, Feb. 24, 1865, Dodge Papers.

5. Seward to Hoxie, Oct. 21, 1861; ORR, ser. 2, vol. 2, pp. 113-14.

6. Dubuque *Herald,* Oct. 24, 1861; James Connor, "The Antislavery Movement in Iowa," *AI* 40 (1970): 474.

7. Dodge to G. M. Dodge, Dec. 12, 1861, Dodge Papers.

8. All documents concerning the Hill affair are in *ORR,* ser. 2, vol. 2, pp. 1321-34; Henry Halleck to Herbert Hoxie, Mar. 15, 1862, ibid, p. 1334. Gurley's decision not to prosecute is found in his letter of Dec. 27, 1861, to J. M. Love, district court judge at Des Moines, who was to try the case. Gurley said nothing about this step opening the way for the State Department to take jurisdiction. The letter is in the Council Bluffs *Nonpareil,* Feb. 8, 1862.

9. Hoxie's letter, Jan. 24, 1862, in the Keokuk *Gate City* (w), Feb. 5, 1862; Council Bluffs *Nonpareil,* Feb. 8, 1862.

10. Kirkwood recommended that Seward devise new ways of selecting jurors. Too many people in the district (probably meaning the area around Des Moines) were of doubtful loyalty. That included some of the "higher" judges and their law clerks, he added. Kirkwood to Seward, Dec. 25, 1861, *ORR,* ser. 2, vol. 2, p. 1324; Joe H. Smith, *History of Harrison County* (Des Moines, 1888), pp. 197-199.

11. For comment concerning how the letters got into the government's hands see John Carl Parish, *George Washington Jones* (Iowa City, 1912), p. 61; Chicago *Times,* July 14, 1862, in Dubuque *Times,* July 18, 1862; *ORR,* Ser. 2, vol. 2, p. 1296; Dubuque *Herald,* Mar. 1, July 10, 1862. The entire State Department report on Jones is in *ORR,* ser. 2, vol. 2, pp. 1295-1302.

12. Ben Samuels to Mason, Dec. 24, 1861, Jan. 16, 1862, Mason Papers, IHD.

13. Mahony to Mason, Dec. 30, 1861; ibid; *Iowa State Register* in Council Bluffs *Nonpareil,* Jan. 4, 1862, including *Nonpareil's* own comment; Buchanan to Jones, Apr. 8, 1862, Pierce to Jones, Oct. 29, 1862, Jones Papers, IHD.

14. Dubuque *Herald,* July 15, 1862; *ORR,* ser. 2, vol. 2, p. 1296; Jones to Summers, May 17, 1861, Summers Papers, IHD. See Burlington *Argus* (w), July 11, 1862, for the letter to Morse.

15. *Constitution,* July 14, 1862; Davenport *Democrat,* July 15, 1862; *Register,* July 19, 1862; *Cass County Gazette* in *Iowa State Register* (w), July 22, 1862; *Argus,* July 11, 1862; Chicago *Times,* July 14, 1862, in Dubuque *Times,* July 18, 1862. Jones's explanation as to the meaning of his letters is in the *Herald,* July 10, 1862.

16. Franklin T. Oldt and P. J. Quigley, eds., *History of Dubuque County, Iowa,* (Chicago, n.d.), pp. 274, 364; Burlington *Hawk-eye,* May 9, 1862; Summers to Jones, July 2, 1862, Jones Papers; Jones to Summers, July 25, 1862, Summers Papers. James Howell of the Keokuk *Gate City* tried to popularize the term "Jonesocracy" for Iowa's "sympathizer" Democrats, but it never caught on. By late summer of 1863, Jones was again politically active in Dubuque where he served as head of the party's county convention. In 1864 he quarreled publicly with those Dubuque Democrats who seemed to him to support the war while talking peace. After Lincoln's assassination he became a strong Johnson supporter. Republicans kept Jones's letters alive. The *Gate City* (w), of Sept. 5, 1865, reprinted the May 17, 1861, letter to Davis; *Iowa State Register* (w) did the same with the Morse letter on May 9, 1866; Dubuque *Herald,* Sept. 13, 1863; Dubuque *Times,* June 23, 1864.

17. Benjamin F. Shambaugh, *The Messages and Proclamations of the Governors of Iowa,* 7 vols. (Iowa City, 1903), 2: 308.

18. Dubuque *Herald,* Jan. 12, 1862; *Gate City* (w), Apr. 23, May 7, 1862.

19. *Keokuk County News* (Sigourney), June 27, 1862.

20. *Courier,* June 4, July 2, 1862; *Iowa State Register* (w), July 19, 1862; *Der Demokrat,* July 24, 31, 1862; Davenport *Democrat,* Sept. 11, 1862.

21. Dubuque *Times,* May 8, 16, 18, 1862; *Iowa State Register* (w), May 20, 23, 1862.

22. Oldt and Quigley, *History of Dubuque County,* p. 287; Dubuque *Herald,* Jan. 18, 1863.

23. Compiled from *Iowa State Register* (w), Nov. 2, 1859, Jan. 15, 1862. There were occasional special elections to fill vacancies which resulted in some seat shifting from one party to another. These have been accounted for in the above totals which differ slightly, therefore, from the *Register's* figures. Some Democratic house members elected on Union party tickets were excluded from participating in the Republican caucus which filled several appointive state offices. In a huff they joined the regular Democratic caucus. *Iowa State Register* (w), Jan. 17, 1862.

24. Benjamin F. Gue, *History of Iowa from the Earliest Times to the Beginning of the Twentieth Century,* 4 vols. (New York, 1903), 2:65.

25. Iowa, General Assembly, House, *Journal*, 1862, p. 676; Iowa, General Assembly, Senate, *Journal*, 1862, pp. 454–55.
26. For a good example of the latter see *Senate Journal*, 1862, pp. 157–59.
27. Apr. 8, 1862.
28. Ibid., Sept. 13, 1862; Gue, *History of Iowa*, 2:74–75.
29. *House Journal*, extra sess., 1862, pp. 58, 61; *Senate Journal*, extra sess., 1862, pp. 45–46.
30. *House Journal*, extra sess., 1862, pp. 17–19, 33, 45.
31. Aug. 15, 1861.
32. Dubuque *Times*, June 25, July 6, 1862; *Iowa State Register* (w), June 29, 1862. Hodnett somehow managed to avoid serving the sentence. Oldt and Quigley, *History of Dubuque County*, pp. 353–54.
33. Thayer's suit included a charge that Mahin had incited a riot in an effort to destroy the *Courier*. *Courier*, Aug. 27–Sept. 5, 1862; *State Democratic Press*, Nov. 29, 1862.
34. Keokuk *Gate City* (d), July 8, 1862, (w), July 16, 1862; Keokuk *Constitution*, July 9, 16, 1862; Davenport *Democrat*, July 17, 1862; Muscatine *Courier*, July 29, 1862. Whether Clagett pushed the suit is unknown.
35. Keokuk *Gate City* (w), Dec. 17, 31, 1862.
36. *Iowa State Register* (w), June 7–8, Aug. 22, 1862.
37. May 8, 10, 1862.
38. In *Des Moines News* (Keosauqua), Jan. 24, 1862.
39. May 9, July 13, 30–31, Aug. 1–2, 1862.
40. Davenport *Democrat*, July 11, 14, 1862.
41. *North Iowa Times*, July 16, 30, 1862; *Register*, Aug. 9, 1862; *Constitution*, Aug. 13, 26, Dec. 24, 1862. Clagett printed figures at the end of the year purporting to show that Lee county's "abolition" townships had by far the poorest enlistment records. Muscatine *Courier*, June–August, 1862. See especially July 22–24, Aug. 9, 1862.
42. Fairfield *Constitution and Union* in Fairfield *Ledger*, July 31, 1862; *Times*, Aug. 5, 1862.
43. Dubuque *Herald*, Sept. 23, Oct. 1, 1862; Oldt and Quigley, *History of Dubuque County*, p. 284.
44. Dubuque *Herald*, Dec. 27, 1862.
45. Solon Langworthy diary, Sept. 28, 1862; Jan. 23, June 26, 1863, Langworthy Collection, IHS; Solon M. Langworthy, "Autobiographical Sketch of Solon M. Langworthy," *IJHP* 8 (1910): 339.
46. Oldt and Quigley, *History of Dubuque County*, pp. 284–91; Dubuque *Herald*, Aug. 22, Sept. 7, 1862; Dubuque *Times*, Aug. 24, 29, Dec. 24, 1862; Nathan H. Brainerd (Kirkwood's secretary), to John T. Brazill, Aug. 12, 1862, Governor's Letterbook Military Record (Samuel J. Kirkwood), IHD.
47. Gue, *History of Iowa*, 2:73–74; Davenport *Democrat*, Sept. 4–11, 1862.
48. *Iowa State Register* (d), Sept. 7, Oct. 9, 1862; *Hawk-eye* in Sioux City *Register*, Sept. 20, 1862; *Times*, Oct. 11, 1862 *Cedar Valley Times* (Cedar Rapids), Sept. 4, 1862.
49. Keokuk *Gate City* (w), Oct. 29, 1862.
50. Davenport *Democrat*, Sept. 12, 1862; Oskaloosa *Times*, Sept. 18, 1862, in David Lendt, *Demise of the Democracy: The Copperhead Press in Iowa* (Ames, Iowa, 1973), p. 88.
51. Dubuque *Herald*, July 31, Aug. 3–6, 8, 10, 13, Sept. 25, 1862; Dubuque *Times* in Fairfield *Ledger*, Aug. 28, 1862; Davenport *Democrat*, Aug. 6, 1862; *Hamilton Freeman* (Webster City), Aug. 30, 1862; Council Bluffs *Nonpareil*, Aug. 23, 1862; Oldt and Quigley, *History of Dubuque County*, pp. 284–85.
52. Dan E. Clark, *Samuel Jordan Kirkwood* (Iowa City, 1912), pp. 230–34; Gue, *History of Iowa*, 2:73–74; John E. Briggs, "The Enlistment of Iowa Troops During the Civil War," *IJHP* 15 (1917): 323–92.
53. Charles Mason "X" letters in Dubuque *Herald*, Dec. 24, 31, 1861; Mount Pleasant *Home Journal*, Jan. 11, 1862; Dubuque *Times*, Aug. 14, 1862.
54. Kirkwood Military Letterbook, pp. 126, 169, 224, 236, 255, 259, 268: Brainerd to Charles Thorp, Apr. 26, 1862; Brainerd to William Marshall, June 20, 1862; Brainerd to J. W. Cardiff, July 24, 1862; Brainerd to J. W. Coolidge, July 30, 1862; Brainerd to J. H. White, Aug. 9, 1862; Brainerd to M. H. Pinkham, Aug. 12, 1862; Brainerd to L. B. Fleak, Aug. 15, 1862; Brainerd to J. Wasson, Aug. 16, 1862. See A. H. Prizer to N. B. Baker, Aug. 11, 1862, DSF, for very specific questions about procedures and evidence needed in order to make arrests.

55. *ORR,* ser. 2, vol. 2, pp. 321–22; Kirkwood to Stanton (copy), Sept. 11, 1862, Kirkwood Military Correspondence; James G. Randall and David Donald, *The Civil War and Reconstruction,* 2d. ed. rev. (Lexington, Mass., 1969), p. 301.

56. Wilson to Stanton, July 28, 1862, *ORR,* ser. 3, vol. 2, pp. 265–66.

57. White to Kirkwood, Aug. 7, 1862; McKim to Kirkwood, Aug. 18, 1862, "War Matters, 1858–1888" Box, IHD; also J. Wasson (LaPorte City), to Kirkwood, Aug. 9, 1862, ibid. At Iron Hill in Jackson county, listeners at a Union meeting egged a speaker, severely beat one man, and warned him and his "union friends" to get out of the area within a week. S. S. Farwell to brother, Aug. 6, 1862, Farwell Collection, IHS.

58. Udell to Kirkwood, Mar. 13, 1861, Matthews to Kirkwood, June 24, 1861, DSF; Burlington *Hawk-eye,* July 3, 6, 9, 1861.

59. Frank Klement, "Rumors of Golden Circle Activity in Iowa during the Civil War Years," *AI* 37 (1965): 525–27; Dubuque *Times,* Dubuque *Herald,* Apr.–May, 1862; *Times,* July 20, 1862; Douglas Democrats, said the *Times,* had nothing to do with secret societies; Muscatine *Journal,* Knox-ville *Republican,* Montezuma *Republican,* all in *Iowa State Register* (w), May 8, 11, 24, June 12, 1862; Grinnell to Kirkwood, Aug. 13, 1862, *ORR,* ser. 3, vol. 2, pp. 403–4; *Democrat* in Fairfield *Ledger,* Sept. 11, 1862.

60. Keokuk *Constitution,* Aug. 11–12, 1862; Burlington *Hawk-eye,* Aug. 14, 1862; Keokuk *Gate City* (w), Aug. 13, 1862; Davenport *Democrat,* Aug. 19, 1862. Keokuk's home guard force, in-stituted by the city council, had one company for each ward. Keokuk also had an Executive War Com-mittee. H. W. Sample was secretary. Ward committees were subordinate to it. These committees pro-moted private subscriptions of monies to pay for county enlistment bounties. When some prominent citizens did not subscribe, their respective ward committees published their names. Keokuk *Constitu-tion,* Aug. 13, 1862.

61. Ibid., Aug. 13, 1862; Burlington *Hawk-eye,* Aug. 13, 1862. What Hiatt did in this case is not clear, but he sometimes released arrestees when he thought there was no substance to the charges against them. See Keokuk *Gate City* (w), Aug. 27, 1862. For a slightly similar case, that involving Philander Swisher, a disabled veteran, his brother and three friends from Washington county, see Davenport *Democrat,* Aug. 13, 18, 1862.

62. Muscatine *Courier,* Aug. 14, 1862; Burlington *Hawk-eye,* Aug. 16, 1862; Davenport *Democrat,* Aug. 20, 1862; *Iowa State Register* (w), Aug. 20, 1862.

63. Keokuk *Constitution,* Aug. 19–20, 1862.

64. Ibid., Aug. 23, 1862.

65. *Iowa State Register* (w), Aug. 14, 20, 1862. Burlington *Argus* in Dubuque *Herald,* Sept. 11, 1862; Davenport *Democrat,* Aug. 15, 1862.

66. Keokuk *Constitution,* Aug. 23, 25, 27, Sept. 15, 1862; *Iowa State Register* (w), Aug. 26, 1862; Edward H. Stiles, *Recollections and Sketches of Notable Lawyers and Public Men of Early Iowa* (Des Moines, 1916), pp. 973–74. Bailey, who died in 1903 at the age of 95, recalled the arrest in his old age with amusement—"as a good joke."

67. *CM,* Aug. 18, 23–26, Sept. 14, 21, Oct. 13, Nov. 10, 16, 1862; Dennis Mahony, *Prisoner of State* (New York, 1863), pp. 400–3; *ORR,* ser. 2, vol. 5, pp. 117–19.

68. Dubuque *Herald,* July 31, Aug. 5–6, 1862; also May 8, 24, Aug. 2–3, 8, 10, 13, 1862. A more compelling reason, though no documentary material exists which could prove it, is that offered by Leland L. Sage. Mahony was the likely Democratic candidate for Congress from the Iowa Third District. Dubuque's William B. Allison, a friend of Herbert Hoxie, was the Republican nominee. Sage thinks it is reasonable to assume that they wanted Mahony out of the way during the campaign. Sage, *William B. Allison,* pp. 52–54.

69. Keokuk *Constitution,* Aug. 27, 1862; Muscatine *Courier,* Aug. 22, 1862.

70. Hoxie to Kirkwood, Sept. 22, 1862, DSF; Keokuk *Gate City* (w), Sept. 24, 1862. Hoxie told Grenville Dodge, Sept. 18, 1862, G. M. Dodge Papers, that the KGCs intended to "bully the Republicans and thus keep them away from the polls."

71. George Rose deposition (copy), to George C. Tichenor, Sept. 19, 1862, DSF.

72. Kirkwood to Stanton, Sept. 11, 1862, Governor's Department Military Correspondence (Samuel J. Kirkwood), IHD; Frank Klement, "Rumors of Golden Circle Activity," p. 528, nn. 18, 21; "Statement of Melvin McGrew," E. H. Harlan Correspondence, IHD.

73. *Iowa State Register,* in Keokuk *Gate City* (w), Oct. 1, 1862; Dubuque *Times,* Oct. 3, 1862.

74. Dubuque *Herald* and Dubuque *Times,* Aug. 19, 1862; Mahony, *Prisoner of State,* pp. 117–20. Other reports of arrests are in the Keokuk *Gate City* (w), Sept. 4, 10, 24, 1862.

75. Keokuk *Gate City* (w), Sept. 17, 1862; Judge Advocate to Hoxie, Sept. 27, 1862, *ORR*, ser. 2, vol. 4, pp. 567-68; Klement, "Rumors of Golden Circle Activity," pp. 527, 528, n.18; David Lendt, "Iowa's Civil War Marshal: A Lesson in Expediency," *AI* 43 (1975): 132-39. See p. 136 for Lendt's perceptive comment on Hoxie's reports to and his relations with officials in the Judge Advocate's office in Washington.

76. Dubuque *Herald*, Nov. 16, Dec. 24, 1862; Keokuk *Constitution*, Nov. 19, 1862; Burlington *Argus*, Dec. 5, 1862; *Iowa State Register* (w), Dec. 16, 21, 1862.

77. Open letters, Mahony to Kirkwood, Mahony to Lincoln, in Dubuque *Herald*, Dec. 2, 7, 1862, respectively; *State Democratic Press*, Jan. 3, 1863; Hoxie to Kirkwood, Nov. 9, 1862, DSF; Council Bluffs *Bugle*, Nov. 26, 1862.

78. Muscatine *Courier*, Dec. 27, 1862.

79. *Ledger*, Mar. 6, 1872; Ottumwa *Courier* in Keokuk *Gate City* (w), Sept. 10, 1862.

80. Burlington *Hawk-eye*, Feb. 19-20, 1862; Washington *Democrat*, Mar. 11, Apr. 7, 1862; Keokuk *Constitution*, Mar. 17, 1862; *State Democratic Press*, Apr. 16, 1862; *History of Jones County* (Chicago, 1879), pp. 371.

81. Hewes to Kirkwood, Dec. 30, 1862, DSF; John Palmer, William Davis, J. F. Logan to Baker, Aug. 31, 1864, ibid.

82. Dec. 25, 1862, Jan. 21, 1863.

83. Burlington *Hawk-eye*, May 13, 1862; *Hawk-eye*, Feb. 12, 1862; *Linn County Register* (Cedar Rapids), July 25, 1862, in Dubuque *Times*, July 29, 1862; *Iowa State Register* (w), Aug. 22, 1862; Oskaloosa *Herald* in *Register* (w), May 11, 1862.

84. *Herald*, Apr. 21, 1862; *State Democratic Press*, Aug. 30, Sept. 6, 1862; see also Harrison John Thornton, "The State University of Iowa and the Civil War," *AI* 30 (1950): 198-209.

85. Kirkwood to W. W. Thomas (Wayne county), and to others in other counties, Sept. 11, 1862, *Reports of the Adjutant General and Acting Quartermaster of the State of Iowa, 1863,* 2: 879. Adjutant General Baker believed reports from some angry Republicans that some Democrats who secured commissions to raise and command militia units enlisted Democrats only in those units. Baker to Thomas, Sept. 22, 1862, Governor's Letterbook (Kirkwood), p. 29.

CHAPTER 5

1. Shambaugh, *The Messages and Proclamations of the Governors of Iowa,* 7 vols. (Iowa City, 1903), 2: 306-7.

2. Monroe and Lowell to Mason, Jan. 23, 1862, Mason Papers, IHD; *Iowa State Register* (w), May 15, 1862.

3. Dubuque *Herald*, Mar. 27, 1862; *Iowa Homestead*, Apr. 10, 1862; Fairfield *Ledger*, Apr. 11, 1862; Dubuque *Times*, July 16, 1862; Franklin T. Oldt and P. J. Quigley, eds., *History of Dubuque County, Iowa* (Chicago, n.d.), p. 144.

4. Charles J. Fulton, "A Wartime Doctor's Account Book, 1861-1862," *AI* 14 (1925): 543. Besides foodstuffs, Dr. Dial accepted payment in dry goods, stocking yarn, vials, bottles, a vest, a violin, and an oil painting. Services he accepted included tailoring, making a linen coat, making pants, cutting wood, shoeing a horse, and repairing sulkey springs.

5. *Iowa Agricultural Report 1862,* p. 8; Keokuk *Constitution*, Feb. 17, 1862; *Herald*, June 4, 1862; *Courier*, June 3, 1862; *Iowa State Register* (w), May 11, 1862.

6. Davenport *Democrat*, June 20, July 26, 1862; Burlington *Hawk-eye*, July 30, Oct. 29, 1862; Muscatine *Courier*, Dec. 31, 1862; Iowa, General Assembly, Senate, *Journal*, 1862, p, 564.

7. The *Iowa Homestead*, oriented toward farmers, appears to have emphasized the rate issue and the blockade earlier and more consistently than most papers. In the last month and a half of 1862 everybody else followed suit. *Iowa Homestead*, Feb. 20, 27, Dec. 11, 1862; Keokuk *Gate City* (w), Dec. 10, 1862; Council Bluffs *Nonpareil*, Nov. 29, 1862; Dubuque *Times*, Dec. 11, 1862; Burlington *Hawk-eye*, Dec. 22, 1862. *Iowa State Register* (w), Dec. 27, 1862; *Agricultural Report 1861-62,* pp. 126-27, 245. John Wallace, agricultural society secretary, called for the state to pass a law mandating rates which would at least protect the farmer until his goods left Iowa, ibid., p. 126.

8. Faye E. Harris, "A Frontier Community: The Economic, Social and Political Development of Keokuk, Iowa from 1820 to 1866" (Ph.D. diss., University of Iowa, 1965), p. 367; Keokuk *Constitution*, July 14, Nov. 18, Dec. 15-16, 1862; *Gate City* (w), Nov. 5, 1862; Dubuque *Times*, Dec. 11, 1862; Gerald Kennedy, "U.S. Army Hospital: Keokuk, 1862-1865," *AI* 40 (1969): 118-19.

242   NOTES TO PAGES 74–81

9. George A. Boeck, "An Early Iowa Community: Aspects of Economic, Social and Political Development in Burlington, Iowa, 1833–1866" (Ph.D. diss., University of Iowa, 1961), pp. 312–14; Burlington *Hawk-eye*, Oct. 31, 1862.

10. *Democrat*, May 6–7, June 16, Aug. 23, Oct. 16–17, 1862; Muscatine *Courier*, July 28, 1862; Dubuque *Times*, Oct. 3, 1862.

11. *Herald*, Jan. 21, Feb. 21, Apr. 6–10, May 14, June 17, July 1, Sept. 30, Nov. 27, 1862; *Times*, Jan. 24, Feb. 18, June 7, 12, 1862; *Iowa State Register* (w), May 4, 1862; Oldt and Quigley, *History of Dubuque County*, pp. 142, 144, 149, 248.

12. *Iowa State Register* (w), Nov. 5, Dec. 3, 1862, Jan. 3, 1863; Johnson Brigham, *Des Moines Together with the History of Polk County, Iowa*, 2 vols. (Chicago, 1911) 2: 214.

13. *Register*, May 31, 1862; *Nonpareil*, July 26, 1862.

14. *Iowa Homestead*, Jan. 1, 1863.

15. Ibid., May 22, 1862; *Report of the Iowa State Agricultural Society, 1861–1862*, p. 129; ibid., 1866, p. 14; *State Democratic Press*, June 7, 1862; John A. Hopkins, Jr., "Economic History of the Production of Beef Cattle in Iowa," pt. 1, *IJHP* 26 (1928): 89–90; pt. 3, (1925), p. 444; Waterloo *Courier*, May 7, 1862; S. S. Farwell to brother, Aug. 6, 1862, S. S. Farwell Papers, IHS.

16. Earle D. Ross, *Iowa Agriculture: An Historical Survey* (Iowa City, 1951), p. 53.

17. Council Bluffs *Bugle*, Dec. 17, 1862.

18. Keokuk *Gate City* (w), Apr. 20, 1862.

19. V. Jacque Voegeli, *Free But Not Equal: The Midwest and the Negro during the Civil War* (Chicago, 1967), pp. 26–28; Iowa, General Assembly, House, *Journal*, extra sess., 1862, pp. 179, 187; Senate, *Journal*, extra sess., 1862, pp. 19, 38, 47; House, *Journal*, extra sess., 1862, pp. 11, 20, 29, 59, 71, 77, 92, 95.

20. Dubuque *Herald*, July 22, Oct. 14, 1862; Keokuk *Constitution*, Nov. 10, 1862.

21. June 18, 1862.

22. June 23, 1862.

23. Davenport *Democrat*, Aug. 1, 1862; Mildred Throne, ed., "Document: A Commissary in the Union Army: Letters of C. C. Carpenter," *IJH* 54 (1955): 69, William Thompson to Jane Thompson, Sept. 25, 1862, in Edwin C. Bearss, ed., "Civil War Letters of Major William Thompson," *AI* 36 (1966): 440–41.

24. Keokuk *Constitution*, Oct. 21, 24, 1862; also, July 12, 1862.

25. Keokuk *Gate City* (w), May 28, July 9, 1862; *Times*, Sept. 12, 20, Dec. 12, 1862; Feb. 6, 1863.

26. *Hawk-eye*, Oct. 10, 1862; Keokuk *Gate City* (w), Oct. 23, 1862.

27. Baldwin to Dodge, Sept. 24, 1862, G. M. Dodge Papers, IHD.

28. Jan. 21, 1862.

29. Dubuque *Herald*, June 13–14, 1862; Dubuque *Times*, June 14, 22, 1862; Davenport *Democrat*, June 18, 1862.

30. Davenport *Democrat*, May 1, 1862; Keokuk *Constitution*, June 30, July 4, 15, 1862.

31. Des Moines *Times* in Dubuque *Times*. Aug. 21, 1862; Dubuque *Times*, Aug. 20, Sept. 2, 3, 6, 26, 1862; Edward Younger, *John A. Kasson: Politics and Diplomacy from Lincoln to McKinley* (Iowa City, 1955), p. 136.

32. Aug. 26, 1862.

33. Dubuque *Herald*, Oct. 3, 11, 1862; Muscatine *Courier*, Oct. 3–4, 8, 11, 1862; Davenport *Democrat*, Oct. 4, 1862; Keokuk *Constitution*, Oct. 9–10, 1862.

34. *Des Moines News* (Keosauqua), in Fairfield *Ledger*, Dec. 4, 1862.

35. Nov. 25, 1862.

36. Dubuque *Herald*, Nov. 30, 1862. Hutchins himself never passed up an opportunity to make money. See Edward J. Gallagher, *Stilson Hutchins, a Biography of the Founder of the Washington Post* (Laconia, N. H., 1965), pp. 9–11, 19–21.

37. Nov. 25, 1862.

38. *Fayette County Pioneer* (West Union), Mar. 24, 1862.

39. Keokuk *Constitution*, May 16, 1862; Charles Mason, *The Election in Iowa*, No. 11 of Papers from the Society for the Diffusion of Political Knowledge (New York, 1863), pp. 2–3.

40. Council Bluffs *Bugle*, Nov. 5, 1862.

41. Clark to Kirkwood, Mar. 20, 1862, Kirkwood Correspondence, IHD; Shambaugh, *Messages and Proclamations*, 2: 303–5.

42. May 20, 1862.

43. Thompson to Jane Thompson, Oct. 14, 1862, Bearss, "Thompson Letters," pp. 447–48; *Der Demokrat*, July 10, 1862.

44. Nov. 10, 1862.
45. Burlington *Hawk-eye*, Feb. 11, 1862.
46. Keokuk *Gate City* (w), Mar. 5, 1862; Dubuque *Times*, July 27, 1862; *Der Demokrat*, Aug. 28, 1862; Irving B. Richman, "Congregational Life in Muscatine, 1843-1893," *IJHP* 21 (1923): 358.
47. *Register*, Oct. 4, 1862; *Nonpareil*, Nov. 2, 1862.
48. *Republican*, Oct. 1, 1862; *Der Demokrat*, Oct. 9, 1862.
49. Mildred Throne, ed., "An Iowa Doctor in Blue: The Letters of Seneca B. Thrall, 1862-1864," *IJH* 58 (1960): 109-110; Mildred E. Throne, ed., *The Civil War Diary of Cyrus F. Boyd, Fifteenth Iowa Infantry, 1861-1863* (Millwood, N.Y., 1977), pp. 110, 132.
50. Feb. 1, 1862.
51. Davenport *Democrat*, Mar. 5, 7, June 10, 1862; *Herald*, Mar. 8, 1862; Keokuk *Constitution*, Mar. 6, Apr. 2, 1862.
52. *Herald*, June 18, 1862; Davenport *Democrat* July 4, 1862; Keokuk *Constitution*, July 7, 19, 1862.
53. *CM*, Sept. 23, Oct. 4, 1862.
54. Dubuque *Herald*, Sept. 24, Oct. 8, 1862; Davenport *Democrat*, Sept. 24, 26, 1862; *Cedar Valley Times* (Cedar Rapids), Oct. 16, 1862. Hollis told fellow Republicans that disloyalty was no charge to fling around carelessly, a rare display of objectivity at that time.
55. Sept. 29, Nov. 13, Dec. 9, 25, 1862. A Clagett headline over an editorial on Jan. 31, 1863, had the Clagett imprint. It read, "To exterminate the White Population of the South, and People it with Abolitionists and Negroes is now the Policy of the Administration—The War to be Hereafter Conducted Primarily for that Purpose." However, the editorial was a report of extreme abolitionist proposals for reconstructing the South, not actual administration objectives, nor a signal that Clagett was now for peace. In an age of florid expression, the Keokuk editor frequently exceeded the norm.
56. *Courier*, Dec. 12, 1862; *Democrat*, Oct. 7, 1862; *Argus*, Dec. 30, 1862.
57. Jan. 9, 1863.
58. Mason "X" letter in the Dubuque *Herald*, Jan. 8, 1863.
59. The paper approved the Dubuque city Democratic platform which announced that there would be no peace "till the treason of abolitionism should be treated as a crime by the government. . . ." ibid., Mar. 25, 1862.
60. Ibid., Jan. 28, 1862; *Democrat*, Feb. 3, 1862.
61. Fairfield *Constitution and Union*, in Burlington *Hawk-eye*, Apr. 6, 1862; Keokuk *Constitution*, June 10, 16, 24, 1862.
62. *Register* and *Cass County Democrat* (Atlantic), in Council Bluffs *Nonpareil*, June 14, 28, 1862, respectively. The *Nonpareil* believed that "by far the greater portion" of the Iowa Democrats agreed with these papers.
63. *Argus* in Dubuque *Times*, July 29, 1862.
64. Davenport *Democrat*, July 21, 1862.
65. Olynthus Clark, *The Politics of Iowa During the Civil War and Reconstruction* (Iowa City, 1911), p. 156; Tichenor to Frank Palmer in *Iowa State Register*, Sept. 28, 1862; Burlington *Argus*, Jan. 15, 1863; J. F. Brown to C. C. Carpenter, May, 1862, Cyrus C. Carpenter Papers, IHS.
66. Dubuque *Herald*, Aug. 22, 1862; Leland L. Sage, *William Boyd Allison: A Study in Practical Politics* (Iowa City, 1956), pp. 55, covers Mahony's nomination and the reaction to it in succinct and interesting fashion; Mahony to Mason, June 24, 1862, Mason Papers; Hutchins to Mason, Aug. 28, 1862, ibid; Chicago *Times* in Mount Pleasant *Home Journal*, Aug. 30, 1862.
67. Grimes to Chase, Oct. 20, 1862, in William Salter, *James W. Grimes* (New York, 1876), p. 218.
68. *Iowa Election Records, 1839-1890* (Iowa City, University Microfilms). For convenience, the Republican and Constitutional Union votes are included together under the Republican percentage in 1860. Northern and Southern Democratic votes are lumped together in the Democratic figure. For 1861, Union party votes are counted with the Republicans while "scattering" are assigned to the Democrats.
69. *State Democratic Press*, Oct. 11, 1862; *Iowa State Register* (w), Oct. 22, 1862, in Edward Benton, "Soldier Voting in Iowa," *IJHP* 24 (1951): 35.
70. Hunter to Mary Hunter, Oct. 15, 1862, Jacob Hunter Letters (microfilm), IHD. Private Hunter was incensed at his wife's report that some Democrats in his home, Monroe, voted illegally. Hunter to Mary Hunter, Oct. 20, 1862.
71. Bussey to Kirkwood, Oct. 19, 1862, Kirkwood Correspondence.
72. Jacob R. Perkins, *Trails, Rails and War: The Life of Grenville M. Dodge* (Indianapolis, 1929), p. 104.

73. For diametrically opposite views on the same incident see Dubuque *Herald,* Oct. 18, 1862, and *Fayette County Pioneer,* Oct. 27, 1862, on one side, and Dubuque *Times* in Keokuk *Gate City* (w), Nov. 12, 1862, on the other. The same issue of the *Gate City* also reported bungled vote taking in the Nineteenth Iowa. Seth Wheaton's report is in the *Herald,* Oct. 30, 1862. Seevers' and Sheafor's are in the *Herald* of Nov. 11, 1862. The Dubuque *Times* letter on ballot burning appeared on Oct. 9, 1862. See also *State Democratic Press,* Nov. 1, 1862, and Keokuk *Constitution,* Oct. 24, 1862. The *Constitution*'s story, by a chaplain with the Fifteenth Iowa, verified the report that the Fifteenth had Republican but no Democratic ballots. Surprisingly, the Democratic Des Moines *Times* accepted the word of civilian commissioners that they acted impartially. Des Moines *Times* in Dubuque *Times,* Nov. 5, 1862.

74. Muscatine *Courier,* Oct. 27, 1862; see Keokuk *Gate City,* Oct. 20, 1862; Dubuque *Times,* Oct. 26, 1862.

75. *Iowa State Register* (w), Dec. 16, 1862.

76. Keokuk *Gate City* (w), Nov. 26, 1862; *Ledger,* Nov. 27, 1862.

77. *Herald,* Aug. 15, Nov. 13–14, 1862; Hutchins to Mason, Sept. 17, 1862, Mahony to Mason, Oct. 4, 1862, Mason Papers; Oldt and Quigley, *History of Dubuque County,* p. 144; Roger Sullivan, "Mahony, the Unterrified" (B.A. thesis, Loras College, 1948), p. 49. Since nobody ever referred to the paper as anything but the *Herald,* the word *Democratic* is not used herein.

78. Mrs. Sheward to Sheward (copy), Sept. 23, 1862, Mason Papers; Sage, *William B. Allison,* p. 55.

79. *Herald,* July 30, 1862, in Dubuque *Times,* Oct. 8, 1862; *North-West Democrat,* in Keokuk *Gate City* (w), Oct. 8, 1862; Dubuque *Times,* Oct. 12, 1862.

80. *Free But Not Equal,* p. 56; Burlington *Hawk-eye,* Oct. 16, 18, 1862.

81. Keokuk *Constitution,* Nov. 25, 1862; Keokuk *Gate City* (w), Nov. 19, 1862.

82. *Tribune* in *National Intelligencer,* Dec. 10, 1862; Dubuque *Herald,* Oct. 14, 1862.

83. Muscatine *Courier,* Nov. 4, 1862; *CM,* Nov. 9, 1862; Dubuque *Herald,* Jan. 11, 1863; *Agricultural Report, 1862,* pp. 221–24.

84. *CM,* Jan. 26, Feb. 9, 16, 18, Mar. 7, May 18, June 26, July 6, 1862.

85. Feb. 18, 25, 1862.

86. Davenport *Democrat,* Apr. 10, 12, 1862; Keokuk *Constitution,* Apr. 23, 28, 1862.

87. Burlington *Hawk-eye,* May 7, 1862. I have made no effort to do a content analysis to verify or deny the *Hawk-eye* contention, but long before reading Dunham's jaundiced comment it seemed from my perusal of the Iowa wartime Democratic press that Meade, McClellan, Sickles, and other Democrats did acquire proportionately more favorable notices in Democratic papers even when losing, or sometimes in the *Herald,* especially when losing. So, it appears, did Ben Butler, even through much of his New Orleans period. The impression gleaned from Iowa Republican papers is that they wanted victories so badly that they didn't care who won them.

88. July 5, 1862.

89. Apr. 23, Nov. 26, 1862.

CHAPTER 6

1. There were a few peace meetings in early 1861, these in Davis, Wapello and Van Buren counties, all in the southeastern part of the state, and all having large numbers of persons with Southern or border state antecedents. Ottumwa *Weekly Democratic Union,* Mar. 21, May 9, 1861; *Des Moines News* (Keosauqua), June 29, 1861.

2. *Iowa State Register* (w), July 27, 1862. Peace men dominated some county Democratic conventions in 1862, including Montgomery, Jones, Jefferson, Howard, and Scott, where Democrats were usually in the minority.

3. Dubuque *Herald,* Feb. 13, 22, 1863.

4. Peace meeting coverage in 1863 is found in all Iowa papers of the times. See especially Fairfield *Ledger,* Jan. 8, Feb. 5, June 4; Burlington *Hawk-eye,* Jan. 22; Burlington *Argus,* Feb. 5, 12, 19, 26, Mar. 5, 12, 26, Apr. 2, 9, 26, May 21; Council Bluffs *Nonpareil,* Mar. 7; Dubuque *Herald,* Feb. 7, 13, 22, 24, Mar. 17, 26, Apr. 14, May 6, 15, July 7; Keokuk *Gate City* (w), Feb. 11, 18, Mar. 4, 11, Apr. 10 (d); Keokuk *Constitution,* Feb. 16; *Iowa State Register* (w), Apr. 8; Charles J. Fulton, ed., *History of Jefferson County, Iowa* (Chicago, 1914), 358; Capt. H. B. Horn to N. B. Baker, Mar. 2, 1863, *Reports of the Adjutant General and Acting Quartermaster of the State of Iowa, 1863,* p. 678; *Pioneer History of Davis County, Iowa* (Bloomfield, Ia., 1927), p. 555; W. W. Merritt, *A History of*

the County of Montgomery (Red Oak, Ia., 1906), pp. 57-61; Realto Price ed., *History of Clayton County* (Chicago, 1916), 1: 149.

5. Burlington *Hawk-eye*, Jan. 6, 1863; Fairfield *Ledger*, Mar. 12, 1863; Rorer to A. D. Green, Feb. 20, 1863, David Rorer Papers, IHS.

6. Kirkwood to James Grimes, James Harlan, and Wilson (copies), Feb. 3, 1863, Governor's Department Military Correspondence (Samuel J. Kirkwood), IHD; Van Benthusen to Kirkwood, Jan. 23, 1863; Crockett to Baker, Mar. 9, 1863; Conger to Baker, Feb. 17, 1863, DSF; Jane Thompson to Major William Thompson, Mar. 11, 20, 1863, William and Jane Thompson Papers, IHD; S. S. Daniels to Kirkwood, Jan. 11, 1863, L. B. Fleak to Kirkwood, Feb. 18, 1863, DSF.

7. Fulton, *History of Jefferson County*, pp. 358-59; Burlington *Argus*, May 21, 1863; Keokuk *Gate City* (w), Mar. 4, 11, 1863. See the *Argus* of July 25, 1863, for a typically bellicose resolution on the draft.

8. *State Democratic Press*, Sept. 26, Oct. 10, 1863; Franklin T. Oldt and P. J. Quigley, eds., *History of Dubuque County, Iowa* (Chicago, n.d.), p. 361.

9. Jan. 3, 10, Feb. 18, June 28, 1863.

10. Nov. 24, Dec. 8, 1862; Jan. 5, 26, 1863. Thayer supported the war and enlistment drives editorially right up to Mahony's arrest. This and other arbitrary arrests in August and September cooled that support, but did not convert him to peace immediately. See *Courier*, June to mid-August, 1862, especially Aug. 9, Aug. 14, 1862, for Thayer as war proponent. Then see Aug. 22, 1862, for a shift in his attitude.

11. Jan. 31, Feb. 21, and Feb. 28, 1863.

12. Feb. 18, 1863.

13. *Democratic Clarion*, Mar. 18, 1863; *Des Moines News*, Feb. 20, 1863; *Argus*, Mar. 19, 1863. This hardly exhausts the list of papers which at one time or another favored a peace policy. Among them were the Oskaloosa *Times*, Independence *Civilian*, Indpendence *Crisis*, Anamosa *News*, and John Duncombe's Fort Dodge *Democrat*.

14. July 14, 1863.

15. May 5-6, 1863.

16. Des Moines *Times* in Fairfield *Ledger*, Mar. 26, 1863.

17. *Gazette*, May 22-23, 1863; Davenport *Democrat*, May 23, 1863.

18. Davenport *Democrat*, May 14, 1863; *Fayette County Pioneer*, Aug. 10, 1863.

19. Apr. 2, 1863.

20. *Herald*, Feb. 12, 25, 1863.

21. Ibid., Feb. 19, 1863; Dubuque *Times*, Apr. 15, 1863.

22. Kelsey to Summers, Feb. 25, 1863, Laurel Summers Papers, IHD; Kelsey to Summers, Mar. 26, July 25, 1863.

23. Mar. 25, 1863; Muscatine *Courier*, Mar. 30, 1863. Mildred Throne, ed., *The Civil War Diary of Cyrus F. Boyd, Fifteenth Iowa Infantry, 1861-1863* (Millwood, N.Y., 1977), pp. 132-34.

24. Burlington *Argus*, Feb. 5, 1863; Dubuque *Herald*, Feb. 13, 1863.

25. Dubuque *Herald*, Feb. 19, Apr. 16, May 6, 1863; Burlington *Argus*, Apr. 9, 16, 1863; Davenport *Democrat*, Apr. 9, May 3, 1863.

26. Mar. 7, 1863.

27. Throne, *Cyrus Boyd Diary*, pp. 120, 121.

28. Keokuk *Constitution*, July 9, 1862.

29. *Fayette County Pioneer*, Jan. 5, 1863.

30. *CM*, Mar. 6, 1865. "The loyal people have a great ball tonight at the Patent Office," he wrote at this time.

31. Jan. 24 and Feb. 3, 1863. Strangely, Butternut tended to displace Copperhead in the September *Hawk-eye* as an odious term, a development not noticeable elsewhere.

32. Sioux City *Register*, Dec. 6, 20, 1862; Jan. 10, 17, 31, Mar. 7, 21, May 16, 1863; *Iowa State Register* (w), Mar. 18, May 20, 27, 1863. For further elucidation on terminology see Burlington *Hawk-eye*, Mar. 14, 1863; Dubuque *Times*, Apr. 28, Sept. 6, Dec. 11, 1863; *Iowa State Register* (w), Dec. 2, 1863, reprinted in *Hawk-eye*, Dec. 4, 1863; *Register* (w), Dec. 9, 1863.

33. Keokuk *Gate City* (w), Sept. 28, 1863; Keokuk *Constitution*, Sept. 29, 1863; *Gate City* (w), Oct. 14, 1863.

34. Oct. 1, 1863.

35. June 10, 1864.

36. *Courier*, Mar. 3, 1863; *Democrat*, Mar. 10, Apr. 7, 1863.

37. *Times*, Apr. 9, 1863 in Keokuk *Gate City* (w), Apr. 15, 1863; *Argus*, Apr. 30, 1863; *CM*, June 3, 1863.

38. Davenport *Democrat*, Sept. 8, Nov. 19, 1863.

39. *Herald*, Mar. 6, 18, 1863; *Times*, May 24, 1864.

40. Nov. 10, 1864.

41. *Iowa State Register* (w), May 27, Aug. 5, 9, 1863; *Statesman*, Aug. 7-8, 1863.

42. Feb. 25, 1864.

43. Benjamin F. Gue, *History of Iowa, From the Earliest Times to the Beginning of the Twentieth Century*, 4 vols. (New York, 1903), 2:361-66; Lurton D. Ingersoll, *Iowa and the Rebellion* (Philadelphia, 1866), pp. 669-71; Burlington *Argus*, Nov. 5, 1863; Keokuk *Constitution*, Aug. 29, 1862; *CM*, Sept. 20, 1863. The Fortieth was the only Iowa regiment to ever cast any Democratic majority in any wartime election; the vote for General Tuttle was the one time that occurred.

44. Hunter to Mary Hunter, Jan. 29, 1863, Hunter Letters (microfilm), IHD.

45. Muscatine *Courier*, Mar. 30, 1863; Dubuque *Herald*, Apr. 15, 1863; Dubuque *Times*, Apr. 20, 1863.

46. Jane Thompson to William Thompson, Feb. 20, 1864, Thompson Letters.

47. Burlington *Hawk-eye*, Dec. 29, 1864; Keokuk *Gate City* (w), Jan. 4, 1865.

48. *Marion County Republican* (Knoxville), in *Iowa State Register* (w), June 18, 1862.

49. Seth J. Temple, "Camp McClellan During the Civil War," *AI* 21 (1937): 17-55; Ted Hinckley, "Davenport and the Civil War," ibid., 34 (1958): 401-19; *Iowa State Register* (w), Dec. 14, 16, 1862; Davenport *Democrat* and Davenport *Gazette* in Keokuk *Constitution*, Dec. 19, 1862.

50. In Davenport *Democrat*, Dec. 30, 1862.

51. Dec. 30, 1862, Jan. 20, Mar. 12, 14, 16-17, Dec. 29-30, 1863, Jan. 5, 1864.

52. Stanley P. Hirshon, *Grenville, M. Dodge: Soldier, Politician, Railroad Pioneer* (Bloomington, Ind., 1967), p. 66; Washington *Democrat*, Mar. 16, 1863.

53. Dubuque *Herald*, Feb. 18, June 17, 1863.

54. Ibid., July 3, 1863.

55. "Peter Wilson in the Civil War, 1863-1865," *IJHP* 40 (1942): 377.

56. The *Herald* of Jan. 8, 1863, insisted on a figure by extrapolation of 30,000 federal casualties. The *Gate City* (w), Jan. 28, 1863, accepted figures of 1,474 killed, 6,874 wounded and 2,000 prisoners. Dubuque *Times*, May 16, 1863. Federal totals from Thomas L. Livermore, *Numbers and Losses in the Civil War in America, 1861-1865* (New York, 1901), p. 97, are 1,677 killed, 7,543 wounded and 3,686 missing.

57. Dubuque *Times*, May 16, 1863; *Herald*, June 25, July 16, 1863.

58. Ibid., June 27, July 8-9, 1863; Burlington *Hawk-eye*, July 10, 1863; Dubuque *Times*, July 12, 19, 1863.

59. *Herald*, Nov. 15, 1863; *Times*, Nov. 17, 1863.

60. Fairfield *Ledger*, July 16, 1863.

61. *Democrat*, July 6-7, 1863; *Courier*, July 8, 1863.

62. July 10, 1863.

63. *State Democratic Press*, July 11, 1863; *Statesman*, July 7, 14, 1863.

64. July 15, 1863.

65. Dec. 20, 1863.

66. Mahony's letter to Kirkwood appeared in the *Herald* of Dec. 2 and the one to Lincoln on Dec. 7, 1862. Neither his letter to Greeley nor Greeley's reply appeared in the *Herald;* both ran in the New York *Tribune* on Nov. 26, 1862. The accommodating Dubuque *Times* of Dec. 7, 1862, printed Greeley's bristling response.

67. U.S. Congress, Senate, *Congressional Globe*, 37th Cong., 3d sess., 1863, 1: 108, 140, 155, 183, 2: 1131-35; the Burlington *Hawk-eye*, Jan. 10, 1863, printed Stanton's documents.

68. Basil Leo Lee, *Discontent in New York City, 1861-1865* (Washington, 1943), pp. 233-34, 237; *Herald*, Mar. 18-19, 1863.

69. *Herald*, Feb. 6, Mar. 25, 1863; Mahony to Mason, Mar. 3, 1863, Mason Papers IHD; Dennis Mahony, *Prisoner of State* (New York, 1863), pp. 45, 189; Mahony, *The Four Acts of Despotism: Comprising I, the Tax Bill with all Amendments; II, the Finance Bill; III, the Conscription Act; IV, the Indemnity Bill, with Introduction and Comments* (New York, 1863), p. 5.

70. *Times*, July 18, 1863.

71. Ibid., Aug. 2, 20, 1863.

72. *Herald*, Aug. 11, Oct. 15, 1863.

73. *Iowa State Register* in Dubuque *Times*, June 12, 1862; *Times*, Nov. 2, 1862, June 11, 1863; Keokuk *Constitution*, Nov. 4, 1863.

74. Jan. 29, Mar. 12, July 2, 1863.

75. *Herald*, Feb. 15, 21, Nov. 17, 1863; *Courier* and Dubuque *Times* in *Times*, May 24, 1863; Robert K. Thorp, "The Copperhead Days of Dennis Mahony," *JQ* 43 (1966): 684.

76. *Herald*, Nov. 17, 1863.

77. *Herald*, Jan. 24, 26, Feb. 28, Mar. 15, May 26, 1863; Cedar Falls *Gazette*, Mar. 13, 1863; Dubuque *Times*, Mar. 17, May 26, 1863.

78. *Herald*, Apr. 26, May 2, 1863.

79. *Der Demokrat*, July 3, 1862.

80. *Journal*, Aug. 25, 1862, Muscatine *Courier*, Aug. 26, 1862; the Dubuque *Times*, Feb. 20, 1863, said the government has as much right to suppress papers as it did to spike an enemy's cannon; Kasson to Dodge, Jan. 21, 1863, G. M. Dodge Papers, IHD; Council Bluffs *Nonpareil*, Mar. 7, 1863.

81. *Republican*, Apr. 29, 1863; Burlington *Hawk-eye*, May 13, 1862.

82. *Constitution*, Feb. 14, 19, 1863; Gerald Kennedy, "U.S. Army Hospital: Keokuk, 1862–1865, *AI* 40 (1969): 133; *Gate City* (d), Feb. 20, and (w), Feb. 25, 1863; Davenport *Democrat*, Feb. 23, 1863; Burlington *Argus*, Feb. 26, May 28, 1863; Sioux City *Register*, Mar. 7, 1863; *Iowa State Register* (w), July 29, 1863 (General Roberts's report); Burlington *Hawk-eye*, Aug. 17, 1863 (Kirkwood's letter to Clagett). See also Council Bluffs *Nonpareil*, Apr. 4, 1863, for a wrist slap-type reprimand administered to one of the soldiers involved in the incident. Washington *Democrat*, June 2, 1863.

83. *Fayette County Pioneer*, May 15, June 15, July 20, 1863; *Iowa State Register* (w), May 20, 1863; Waterloo *Courier*, Nov. 4, 1863; *History of Fayette County* (Chicago, 1878), pp. 456–57.

84. Fairfield *Ledger*, Feb. 5, Aug. 20, 1863; "Petition of Joseph B. Shollenbarger for loss sustained in 'Tally War in Keokuk Co.,' " IHD.

85. Cedar Falls *Gazette* in Charles City *Intelligencer*, May 7, 1863; Dubuque *Herald*, May 13, 1863; *Pocket City News*, in *Intelligencer*, June 4, 1863.

86. May 19, 23, 1863.

87. Dubuque *Times*, July 18, 1863; *Cedar Valley Times* (Cedar Rapids), July 9, 1863.

88. *Iowa State Register* (w), Aug. 5, 1863.

89. Burlington *Argus*, May 7, 1863; *Des Moines News* (Keosauqua), May 8, 1863; Fairfield *Ledger*, Aug. 6, 1863; Burlington *Hawk-eye*, Aug. 13, 1864.

90. Washington *Democrat*, May 12, 1863.

91. *History of Mahaska County, Iowa* (1878), pp. 376–77; Keokuk *Gate City* (w), Aug. 26, 1863.

92. Dubuque *Herald*, Sept. 19, 1863.

93. J. L. Swift, "The Death of Cyphert Tally," *AI* 41 (1972), pp. 834–42, is the best account of the shooting. Complete accounts of the whole affair, August 1–8 (as complete as they could be without the information Swift has), are found in *Adjutant General's Report 1863–64*, pp. 687–91, and *History of Mahaska County*, pp. 375–76. See also, Dan E. Clark, *Samuel Jordan Kirkwood* (Iowa City, 1917), pp. 270–74; *ORR*, ser. 3, vol. 3, pp. 632–33, 637–39: Kirkwood to Stanton, Aug. 7, 1863; Stanton to Kirkwood, Aug. 8, 1863; Pope to Roberts, Aug. 7, 1863. See *State Democratic Press*, Nov. 4, 1863, for an example of Democratic anger at the way the courts handled the case.

94. Aug. 27, 1863.

95. Jacob Hunter to Mary Hunter, Dec. 11, 1862, Jan. 15, Feb. 8, 1863, Hunter Letters.

96. Mrs. E. J. Runyon to Samuel Kirkwood, July 2 [1862 or 1863], DSF.

97. In Dubuque *Times*, July 23, 1863.

98. Jacob R. Perkins, *Trails, Rails and War: The Life of General Grenville M. Dodge* (Indianapolis, 1929), pp. 94–95.

99. Dubuque *Times*, Nov. 18, 1863. The present day publisher of the DeWitt *Observer*, Bob Parrott, informed the author that the Civil War publisher of the paper, a bitter foe of local Copperheads, was burned out twice in his career. Contemporaries believed, however, that the liquor interests whom he also fought, not Copperheads, were more likely the arsonists. Letter, Parrott to author, Jan. 10, 1977.

100. C. W. Joerns and others to Samuel Kirkwood, July 3, 1863, DSF; F. E. Bissell to Kirkwood, July 20, 1863, ibid., on Republican fears. Kirkwood wrote "file" on the Bissell letter.

101. General Order No. 117, July 14, 1863, *Adjutant General's Report 1863–64*, pp. 718–19. Provost Marshal P. H. Conger was politically ambitious, but he was not alone in a city which was top-heavy with such men. The order hardly pleased the *Herald* which predicted Civil War in Dubuque county if it went into effect. *Herald*, July 23, 1863.

CHAPTER 7

1. F. A. C. Foreman to Kirkwood, Aug. 10, 1862, Governor's Department Military Correspondence (Samuel J. Kirkwood), IHD.

2. Ibid.: Petition for Disbandment of Bloomfield Border Brigade Company; F. T. Wilson and William Hill to Kirkwood, Nov. 23, 1862; Hosea Horn to Kirkwood, Nov. 25, 1862; Davis county board of supervisors Memorial to Kirkwood, Dec. 6, 1862; J. Kister to N. B. Baker, Dec. 6, 1862.

3. Hewes to Kirkwood, Dec. 30, 1862, Flick to N. B. Baker, Jan. 5, 1863, DSF.

4. *ORR*, ser. 1, vol. 22, pt. 2, pp. 104–7: Johnson to Hiatt, Feb. 5, 1863; Hiatt to Gallagher, Feb. 9, 1863; Gallagher to Maj. Gen. S. R. Curtis, Feb. 10, 1863; Hiatt to Curtis, Feb. 10, 1863.

5. DSF: Holiday to Kirkwood, with Kirkwood notation to Baker, Feb. 23, 1863; Hoxie to Kirkwood, Feb. 24, 1863; Peter Myers to John Kasson, Hoxie to Kasson, Feb. 25, 1863.

6. *ORR*, ser. 3, vol. 2, pp. 82–84: Everett to Kirkwood, Mar. 13, 1863; Kirkwood to Stanton Mar. 23, 1863; Kirkwood Proclamation, Mar. 23, 1863.

7. Burlington *Argus* in Washington *Democrat*, Aug. 4, 1863.

8. Lt. Col. E. H. Sears to Baker, Oct. 30, 1863, *Reports of the Adjutant General and Acting Quartermaster of the State of Iowa 1863–64*, p. 680; *History of Fremont County, Iowa* (Des Moines, 1881), pp. 483–84.

9. Frank L. Klement argues persuasively that the Iowa KGC existed largely in the minds of Republicans. Klement, "Rumors of Golden Circle Activity in Iowa During the Civil War Years," *AI* 37 (1965): 523–36. See also H. H. Wubben, "The Maintenance of Internal Security in Iowa, 1861–1865," *CWH* 10 (1964): 401–15.

10. Fairfield *Ledger*, Feb. 12, 1863.

11. Fleak to Kirkwood, Mar. 5, 1863, DSF.

12. James Grimes to Edwin Stanton, Apr. 20, 1863, *ORR*, ser. 3, vol. 3, pp. 124–25; see also William Swiney to Kirkwood, Mar. 11, 1863, Horace Everett to Kirkwood, Mar. 13, 1863, DSF.

13. *ORR*, ser. 3, vol. 3, pp. 66–72: Hoxie to Maj. L. D. Turner, Feb. 21, 24, 25, 1863 (with enclosures); Kirkwood to Stanton, Mar. 13, 1863.

14. "Secret Societies During the Rebellion," Civil War Miscellaneous, Governor's Records (Samuel J. Kirkwood), IHD.

15. Keokuk *Gate City* in Dubuque *Times*, May 17, 1863.

16. In Dubuque *Times*, May 7, 1863.

17. Affidavit of H. B. Rogers, Aug. 6, 1863, in Sigourney *News*, Sept. 16, 1863; *Iowa State Register* (w), Sept. 23, 1863.

18. Klement, "Golden Circle Rumors," pp. 533–35.

19. Council Bluffs *Bugle*, Mar. 4, 1863; *Herald*, Mar. 14, Apr. 12, June 7, 1863; Dubuque *Times*, May 5, 1863; Franklin T. Oldt and P. J. Quigley, eds., *History of Dubuque County, Iowa* (Chicago, n.d.) p. 301.

20. Burlington *Argus*, July 25, 1863.

21. *CM*, Oct. 22, 25, 1863.

22. Merritt to Mason, Feb. 21, 1864, Charles Mason Papers, IHD.

23. Negus to Mason, Feb. 14, 1863, ibid.

24. DSF: Deposition of George Rose before George C. Tichenor, Sept. 19, 1862; "Secret Societies during the Rebellion"; deposition of Richard Root (copy), 1st. Lt., Company K, Eighteenth Iowa Infantry before Rush Clark, Apr. 21, 1863; deposition of J. T. F. Carr (copy), before John P. Grantham, Apr. 24, 1863; *Iowa State Register* (w), Sept. 23, 1863; deposition of H. B. Rogers before Johnson county notary public, Aug. 6, 1863; E. H. Harlan Correspondence, IHD: "Statement of Melvin McGrew"; manuscript, Jan. 25, 1909, IHD: J. A. Keck, "Sons of Liberty versus Knights of the Golden Circle."

25. W. A. to My Dear Brother of the X + X Order of the KGC, Mar. 9, 1863 and Order No. 198 and Order No. 199, _?_, 1863, DSF.

26. E. A. F. to Kirkwood, Mar. 16, 1863, note by Daniels appended, ibid.

27. Frank Hickenlooper, *An Illustrated History of Monroe County, Iowa* (Albia, Iowa, 1896), pp. 145–46.

28. *History of Mahaska County, Iowa*, p. 374.

29. C. Ray Aurner, ed., *A Topical History of Cedar County, Iowa* (Chicago, 1910), 1: 335. Joyce Giaquinta, manuscript librarian at the State Historical Society of Iowa City, called my attention to the original signed roster of the Independent Riflemen and their statement of purpose. The county history

only contains the statement of purpose and the editor's explanation of the objectives behind the statement. Mrs. Giaquinta checked the delinquent tax lists for 1861 which appeared in the September, 1862, issues of the Tipton *Advertizer*. There she discovered what appears to be a correlation between the Riflemen's membership and those who paid no 1861 tax.

30. Hoxie to Dodge, May 21, July 6, July 25, 1863, G. M. Dodge Papers, IHD.

31. *Iowa State Register* (w), July 8, 1863.

32. Ibid., July 29, 1863; Fairfield *Ledger*, July 30, 1863; *Mercury* in *Des Moines News* (Keosauqua), July 31, 1863.

33. Des Moines *Statesman*, July 15, 19, 28, Oct. 24, Nov. 6, 1863, Oct. 21, 28, 1864; Washington *Democrat*, July 21, 1863; Muscatine *Courier*, Aug. 22, 1863; Burlington *Argus*, Oct. 13, Nov. 12, 1863; *Iowa State Register* (w), Nov. 18, 1863; Council Bluffs *Bugle*, June 7, 1864; *Hamilton Freeman* (Webster City), Oct. 29, 1864; Keokuk *Constitution*, June 2, 4, Oct. 24, 28, Nov. 2, 1864; *History of Mahaska County*, pp. 373-74.

34. Hoxie to Dodge, May 21, 1863, G. M. Dodge Papers; Capt. James F. Dwight, Provost-Marshal-General, St. Louis, to Hiatt, June 7, 1863, *ORR*, ser. 2, vol. 5, p. 757; Burlington *Argus*, May 21, July 9, 1863.

35. Dean to Gideon S. Bailey, June, 1863, Gideon Bailey Collection, IHD; Dean to Mahony, June 3, 1863, in Dubuque *Herald*, June 18, 1863; Dean to Mason, May 30, 1863, Mason Papers.

36. *Iowa State Register* (w), June 3, 10, 1863.

37. Thrall to Mrs. Thrall, June 6, 1863, in Mildred Throne ed., "An Iowa Doctor in Blue: The Letters of Seneca B. Thrall, 1862-1864," *IJH* 58 (1960): 155-57.

38. Miller to Baker, Oct. 1864, DSF.

39. *Iowa State Register* (w), July 15, 1863.

40. DSF: S. S. Cook to N. B. Baker, Jan. 6, 1863; Hoxie to Kirkwood, Feb. 21, 1863; Holiday and petitioners to Kirkwood, Feb. 23, 1863; *ORR*, ser. 3, vol. 3, p. 71: Henry to Kirkwood, Feb. 24, 1863, in Kirkwood to Stanton, Mar. 13, 1863.

41. Kirkwood to Stanton, Mar. 10, 1863, ibid., p. 62.

42. DSF: Fleak to Kirkwood, Feb. 27, Mar. 10, 1863; 1st Lt. W. P. Benton, Eighth Iowa, to Col. Geddes, n.d., 1863; G. A. Bass and Alvin Thayer to Kirkwood, Mar., 1863; Samuel J. Kirkwood Correspondence, IHD: E. W. Lucas to Kirkwood, Feb. 25, 1863; "Peter Wilson in the Civil War, 1863-1865," *IJH* 40 (1942): 353.

43. "To the Officers and Soldiers of the Iowa Volunteer Regiments," Mar. 23, 1863, in Benjamin F. Shambaugh, *The Messages and Proclamations of the Governors of Iowa*, 7 vols. (Iowa City, 1903), 2:514-15; *Adjutant General's Report 1863*, pp. 699-700; Hoxie to Dodge, Apr. 14, 1863, Dodge Papers.

44. W. H. F. Gurley, U.S. Attorney for Iowa, Herbert Hoxie, and others to Abraham Lincoln, *ORR*, ser. 1, vol. 27, pt. 2, p. 923; *Herald*, June 17, 1863.

45. Ibid., July 14, 1863; Muscatine *Courier*, July 23, 1863; Davenport *Democrat*, July 18, 23, 1863.

46. Pope to Henry W. Halleck, July 13, 1863, *ORR*, ser. 2, vol. 3, pp. 520-21.

47. Dubuque *Herald*, July 21, 23-24, 1863; Dubuque *Times*, July 21, 1863; Burlington *Hawk-eye*, July 23, 1863; *Fayette County Pioneer*, Aug. 3, 1863; Oldt and Quigley, *History of Dubuque County*, pp. 297-98.

48. Dubuque *Herald*, Aug. 20, 30, 1863; Oldt and Quigley, *History of Dubuque County*, p. 299.

49. Muscatine *Journal* in Fairfield *Ledger*, July 30, 1863; Dubuque *Times*, Aug. 13, 1863.

50. In *Iowa State Register* (w), Sept. 16, 1863.

51. Dennis A. Mahony, *The Four Acts of Despotism: Comprising I, the Tax Bill with All Amendments; II, the Finance Bill; III, the Conscription Act; IV, the Indemnity Bill; with Introduction and Comments* (New York, 1863), pp. 6, 23; Dubuque *Herald*, Sept. 6, 1863; Muscatine *Courier*, Sept. 26, 1863; Council Bluffs *Bugle*, Dec. 17, 1863.

52. Fairfield *Ledger*, Dec. 17, 1863; Davenport *Der Demokrat*, July 30, 1863.

53. Sept. 3, 1863.

54. James B. Fry to Kirkwood, Oct. 6, 1863, *ORR*, ser. 3, vol. 3, p. 865.

55. Dubuque *Times*, Aug. 25, 1863; Davenport *Democrat* in ibid., Aug. 27, 1863.

56. *Adjutant General's Report 1863*, pp. 725-35; *Adjutant General's Report 1864*, iv-v. The 1863 report revealed that some exemption claimants had resided in the country for as long as sixteen years.

57. *State Democratic Press,* Nov. 25, 1863; Keokuk *Constitution,* Nov. 4, 1863.

58. Oldt and Quigley, *History of Dubuque County,* p. 299; Keokuk *Gate City* (w), Aug. 12, 1863; Dubuque *Herald,* Feb. 18, 1863.

59. Dubuque *Herald,* Oct. 11, 1863; Keokuk *Gate City* (w), Aug. 12, 1863; *Iowa State Register* (w), Aug. 19, 1863.

60. Joe H. Smith, *History of Harrison County, Iowa* (Des Moines, 1883), p. 333.

61. Davenport *Democrat,* Aug. 8, 1862; *Times,* July 12, 1862; *Republican,* May 7, 1862; Davenport *Der Demokrat,* Aug. 14, 1862.

62. Brainerd to Clark, Aug. 8, 1862, Military Letterbook (Kirkwood), p. 253; Kirkwood to Harriet N. Kellogg, Mar. 28, 1862, ibid., 239–40; Kirkwood to Halleck, Aug. 5, 1862, in V. Jacque Voegeli, *Free But Not Equal: The Midwest and the Negro during the Civil War* (Chicago, 1967), p. 102; Davenport *Democrat,* Jan. 20, 1862.

63. Mildred Throne, ed., *Diary of Cyrus F. Boyd, Fifteenth Iowa Infantry, 1861–1863* (Millwood, N.Y., 1977), Aug. 24, 1862, Feb. 9, 1863, pp. 118–19. Boyd sympathized with blacks and reported instances of their being meanly treated by Iowa soldiers. Soldier letter in *North Iowa Times* (McGregor), Feb. 4, 1863; Davenport *Democrat,* Feb. 28, 1863; Washington *Democrat,* Mar. 16, 1863.

64. Keokuk *Gate City* (w), June 17, 1863; *Iowa State Register* (d), June 23, 1863; Council Bluffs *Nonpareil,* July 25, 1863.

65. *ORR,* Ser. 3, vol. 3, pp. 563, 576, 993, 1113: Kirkwood to Stanton, July 24, 1863; C. W. Foster, Ass't Adj. Gen. (U.S.) to Kirkwood, July 27, 1863; Maj. Gen. J. M. Schofield and O. D. Green to Kirkwood, Nov. 4, 1863; C. W. Foster to Stanton, Oct. 31, 1863; Military Letterbook (Kirkwood): N. H. Brainered, to C. C. Nourse, Aug. 19, 1863; John E. Briggs, "The Enlistment of Iowa Troops during the Civil War," *IJHP* 15 (1917): 363; Benjamin F. Gue, *History of Iowa from the Earliest Times to the Beginning of the Twentieth Century,* 4 vols. (New York, 1903), pp. 366–67; G. Galin Berrier, "The Negro Suffrage Issue in Iowa—1865-1868," *AI* 39 (1968): 243.

66. Aug. 29, 1863; *Herald,* Oct. 30, 1863.

67. Only a few examples of many are the following papers, each listed with one or more dates containing derogatory news or comment about black troops: Muscatine *Courier* (d), Aug. 12, 1863; and (w), Dec. 10, 1863; Dubuque *Herald,* Sept. 12, Dec. 5, 1863; *Fayette County Pioneer,* Dec. 14, 1863, May 9, 1864; Des Moines *Statesman,* Dec. 23, 1863, Jan. 13, Mar. 13, May 13, 1864.

68. *Iowa State Register* (w), Dec. 2, 1863; Fairfield *Ledger,* Feb. 11, 1864; Keokuk *Gate City* (w), Mar. 8, 1864; Dubuque *Times,* June 16, 1864; Muscatine *Journal* in Burlington *Hawk-eye,* *Hawk-eye* editorial agreement, June 22, 1864.

69. Keokuk *Constitution,* Oct. 19, 1864.

70. *CM,* Feb. 25, 1865.

71. *Herald,* Mar. 19–20, 22, June 18, 1863; Davenport *Democrat,* Aug. 27, 1863.

72. Almost every Iowa Democratic paper of 1863 will serve to document this clear rise in anti-black news and editorial opinion. Besides the *Herald,* John Gharkey in the *Fayette County Pioneer* and Lysander Babbitt in the Council Bluffs *Bugle* were especially strident. For specific examples among these three see the *Pioneer,* Feb. 23, Mar. 16, 1863; *Bugle,* Feb. 25, 1863; *Herald,* Feb. 12, Mar. 10, 13, June 12, Aug. 14, 22, 25, Sept. 6–9, 1863; also Des Moines *Statesman,* July 9, 1863; Davenport *Democrat,* Mar. 20, 1863. The *Times's* thrusts at the *Herald's* coverage are in Apr. 21, May 6, 1863, issues.

73. Keokuk *Constitution,* especially Sept. and Oct., 1863. See specifically, Sept. 10, Dec. 8, 1863.

74. Leola Bergmann, *The Negro in Iowa* (Iowa City, [1969]), pp. 28–30; *Iowa State Register* (w), Jan. 6, 21, Feb. 4, 11, 1863; Burlington *Argus,* Feb. 12, 1863; Fairfield *Ledger,* Feb. 12, 1863.

75. *Iowa State Register* (w), Feb. 25, 1863; Horn to Baker, Mar. 2, 1863, in *Adjutant General's Report 1863,* pp. 677–78.

76. Fairfield *Ledger,* Feb. 25, 1863; Dubuque *Herald,* Mar. 14, 1863; *State Democratic Press,* Apr. 4, 1863.

77. *Herald,* Mar. 25, Apr. 7 (from the Iowa City *Republican*), May 19, 28, July 15, 1863.

78. *Iowa State Register* (w), Aug. 5, 1863.

79. Davenport *Democrat,* July 29, 1863.

80. Muscatine *Courier,* May 13, 15, 18, 1863.

81. "Peter Wilson in the Civil War," p. 360; *Iowa State Register* (w), Aug. 5, 1863; Fairfield *Ledger,* Mar. 26, 1863; Burlington *Hawk-eye,* May 16, 1863; *Nonpareil,* Aug. 15, 1863, pass.

82. Mount Pleasant *Home Journal,* June 13, Dec. 26, 1863, Feb. 6, 1864; *Iowa State Register* in Dubuque *Times,* Oct. 10, 1863.

83. Davenport *Democrat*, Mar. 11, 1864.

84. Paul W. Gates, *Agriculture and the Civil War* (New York, 1965), p. 184; *Reports of the Iowa State Agricultural Society 1863*, pp. 5–6; *Agricultural Report 1864*, p. 15; Norman V. Strand, "Prices of Iowa Farm Products, 1851–1940," *Iowa State College Research Bulletin* 303 (1942): 960.

85. June 20, Sept. 23, 1863.

86. Burlington *Hawk-eye*, Jan. 14, July 30, Nov. 7, 1863; George A. Boeck, "An Early Iowa Community: Aspects of Economic, Social and Political Developments in Burlington, Iowa, 1833–1866" (Ph.D. diss., University of Iowa, 1961), pp. 305, 312, 314. Hog raisers in 10 of the county's 12 townships had lost 39,478 hogs to hog cholera the previous year, 1862. *Hawk-eye*, June 7, 1863; John F. Henry, Jr., to Mason, Jan. 21, 1863, Mason Papers.

87. Keokuk *Gate City* (w), Jan. 14, Mar. 11, Oct. 7, Nov. 18, 24, 1863; Keokuk *Constitution*, Feb. 16, 1863; Faye E. Harris, "A Frontier Community: The Economic, Social and Political Development of Keokuk, Iowa from 1820 to 1866" (Ph.D. diss., University of Iowa, 1965), pp. 369–70.

88. Davenport *Democrat*, Mar. 3, Aug. 31, Sept. 25, Oct. 1, 13, 1863; Dubuque *Times*, June 2, 1863; Mar. 3, 1863.

89. *Herald*, Jan. 31, Mar. 14, 1863; Oldt and Quigley, *History of Dubuque County*, p. 146.

90. *Herald*, Oct. 9, 23, 1863.

91. Ibid., Dec. 8, 1863.

92. Ibid., Apr. 22, 1863.

93. Oct. 30, 1863; May 9, 1863.

94. Dec. 1, 1863.

95. Nov. 10, 1863.

96. *Bugle*, Apr. 8, 1863; *Nonpareil*, June 20, 1863.

97. *State Democratic Press*, Apr. 18, 25, 1863.

98. Fairfield *Ledger*, Dec. 11, 1862.

99. Dubuque *Herald*, Dec. 20, 1862; Feb. 14, 21, 28, Mar. 10, 1863.

100. In Burlington *Hawk-eye*, Feb. 10, 1863; Fairfield *Ledger*, Apr. 23, 1863.

101. Davenport *Democrat*, Mar. 20, 1863; *Iowa Homestead*, Jan. 8, Feb. 19, 1863; Keokuk *Constitution*, Feb. 17, 1863; Washington *Democrat*, May 12, 1863; Des Moines *Statesman*, Oct. 31, Nov. 8, Dec. 29, 1863.

102. Keokuk *Gate City* (w), Jan. 28, 1863; Burlington *Hawk-eye*, Mar. 4, 1863.

103. Burlington *Hawk-eye*, Feb. 22, May 15, 1863, Des Moines *Statesman*, Oct. 11, 1863; Dubuque *Times*, Dubuque *Herald*, Dec. 11, 1863.

104. Keokuk *Constitution*, Jan. 13, 1863; Dubuque *Times*, Feb. 18, 1863; Dubuque *Herald*, Jan. 30, Feb. 18, 22, Mar. 12, 19, 1863.

105. *Herald*, Apr. 2–3, 1863; *Times*, Apr. 3, 1863.

106. Dubuque *Times*, May 5, 1863.

107. July 16, 1863.

108. Davenport *Democrat*, Mar. 25, July 13, 1863; Muscatine *Courier*, July 13, 1863.

109. *Iowa State Register* (w), Nov. 11, 1863; *Statesman*, Jan. 20, 23, 1864.

110. In Keokuk *Gate City* (w), Apr. 15, 1863, and the Montrose incident is in the same issue; Oskaloosa *Herald* in *Iowa State Register* (w), July 8, 1863. See reports on Democratic infighting in Dubuque *Times*, Mar. 7, 1863; Burlington *Hawk-eye*, Mar. 20, 1863; Sioux City *Register*, Mar. 21, 1863; Muscatine *Journal* in *Gate City* (w), Apr. 22, 1863; Council Bluffs *Bugle* in Fairfield *Ledger*, Apr. 2, 1863; C. C. Cole to Kirkwood, Apr. 22, 1863, Kirkwood Correspondence.

111. July 2, 1863.

112. Dubuque *Herald*, July 12, 1863; Davenport *Democrat*, July 14, 1863; Keokuk *Constitution*, Sept. 3, Oct. 2, 1863.

113. Clinton *Herald*, Sioux City *Register*, Apr. 15, 1863; Burlington *Hawk-eye*, Aug. 6, 1863.

114. The platform and complete convention proceedings are printed in the Davenport *Democrat*, July 14, 1863; see also *Iowa State Register* (w), July 15, 1863; Keokuk *Constitution*, Sept. 3, 1863; Dubuque *Herald*, July 15, 1863. Fisher's letter of withdrawal is in the *Democrat* of July 28, and Aug. 3, 1863. The complete story of the committee meeting at which Byington and Plum found themselves outmaneuvered is in Plum to Laurel Summers, Aug. 11, 1863, Summers Papers, IHD.

115. Kirkwood to Dr. Fred Lloyd, Sept. 22, 1863, Military Letterbook (Kirkwood); M. M. Crocker to G. M. Dodge, July 2, 21, Aug. 27, 1863; Herbert Hoxie to Dodge, July 6, 1863, G. M. Dodge Papers; *Hawk-eye*, Aug. 20, 1863.

116. Tuttle's letter of acceptance, "To the People of Iowa," Aug. 13, 1863, is in the Davenport *Democrat*, Aug. 20, 1863; Chicago *Evening Journal* in Charles City *Intelligencer*, Sept. 3, 1863.

117. Gue, *History of Iowa*, 2: 94–96; *Iowa State Register* (w), Mar. 4, 1862.

118. "Peter Wilson in the Civil War," p. 393; Carpenter to Emmett Carpenter, Sept. 13, 1863, Cyrus C. Carpenter Papers, IHS.
119. Davenport *Democrat,* July 15, 1863; *Argus,* Oct. 8, 1863; Dubuque *Herald,* July 15, 1863; Burlington *Hawk-eye* in *Cedar Valley Times* (Cedar Rapids), Sept. 17, 1863.
120. Dubuque *Times,* Aug. 28, 30, Oct. 4, 1863.
121. Davenport *Der Demokrat,* Sept. 25, 1863; Davenport *Democrat,* Sept. 25-26, 1863; Keokuk *Constitution,* Sept. 26, 1863; Muscatine *Courier,* Oct. 8, 1863; *Iowa State Register* (w), Oct. 28, 1863; *Hawk-eye* (w), Oct. 17, 24, 1863.
122. Muscatine *Courier,* Oct. 14 (d), *Courier* (w), Oct. 29, 1863; Keokuk *Constitution,* Oct. 29, 1863.
123. Keokuk *Constitution,* Oct. 14, 1863; Des Moines *Statesman,* Oct. 22, 1863; *Fayette County Pioneer,* Oct. 27, 1863; Nannie M. Tilley ed., *Federals on the Frontier: the Diary of Benjamin F. McIntyre, 1862-1864* (Austin, Tex., 1963), p. 234 *n* 129; Herbert Hoxie to G. M. Dodge, Aug. 13, 1863, in Stanley P. Hirshon, *Grenville M. Dodge: Soldier, Politican, Railroad Pioneer* (Bloomington, Ind., 1967), p. 78; Throne, "Iowa Doctor in Blue," 171-72; *Iowa State Register* (w), Dec. 9, 1863.
124. William M. Stone to Kirkwood, n.d., 1863, Samuel J. Kirkwood Box, IHD; Iowa Election Records (Iowa City, Iowa: Univ. Microfilms, 1839-1890).
125. Keokuk *Constitution,* Oct. 19, Nov. 2, 1863.
126. Dubuque *Herald,* Oct. 21, 1863.
127. *Iowa State Register* (w), Apr. 13, 1864; Herbert G. Gutman, *The Black Family in Slavery and Freedom, 1750-1925* (New York, 1976), pp. 23-24; Burlington *Hawk-eye,* May 5, 1864.

CHAPTER 8

1. Negus to Mason, Nov. 9, 1863, Mason Papers, IHD.
2. The Democratic senators were: John Jennings and F. M. Knoll, Dubuque; George Gray, Allamakee; Fred Hesser, Lee. The Democratic representatives were: John Christoph, Daniel Cort, D. O'Brien, and B. B. Richards, Dubuque; E. A. Cary, Van Buren; Charles Paul, Allamakee.
3. Stone's First Inaugural Address is in Benjamin F. Shambaugh, *The Messages and Proclamations of the Governors of Iowa,* 7 vols. (Iowa City, 1903), 3: 13-14.
4. Iowa, General Assembly, House, *Journal,* 1864, pp. 590-91; Iowa, General Assembly, Senate, *Journal,* 1864, pp. 402-4.
5. *Senate Journal,* 1864, pp. 176, 520, 570; *House Journal,* 1864, pp. 86-87, 184-85, 649-50.
6. *House Journal,* 1864, pp. 222-23.
7. *Senate Journal,* 1864, 248-49, 484; *House Journal,* 1864, p. 183.
8. *House Journal,* 1864, p. 44. Stone wanted the State Sanitary Commission to take responsibility for disbursing the funds in order to insure that "disloyal" boards could not subvert the law's intent. The legislature, after sharp debate, left the disbursement power with the county boards. See especially *Senate Journal,* 1864, pp. 492-94.
9. *Fairfield Ledger,* Feb. 4, 1864; *Iowa State Register* (w), Feb. 3, 1864.
10. E. F. Esteb to N. B. Baker, n.d., 1863, DSF; Boonesboro *Times* in *Iowa State Register* (w), Aug. 19, 1863.
11. *Times,* Aug. 17, 1862; *Herald,* June 30, Sept. 23, 1863.
12. The controversy over relief for soldiers and their families was an intermittent one throughout the war and was well covered in both the *Times* and *Herald.* See *Times,* Oct. 23-24, 27, 1863; *Herald,* Oct. 23, 1863, Jan. 9, 1864; Franklin T. Oldt and P. J. Quigley, *History of Dubuque County, Iowa* (Chicago, n.d.), pp. 301, 305, 313, 412.
13. Ivan L. Pollock, "State Finances in Iowa During the Civil War," *IJHP* 16 (1918): 88.
14. *Gate City* (w), Jan. 5, 1864; *Constitution,* Mar. 3, 1864; Clinton *Herald* in Dubuque *Times,* Jan. 28, 1864; A. C. Dodge to Charles Mason, Jan. 28, 1864, Charles Mason Papers, IHD; Burlington *Hawk-eye* (w), Apr. 2, 1864, in George A. Boeck, "An Early Iowa Community: Aspects of Economic, Social and Political Development in Burlington, Iowa, 1833-1866 (Ph.D. diss., University of Iowa, 1961), p. 313. Dodge saw the prosperity in Burlington but said the citizens felt a great storm lay ahead. In April there was noticeable unemployment as well as high real estate prices.
15. *Bugle,* Jan. 14, 1864; *Nonpareil,* Feb. 6, 1864; *Bugle* in Burlington *Hawk-eye,* May 31, 1864.
16. *Iowa Homestead,* Jan. 13, 1864; *Times,* Mar. 2, Sept. 2, 1864. The average price farmers received for butter in Iowa in 1864 was 22¢ a pound. Norman V. Strand, "Prices of Farm Products in Iowa, 1851-1940," *Iowa State College Research Bulletin,* No. 303 (1952): 934-37.

17. Apr. 28, May 6, 1864.

18. *Iowa State Register* (w), Feb. 24, 1864.

19. Keokuk *Gate City* (w), Feb. 3, 1864; Dubuque *Herald,* Feb. 10, 16, 1864.

20. Dubuque *Times,* Feb. 23, Aug. 1, 1864; *Herald,* May 14, June 4, 29, July 14, 1864. Wood dealers took advantage of the times also. The *Herald* (Apr. 1) believed they needed competition from upriver dealers. A price of $10–$12 a cord was "exorbitant."

21. Keokuk *Constitution,* May 19, 1864; Davenport *Democrat,* May 27, 1864; *Iowa State Register* in Burlington *Hawk-eye,* July 23, 1864; *Register* (w), July 27, 1864.

22. *Hawk-eye,* July 16, 1864; *Star* in *Hawk-eye,* July 4, 1864; Davenport *Democrat,* Sept. 12, 1864. See the story on farmer A. C. Felton, living 15 miles west of Davenport, who netted $7,905 (gross income $10,111) for 1863 by intensively farming 62 acres. Keokuk *Constitution,* July 8, 1864; *Hawk-eye,* July 9, 1864.

23. Davenport *Democrat,* July 9, 11–13, 1864; Lyons *Mirror,* July 2, in Burlington *Hawk-eye,* July 9, 1864; *Hawk-eye,* July 14, 1864.

24. *Gate City* (w), Aug. 17, 1864; Burlington *Hawk-eye,* Oct. 25, 1864; Davenport *Democrat,* Nov. 16, 19, 1864.

25. Strand, "Iowa Farm Prices," pp. 934–37. Strand has no monthly figures for hog prices for the months February through September. But they were $5.52, $7, $7.42, and $9 for January, October, November, and December respectively. Ibid., p. 959.

26. *Iowa State Register* (w), June 29, 1864; Aug. 24, 1864; Davenport *Democrat,* Dec. 10, 1864.

27. *Times,* July 2, 1864; Dubuque *Herald,* Dec. 3, 1864.

28. Council Bluffs *Nonpareil,* Mar. 19, 1864.

29. Dubuque *Herald,* June 19, 1864; *Report of the Iowa State Agricultural Society, 1864,* pp. 318, 321, 346–47, 349, 364, 372.

30. Ibid., pp. 161–62; also 222–23.

31. *CM,* Dec. 16, 1864.

32. Keokuk *Gate City* (w), Apr. 13, 1864.

33. *Democrat,* Mar. 9, June 2, 1864; Burlington *Hawk-eye,* July 18, 1864.

34. In Burlington *Hawk-eye,* July 28, Aug. 6, 1864; Davenport *Democrat,* July 27, 1864.

35. *Herald,* Apr. 13, July 12, Aug. 20, 1864; *Times,* July 21, 28, Aug. 12, 1864.

36. Burlington *Hawk-eye,* Nov. 15, 1864.

37. Ibid., Feb. 5, Mar. 30, May 19, 1864; *Journal* in *Times,* May 11, 1864; *Times,* May 12, 24, July 28, 1864; Davenport *Democrat,* Sept. 1, 1864. Governor Stone's call for the "hundred-days" regiments is in the Burlington *Hawk-eye,* Apr. 26, 1864.

38. Dubuque *Times* in Davenport *Democrat,* Sept. 1, 1864.

39. Davenport *Democrat,* Apr. 9, May 2, 18, 1864; Keokuk *Constitution,* June 30, 1864; Council Bluffs *Bugle,* Oct. 27, 1864. Charles Mason converted $5,000 of his assets to gold during the first two years of the war. Then, anticipating a drop, not a rise, he sold $3,500 of it. When the price rose, he found that his speculation had cost him $900. *CM,* May 30, 1864; Willard I. Toussaint, "Biography of a Businessman: Charles Mason, 1804–1882 (Ph.D. diss., University of Iowa, 1963), p. 358.

40. Keokuk *Constitution,* Apr. 4, 1864; Dubuque *Herald,* Oct. 1, 1864; *State Democratic Press,* Oct. 19, 1864. On freight rates see Paul W. Gates, *Agriculture and the Civil War* (New York, 1965), pp. 245–46.

41. *The Conservative* (Independence), Dec. 6, 1864; Dubuque *Herald,* Dec. 1, 6, 10, 1864, Feb. 3, 1865.

42. *CM,* Jan. 3, 1864; Feb. 25, 1864, in *State Democratic Press,* Mar. 16, 1864. Republican papers cited the same experiences of blacks in freedom that Mason cited, but the conclusions were entirely different. See, for example, *Waterloo Courier,* Mar. 3, 1864.

43. Aug. 2, 1864.

44. Aug. 3, 14, 1864.

45. Burlington *Hawk-eye,* Oct. 26, 31, 1864; Keokuk *Constitution,* June 24, 1864.

46. *State Democratic Press,* Mar. 9, 1864; Keokuk *Gate City* (w), Mar. 16, 1864; Fairfield *Ledger,* Mar. 31, 1864; Council Bluffs *Nonpareil,* Apr. 9, 1864; Des Moines *Statesman* in *Gate City* (w), and *Gate City* comment, Apr. 27, 1864; *Herald,* May 21, 1864; Keokuk *Constitution,* Jan. 6, July 10, Aug. 14, 16–17, Sept. 3, 1864.

47. *Herald,* Feb. 19–20, June 5, 1864.

48. *Constitution,* Feb. 11, Oct. 8, 1864; *Times,* May 18, 1864; *Journal* in *Hawk-eye,* May 2, 1864.

49. Dubuque *Times,* Mar. 11, 1864.

50. *Democrat,* Dec. 26, 1863, Jan. 4-5, Mar. 26, Apr. 6, July 5, Sept. 1, Nov. 11, 1864; *Iowa State Register* in Keokuk *Gate City* (w), July 13, 1864.

51. Muscatine *Journal,* May 28, 1864; *Journal* in Davenport *Democrat,* June 25,1864.

52. *Herald,* May 7, 1864; *Fayette County Pioneer* in Dubuque *Times,* May 1, 1864. The *Times* described Gharkey's outburst as "cruel and contemptible prejudice." The paper also reported the La Crosse (Wis.) *Democrat*'s response: that no one could blame the rebels for doing what they did to black troops; that all white men put in their position would do the same.

53. Muscatine *Courier,* Dec. 10, 1863, in David L. Lendt, *Demise of the Democracy: the Copperhead Press in Iowa* (Ames, Ia., 1973), p. 89; Dubuque *Herald,* Sept. 7, 25, 1864; Davenport *Democrat,* Sept. 22, 1864.

54. Dubuque *Herald,* Aug. 26, 1864.

55. Keokuk *Constitution,* Nov. 18, 30, 1864.

56. Burlington *Hawk-eye,* July 16, 1864.

57. In Keokuk *Gate City* (w), July 20, 1864.

58. Apr. 23, May 4, 1864.

59. *Constitution,* July 15, 25, 1864.

60. In Lendt, *Demise of the Democracy,* p. 87; Dubuque *Herald,* Nov. 20, 1863.

61. Davenport *Democrat,* May 9, 1864.

62. *Reports of the Adjutant General and Acting Quartermaster of the State of Iowa, 1864,* pp. 852-53; Curtis to Stone, *ORR,* ser. 1, vol. 34, pt. 2, p. 480.

63. Mildred Throne, "Iowa Farm Letters, 1856-1865," *IJH* 58 (1960): 87; *Gate City* (w), May 25, 1864; Davenport *Democrat,* Dec. 11, 1863.

64. Eugene Murdoch, *One Million Men: The Civil War Draft in the North* (Madison, Wis., 1971), p. 352.

65. *Nonpareil,* Nov. 21, 1863; *Bugle,* Dec. 10, 1863; *Statesman,* Dec. 9, 21, 1863.

66. *History of Fremont County, Iowa* (Des Moines, 1881), pp. 479-80; Waterloo *Courier,* Jan. 20, 1864.

67. *Gate City* (w), Feb. 10, 1864; *Constitution,* Feb. 23, 1864.

68. Mar. 16, 1864.

69. *Constitution,* Sept. 6, Oct. 5, 19, 1864; Muscatine *Journal* in *Constitution,* Oct. 2, 1864.

70. *Times,* Sept. 22-23, 26, 1864; *Herald,* Sept. 23, 27, Oct. 4, 14, 1864; Oldt and Quigley, *History of Dubuque County,* pp. 309-13.

71. James W. Ellis, *History of Jackson County, Iowa,* 2 vols. (Chicago, 1910), 1: 143; Charles J. Fulton, ed., *History of Jefferson County, Iowa,* 2 vols. (Chicago, 1914), 1: 371.

72. Oct. 19, 26, 1864.

73. *Bugle,* Nov. 10, 17, 24, 1864; Thomas Clagett sympathized with Babbitt in Keokuk *Constitution,* Nov. 24, 1864.

74. Jesse Macy to family, Oct. 5, 1864, Macy Letters, IHS.

75. Nov. 3, 1864; *Biographical and Historical Memoirs of Story County* (1890), p. 168.

76. Dodge to Dodge, Dec. 27, 1863, in Stanley P. Hirshon, *G. M. Dodge: Soldier, Politican, Railroad Pioneer* (Bloomington, Ind., 1967) p.85.

77. "Proclamation to the People of Iowa," by Governor Stone, written by N. B. Baker, state adjutant general, Jan. 23, 1865, *ORR,* ser. 3, vol. 4, pp. 1072-73.

78. Davenport *Democrat,* Jan. 20, 1864.

79. *Adjutant General's Report 1864,* pp. 1411-15; *History of Mahaska County, Iowa* (1878), pp. 378-79; *History of Marion County, Iowa* (Des Moines, 1881), p. 462; Charles E. Payne, *Josiah Bushnell Grinnell* (Iowa City, 1938), pp. 172-73; Muscatine *Courier* in Burlington *Argus,* Nov. 3, 1864; Lendt, *Demise of the Democracy,* pp. 103-4.

80. DSF: George B. Wheeler to N. B. Baker, Aug. 15, 1864; George Kinck to William Stone, Aug. 20, 1864; John E. Douglas to Baker, Aug. 27, 1864; William C. Howard to Baker, Sept. 6, 1864.

81. F. T. Townsend to Baker, Aug. 25, 1864, ibid.

82. Ibid.; "A strictly loyalist" to Baker, Aug. 20, 1864; Springer to Baker, July 27, 1864.

83. Brainerd to Baker in Richard L. Hoxie Collection, Hoxie-Banbury Papers, Civil War Materials, IHS.

84. *History of Audubon County, Iowa* (Indianapolis, Ind., n.d.) pp. 168-72.

85. In Dubuque *Herald,* Sept. 1, 1864. The original oath is in the Davenport *Democrat,* Aug. 27, 1864; the new oath is in the Sept. 16, *Democrat.* Stone to Baker, Sept. 12, 1864, in *Adjutant General's Report 1864,* pp. 884-885; DSF: Stephen Feather to Baker, Aug. [?] 1864; R. B. Tuttle to Baker, Sept. 9, 1864; W. B. Davis to Baker, Oct. 23, 1864. Stone claimed that Democrats in the southern three tiers of counties were extremely partisan in organizing units. He also said one elected

captain had been dishonorably discharged from the army for "utterances of treasonable sentiments, and for other conduct unbecoming to an officer and gentleman. . . ." Another, he said, had been a Missouri guerilla.

86. See note by Baker on back of letter from N. E. Rice, Aug. 27, 1864, DSF. "Copperhead stuff" is what Baker wrote on this rambling letter which repeated hearsay and charged that certain individuals were disloyal.

87. Stone to Baker, Sept. 12, 1864, in *Adjutant General's Report 1864*, pp. 883–86; DSF: Stone to Col. [name illegible] Jan. 31, 1865; Stone to Baker, Aug. 12, 1864.

88. R. G. Orwig (Stone's secretary), to A. H. Hemenway, Apr. 9, 1864, Governor's letterbook (William M. Stone), IHD, p. 319; see also pp. 181, 189, 281, 288–90, 312, 320, 365–66, 536, 637, 664.

89. Anderson to Stone, Feb. 9, 1864, DSF; North to Anderson, Feb. 14, 1864, Governor's Letterbook (Stone), pp. 15, 89.

90. Keokuk *Constitution*, Feb. 10, 1864.

91. Shambaugh, *Messages and Proclamations*, 3:216–18; *Adjutant General's Report 1864*, pp. 872.

92. General Orders No. 25 to Southern Border Brigade, *Adjutant General's Report 1864*, pp. 872–73.

93. Glenn to Baker, Oct. 8, 1864, DSF.

94. Des Moines *Statesman*, Nov. 12, 1864; Council Bluffs *Bugle*, June 8, 1865.

95. *Adjutant General's Report 1864*, pp. 1419–28; Benjamin J. Gue, *History of Iowa from the Earliest Times to the Beginning of the Twentieth Century*, 4 vols. (New York, 1903), 2: 93–94; *History of Davis County, Iowa* (Des Moines, 1882), pp. 556–63.

96. *ORR*, ser. 1, vol. 41, pt. 4, pp. 245, 260, 303–4, 396–97, 422–23; Hiatt to Pope, Oct. 17, 1864; Ten Broeck to Maj. J. F. Milne, Oct. 25, 1864; Smith to Milne, Oct. 26; William Stone to Pope, Nov. 1, 1864; Pope to Smith, Nov. 3, 1864. Other communications in the same source on this subject are on pp. 124–25, 407, 895.

97. Keokuk *Constitution*, Feb. 16, 1864; Col. Harry J. B. Cummings to Mrs. Cummings, Apr. 29, 1864, Harry J. B. Cummings Papers, IHD; Des Moines *Statesman* in June 6, 1864, Dubuque *Herald*; Burlington *Argus*, May 19, 1864.

98. Des Moines *Statesman*, Apr. 12, 17, 29, 1864.

99. William H. Francis to Baker [probably Feb.], 1865, DSF.

100. *Herald*, Mar. 15, 19, 1864.

101. Ibid., Mar. 1, June 18–19, 24, Dec. 4, 1864, Jan. 14, 1865; *Times*, Mar. 2, July 9, 16, 1864; *Iowa State Register* (w), Sept. 21, 1864.

102. *Hawk-eye*, Jan. 1, 1864; *Constitution*, Jan. 5, 1864; *Argus*, Apr. 21, 1864.

103. *Courier* in Davenport *Democrat*, Apr. 29, 1864; Iowa City *Republican*, Apr. 27, 1864; Dubuque *Herald*, May 1, 1864.

104. *Bugle*, May 12, 19, June 2, 1864; *Nonpareil*, Apr. 18, 1864.

105. Nov. 23, 1864, in Lendt, *Demise of the Democracy*, p. 15.

106. Des Moines *Statesman* in Davenport *Democrat*, Nov. 30, 1864; Burlington *Hawk-eye*, Dec. 5, 1864.

107. *Hawk-eye*, Mar. 21, 1864; Dubuque *Times*, Mar. 31, 1864; Council Bluffs *Nonpareil*, June 10, 1865. Foreman pulled his son out of school after the school board voted to admit an octaroon to young Foreman's classroom. Freed from schooling, the Foreman son demonstrated either his pleasure or displeasure by throwing rocks at the schoolhouse. The principal hauled him inside and administered a spanking. Foreman senior then assaulted the principal. When the *Nonpareil* writer reported what had happened, Foreman assaulted him also.

108. Keokuk *Constitution*, Mar. 1, 1864. Later in the year Clagett won a district court suit against Charles Ball, former hospital commander, "for trespass on plaintiff's property," done on Ball's orders. Ball paid the cost of the suit, plaintiff's attorney fees, and costs for damages done to Clagett's property. Clagett gave up a claim for exemplary damages. This case arose out of some 1863 incident, although it was not clearly identified in the newpaper coverage as being related to the most destructive act against the *Constitution*, that of January, 1863. Ibid., Dec. 9, 1864; Davenport *Democrat*, Dec. 14, 1864.

109. Fairfield *Ledger*, Feb. 11, 1864; Keokuk *Constitution*, Feb. 20, 1864; Council Bluffs *Nonpareil*, Apr, 16, 1864. As early as the summer of 1862, soldiers from Company E had written the *Ledger* excoriating the *Constituion and Union*. One promised that the troops would burn the paper and invite Sheward to leave the state when they returned. *Ledger*, Aug. 14, 1862.

110. Burlington *Hawk-eye*, Apr. 16, 22, 1864; *History of Mahaska County*, pp. 377–78. The *Hawk-eye* had no use for Wheelock but opposed violence to his paper.

111. Dec. 28, 1864.
112. June 6, 1864.
113. *Democrat*, Dec. 27, 1864.
114. Nov. 29, 1864.
115. H. H. Wubben, "Copperhead Charles Mason: A Question of Loyalty," *CWH* (1978): 46–65; *CM*, July 31, 1864; see Dubuque *Times*, Dec. 2, 1864, for a perceptive, if also astringent, commentary on Mason's "X" letters.
116. *Times*, July 22, 1864.
117. Ibid., Oct. 9, 1864.
118. *Herald*, Feb. 4, 1865; Davenport *Gazette*, Jan. 12, 1865.
119. Jane Thompson to William Thompson, Mar. 14, 1864, Thompson Papers, IHD; Edwin C. Bearss, "Civil War Letters of Major William Thompson," *AI* 36 (1966): 432–33.
120. Keokuk *Constitution*, Feb. 6, 1864.
121. Baugh to Laurel Summers, July 20, 1864, Summers Papers; N. Sales to Charles Mason, Aug. 16, 1864, Mason Papers.
122. Keokuk *Constitution*, Feb. 6, 1864.
123. Byington's views are well expressed in the resolutions adopted at the peace rally he orchestrated at Iowa City on August 24. Gue, *History of Iowa*, 2: 123; *History of Cass County, Iowa* (Springfield, Ill., 1884), pp. 172–73. This county history is a better source of party platforms of this era than most Iowa newspapers. See also Byington's prerally platform statement included in his call in Dubuque *Herald*, July 28, 1864, *Hamilton Freeman*, July 23, 1864.
124. Durham to Summers, Apr. 25, 1864, Summers Papers; Council Bluffs *Bugle*, Aug. 18, 1864.
125. Burlington *Argus*, Mar. 31, 1864; Keokuk *Constitution*, Apr. 3, 1864; Sioux City *Register*, Apr. 23, 1864.
126. Dubuque *Herald*, Keokuk *Constitution*, June 20, 1864; *Iowa State Register* (w), June 29, 1864. E. B. Bolens of the Washington *Democrat*, an alternate to the national convention, thought the Byington forces made too much out of nothing. Most of the delegates and alternates, he thought, were basically peace men. How pure they were, he inferred, was quibbling. Washington *Democrat*, July 14, 1864.
127. Muscatine *Courier*, July 11, 1864; Burlington *Argus*, Council Bluffs *Bugle*, July 21, 1864; Gue, *History of Iowa*, 2: 123.
128. Circular, July 28, 1864, announcing Dubuque Peace Rally, Mason Papers; Dubuque *Herald*, Aug. 4, 26, 1864; Oldt and Quigley, *History of Dubuque County*, p. 361.
129. *The Chicago Copperhead Convention* (Washington, D.C., 1864), p. 12; Gue, *History of Iowa*, 2: 119. For preconvention opposition to McClellan see *Iowa State Register* (w), June 29, 1864; Samuel W. Durham, Apr. 8, 1864, N. B. Taylor, June 22, 1864, to Laurel Summers, Summers Papers; Dennis Mahony to Charles Mason, Jan. 16, Aug. 23, 1864, Mason Papers. On Mason's interest in Grant see Silas Hudson to Mason, Dec. 16, 1863, ibid. Mahony finally wrote that he would back McClellan, Mahony to Mason, Sept. 20, 1864, ibid. Babbitt grudgingly caved in late in the campaign, Council Bluffs *Bugle*, Sept. 22, 1864, Davenport *Democrat*, Nov. 3, 1864.
130. Jones to Summers, Oct. 9, 1864, Summers Papers. Byington's actions brought scorn from David Richardson (Davenport *Democrat*, Sept. 29, 1864), and William Merritt (Des Moines *Statesman*, Oct. 4, 1864). Nor was John Irish of the *State Democratic Press* (Oct. 12, 1864), in Iowa City pleased, especially since Byington started a rival newspaper called the *Olive Branch*.
131. Davenport *Democrat*, Sept. 1, 1864.
132. Sales to Laurel Summers, Oct. 6, 1864, Plum to Summers, same date, Summers Papers.
133. *CM*, Nov. 2, 1864.
134. Hoxie to Dodge, July 25, 1864, G. M. Dodge Papers; Bartlett to Summers, Oct. 30, 1864, Summers Papers.
135. Stevens to mother, Sept. 9, 1864, in Richard N. Ellis, "The Civil War Letters of an Iowa Family," *AI* 39 (1969): 585.
136. *National-Demokrat*, Oct. 13, 24, 1864.
137. *Der Demokrat*, Oct. 27, 1864; Dubuque *Herald*, Sept. 11, 1864; Burlington *Argus*, Sept. 15, 1864.
138. Iowa Election Records, 1864 (Iowa City, Univ. Microfilms).
139. Nov. 11, 1864.
140. *State Democratic Press*, Nov. 8, 1864, Dubuque *Herald*, Nov. 10, 1864; Negus to Mason, Nov. 23, 1864, Mason Papers; Keokuk *Constitution*, Dec. 10, 1864.

141. Burlington *Hawk-eye*, Nov. 29, 1864; *CM*, Dec. 6, 1864; Dean to Mason, July 27, 1864, Mason Papers; Gear to Mason, Feb. 8, 1865, ibid. On Apr. 17, 1864, Mason wrote in his diary that he wished McClellan had overthrown Lincoln when the President issued the preliminary Emancipation Proclamation. McClellan might have restored peace at that time, he said.

142. Dean to Summers, Feb. 21, 1865, Summers Papers.

CHAPTER 9

1. *Herald,* Mar. 29, May 24, 1862; Keokuk *Gate City* (w), May 21, 1862.
2. Davenport *Democrat,* Sept. 8–13, 1862; Nathan Brainerd to elders, Amana Society, Aug. 27, 1862, Governor's Letterbook Military Record (Samuel J. Kirkwood), IHD, p. 278.
3. *State Democratic Press,* Nov. 1, 1862. No evidence found to date supports this criticism. Kirkwood could be blunt, but he was not prone to make invidious distinctions among denominations.
4. Council Bluffs *Bugle,* Dec. 24, 1862.
5. Fairfield *Ledger,* Jan. 23, 1863; Muscatine *Courier,* Mar. 26, 1863.
6. Burlington *Hawk-eye,* May 19, 1863.
7. Davenport *Democrat,* Sept. 21, 1863.
8. Aug. 4, 1863; *Republican* in Dubuque *Times,* Nov. 22, 1863; *Iowa State Register* (w), Nov. 25, 1863.
9. Des Moines *Statesman,* Dec. 25, 1863; Keokuk *Gate City* (w), Dec. 30, 1863; Burlington *Argus,* May 19, 1864.
10. Council Bluffs *Nonpareil,* May 30, June 20, 1863.
11. Fairfield *Ledger,* June 11, Aug. 13, Nov. 26, 1863; Keokuk *Gate City* (w), Sept. 16, 1863; *State Democratic Press,* Nov. 4, 1863.
12. Irving B. Richman, ''Congregational Life in Muscatine, 1843–1893,'' *IJHP* 21 (1923): 385; Burlington *Hawk-eye,* June 6, 1863.
13. Burkholder to Carpenter, Feb. 19, 1863, Cyrus C. Carpenter Papers, IHS; *Biographical and Historical Memoir of Story County* (Chicago, 1890), p. 162.
14. Oskaloosa *Herald* in *Iowa State Register* (w), May 11, 1862; *Register,* Nov. 25, 1863.
15. The Dubuque *Herald,* Dec. 27, 1863, carried a story on Curtis's supposed expulsion and the charges against him; *Iowa State Register* (w), Jan. 21, 1864; Burlington *Argus,* Jan. 21, 1864.
16. Aug. 2, 1864.
17. *Iowa State Register* in Dubuque *Times,* Jan. 9, 1864.
18. Jane Thompson to Maj. William Thompson, Feb. 20, 1864, Thompson Letters.
19. Dean to Charles Mason, July 4, 1864, Charles Mason Papers, IHD. See also the letter from ''Ignatius'' addressed to ''The Rev. Mr. Teeters and the other Clergymen of Keokuk who are engaged in political discussion and stump speaking,'' Keokuk *Constitution,* Oct. 12, 1864.
20. Nov. 15, 1862.
21. Apr. 22, May 3, Aug. 30, 1863.
22. May 13, 1863.
23. Oct. 27, 1863.
24. Clarence R. Aurner, ''Historical Survey of Civic Instruction and Training for Citizenship in Iowa,'' *IJHP* 17 (1919): 145, 149.
25. *Herald,* Jan. 15–16, 21, 1863.
26. Ibid., Jan. 21, Mar. 1, 10, Apr. 11, 1863; Dubuque *Times,* Mar. 3, 10, 1863.
27. Mar. 9, 11, 1863.
28. Keokuk *Gate City* (w), Mar. 11, 1863; Johnson Brigham, *Des Moines Together with the History of Polk County, Iowa,* 2 vols. (Chicago, 1911), 2: 216.
29. *Ledger,* Apr. 23, 1863; Burlington *Hawk-eye,* Mar. 18, 1863; *Iowa State Register,* Mar. 25, 1863.
30. May 29, Aug. 28, Sept. 25, 1863.
31. June 26, 1863.
32. *Constitution,* Mar. 14, 1864; *The Hawkeye Flag* (Winterset), in Dubuque *Times,* Mar. 31, 1864.
33. *State Democratic Press,* July 27, 1864.
34. Keokuk *Gate City* (w), Sept. 7, 1864.
35. Aug. 25, 1864.

36. In Burlington *Hawk-eye,* Apr. 1, 1864.

37. Dubuque *Times,* Feb. 25, 1863.

38. Jan. 11, 1863.

39. Thompson to Thompson, Sept. 18, 1862, in Edwin C. Bearss, ed., "Civil War Letters of Major William Thompson," AI 36 (1966): 437–38.

40. Dubuque *Herald,* July 16, 1862; Dubuque *Times* in Keokuk *Gate City* (w), June 1, 1864; *News* in Burlington *Hawk-eye,* May 24, 1864.

41. July 30, Aug. 15, 1862.

42. Dec. 2, 1862.

43. Council Bluffs *Nonpareil,* Dec. 5, 1863.

44. Dubuque *Times,* Mar. 8, 1864; *Iowa State Register* (w), Mar. 9, 1864.

45. Dubuque *Times,* June 21, 1864.

46. Sept. 25, 1863.

47. *Times,* July 7, 21, 25, 1864; *Herald,* July 21, Aug. 25, 1864.

48. Mar. 5, 1862.

49. Apr. 6, 1862.

50. Jan. 24, 1862.

51. Ibid., May 1, 1864.

52. Aug. 25, Sept. 15, 1864.

53. *Constitution,* July 8, Nov. 8, 1864; *Statesman,* Nov. 26, 1864.

54. In Burlington *Hawk-eye,* Mar. 7, 1865; Albia *Union* in *Hawk-eye,* Nov. 16, 1865.

55. *Times,* Jan. 21, 1862; ibid., Feb. 25, 1862.

56. *State Democratic Press,* June 21, Nov. 29, 1862.

57. *Democrat,* Jan. 12, 1863; *Herald,* Oct. 4, 18, 1863; Waverly *Phoenix* in Dubuque *Times,* Dec. 12, 1863.

58. *Nonpareil,* Jan. 17, 1863; *Democrat,* Jan. 13, 23, Mar. 6, 19, 1863; Mary Jo Mason Diary, IHD, July 23, 1863.

59. *State Democratic Press,* Aug. 29, 1863; *Constitution,* Sept. 29, 1863; *Herald,* July 8, Oct. 28–29, 1863.

60. Iowa, *Legislative Documents,* 10th General Assembly, 1864: *Report of the Secretary of State in Relation to the Criminal Returns of the State of Iowa for the Years 1862–1863,* p. 66; *Report of the Warden of the Iowa Penitentiary to the Governor for the Two Years Commencing Oct. 1, 1861, and Ending Sept. 30, 1863,* p. 24.

61. *Democrat,* May 17, 1864.

62. *Times,* Nov. 3, 11, 16, 1864; *Herald,* Mar. 8, Apr. 7, 1865.

63. Mar. 22, 1864.

64. *Star,* July 8, 1864; Dubuque *Times,* July 13, 1864.

65. *Herald* in Davenport *Democrat,* Jan. 18, 1865, Burlington *Hawk-eye,* Mar. 13, 1865.

66. Dec. 19–21, 1864.

67. Mildred Throne, "Iowa Farm Letters, 1856–1865," *IJH* 58 (1960): 85–86; *Herald,* July 12, 1863; Independence *Guardian* in Waterloo *Courier,* Sept. 23, 1863.

68. Muscatine *Courier* in Dubuque *Times,* Nov. 1, 1863.

69. *Times,* Jan. 28, Oct. 1, 1862; *Bugle,* Dec. 3, 1862.

70. *Herald,* Jan. 3, Sept. 22, 1863; Dubuque *Times,* Nov. 1, 1863.

71. *Nonpareil,* Apr. 25, 1863; *Bugle,* Oct. 22, 1863; Keokuk *Constitution* in *Times,* Oct. 17, 1863; *Times,* Sept. 25, Oct. 31, 1863.

72. Dodge to Mason, Jan. 28, 1864, Mason Papers; *Herald,* Oct. 30, 1864.

73. Davenport *Democrat,* Feb. 5, 1864; Dubuque *Herald,* Apr. 13–14, July 9, 1864. Agassiz got $100 for the first lecture and $50 each for the other two. Besides season ticket holders for the city's lecture series, he attracted $150 in general admissions. The professor announced that he would return in 1865 to examine the geologic formations in the area which he called some of the "most wonderful in the world." What the *Times,* and presumably many other Dubuquers, valued in public figures and their wives is interesting. Agassiz was a man whose heart was equal to his intellect. He put on no airs, nor did he act superior. Mrs. Agassiz was a "winning, childlike creature, being in the rear rather than in the front of fashion," *Times,* Mar. 1, 1864; Iowa City *Republican* in *Times,* July 9, 1864.

74. *Times,* Apr. 24, 1864; *Herald,* Apr. 20, 1865.

75. *Times,* May 8, 18, 1864.

76. *State Democratic Press,* June 22, 1864; *The Conservative,* July 6, 1864; stories from the *Linn County Patriot, Home Journal, Buchanan County Guardian,* in *Times,* July 25, 1864; *Times,* Aug. 3, 1864.

77. Jacob Hunter Letters (Microfilm), IHD.

CHAPTER 10

1. Keokuk *Constitution*, Feb. 26, 28, 1865; Burlington *Hawk-eye*, Davenport *Democrat*, Feb. 23, 1865.
2. Jan. 25, Mar. 1, 29, 1865.
3. Council Bluffs *Bugle*, Feb. 9, 1865; *CM*, Dec. 25, 1864, Jan. 8, 29, Feb. 19, 25, Mar. 12, 19–20, Apr. 9, 1865.
4. *Herald*, Feb. 5, 15, Mar. 21 (the *Catholic Telegraph* story and response), Apr. 4, 6, 15, 1865; Davenport *Democrat*, Apr. 14, 1865.
5. *Hawk-eye*, Apr. 4, 15, 21, 1865; *Gate City* (d), Apr. 10, (w), Apr. 12, 1865.
6. *Democrat*, Jan. 25, Mar. 18, 1865; *Hawk-eye*, Feb. 3, 1865; *Herald*, Mar. 23, Apr. 5, 1865.
7. Ibid., Feb. 4, 7, 1865.
8. *CM*, Mar. 13, 1864, Jan. 8, May 23, 27, 1865; "X" letters Dubuque *Herald*, Mar. 4, 20, 1864; Mason to Yewell, Nov. 4, 1861, in George H. Yewell, "Reminiscences of Charles Mason," *AI* 5 (1901): 174; Charles Babbitt, Third Iowa Battery, Little Rock, Ark., in Council Bluffs *Bugle*, July 13, 1865.
9. *Iowa State Register* (w), Feb, 12, 1865; *Constitution*, Feb. 17, 24, Mar. 21, 1865; *Gate City* (w), Mar. 20, 1865.
10. Mar. 14, 1865.
11. In the Burlington *Hawk-eye*, Jan. 27, 1865.
12. *Herald*, July 21, 1865; *Democrat*, July 21, 1865. Baker's explanation, July 13, 1865, is in the *Iowa State Register* (w), July 26, 1865.
13. *Journal* in Davenport *Democrat*, Mar. 2, 1865; *Democrat*, Mar. 9, 1865; *Iowa State Register* in the *Democrat*, Aug. 7, 1865; Keokuk *Constitution*, Mar. 18, 1865.
14. Davenport *Democrat*, Apr. 15, 29, 1865; *Iowa State Register* (w), Apr. 26, 1865; *Herald*, Apr. 15, 21–22, 25, 1865.
15. Council Bluffs *Bugle*, Apr. 20, Oct. 26, 1865; *State Democratic Press*, Apr. 26, 1865.
16. *CM*, Apr. 16, Oct. 29, 1865. Mason's daughter did reveal that the Mason family had at first hoped for Lincoln's survival because it feared a Johnson presidency worse. *MJM*, Apr. 16, 1865.
17. *Iowa State Register* (w), May 3, 1865; Burlington *Hawk-eye*, Apr. 18, 20–21, 24–25, 28, May 2–6, 8, 1865; Dubuque *Times*, Apr. 23, 1865; Franklin T. Oldt and P. J. Quigley, eds., *History of Dubuque County, Iowa* (Chicago, n.d.), p. 316.
18. July 26, 1865.
19. *CM*, June 14, 18, 1865; Jones to Mason, July 17, 1865, Mason Papers, IHD; Mason to Jones, July 22, 1865, George W. Jones Papers, IHD.
20. George H. Parker to Mason, July 12, 1865, Jones to Mason, July 17, 1865, Mason Papers; *Iowa State Register* (w), July 19, 1865.
21. *Iowa State Register* (w), July 21, 1865; Benjamin F. Gue, *History of Iowa from the Earliest Times to the Beginning of the Twentieth Century*, 4 vols. (New York, 1903), 3: 2.
22. Mason to Jones, July 22, Sept. 9, 1865, Jones Papers; Jones to Laurel Summers, n.d., Laurel Summers Papers, IHD; *CM*, June 18, 1865.
23. Blair to Jones, Aug. 4, 1865, Jones Papers; Buchanan to Jones, Aug. 3, 1865, Jones Papers.
24. For a sophisticated treatment of the Republican response see Robert R. Dykstra, "Iowa: Bright Radical Star," in James C. Mohr, ed., *Radical Republicans in the North: State Politics during Reconstruction* (Baltimore, 1976), pp. 167–93; also G. Galen Berrier, "The Negro Suffrage Issue in Iowa—1865–1868," *AI* 39 (1968): 241–61; Gue, *History of Iowa*, 3: 1–2; Council Bluffs *Nonpareil*, June 17, 1865; *Marshall County Times* (Marshalltown), June 28, 1865.
25. Mildred Throne, "Erastus Soper's History of Company D, 12th Iowa Infantry, 1861–1866," pt. 3, *IJH* 56 (1958): 343–44. The Twelfth's soldiers didn't see themselves as extremists. They came out against both the *Iowa State Register* and the Dubuque *Herald*; Keokuk *Constitution*, July 16, 30, 1865; Miller to Mason, Sept. 1, 1865, Mason Papers; Oskaloosa *Herald* in Davenport *Democrat*, Sept. 12, 1865.
26. July 28, 1865.
27. George Tichenor to G. M. Dodge, Aug. 25, 1865, G. M. Dodge Papers, IHD; W. O. Payne, *History of Story County*, 2 vols. (Chicago, 1911), 1: 365–67. This county historian noted that Story county Republicans, after 1865, liberally sprinkled their county slates with ex-soldiers.
28. *Iowa State Register* (w), Aug. 9, 1865; Herbert S. Fairall, ed., *Manual of Iowa Politics* (Iowa City, 1881), p. 70; Gue, *History of Iowa*, 3: 5–6.
29. *Iowa State Register* (w), Aug. 30, 1865; Fairall, *Manual of Iowa Politics*, pp. 71–72.
30. Copy of letter of acceptance, Thomas H. Benton to Capt. George W. Clark, Capt. A. T. Ault, and the Reverend A. J. Barton, Aug. 28, 1865, Mason Papers; *CM*, Sept. 17, 1865.

31. Circular issued by LeGrand Byington and others, Council Bluffs *Nonpareil*, Aug. 26, 1865.
32. Washington *Democrat*, Sept. 26, 1865; *Iowa Sate Register* (w), Sept. 27, 1865; Council Bluffs *Nonpareil*, Sept. 30, 1865; George Jones to Charles Mason, Oct. 3, 1865, Mason Papers.
33. Glenwood *Opinion*, Sept. 23, 1865.
34. Grinnell to Benton, Sept. 9, 1865, in Glenwood *Opinion* and Council Bluffs *Nonpareil*, Sept. 30, 1865; Marcellus Crocker to Stone, July 6, 1865, in *Iowa State Register* (w), Oct. 4, 1865, *Nonpareil*, Sept. 30, 1865.
35. Grimes to Edward H. Stiles, Sept. 14, 1865, in *Nonpareil*, Sept. 30, 1865. Shrewd James Howell knew even two months earlier exactly what Mason was doing and why. Keokuk *Gate City* (w), July 26, 1865.
36. Sept. 30, 1865; Oskaloosa *Herald* in Keokuk *Gate City* (w), Sept. 26, 1865.
37. *Iowa State Register* (w), Oct. 18, 1865.
38. Iowa Election Records, 1865 (Iowa City, Univ. Microfilm); Henry Trimble to Charles Mason, Nov. 13, 1865, Mason Papers; Dubuque *Herald* in *Iowa State Register* (w), Nov. 15, 1865.

CHAPTER 11

1. The voting percentages are derived from Iowa Election Records, 1839–1890 (Iowa City, Univ. Microfilms).
2. Dubuque *Herald*, Feb. 7, 1860; Franklin T. Oldt and P. J. Quigley, eds., *History of Dubuque County, Iowa* (Chicago, n.d.), p. 486.
3. George H. Daniels, "Immigrant Vote in the 1860 Election: The Case of Iowa," *Mid-America* 44 (1962): 146–162; also, Daniels's original seminar paper, "Frontier Populations and the Problems of Political Analysis: The Case of Iowa, 1850–1860." This paper, at the Iowa University history department, lists all 80 of the Daniels townships, the nativities of the major voting group or groups in each, and the Democratic voting percentage each township recorded in 1860 (app. B, Table 7, pp. 35–39).
4. Keokuk *Constitution*, Oct. 16, 1862.
5. Newspapers used which contained official votes by township were: Dubuque *Times*, Oct. 22, 1861, Oct. 17, 22, 1862, Oct. 17, 1863, Nov. 11, 1864; Dubuque *Herald*, Oct. 25, 1865; Burlington *Hawk-eye*, Nov. 14, 1860, Oct. 16, 1861, Oct. 22, 1862, Oct. 24, 1863, Nov. 15, 1864, Oct. 17, 1865; *Fayette County Pioneer*, Nov. 16, 1860, Oct. 21, 1861, Oct. 27, 1862, Oct. 26, 1863; Mount Pleasant *Home Journal*, Nov. 10, 1860, Oct. 19, 1861, Nov. 1, 1862, Oct. 24, 1863, Nov. 19, 1864; Iowa City *Republican*, Nov. 21, 1860, Oct. 21, 1863, Nov. 9, 1864, Oct. 18, 1865; Anamosa *Eureka*, Nov. 9, 1860, Oct. 18, 1861, Oct. 24, 1862, Oct. 23, 1863, Nov. 18, 1864, Oct. 19, 1865; *Des Moines Valley Whig*, Nov. 16,1860, Oct. 21, 1861; Keokuk *Gate City* (w), Oct. 28, 1863, Oct. 24, 1865; Linn County *Register*, Nov. 17, 1860, Oct. 23, 1862; Linn County *Patriot*, Oct. 24, 1864; Muscatine *Journal* (w), Nov. 16, 1860, Oct. 18, 1861, Nov. 24, 1862; Muscatine *Courier* (w), Oct. 29, 1863, Oct. 20, 1865; Davenport *Democrat*, Oct. 16, 1861, Oct. 22, 1862, Oct. 15, 1863, Nov. 15, 1864, Nov. 18, 1865; Story County *Advocate*, Nov. 15, 1860, Oct. 17, 1861; Republican *Reville* (Nevada), Oct. 22, 1863; Story County *Aegis*, Nov. 16, 1864; Washington *Press*, Nov. 14, 1860, Oct. 16, 1861, Oct. 29, 1862, Oct. 28, 1863, Nov. 16, 1864, Nov. 1, 1865; Tipton *Advertizer*, Nov. 22, 1860, Oct. 24, 1861, Oct. 30, 1862, Nov. 17, 1864, Oct. 19, 1865; Vinton *Eagle*, Nov. 14, 1860, Nov. 6, 1861, Oct. 21, 1863, Nov. 16, 1864, Oct. 25, 1865.
6. *Iowa Official Register, 1915–1916*, in Leland L. Sage, *A History of Iowa* (Ames, Iowa 1974) p. 310.
7. All calculations in the section on the vote in the midwestern states in 1860, 1862, and 1863 are based on election returns found in the New York *Tribune Almanac*, 1861, pp. 55–63; ibid., 1863, pp. 55–63; ibid., 1864, pp. 60–66.
8. Frank L. Klement, *The Copperheads in the Middle West* (Chicago, 1960), pp. 25–27.
9. Wood Gray, *The Hidden Civil War: The Story of the Copperheads* (New York, 1942), p. 27.
10. P. E. Brown, *Soils of Iowa* (Ames, Iowa, 1936), pp. 248–51. The 13 top Republican counties with Grade I soil predominating are Blackhawk, Bremer, Cerro Gordo, Chickasaw, Clarke, Floyd, Hamilton, Hardin, Henry, Louisa, Marshall, Mitchell, and Page. The seven top Democratic counties with Grade I soil are Boone, Fremont, Guthrie, Marion, Pottawattamie, Wayne, and Webster.
11. Rutland, "The Copperheads of Iowa, A Re-examination," *IJH* 52 (1954): 24.
12. See Robert R. Dykstra and Harlan Hahn, "Northern Voters and Negro Suffrage: The Case

of Iowa, 1868,'' *Public Opinion Quarterly* 32 (1968): 202–15, especially 213–14. Dykstra has since stated that some of the findings in this article are open to serious question. They will be revised in his forthcoming work on Iowa Radical Republicanism. Dykstra in James C. Mohr, ed., *Radical Republicans in the North: State Politics During Reconstruction* (Baltimore, 1976), p. 180 n. 8.

13. Paul Kleppner, *The Cross of Culture: A Social Analysis of Midwestern Politics, 1850–1900* (New York, 1970), especially chaps. 1–2. Conservative Lutheranism as a political factor among one immigrant group is treated in Arlow William Anderson, *The Immigrant Takes His Stand: The Norwegian-American Press and Public Affairs, 1846–1872* (Northfield, Minn., 1953), pp. 51, 58, 71–74, 82.

CHAPTER 14

1. Benjamin F. Shambaugh, ed., *The Messages and Proclamations of the Governors of Iowa,* 3 vols. (Iowa City, 1903), 3: 14.
2. Susan Carpenter to Carpenter, Apr. 20, 1865, Cyrus C. Carpenter Papers, IHS.
3. Byington to Mason, Oct. 21, 1865, Mason Papers, IHD.
4. Oct. 28, 1865.
5. 1: 251.
6. Dunham to Samuel Kirkwood, Jan. 29, 1866 [?], Samuel J. Kirkwood Box, IHD.
7. *CM,* Sept. 2, 1866. His exact words were ''It [partisan use of the patronage] is better than Civil War, which will have to be resorted to before we are through, if the radicals remain in the ascendancy long.''
8. Ibid., Jan. 20, Feb. 3, 1867; see also, Hubert H. Wubben, ''Copperhead Charles Mason, A Question of Loyalty,'' *CWH* (1978): 46–65.
9. *Iowa State Register* (w), July 4, 18, Sept. 5, 1866; Clipping from *The Olive Branch,* Sept. 1, 1866, Laurel Summers Papers, IHD.
10. Aug. 29, 1866.
11. *CM,* June 27, 30, 1867.
12. Both platforms are in *History of Cass County, Iowa,* 2 vols. (Chicago, 1912), pp. 179–180; *Hawk-eye,* Oct. 4, 1867.
13. Robert Dykstra, ''Iowa, Bright Radical Star,'' in James C. Mohr, ed., *Radical Republicans in the North: State Politics During Reconstruction* (Baltimore, 1976), 167–93. Dykstra points out that with the vote on black suffrage the Iowa voters ''provided the nation's first and only grass-roots victory for black political equality where the ballot offered voters a clear alternative to uncompromising racism,'' p. 167.
14. ''The Liberal Republican Party in Iowa, 1872,'' *IJH* 53 (1955): 121–152; and ''The Anti-Monopoly Party in Iowa, 1873–1874,'' ibid. 52 (1954): 289–326.
15. Horace Samuel Merrill, *Bourbon Democracy of the Middle West, 1865–1896,* 2d. ed., rev. (Seattle, 1967), p. 128.
16. Gue, *History of Iowa,* 3: 153–154.
17. Merrill, *Bourbon Democracy of the Middle West,* pp. 204–205. See also Leland Sage, *A History of Iowa* (Ames, Ia., 1974), Chaps. 10–12.
18. Dubuque *Times* and Dubuque *Herald,* Nov. 6, 1879; Dubuque *Telegraph-Herald,* Aug. 27, 1911; Throne, ''Liberal Republican Party,'' p. 142.
19. Des Moines *Register and Leader,* Jan. 27, 1915; Edward J. Gallagher, *Stilson Hutchins, 1838–1912: A Biography of the Founder of the Washington Post* (Laconia, N. H., 1965).
20. Grimes to Mason, Feb. 27, 1871, in Ottumwa *Democrat,* Apr. 18, 1872, and Iowa City *Press,* May 1, 1872, in Throne, ''Liberal Republican Party,'' pp. 126–27; *CM,* Jan. 16, 1876; *MJM,* 7:169.
21. John Carl Parish, *George Washington Jones* (Iowa City, 1912), pp. 246–47.
22. Henry Clay Dean, *Crimes of the Civil War and the Curse of the Funding System* (Baltimore, 1866), *Iowa State Register,* Feb. 13, 1877; Edward H. Stiles, *Recollections and Sketches of Notable Lawyers and Public Men of Early Iowa* (Des Moines, 1916), pp. 573–85; George F. Robeson, ''Henry Clay Dean,'' *Palimpsest* 5 (1924): 321–33.
23. Stiles, *Recollections and Sketches,* pp. 909–11.
24. Throne, ''Liberal Republican Party,'' p. 130; Iowa City *Press,* Nov. 27, 1907, in Stiles, *Recollections and Sketches,* pp. 777–78.

25. H. N. Pratt, *History of Fort Dodge and Webster County* (Chicago, 1913), 2: 5–6.

26. Louis Pelzer, *Augustus Caesar Dodge* (Iowa City, 1908), pp. 252–54.

27. Robert Rutland, "Copperheads of Iowa, a Re-examination," *IJH* 52 (1954): 28–29.

28. P. 929.

29. *History of Madison County* (Des Moines, 1879); *History of Madison County and Its People,* 2 vols. (Chicago, 1915).

30. P. 230.

31. Richard O. Curry, "The Civil War and Reconstruction, 1861–1877: A Critical Overview of Recent Trends and Interpretations," *CWH* 20 (1974): 217.

32. Hubert H. Wubben, "Copperhead Charles Mason: A Question of Loyalty," *CWH* (1978): 58–59, 65.

33. David M. Potter, *The South and the Sectional Conflict* (Baton Rouge, La., 1968), p. 26.

34. Ibid., p. 41.

35. Rutland, "The Copperheads of Iowa," p. 6.

36. *CM*, May 28, June 27, July 14, 1857.

37. Robeson, "Henry Clay Dean," 321–33.

38. Frank L. Klement, " 'Brick' Pomeroy: Copperhead and Curmudgeon," *Wisconsin Magazine of History* 25 (1951): 107–11.

····⟫[*Bibliographical Essay*   ]⟪····

ONE could write a history of Iowa Copperheadism without the Charles Mason diaries and letters (Iowa State Department of History and Archives, Des Moines— IHD), but it would be a poorer history. Mason corresponded with numerous important Democrats on both the state and national scene. His diaries reveal that he was more of a foe of the war and a friend of the South than his friends (or his enemies) suspected. Both the diaries and excerpts from his correspondence were published in a limited edition by his grandson, Charles Mason Remey (*Life and Letters of Charles Mason: Chief Justice of Iowa, 1804-1882*, 12 typescript vols., Washington, 1939). Mason's daughter, Molly, kept a wartime diary also. The originals are in the Des Moines archives. Remey, her son, published these also (*Life and Letters of Mary Josephine Remey, Wife of Rear Admiral George Collier Remey, Daughter of Chief Justice Charles Mason, 1845-1938*, 12 typescript vols., Washington, 1939). Copies of both sets of transcripts are located in several major libraries throughout the country as well as the Des Moines repository and the State Historical Society library at Iowa City. Molly's diaries are helpful to those who want to understand her father and his politics. In addition, they are a sometimes fascinating account of life in wartime Washington. Mason's political tract, *The Election in Iowa*, a publication of the Society for the Diffusion of Political Knowledge (New York, 1863), stressed the complementary nature of Southern slave-based agriculture and the North's mixed industrial-agricultural economy. It also made the case for maintaining white supremacy throughout the nation, without adding anything new to that doctrine. Unlike his diary and his unsigned "X" letters to the Dubuque *Herald*, this publication, printed under his own name, praised Northern soldiers and professed sympathy for their hardships and suffering. The late Willard I. Toussaint's "Biography of an Iowa Businessman: Charles Mason, 1804-1882," (Ph.D. diss., Univ. of Iowa, 1963), reveals that during the war Mason's political beliefs influenced his business judgment, sometimes adversely.

Less extensive than the Mason letters, but still important, are the letters at Des Moines (IHD), of antiwar men Laurel Summers and George Jones and, at

Iowa City (a limited collection on microfilm, IHS), of LeGrand Byington. They exhibit the frustration and anger of those who could not get a majority of their own party to stand with them "on principle."

The various official and private papers of Governor Samuel Kirkwood, the Kirkwood Correspondence, the Samuel J. Kirkwood Box, the Governor's Department Military Correspondence, and the Governor's Letterbook Military Record, are all at Des Moines (IHD). Kirkwood had his faults, but on balance these papers, and others in other collections, do little to disturb the judgment of generations of Iowa scholars that Kirkwood was the right man in the right place at the right time. The Adjutant General's Correspondence, "Disloyal Sentiment, 1861–1865" (Des Moines, IHD) is a fascinating collection of letters written by some Iowans who did not hesitate to tell Adjutant General Nathaniel Baker, Governor Kirkwood, and Kirkwood's successor William Stone just which other Iowans were disloyal. The writers often asked for or offered advice to those officials on how to deal with these irritants.

The political developments in Iowa, 1850–1860 are well covered in Morton M. Rosenberg, *Iowa on the Eve of the Civil War: A Decade of Frontier Politics* (Norman, Okla.: Univ. of Oklahoma Press, 1972), and David Sparks, "The Birth of the Republican Party in Iowa, 1848 to 1860" (Ph.D. diss., Univ. of Chicago, 1951). Rosenberg's Ph.D. dissertation, "The Democratic Party of Iowa, 1850–1860" (Univ. of Iowa, 1957), contains a valuable appendix listing the birthplaces of the residents of each county for the years 1850, 1856, and 1860. The 1856 figures come from a state census of that year. The other two are from the seventh and eighth federal censuses. Three studies, all less narrowly political, throw additional light on this era. They are those by: George A. Boeck, "An Early Iowa Community: Aspects of Economic, Social and Political Development in Burlington, Iowa 1833–1866" (Ph.D. diss., Univ. of Iowa, 1961); Faye E. Harris, "A Frontier Community: The Economic, Social and Political Development of Keokuk, Iowa from 1820 to 1866" (Ph.D. diss., Univ. of Iowa, 1965); and Roland F. Matthias, "The Know Nothing Movement in Iowa" (Ph.D. diss., Univ. of Chicago, 1965). And Robert E. Sterling's excellent dissertation, "Civil War Draft Resistance in the Middle West" (Northern Illinois Univ., 1974), devotes much space to Iowa and shows how uncomfortable local enrollment officers became with putting their neighbors on the draft lists.

Two articles on Iowa Copperheads appeared in the early 1950s. Frank C. Arena's title, "Southern Sympathizers in Iowa During the Civil War," *AI* 30 (1951), accurately reflects his treatment of the subject. More in the revisionist mold of Frank Klement and Richard Curry is Robert Rutland's, "The Copperheads of Iowa: a Re-examination," *IJH* 52 (1954). David L. Lendt's *Demise of the Democracy: the Copperhead Press in Iowa* (Ames, Ia., Iowa State Univ. Press, 1973), contains many examples of editorial opposition to the Lincoln administration. See also my article, "The Maintenance of Internal Security in Iowa, 1861–1865," *CWH* 10 (1964).

The annual *Reports of the Iowa State Agricultural Society* provide a running account of the directions taken in Iowa agriculture during the 1850s and 1860s. They show that Iowa's farmers were nothing if not commercial minded. Not for them, if they could avoid it, was the life of Thomas Jefferson's simple, independent, subsistence yeoman. The *Iowa Homestead* newspaper, oriented toward farmer readers, could declaim on the virtues of rural life while promoting the rewards of efficient commercial agriculture. Louis B. Schmidt, "The Internal Grain Trade of the United States, 1850–1860," *IJHP* 18 (1920), tells of shifts in the grain trade and of the decline of New Orleans as a grain exporter.

On the origins of Iowa's population see: John D. Barnhart, "Sources of Southern Migration into the Old Northwest," *MVHR* 22 (1933): 49–62; Cardinal Goodwin, "The American Occupation of Iowa, 1833–1860," *IJHP* 17 (1919): 83–102; Frank I. Herriott, "Whence Came the Pioneers of Iowa," *AI* 7 (1906): 367–79, 446–65; Henry C. Hubbart, "Pro-Southern Influences in the Free West, 1840–1865," *MVHR* 20 (1933): 45–62; William J. Peterson, "Population Advance to the Upper Mississippi Valley, 1833–1860," *IJHP* 32 (1934): 312–353.

Iowa's county histories range from the useless to the surprisingly informative (and reasonably objective in some cases) so far as coverage of Copperheadism in their areas is concerned. The best are: *History of Davis County* (Des Moines: State Historical Co. 1882); *Pioneer History of Davis County* (Bloomfield, Ia.: Federated Women's Clubs of Davis Co., 1927); J. M. Howell and Heman C. Smith eds., *History of Decatur County Iowa and Its People* (Chicago: S. J. Clarke, 1915); Franklin T. Oldt and P. J. Quigley eds., *History of Dubuque County* (Chicago: Goodspeed Historical Assoc., n.d.); *History of Fremont County* (Des Moines: Iowa Historical Co., 1881); E. B. Stillman, *Past and Present of Greene County* (Chicago: S. J. Clarke, 1907); Joe H. Smith, *History of Harrison County* (Des Moines: Iowa Printing, 1888); Charles J. Fulton ed., *History of Jefferson County*, 2 vols. (Chicago: S. J. Clarke, 1914); *Lee County Iowa History* (Iowa Writers Program, Works Progress Administration, 1942); *History of Mahaska County, Iowa* (1878); Frank Hickenlooper, *An Illustrated History of Monroe County, Iowa* (1896); and W. O. Payne, *History of Story County, Iowa*, 2 vols. (Chicago: S. J. Clarke, 1911). Of lesser but some merit in their coverage of Copperheadism are: Realto E. Price ed., *History of Clayton County, Iowa*, 2 vols. (Chicago: Robert O. Law, 1916); *Dubuque County, Iowa, History* (Iowa Writers Program, Works Progress Administration, 1942); C. Childs, *History of Dubuque County, Iowa* (Chicago: Western Historical Co., 1880); R. M. Corbit, *History of Jones County Past and Present*, 2 vols. (Chicago: Western Historical Co., 1910); *History of Jones County, Iowa* (Chicago: Western Historical Co., 1879); *History of Kossuth County, Iowa* (1913); *History of Lee County, Iowa* (Chicago: Western Historical Co., 1879); Manoah Hedge, *Past and Present of Mahaska County, Iowa* (Chicago: S. J. Clarke, 1906); *History of Montgomery County, Iowa* (Des Moines: Iowa Historical and Biographical Co., 1881); Johnson Brigham, *Des Moines Together with the History of Polk County, Iowa* 2 vols. (Chicago: S. J. Clarke, 1911); *Biographical and Historical Memoirs of Story County, Iowa* (1890).

A surprisingly complete source of wartime political party platforms is *History of Cass County, Iowa* (Springfield, Ill.: Continental Historical Co., 1884).

Except for John Carl Parish's *George Washington Jones* (Iowa City: State Historical Society of Iowa, 1912), no full length scholarly treatment of Iowa's leading Copperheads exists. Biographical sketches for some can be located in Josiah B. Grinnell, *Men and Events of Forty Years* (Boston: D. Lathrop, 1891), Edward H. Stiles, *Recollections and Sketches of Notable Lawyers and Public Men of Early Iowa* (Des Moines: Homestead Publ. Co., 1961), the *Annals of Iowa*, and the *Iowa Journal of History and Politics* (later shortened to *Iowa Journal of History*). Dennis Mahony is the subject of a serviceable B.A. thesis submitted by Roger Sullivan to Loras College in 1948 entitled, "Mahony, the Unterrified." See also Robert K. Thorp, "The Copperhead Days of Dennis Mahony," *Journalism Quarterly* 43 (1966), and my "Dennis Mahony and the Dubuque *Herald*, 1860–1863," *IJH* 56 (1958). Mahony's successor at the Dubuque *Herald*, Stilson Hutchins, has finally received some attention. Journalist Edward J. Gallagher's *Stilson Hutchins, 1838–1912: A Biography of the Founder of the Washington Post* (Laconia, N. H.: Citizen Publ., 1965), is anecdotal, amusing, and in places unreliable. Gallagher, however, does reveal that Hutchins' turbulent career as a young man during the Civil War was only the tip of the iceberg of a life which was to range from the bizarre to the grandiose in style, with some periods of solid achievement throughout.

Besides his *Herald* editorials Mahony wrote two wartime books. His *Prisoner of State* (New York, Carlton Publ., 1863) is an angry recital of his arrest, imprisonment and efforts to win his freedom. *The Four Acts of Depotism: Comprising I, the Tax Bill with All Amendments; II, the Finance Bill; III, the Conscription Act; IV, the Indemnity Bill; with Introduction and Comments* (New York: Van Evrie, Horton, 1863), is a scathing critique of war-inspired federal legislation. It also reveals his reconstruction proposals. Mahony wanted a president and a vice-president, alternately from North and South, each with veto power. He wanted the country to be divided into five sections—East, West, North, South, and Pacific—equal in power and each with an executive head. But the South was to be "most equal" of all; it was to stand as one unit while the rest were to be lumped into another.

Leland L. Sage's *A History of Iowa* (Ames, Ia.: Iowa State Univ. Press, 1974), particularly chapters 6–12, are valuable for an overall understanding of the period 1850–1900, including the long-term effects of the political disaster which overcame the Democrats during the war. His footnotes to those chapters are a bibliographical mine of information. Joseph F. Wall's, *Iowa: A Bicentennial History* (New York, W. W. Norton & Co., 1978), makes a good case for his introductory statement that the "[civil] war with its consequences has remained the single most determinative factor in Iowa's history. . . ." Chapter 6 deals with the war years. Still useful for coverage of the war era is Benjamin F. Gue's second volume of his four volume *History of Iowa from the Earliest Times to the Beginning of the Twentieth Century* (New York: Century Historical Co., 1903).

One of the best Iowa Civil War soldier diaries is that of Cyrus Boyd: Mildred Throne ed, with a new introduction by E. B. Long, *The Civil War Diary of Cyrus F. Boyd, Fifteenth Iowa Infantry, 1861-1863* (Millwood, N.Y.: Krauss Reprint Co., 1977). Boyd was an astute observer and recorder of soldier political attitudes and of soldier views on blacks, on army officers, and on Southern life. The Jacob Hunter Letters (Microfilm, IHD) are an exceptionally moving record of a man who felt impelled to enlist to do his part to save the Union and to end slavery, leaving behind a wife and four children. He died of illness before ever having been in combat, but not before learning, to his great sorrow, that few soldiers were as Christian or as committed as he to either Union or abolition. The William and Jane Thompson Letters (Des Moines: IHD) are entirely different. A lawyer before entering the service, Thompson was under no illusions about the nature of man and certainly not about the day to day commitment of the average Iowa trooper to the grand and humane objectives which motivated Private Hunter. Mrs. Thompson kept the Major well informed about life in the town of Marion. He in turn kept her well informed about his activities and commented freely upon conditions in what he regarded as the backward South.

It is a rewarding task to read Iowa's Civil War newspapers, especially if one doesn't rush the job. In no other way can one get the flavor of what life was like in the state in that time. Most of them are now on microfilm at the historical library in Iowa City. The Des Moines repository has a good bound collection also. At the time this study was underway the Des Moines *Iowa State Register* file was incomplete. Hopefully that will not be the case much longer. Over seventy papers, dailies and weeklies, figured in this study, and nearly all supplied useful information. Absolutely essential were the Dubuque *Herald* and its Republican opponent, the *Times*. Dubuque was where much of the action in Iowa was, and these two papers between them covered all of it. The best of the rest among Democratic papers were: the Burlingtron *Argus;* the Council Bluffs *Bugle* of sulfurous Lysander Babbitt; the Davenport *Democrat* run by the relatively calm David Richardson; the Des Moines *Statesman;* the Iowa City *State Democratic Press;* the Keokuk *Constitution* published by profane and excitable Thomas Clagett who had good reason for being both; Edward Thayer's Muscatine *Courier;* the always prowar Sioux City *Register;* and the West Union *Fayette County Pioneer.* Important Republican papers used besides the *Iowa State Register* were the Burlington *Hawk-eye* which could be just as tough as the Dubuque *Herald* when editor Clark Dunham put his mind to it; the Council Bluffs *Nonpareil;* the Davenport *Gazette;* the Fairfield *Ledger* whose W. W. Junkin had a keener understanding of what a free press was than many of his fellow editors; the Iowa City *Republican;* James Howell's Keokuk *Gate City;* the Muscatine *Journal;* and the Webster City *Hamilton Freeman.* The most useful German language newspapers were Dubuque's *Der National Demokrat* and Davenport's *Der Demokrat.*

Many of these papers are still operating today. The Des Moines *Register* has a national reputation for excellence. The Dubuque *Herald* is now the *Telegraph-*

Herald, still independently owned. Dennis Mahony would like that. Those who knew the *Herald* of the Civil War era will be interested in Ben Bagdikian's "The Little Old Daily of Dubuque," (*New York Times Magazine*, Feb. 3, 1974).

The *Annals of Iowa* and the *Iowa Journal of History* (until its unfortunate demise in 1961) are indispensable sources for students of Iowa history. One who takes the trouble to check their contents will find much good historical writing and discover leads to other sources and ideas which would be much harder to come by otherwise.

Index

Abingdon, 69, 93
Abolition and abolitionists, 29, 37, 52, 80, 183; antagonism toward, 22–24, 27, 30, 39; defense of, 40; Democrats and, 139; growth of, 7–8; hiring blacks, 80, 132, 155; Republicans and, 38; and schools, 179–81. *See also* Underground Railroad
Adams, Shubael, 166
Adel, 165
Agassiz, Louis, 191, 258 *n*73
Agriculture: average prices (1863–64), 149; commodity prices, 12, 36, 74–76, 134–36, 148–49; farmers club, 190; land values (1860), 37; livestock prices, 75, 135–36; markets, 11; and railroads, 12; wages, 36, 73, 138, 149; women in, 182–83. *See also* East-West trade; North-South trade
Ainsworth, Lucian L., 219
Albia, 93, 114, 186
Aldrich, Charles, 42
Allamakee County, 46, 93, 145, 205, 221
Allison, William B., 41, 186
Altman, Henry, 46
Amana Society, 162, 175
Amity, 44–45
Amsden, E. M., 124–25
Anamosa, 170, 199
Anamosa *News*, 245 *n*13
Anderson, William, 164
Anti-Monopoly Party, 219
Appanoose County, 65, 75, 149, 205, 214, 221
Arrests, 51–54, 65–68, 118, 123–25, 127; treatment of arrestees, 69, 124
Atchison County, Mo., 44
Audubon County, 43, 163, 205, 221

Babbitt, Charles, 160–61, 197
Babbitt, Lysander, 10, 26, 37, 92, 164, 188, 190, 202, 222; battles *Nonpareil*, 59, 161, 167; and blacks, 20, 81; on the draft, 159–61; on the economy, 76, 153; on Lincoln's death,

198; on Methodist church, 175–76; opposes war, 96, 170; postwar career, 220; on secession, 25, 27, 195; on war's legality, 32
Bailey, Gideon S., 33, 67, 202, 204, 240 *n*66
Baker, Nathaniel B., 42, 65, 94, 118, 121, 125, 163; on alien exemptions, 128, 198; appointed adjutant general, 34; and border problems, 164; and enlistments, 128, 197; leaves Democratic party, 86; in legislature, 33–34; on Mahony's loyalty, 41, 43; and militia, 116, 162–64; organizes Border Brigade, 45; "shoot to kill" order, 164; and Union Party, 47–49
Baldwin, Caleb, 79
Ball, Charles, 255 *n*108
Baltimore convention (1860), 19
Banks and banking, 4, 11, 36–37
Bartlett, E. P, 173
Baseball, 191–92
Bates, J. F., 56, 160
"Battle of Athens" (Mo.), 45–46
Baugh, D., 170
Becker's Clothing House, 137–38
Belfield, H. H., 179–80
Belknap, William W., 23–24, 67, 98, 139
Bell-Everett men, 19, 232 *n*6
Bellevue *Argus,* 97
Bennett, M. V. B., 102–3
Benton, Thomas H., 201–4
Benton County, 181
Bill, A. J., 203
Blackhawk County, 159, 183
Blacks: aid for, 134, 154; antagonism toward, 7–8, 79, 131–34, 156, 181, 198; and civil rights, 8, 77, 144; defense of, 20, 82, 154; deportation sought, 79; equality issue, 20, 158; exclusion law of 1851, 7, 230 *n*18; exclusion sentiment, 77, 79, 131, 133; expulsion proposed, 79, 145; First Iowa African Infantry, 130; and fitness for slavery, 131; and labor force, 78–81, 90, 132–33, 158;

Dunlavy, Harvey, 77, 103
Dunlavy, James, 103
Dunn, Richard P., 164
Durham, Jeff, 103
Durham, Samuel, 103, 170, 178
Dykstra, Robert, 261 *n*13

East-West trade, 12–17, 35, 148
Eastman, Enoch, 86
Eddyville, 66, 188, 199, 229 *n*2
Eddyville *Star,* 116, 149, 188
Edwards, John, 236–37 *n*91
Education, 71, 178–82; blacks and, 8–9, 52, 154–55
Elections: prewar, 5–10, 21; 1861, 49, 211; 1862, 80, 85, 87, 90, 212–13; 1863, 143, 145, 212; 1864, 173–74; 1865, 204, 211; postwar, 204, 211, 217–19
Ellwood, James, 49
Emancipation Proclamation, 38, 82–83, 87, 157; Democratic response, 84–85, 93–96, 126–27, 136, 223; Republican response, 82–83
English, J., 156
English, J. M., 101
English, Nathan, 116
Enlistments, 32, 42–44, 60–62, 66, 161; of blacks, 129–31; bounties for, 61, 129, 147, 159–60; discouragement of, 64, 126; numbers of, 63, 128; political arguments over, 42–43, 60, 129
Entertainment, 186, 189–93
Esteb, E. F., 118
Evans, Joseph K., 67
Evans, William, 67
Everett, Horace, 118
Everingham, B. D., 97

Fairfield, 36, 93, 112–14, 132, 154, 180; blacks in, 132; disloyalty alleged in, 33, 39, 94, 106
Fairfield *Constitution and Union,* 33, 59, 89, 96; problems of, 112–13, 168
Fairfield *Ledger,* 59, 116, 146
"Farmers revolt" (1870s), 218–19
Farmington, 114, 180
Farwell, Samuel, 76
Faville, Oran, 160
Fay, Pliny, 158
Fayette County Pioneer (West Union), 59, 112
Felt, Andrew J., 112
Finch, Daniel, 226
Fisher, Maturin L., 48, 140
Fishlow, Albert, 15–16
Fleak, L. B., 119, 126
Flick, John, 117
Flint, C. C., 41
Floyd County, 93, 183
Foreign born: antagonism toward, 6, 21, 198; defense of, 21; and Democratic party, 3–4, 90, 142; and the draft, 62–63, 128, 161,

198; and Republican party, 5, 19, 142; and secret societies, 120. *See also* Irish; Germans; Hollanders
Foreman, Joe, 167–68, 255 *n*107
Fort Dodge, 42, 177, 216, 220
Fort Dodge *Democrat,* 42, 59, 245 *n*13
Fort Donelson, 74, 91
Fort Madison, 93, 150, 187
Fort Madison *Plain Dealer,* 167
Fort Pillow massacre, 156
Fort Sumter, 27–28, 30
Frame, George, 155
Francis, William H., 166
Frane, George, 52
Franklin County, 150
Franklin, Cyrus, 57
Free Soilers, 3, 7
Fremont County, 44, 118, 159, 164
Frost, J. Lyman, 163
Fugitive slave law, 7–8, 230 *n*24
Fuller, Meville, 225
Funk, George P., 184

Gallagher, W. D., 117
Gaston, William, 95
Gates, Paul, 14
Gear, E. G., 174
Germans, 132, 149, 227; and alienage exemptions, 62, 128, 198; and Democratic party, 3, 5, 142; in Dubuque schools, 179; and 1860 campaign, 21; German press, 21, 59, 161, 173; and the Iowa vote, 205–9; and Republican party, 5, 19, 142; in West Point Township (Lee County), 159, 162
Gettysburg (battle), 106
Gharkey, John, 35–36, 81, 97, 222; on blacks, 156; on the draft, 127; newspaper attacked, 112
Giaquinta, Joyce, 248–49 *n*29
Gibson, Levi, 66
Gideon, Joseph, 67–68
Gideon, V. M., 67
Gleason, Pat, 162
Glenn, Samuel, 164
Goodenow, Mr., 192
Grangers, 219
Grant, John Henry, 132
Grant, Judge, 174
Grant, Ulysses S., 156, 166, 172, 196, 218
Gray, George W., 86, 139, 252 *n*2
Gray, Wood, 14
Greeley, Horace, 107–8
Greenback movement, 218–19
Greenbush (Warren County), 177
Greene County, 163
Grimes, James, 25, 119, 203, 220; on blacks, 80, 130; and Emacipation Proclamation, 87; and Hill case, 53–54; and Mahony, 108; and rise of Republican party, 3, 5, 7–9